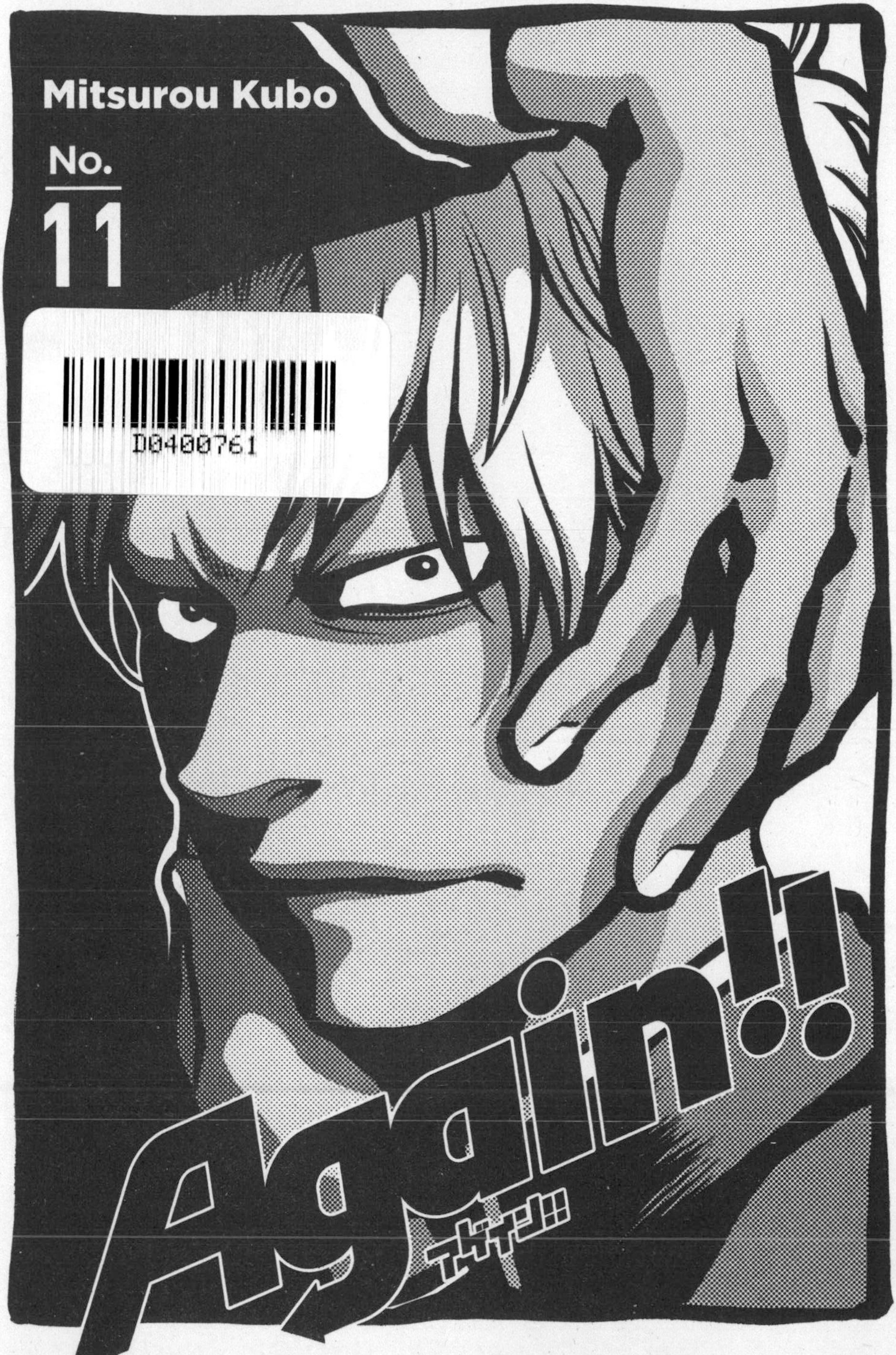
Mitsurou Kubo
No.
11
Again!!
アゲイン!!

contents

112. THE OUENDAN IS TOO MUCH!

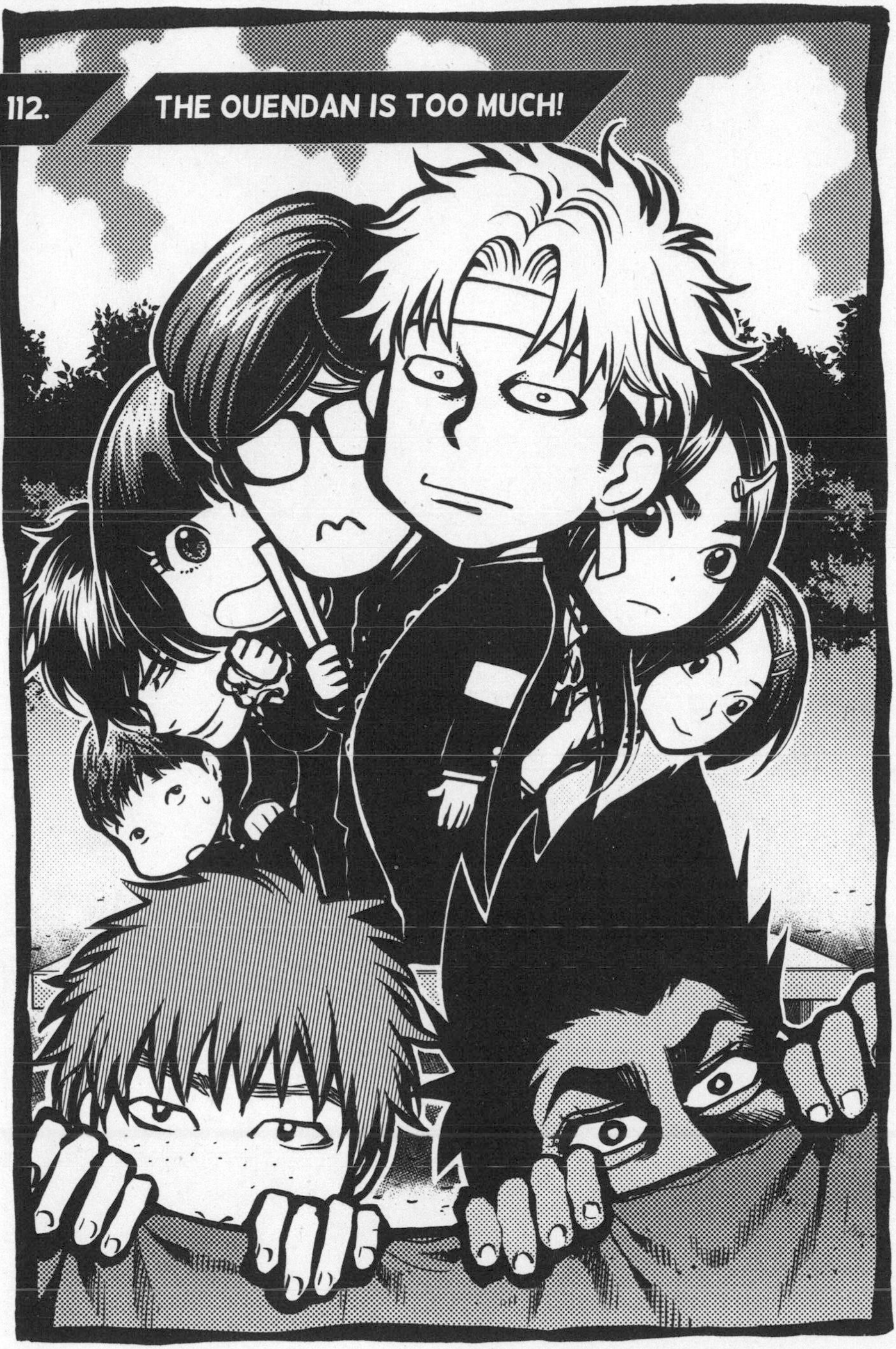

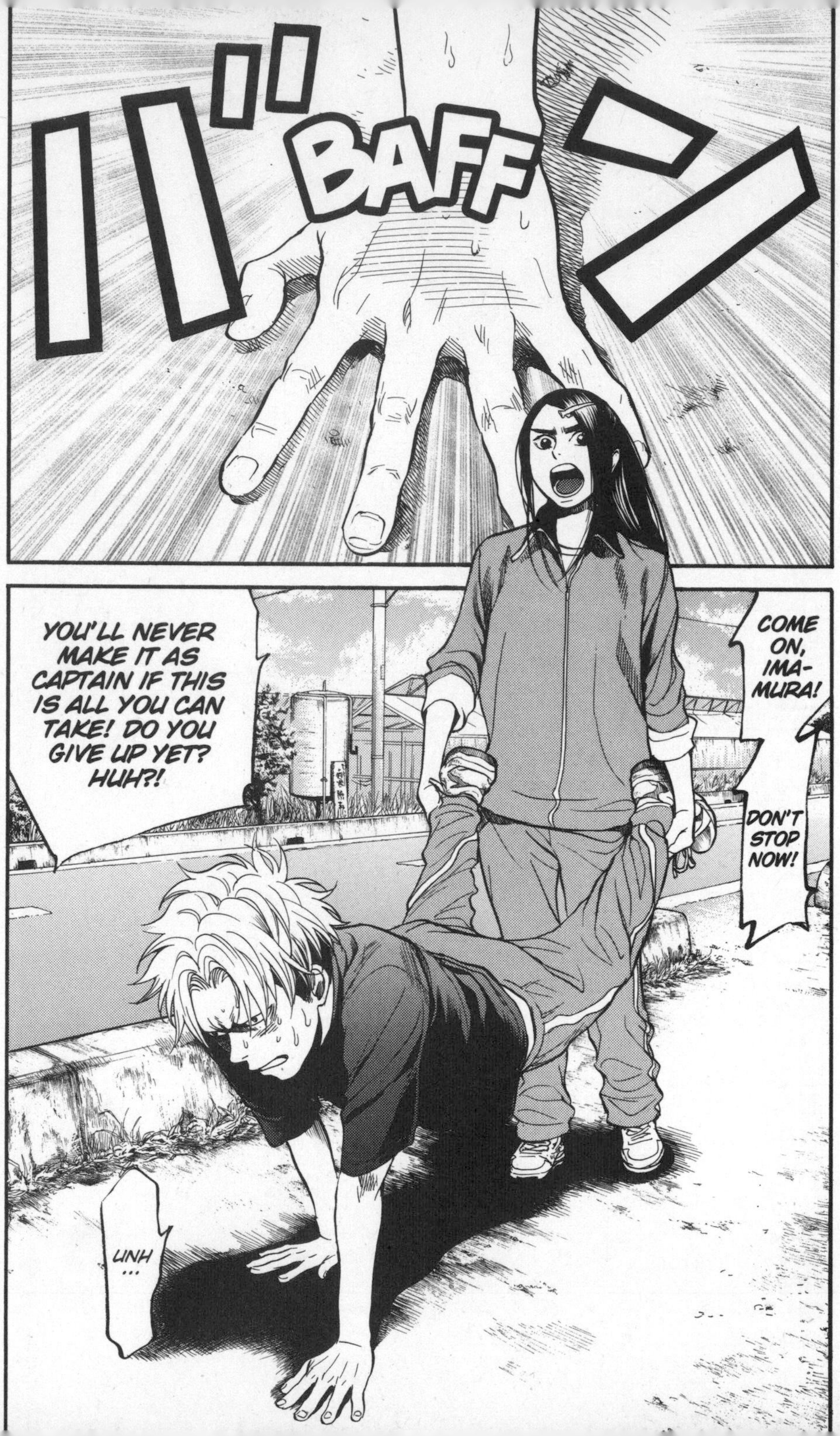
BAFF
COME ON, IMA-MURA!
DON'T STOP NOW!
YOU'LL NEVER MAKE IT AS CAPTAIN IF THIS IS ALL YOU CAN TAKE! DO YOU GIVE UP YET? HUH?!
UNH ...

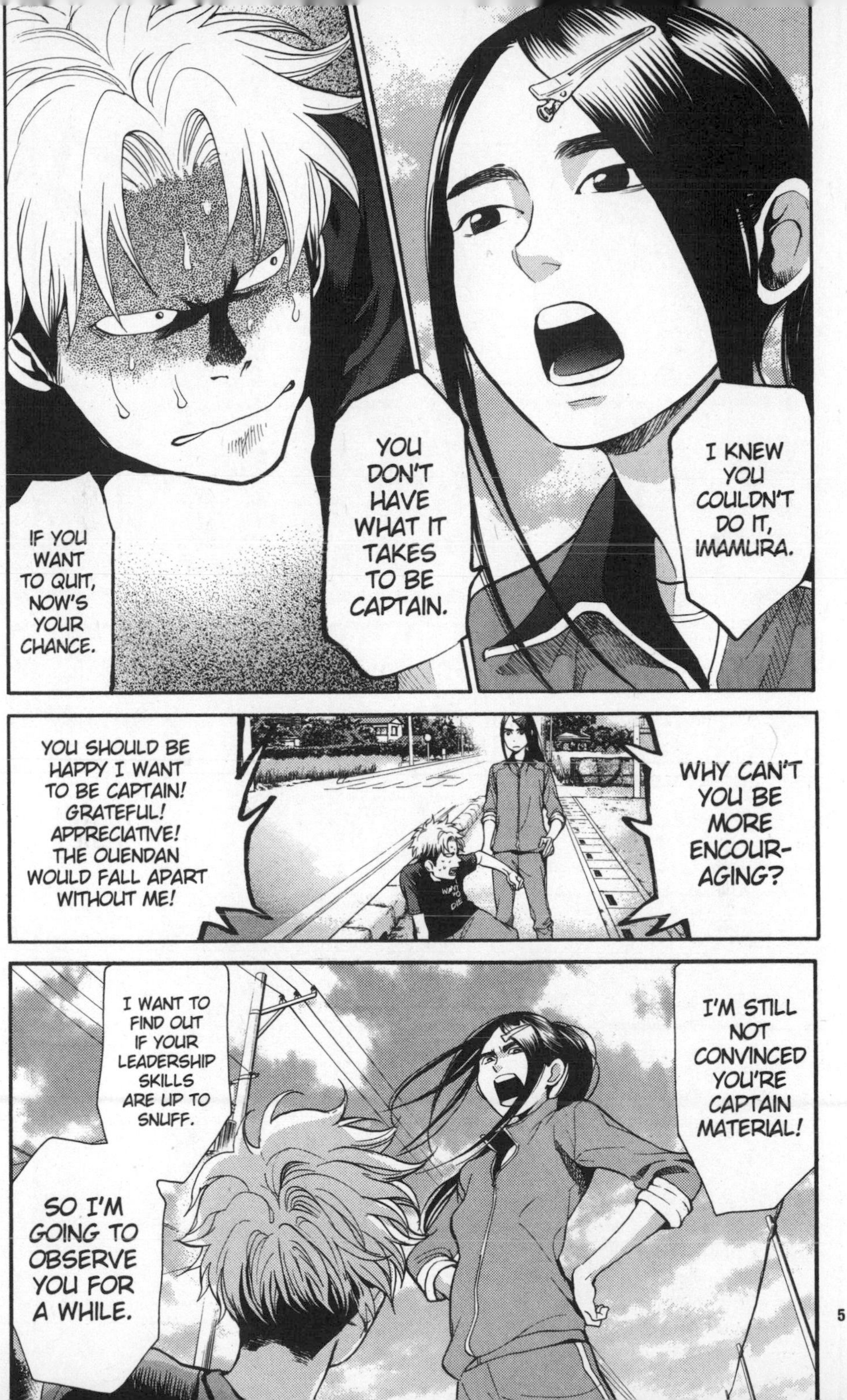
I KNEW YOU COULDN'T DO IT, IMAMURA.
YOU DON'T HAVE WHAT IT TAKES TO BE CAPTAIN.
IF YOU WANT TO QUIT, NOW'S YOUR CHANCE.
WHY CAN'T YOU BE MORE ENCOUR-AGING?
YOU SHOULD BE HAPPY I WANT TO BE CAPTAIN! GRATEFUL! APPRECIATIVE! THE OUENDAN WOULD FALL APART WITHOUT ME!
I'M STILL NOT CONVINCED YOU'RE CAPTAIN MATERIAL!
I WANT TO FIND OUT IF YOUR LEADERSHIP SKILLS ARE UP TO SNUFF.
SO I'M GOING TO OBSERVE YOU FOR A WHILE.

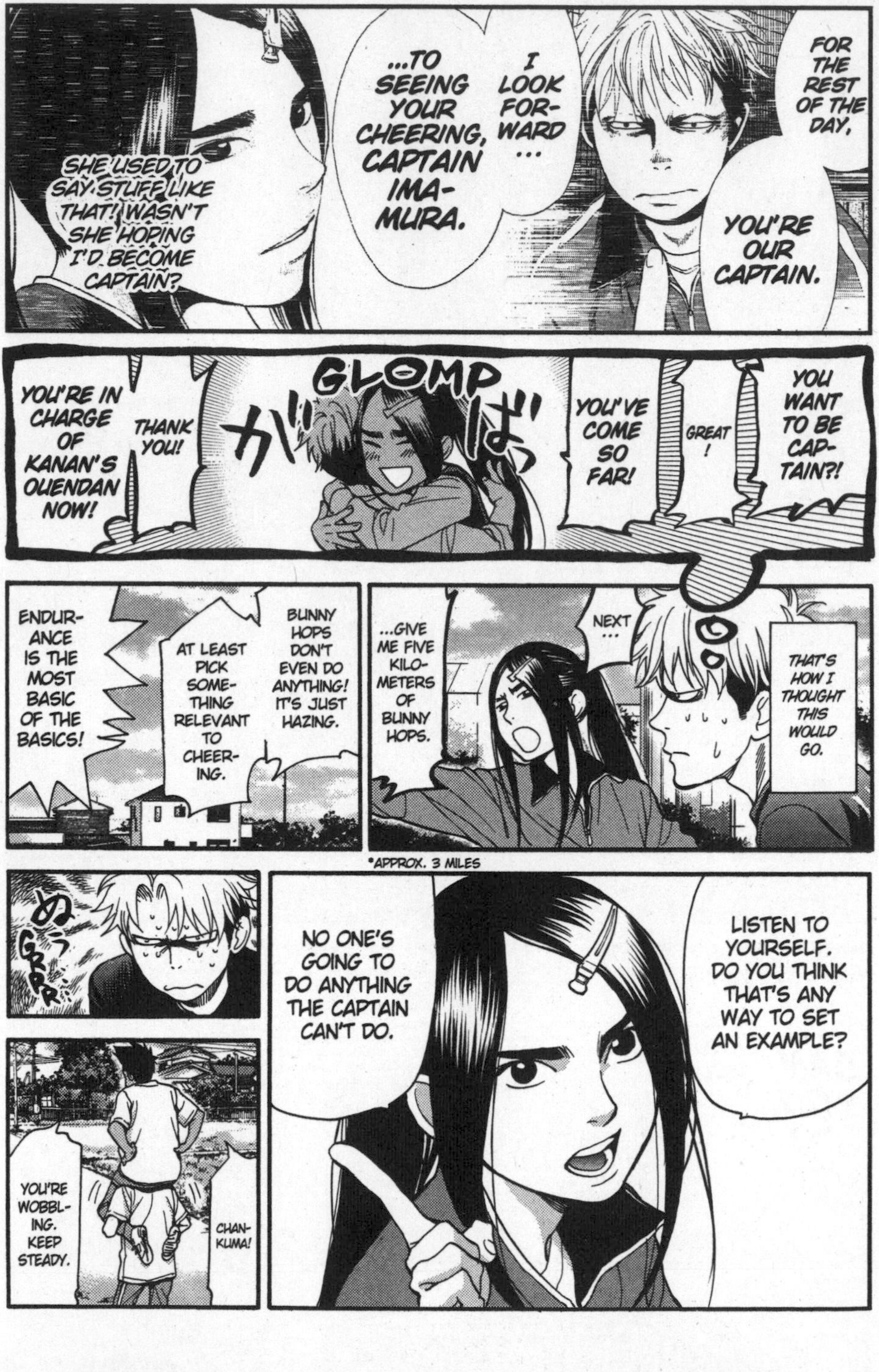
FOR THE REST OF THE DAY,
YOU'RE OUR CAPTAIN.
I LOOK FORWARD...
...TO SEEING YOUR CHEERING, CAPTAIN IMAMURA.
SHE USED TO SAY STUFF LIKE THAT! WASN'T SHE HOPING I'D BECOME CAPTAIN?
YOU WANT TO BE CAPTAIN?!
GREAT!
YOU'VE COME SO FAR!
GLOMP
がばっ
THANK YOU!
YOU'RE IN CHARGE OF KANAN'S OUENDAN NOW!
THAT'S HOW I THOUGHT THIS WOULD GO.
NEXT...
...GIVE ME FIVE KILOMETERS OF BUNNY HOPS.
BUNNY HOPS DON'T EVEN DO ANYTHING! IT'S JUST HAZING.
AT LEAST PICK SOMETHING RELEVANT TO CHEERING.
ENDURANCE IS THE MOST BASIC OF THE BASICS!
*APPROX. 3 MILES
LISTEN TO YOURSELF. DO YOU THINK THAT'S ANY WAY TO SET AN EXAMPLE?
NO ONE'S GOING TO DO ANYTHING THE CAPTAIN CAN'T DO.
ぬぅ
GRRR
CHANKUMA!
YOU'RE WOBBLING. KEEP STEADY.

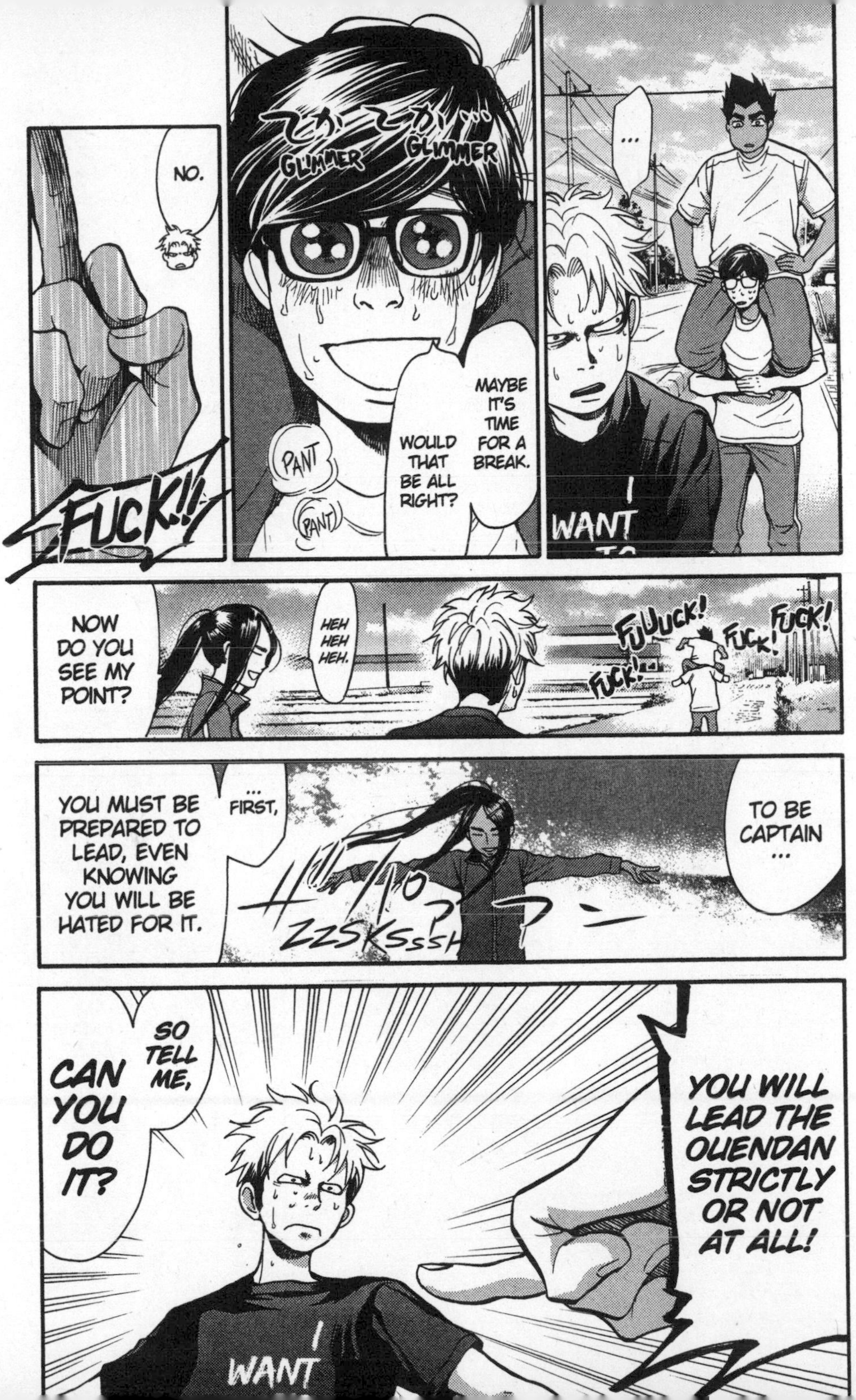
...
I WANT TO
てかてか
GLIMMER GLIMMER
MAYBE IT'S TIME FOR A BREAK.
WOULD THAT BE ALL RIGHT?
PANT
PANT
NO.
FUCK!!
FUCK!
FUCK!
FUCK!
FUUUCK!
HEH HEH HEH.
NOW DO YOU SEE MY POINT?
TO BE CAPTAIN ...
ZZSKSssh
... FIRST,
YOU MUST BE PREPARED TO LEAD, EVEN KNOWING YOU WILL BE HATED FOR IT.
YOU WILL LEAD THE OUENDAN STRICTLY OR NOT AT ALL!
SO TELL ME,
CAN YOU DO IT?
I WANT

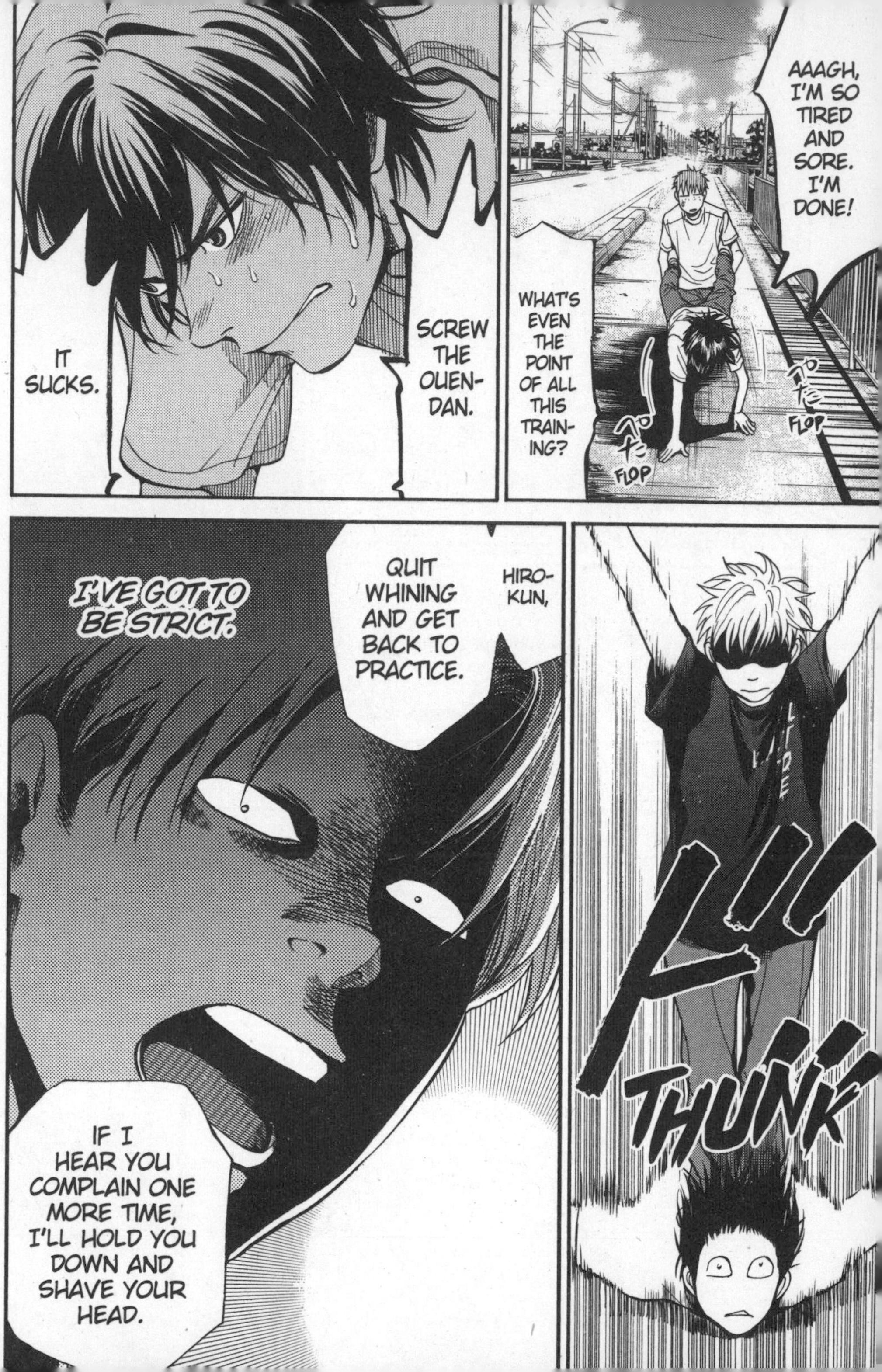
AAAGH, I'M SO TIRED AND SORE. I'M DONE!
WHAT'S EVEN THE POINT OF ALL THIS TRAIN-ING?
FLOP
FLOP
SCREW THE OUEN-DAN.
IT SUCKS.
THUNK
HIRO-KUN,
QUIT WHINING AND GET BACK TO PRACTICE.
I'VE GOT TO BE STRICT.
IF I HEAR YOU COMPLAIN ONE MORE TIME, I'LL HOLD YOU DOWN AND SHAVE YOUR HEAD.

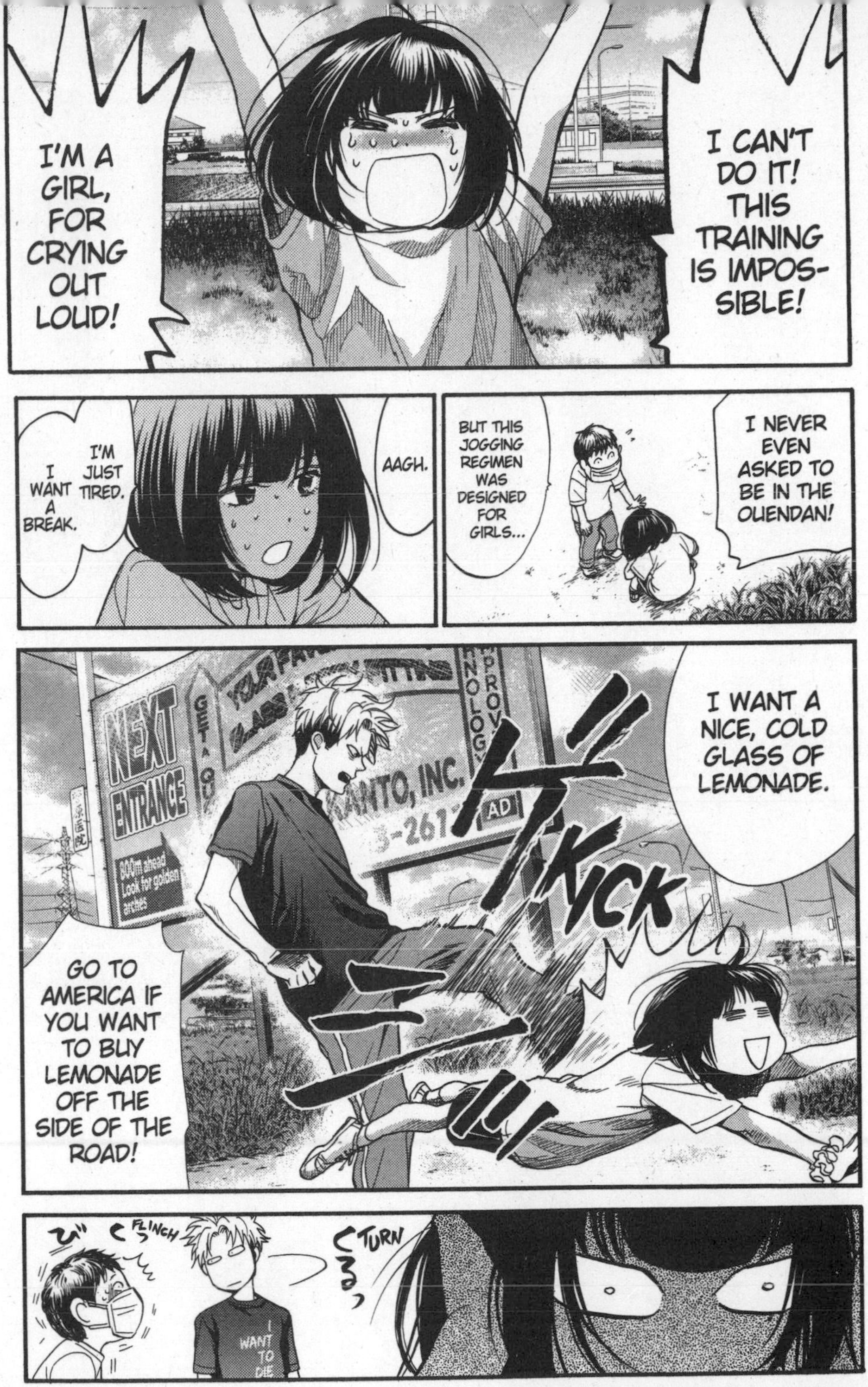
I CAN'T DO IT! THIS TRAINING IS IMPOS-SIBLE!
I'M A GIRL, FOR CRYING OUT LOUD!
I NEVER EVEN ASKED TO BE IN THE OUENDAN!
BUT THIS JOGGING REGIMEN WAS DESIGNED FOR GIRLS...
AAGH.
I'M JUST TIRED.
I WANT A BREAK.
I WANT A NICE, COLD GLASS OF LEMONADE.
KICK
NEXT ENTRANCE
800m ahead Look for golden arches
KANTO, INC.
AD
GO TO AMERICA IF YOU WANT TO BUY LEMONADE OFF THE SIDE OF THE ROAD!
TURN
FLINCH
I WANT TO DIE

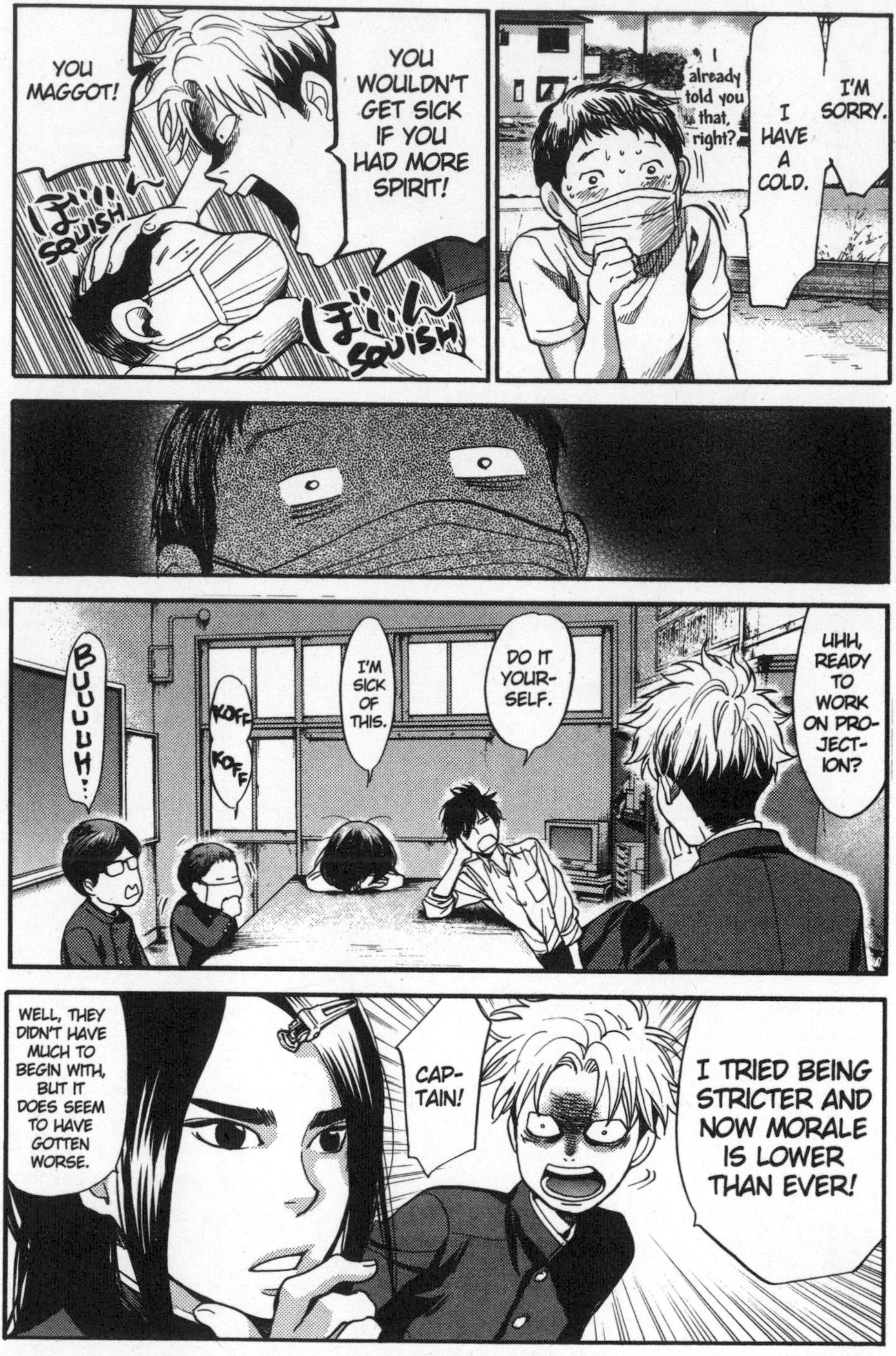

I'M SORRY.
I HAVE A COLD.
I already told you that, right?
YOU WOULDN'T GET SICK IF YOU HAD MORE SPIRIT!
YOU MAGGOT!
SQUISH
SQUISH
UHH, READY TO WORK ON PRO-JECT-ION?
DO IT YOUR-SELF.
I'M SICK OF THIS.
KOFF
KOFF
BUUUUH...!
I TRIED BEING STRICTER AND NOW MORALE IS LOWER THAN EVER!
CAP-TAIN!
WELL, THEY DIDN'T HAVE MUCH TO BEGIN WITH, BUT IT DOES SEEM TO HAVE GOTTEN WORSE.

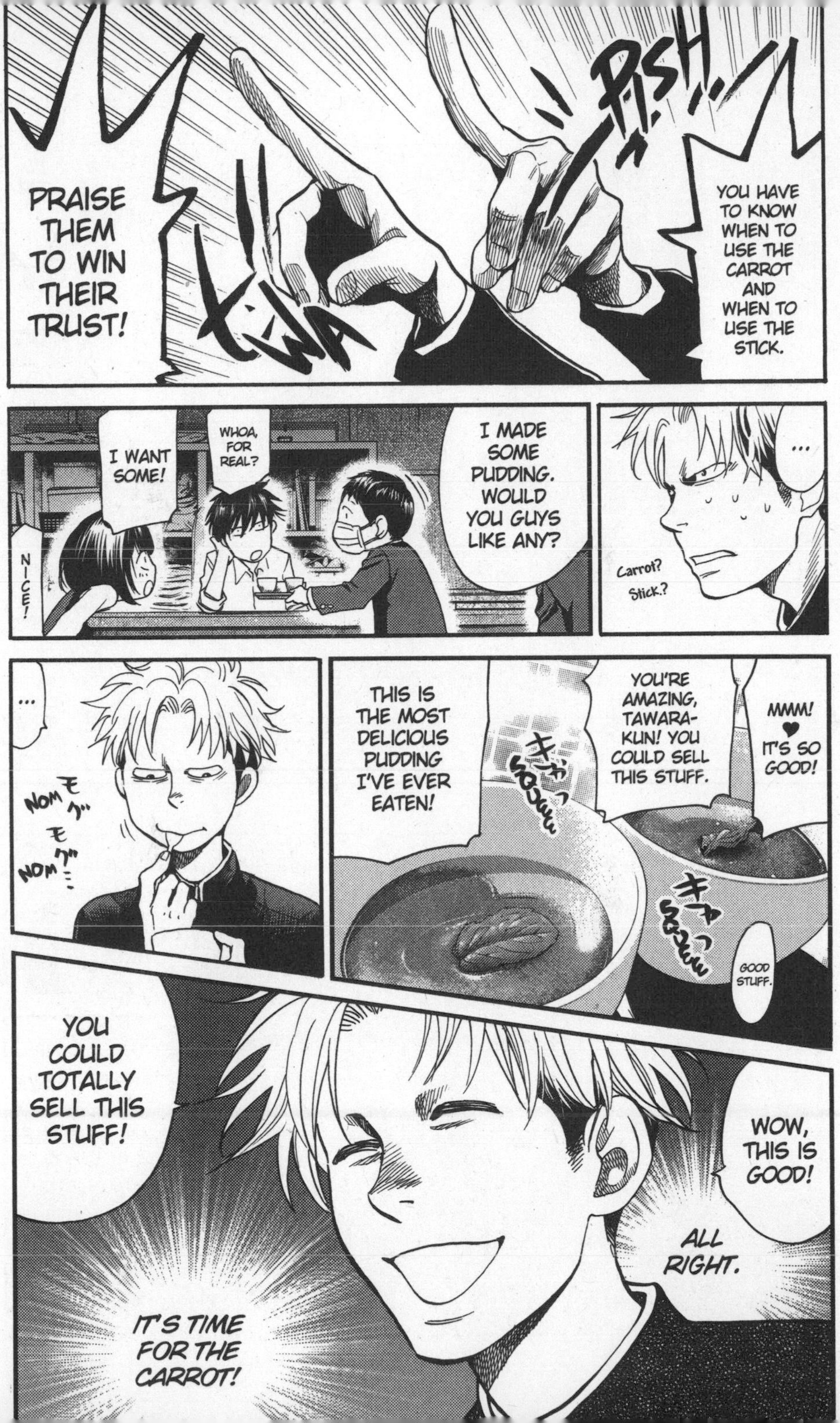
PISH!!
YOU HAVE TO KNOW WHEN TO USE THE CARROT AND WHEN TO USE THE STICK.
PRAISE THEM TO WIN THEIR TRUST!
...
Carrot? Stick.?
I MADE SOME PUDDING. WOULD YOU GUYS LIKE ANY?
WHOA, FOR REAL?
I WANT SOME!
NICE!
MMM! ♥ IT'S SO GOOD!
YOU'RE AMAZING, TAWARA-KUN! YOU COULD SELL THIS STUFF.
THIS IS THE MOST DELICIOUS PUDDING I'VE EVER EATEN!
GOOD STUFF.
...
NOM モグ
NOM モグ
WOW, THIS IS GOOD!
ALL RIGHT.
YOU COULD TOTALLY SELL THIS STUFF!
IT'S TIME FOR THE CARROT!

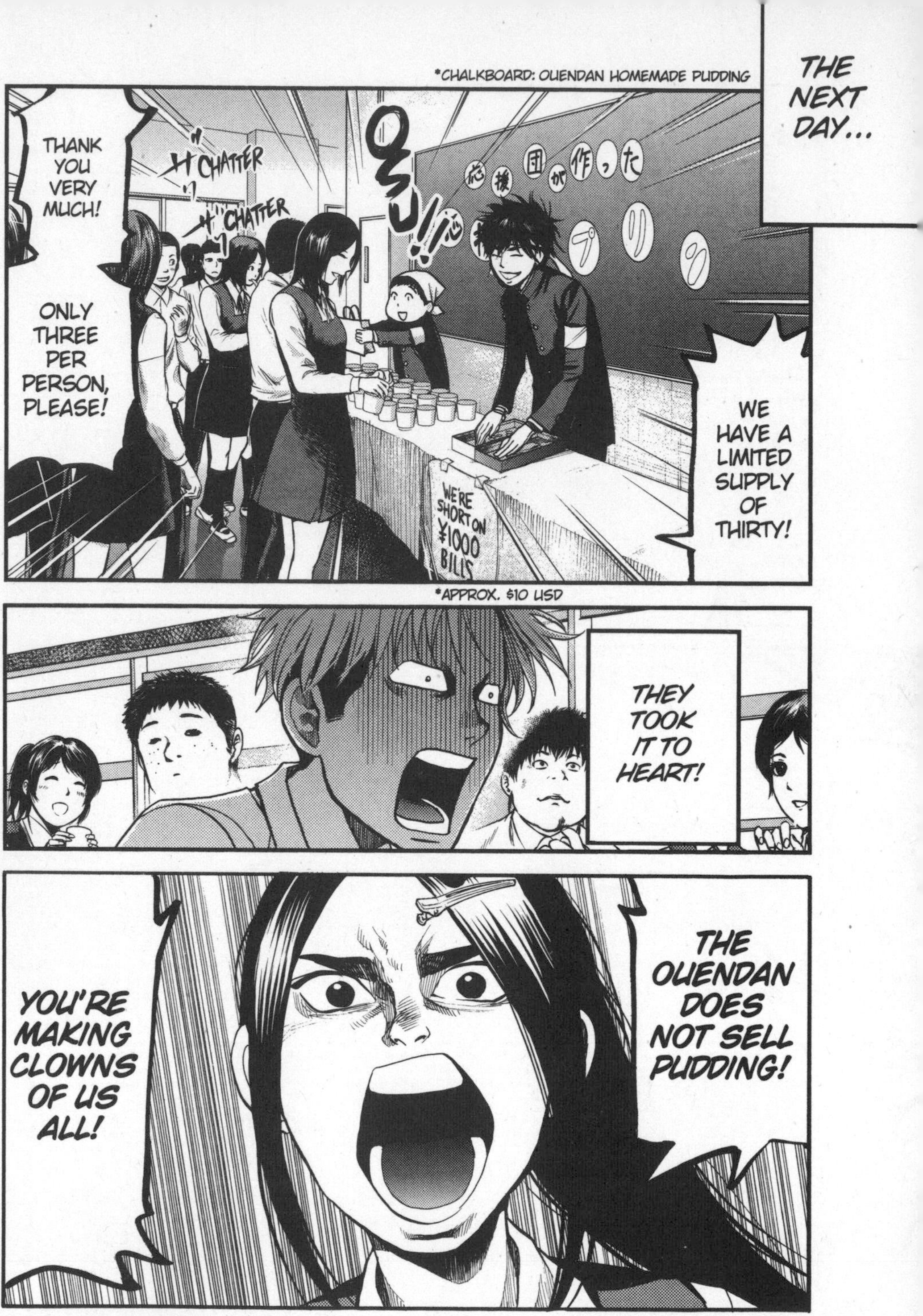
THE NEXT DAY...
*CHALKBOARD: OUENDAN HOMEMADE PUDDING
OSU!!
WE HAVE A LIMITED SUPPLY OF THIRTY!
WE'RE SHORT ON ¥1000 BILLS
THANK YOU VERY MUCH!
CHATTER
CHATTER
ONLY THREE PER PERSON, PLEASE!
*APPROX. $10 USD
THEY TOOK IT TO HEART!
THE OUENDAN DOES NOT SELL PUDDING!
YOU'RE MAKING CLOWNS OF US ALL!

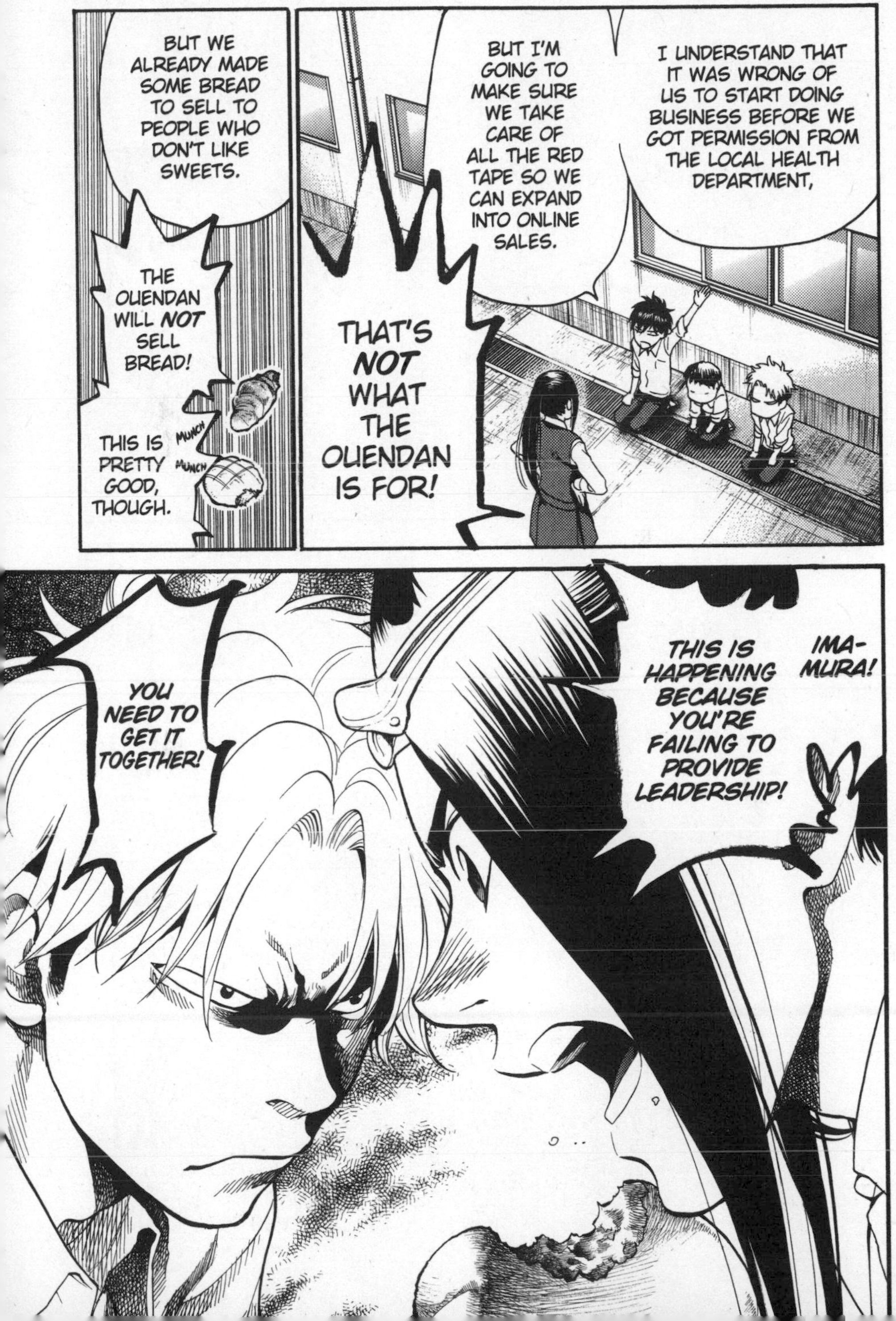
I UNDERSTAND THAT IT WAS WRONG OF US TO START DOING BUSINESS BEFORE WE GOT PERMISSION FROM THE LOCAL HEALTH DEPARTMENT,
BUT I'M GOING TO MAKE SURE WE TAKE CARE OF ALL THE RED TAPE SO WE CAN EXPAND INTO ONLINE SALES.
THAT'S *NOT* WHAT THE OUENDAN IS FOR!
BUT WE ALREADY MADE SOME BREAD TO SELL TO PEOPLE WHO DON'T LIKE SWEETS.
THE OUENDAN WILL *NOT* SELL BREAD!
MUNCH
MUNCH
THIS IS PRETTY GOOD, THOUGH.
IMA-MURA!
THIS IS HAPPENING BECAUSE YOU'RE FAILING TO PROVIDE LEADERSHIP!
YOU NEED TO GET IT TOGETHER!

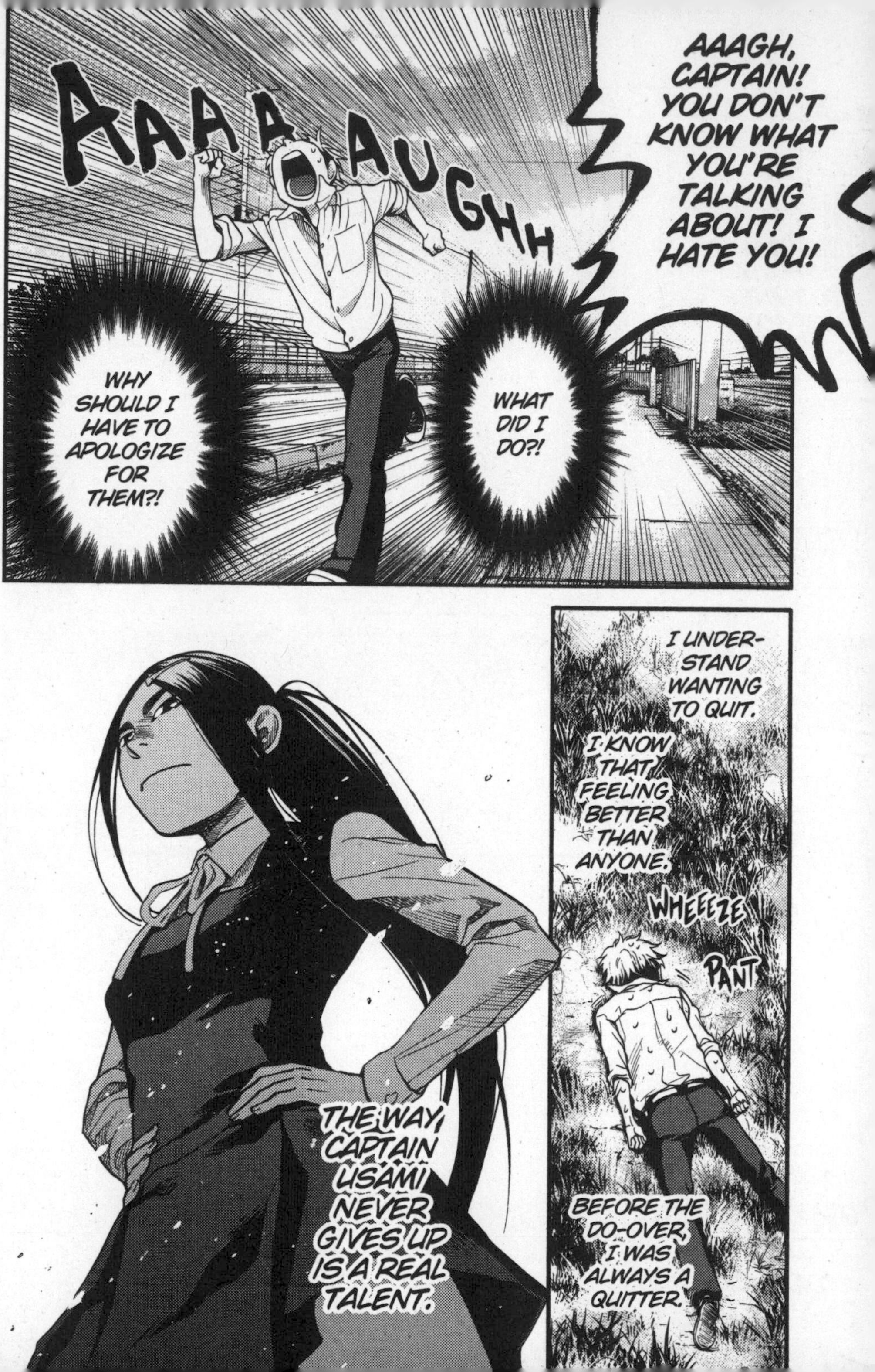
AAAGH, CAPTAIN! YOU DON'T KNOW WHAT YOU'RE TALKING ABOUT! I HATE YOU!
AAAAAUGHH
WHAT DID I DO?!
WHY SHOULD I HAVE TO APOLOGIZE FOR THEM?!
I UNDER-STAND WANTING TO QUIT.
I KNOW THAT FEELING BETTER THAN ANYONE.
WHEEEZE
PANT
BEFORE THE DO-OVER, I WAS ALWAYS A QUITTER.
THE WAY CAPTAIN USAMI NEVER GIVES UP IS A REAL TALENT.

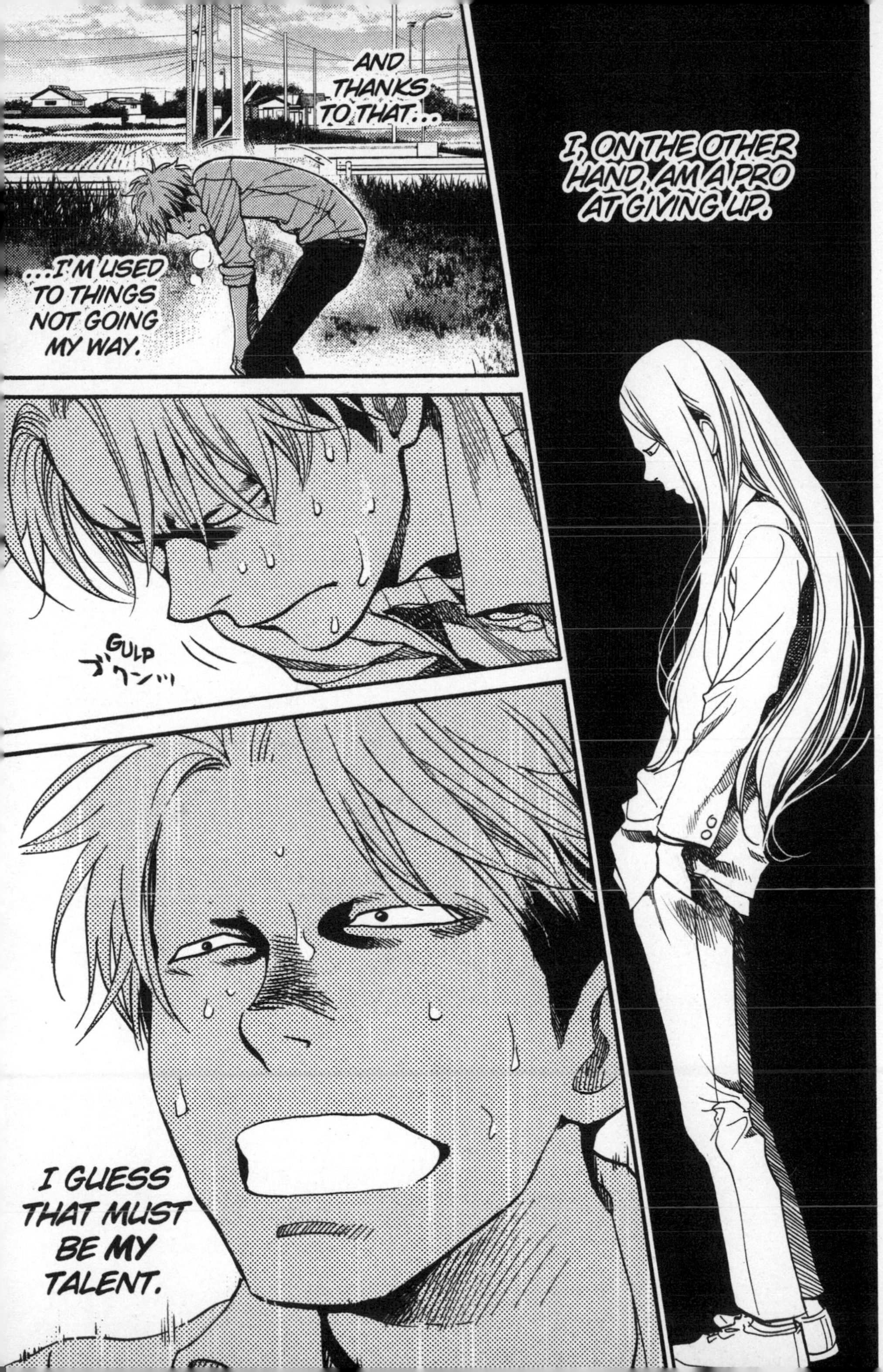
I, ON THE OTHER HAND, AM A PRO AT GIVING UP.
AND THANKS TO THAT...
...I'M USED TO THINGS NOT GOING MY WAY.
GULP
ゴクンッ
I GUESS THAT MUST BE MY TALENT.

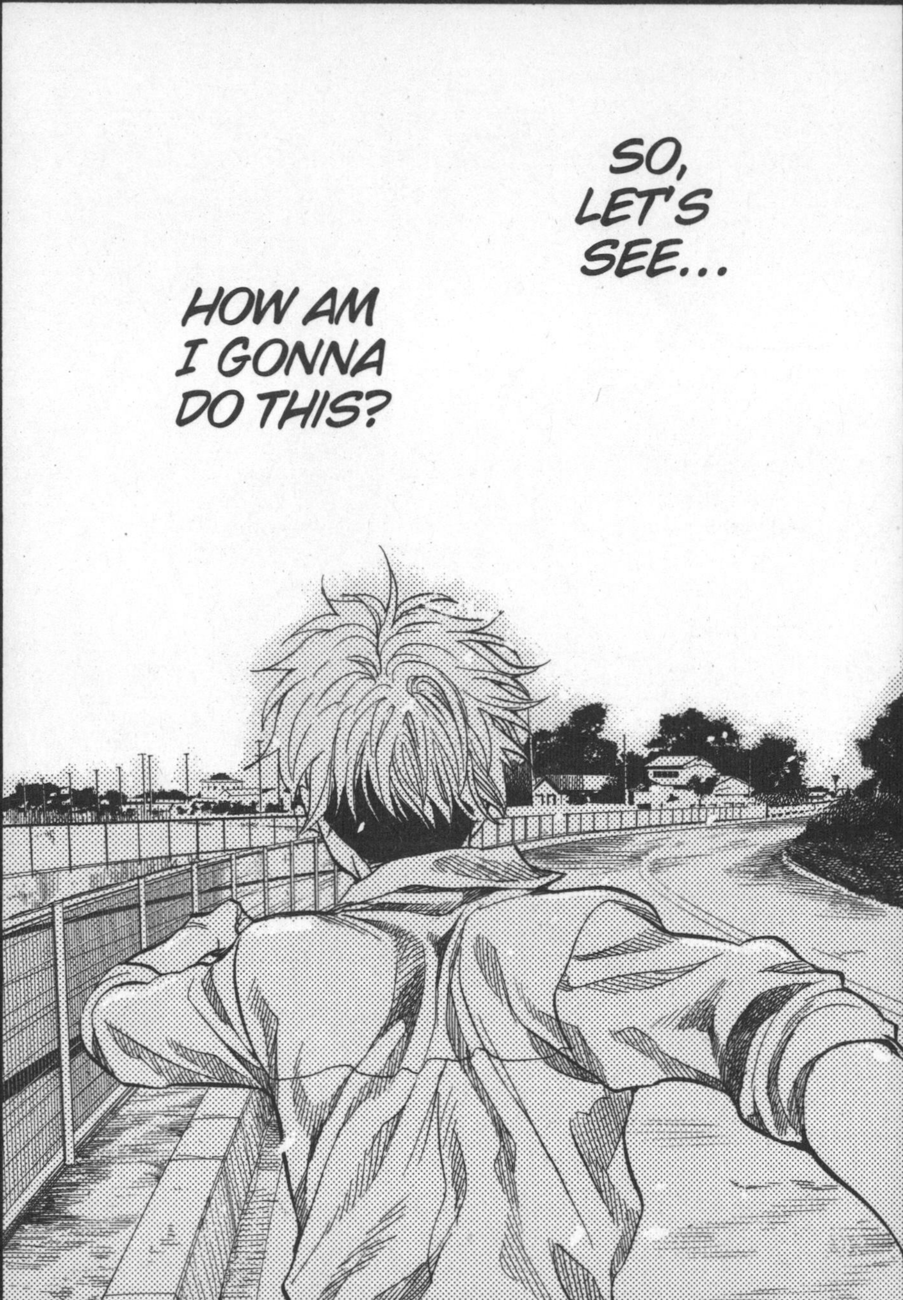
SO, LET'S SEE...
HOW AM I GONNA DO THIS?

113. EVERY CAPTAIN'S DIFFERENT

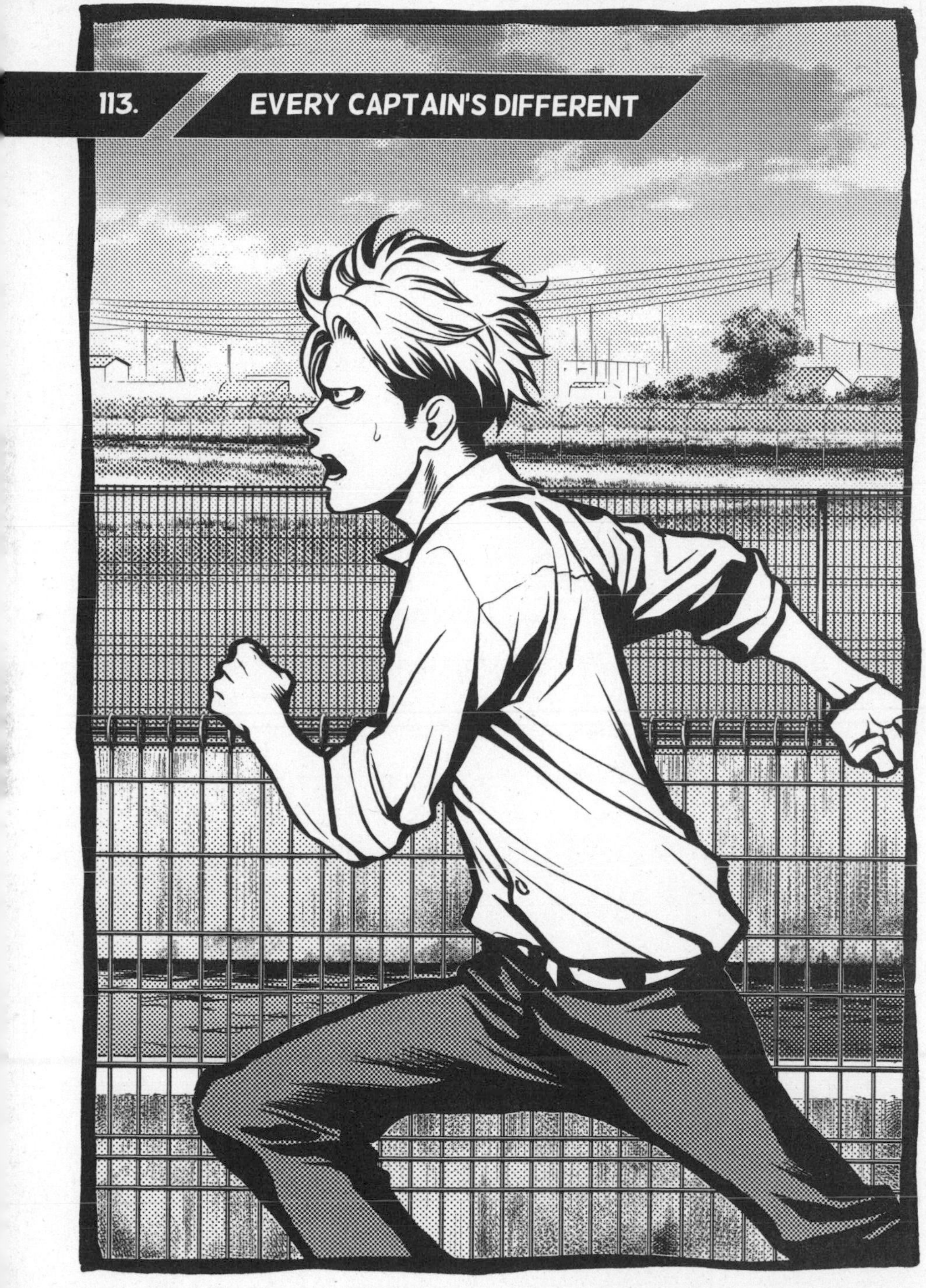

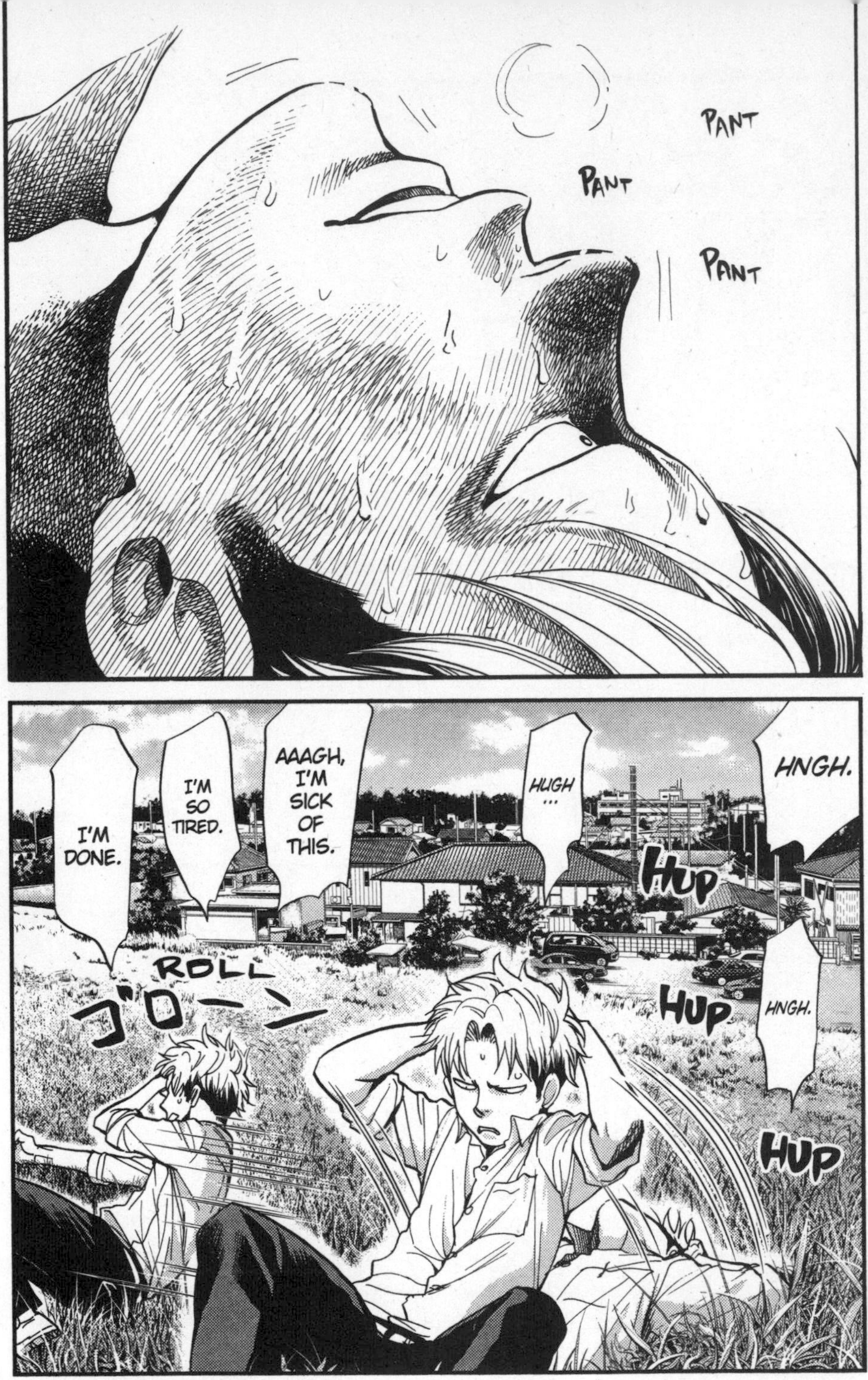
PANT
PANT
PANT
HNGH.
HUGH ...
HUP
AAAGH, I'M SICK OF THIS.
I'M SO TIRED.
I'M DONE.
HNGH.
HUP
ROLL
ゴローン
HUP

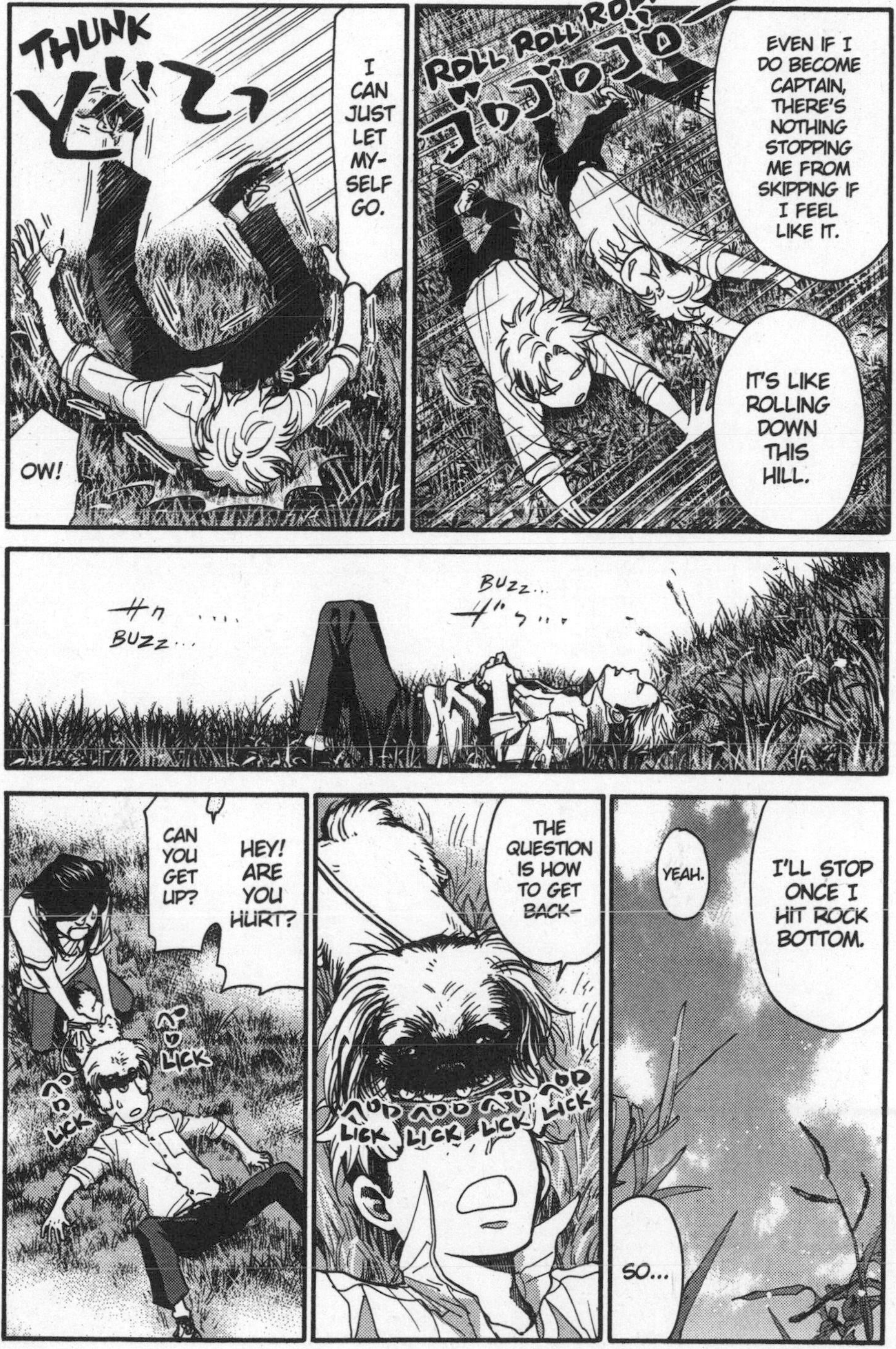
ROLL ROLL ROLL
EVEN IF I DO BECOME CAPTAIN, THERE'S NOTHING STOPPING ME FROM SKIPPING IF I FEEL LIKE IT.
IT'S LIKE ROLLING DOWN THIS HILL.
THUNK
I CAN JUST LET MY-SELF GO.
OW!
BUZZ...
BUZZ...
I'LL STOP ONCE I HIT ROCK BOTTOM.
YEAH.
SO...
THE QUESTION IS HOW TO GET BACK-
LICK LICK LICK LICK
HEY! ARE YOU HURT?
CAN YOU GET UP?
LICK
LICK

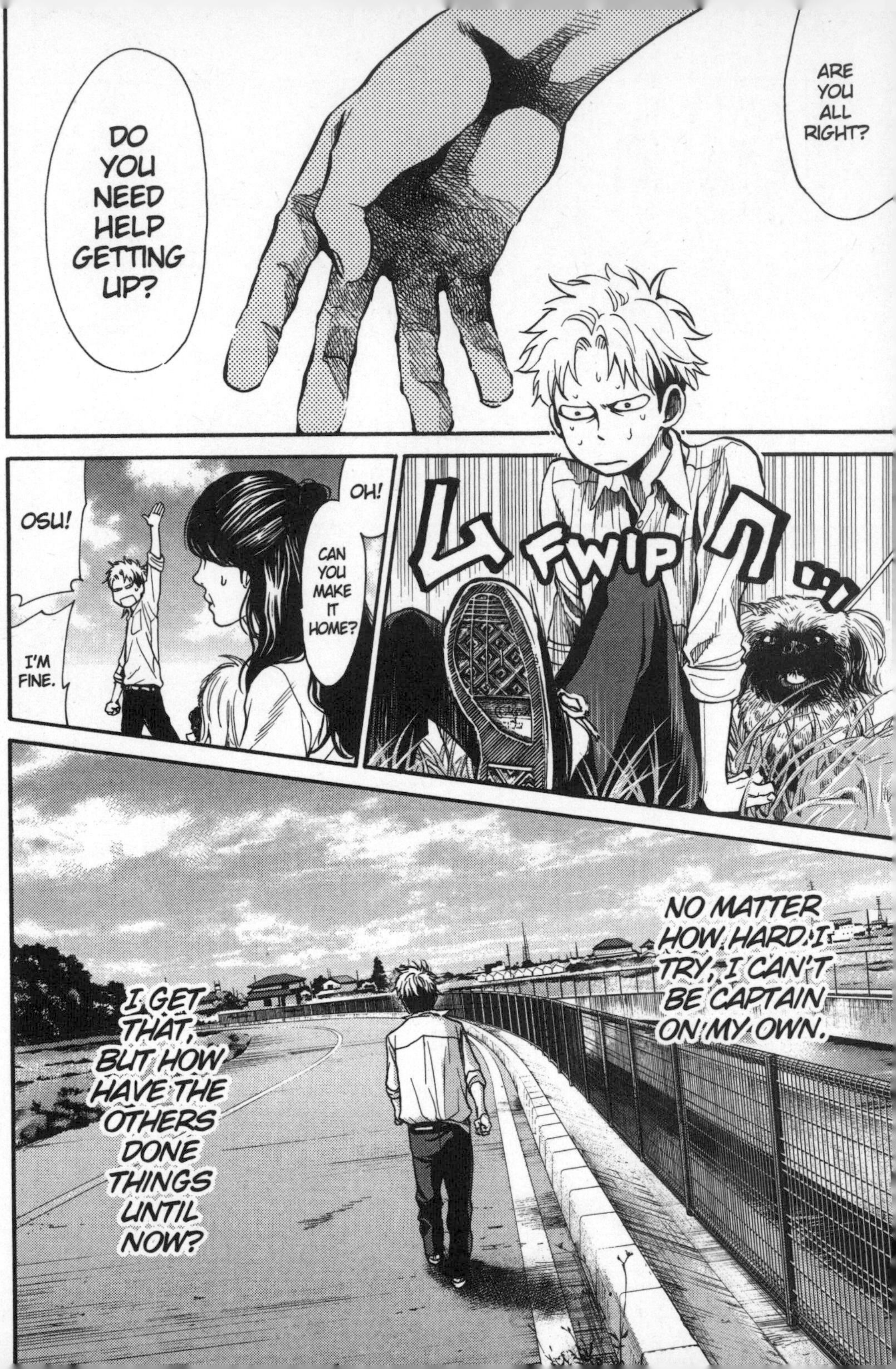
ARE YOU ALL RIGHT?
DO YOU NEED HELP GETTING UP?
FWIP
OH!
CAN YOU MAKE IT HOME?
OSU!
I'M FINE.
NO MATTER HOW HARD I TRY, I CAN'T BE CAPTAIN ON MY OWN.
I GET THAT, BUT HOW HAVE THE OTHERS DONE THINGS UNTIL NOW?

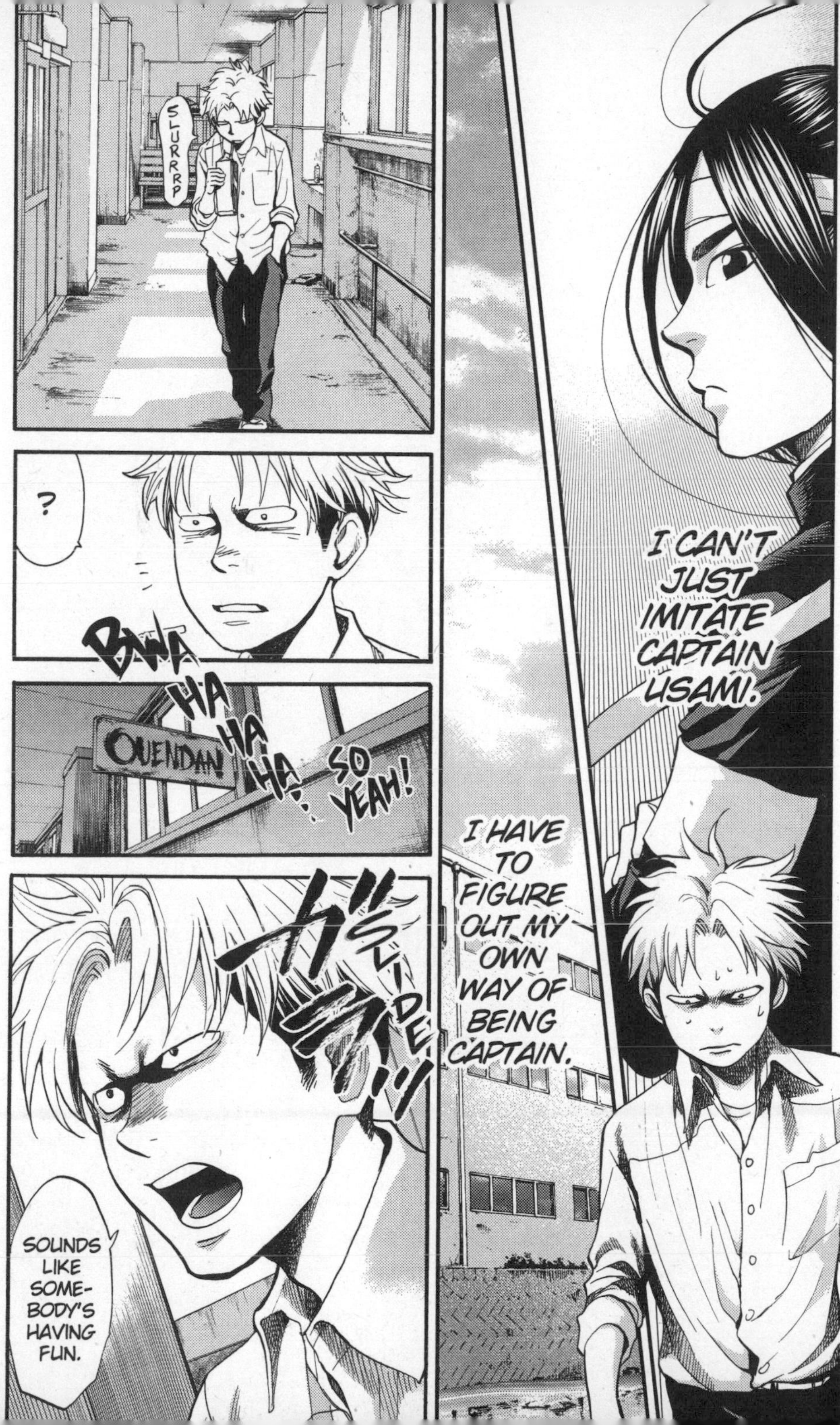
I CAN'T JUST IMITATE CAPTAIN USAMI.
I HAVE TO FIGURE OUT MY OWN WAY OF BEING CAPTAIN.
SLURRRP
?
BWA HA HA HA...
OUENDAN
SO YEAH!
SLIDE!!
SOUNDS LIKE SOME-BODY'S HAVING FUN.

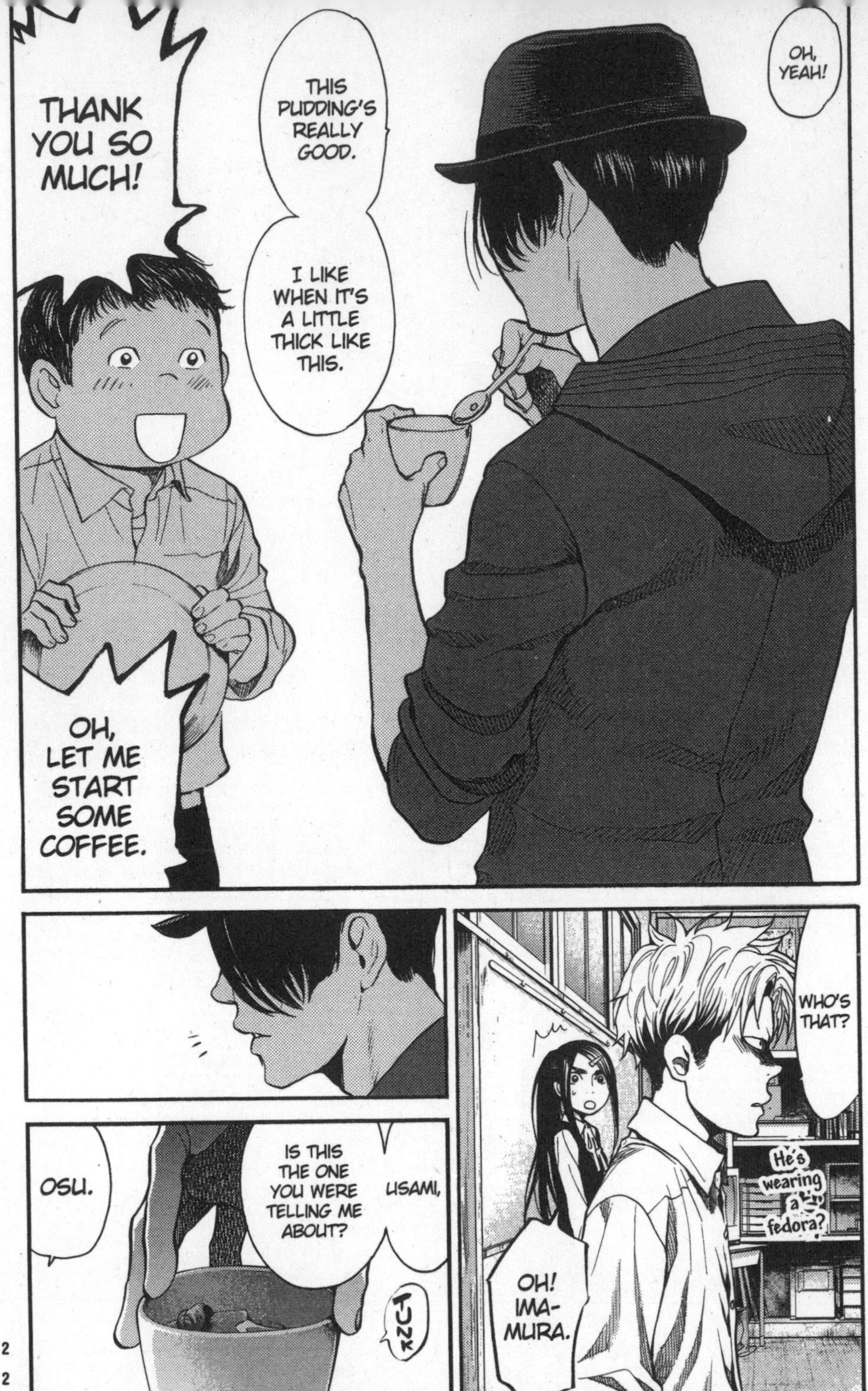
OH, YEAH!
THIS PUDDING'S REALLY GOOD.
I LIKE WHEN IT'S A LITTLE THICK LIKE THIS.
THANK YOU SO MUCH!
OH, LET ME START SOME COFFEE.
WHO'S THAT?
He's wearing a fedora?
OH! IMA-MURA.
USAMI,
IS THIS THE ONE YOU WERE TELLING ME ABOUT?
OSU.
JUNK

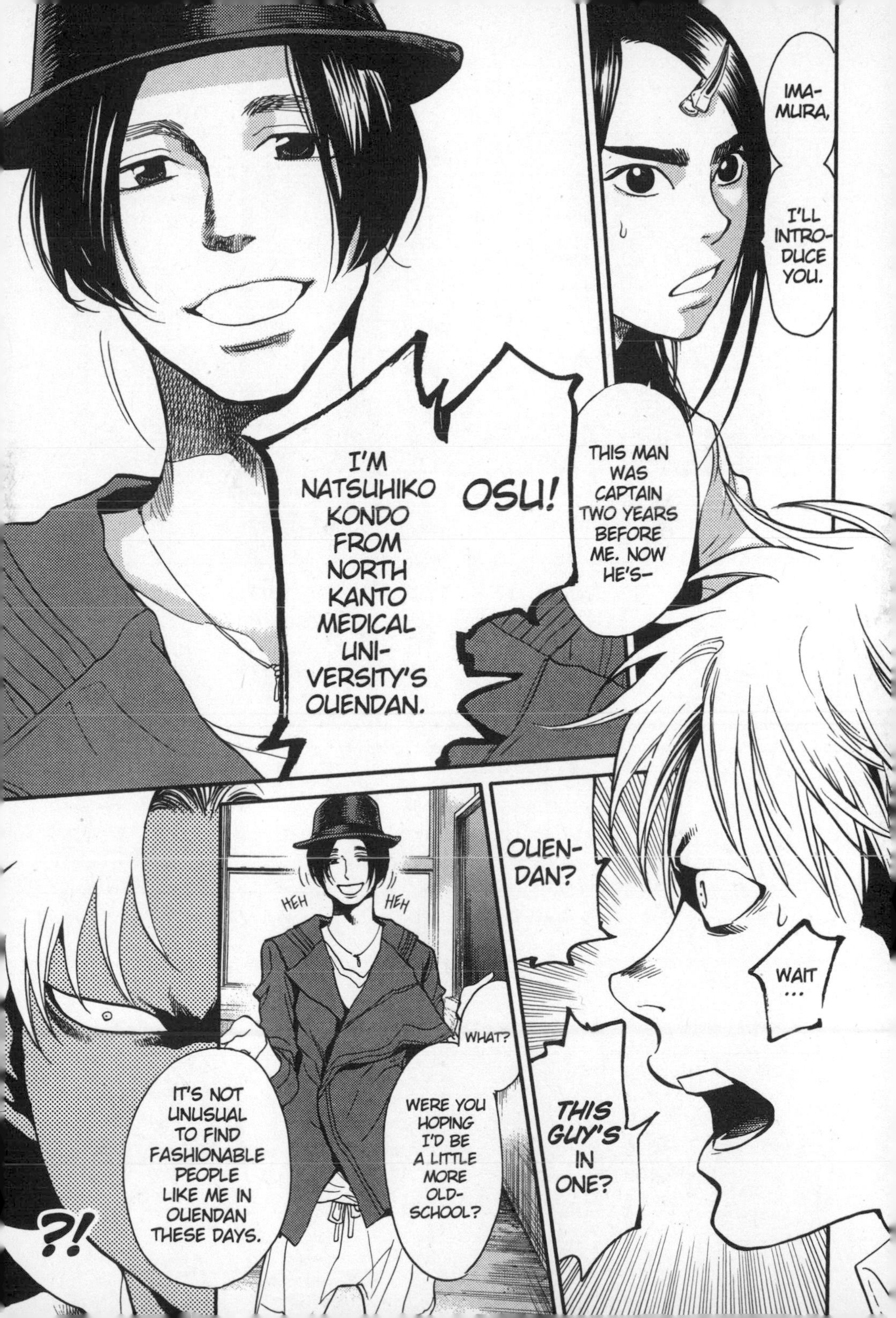
IMA-MURA,
I'LL INTRO-DUCE YOU.
THIS MAN WAS CAPTAIN TWO YEARS BEFORE ME. NOW HE'S-
OSU!
I'M NATSUHIKO KONDO FROM NORTH KANTO MEDICAL UNI-VERSITY'S OUENDAN.
OUEN-DAN?
WAIT ...
THIS GUY'S IN ONE?
WHAT?
HEH HEH
WERE YOU HOPING I'D BE A LITTLE MORE OLD-SCHOOL?
IT'S NOT UNUSUAL TO FIND FASHIONABLE PEOPLE LIKE ME IN OUENDAN THESE DAYS.
?!

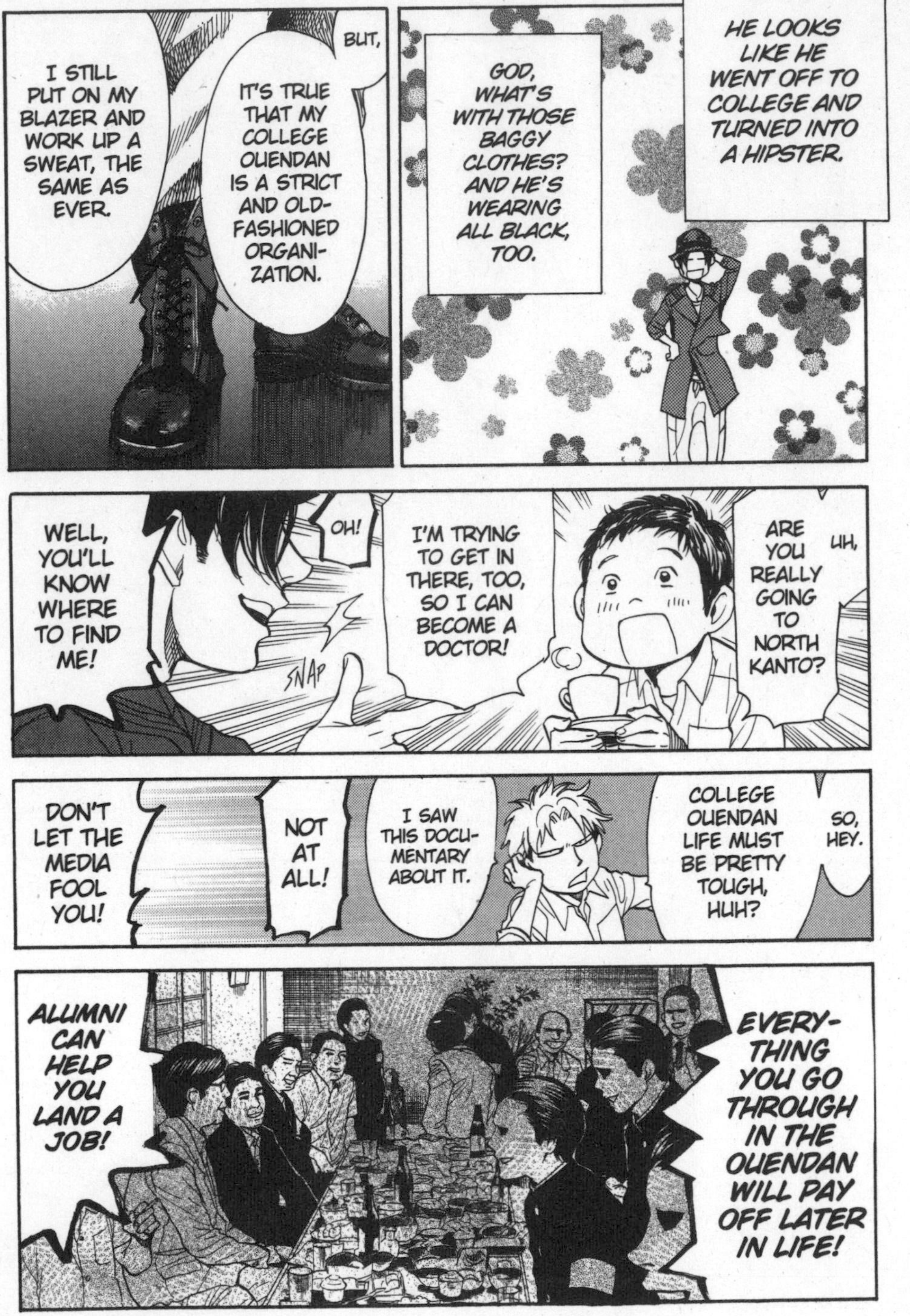
HE LOOKS LIKE HE WENT OFF TO COLLEGE AND TURNED INTO A HIPSTER.
GOD, WHAT'S WITH THOSE BAGGY CLOTHES? AND HE'S WEARING ALL BLACK, TOO.
BUT,
IT'S TRUE THAT MY COLLEGE OUENDAN IS A STRICT AND OLD-FASHIONED ORGANIZATION.
I STILL PUT ON MY BLAZER AND WORK UP A SWEAT, THE SAME AS EVER.
UH,
ARE YOU REALLY GOING TO NORTH KANTO?
I'M TRYING TO GET IN THERE, TOO, SO I CAN BECOME A DOCTOR!
OH!
SNAP
WELL, YOU'LL KNOW WHERE TO FIND ME!
SO, HEY.
COLLEGE OUENDAN LIFE MUST BE PRETTY TOUGH, HUH?
I SAW THIS DOCUMENTARY ABOUT IT.
NOT AT ALL!
DON'T LET THE MEDIA FOOL YOU!
EVERYTHING YOU GO THROUGH IN THE OUENDAN WILL PAY OFF LATER IN LIFE!
ALUMNI CAN HELP YOU LAND A JOB!

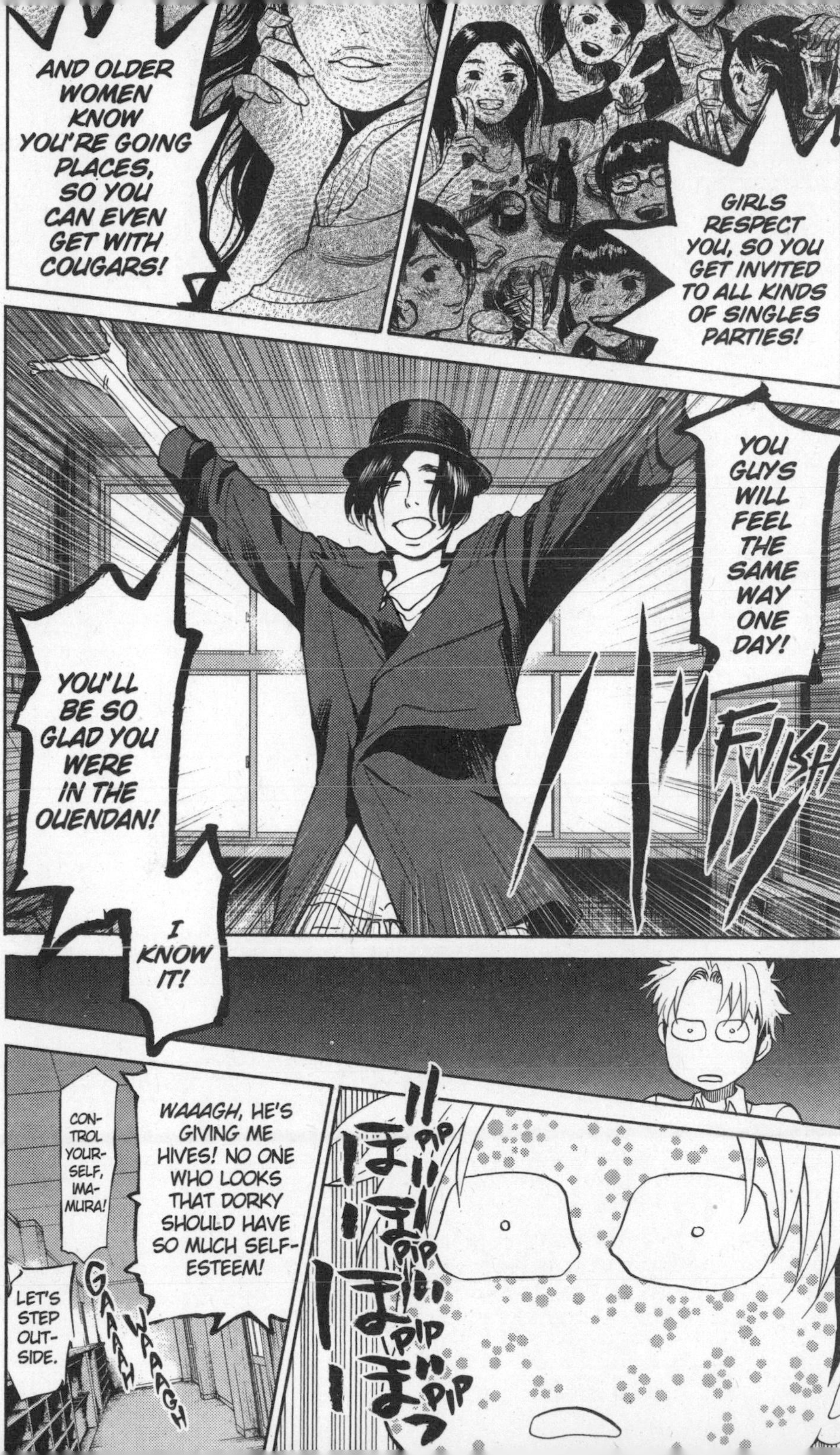
GIRLS RESPECT YOU, SO YOU GET INVITED TO ALL KINDS OF SINGLES PARTIES!
AND OLDER WOMEN KNOW YOU'RE GOING PLACES, SO YOU CAN EVEN GET WITH COUGARS!
YOU GUYS WILL FEEL THE SAME WAY ONE DAY!
FWISH
YOU'LL BE SO GLAD YOU WERE IN THE OUENDAN!
I KNOW IT!
ぽぽぽぽっ
PIP PIP PIP PIP
WAAAGH, HE'S GIVING ME HIVES! NO ONE WHO LOOKS THAT DORKY SHOULD HAVE SO MUCH SELF-ESTEEM!
CONTROL YOURSELF, IMAMURA!
GAAAAH
WAAAGH
LET'S STEP OUTSIDE.

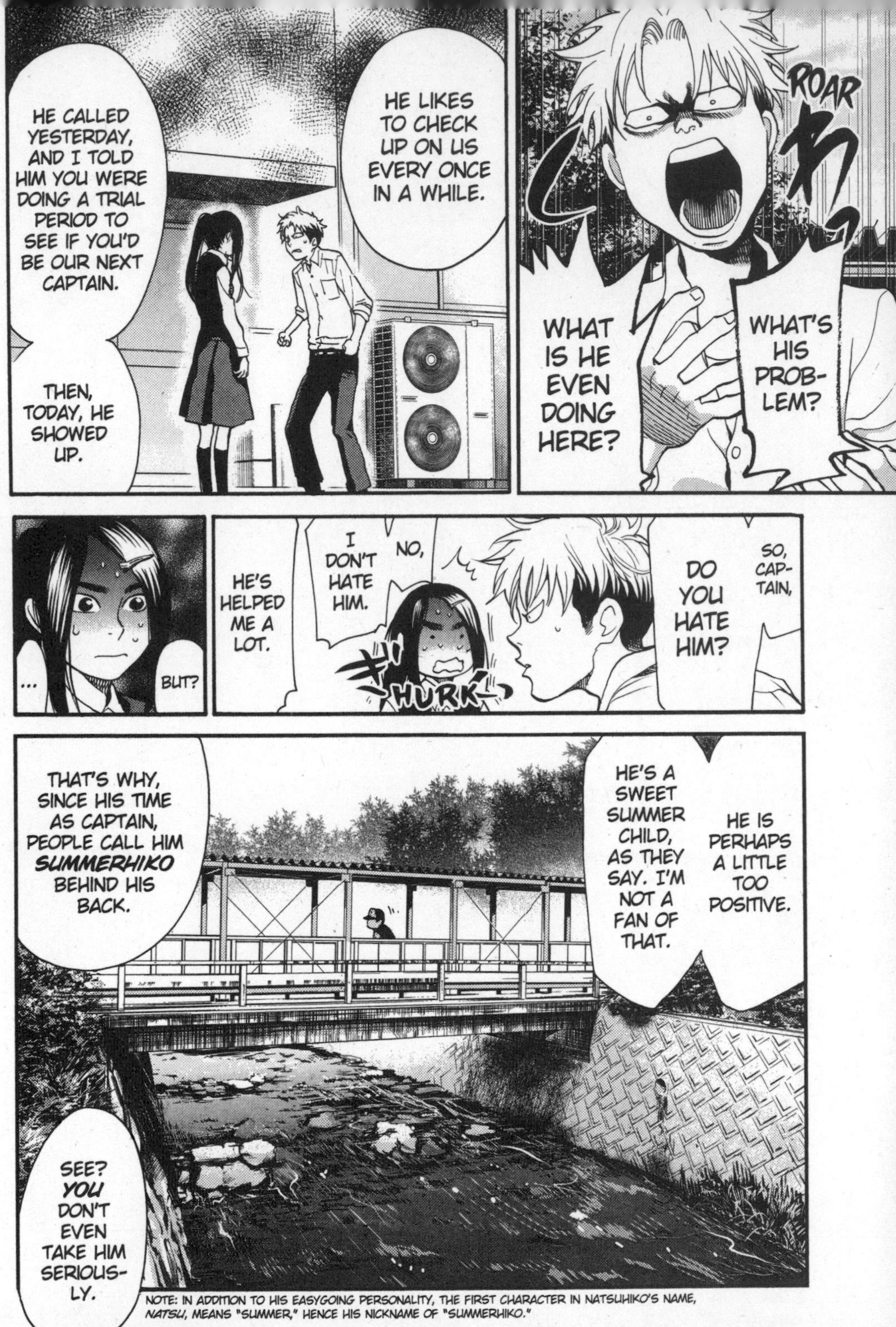
ROAR
WHAT'S HIS PROBLEM?
WHAT IS HE EVEN DOING HERE?
HE LIKES TO CHECK UP ON US EVERY ONCE IN A WHILE.
HE CALLED YESTERDAY, AND I TOLD HIM YOU WERE DOING A TRIAL PERIOD TO SEE IF YOU'D BE OUR NEXT CAPTAIN.
THEN, TODAY, HE SHOWED UP.
SO, CAPTAIN,
DO YOU HATE HIM?
NO,
I DON'T HATE HIM.
HE'S HELPED ME A LOT.
HURK
BUT?
...
HE IS PERHAPS A LITTLE TOO POSITIVE.
HE'S A SWEET SUMMER CHILD, AS THEY SAY. I'M NOT A FAN OF THAT.
THAT'S WHY, SINCE HIS TIME AS CAPTAIN, PEOPLE CALL HIM ***SUMMERHIKO*** BEHIND HIS BACK.
SEE? ***YOU*** DON'T EVEN TAKE HIM SERIOUSLY.

NOTE: IN ADDITION TO HIS EASYGOING PERSONALITY, THE FIRST CHARACTER IN NATSUHIKO'S NAME, *NATSU*, MEANS "SUMMER," HENCE HIS NICKNAME OF "SUMMERHIKO."

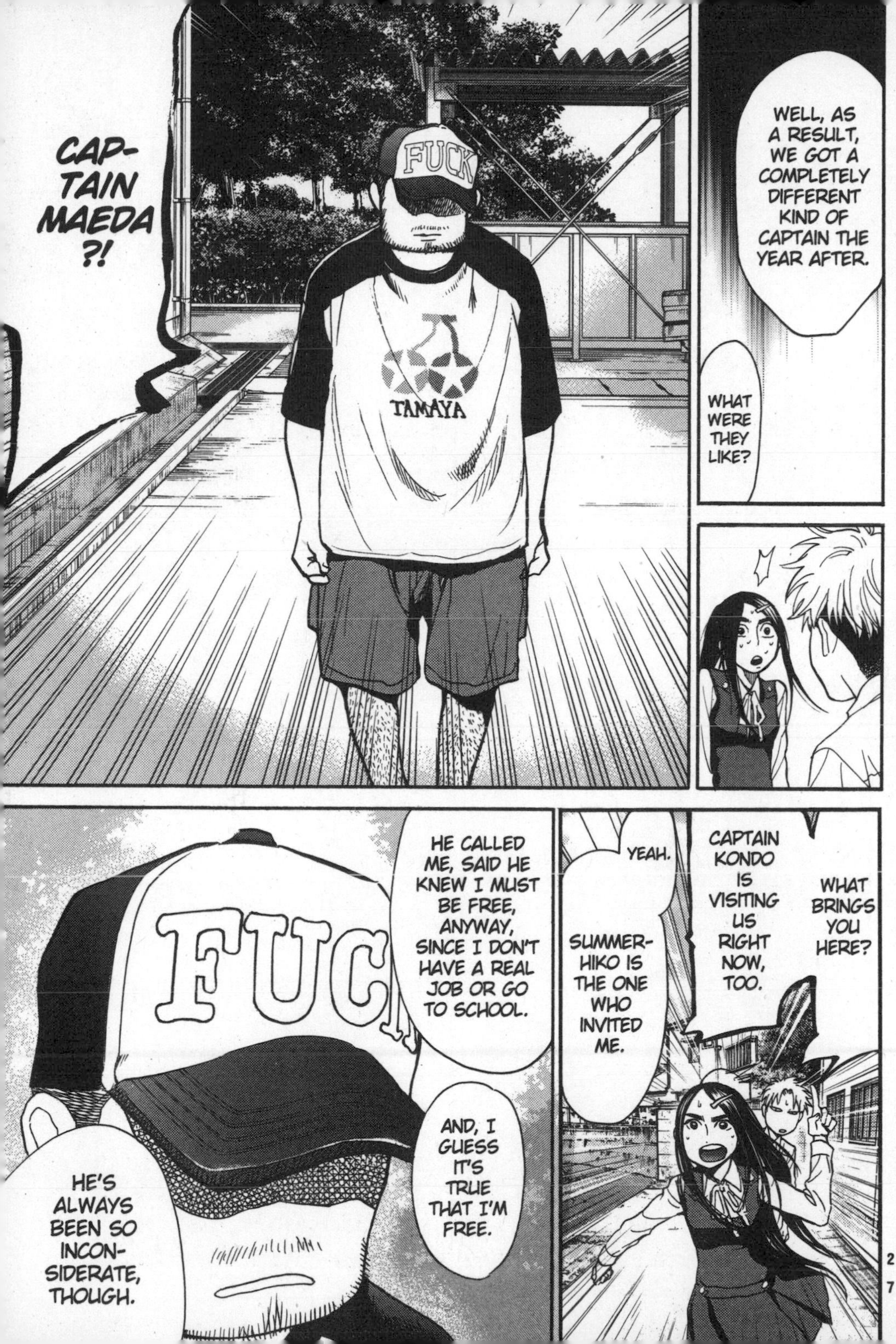
WELL, AS A RESULT, WE GOT A COMPLETELY DIFFERENT KIND OF CAPTAIN THE YEAR AFTER.
WHAT WERE THEY LIKE?
CAPTAIN MAEDA ?!
FUCK
TAMAYA
WHAT BRINGS YOU HERE?
CAPTAIN KONDO IS VISITING US RIGHT NOW, TOO.
YEAH.
SUMMERHIKO IS THE ONE WHO INVITED ME.
HE CALLED ME, SAID HE KNEW I MUST BE FREE, ANYWAY, SINCE I DON'T HAVE A REAL JOB OR GO TO SCHOOL.
FUC
AND, I GUESS IT'S TRUE THAT I'M FREE.
HE'S ALWAYS BEEN SO INCONSIDERATE, THOUGH.

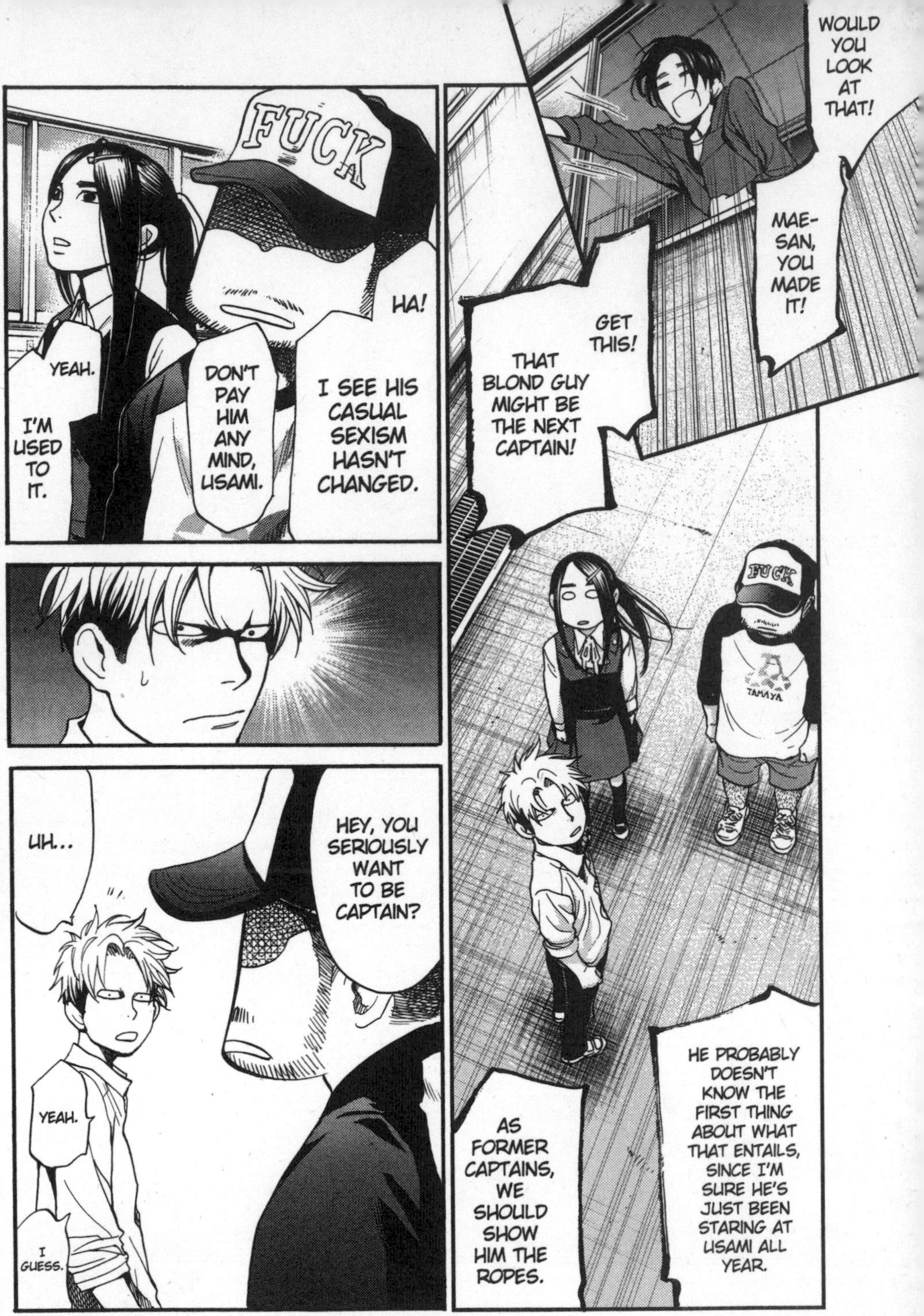
WOULD YOU LOOK AT THAT!
MAE-SAN, YOU MADE IT!
GET THIS!
THAT BLOND GUY MIGHT BE THE NEXT CAPTAIN!
HE PROBABLY DOESN'T KNOW THE FIRST THING ABOUT WHAT THAT ENTAILS, SINCE I'M SURE HE'S JUST BEEN STARING AT USAMI ALL YEAR.
AS FORMER CAPTAINS, WE SHOULD SHOW HIM THE ROPES.
HA!
I SEE HIS CASUAL SEXISM HASN'T CHANGED.
DON'T PAY HIM ANY MIND, USAMI.
YEAH.
I'M USED TO IT.
HEY, YOU SERIOUSLY WANT TO BE CAPTAIN?
UH...
YEAH.
I GUESS.

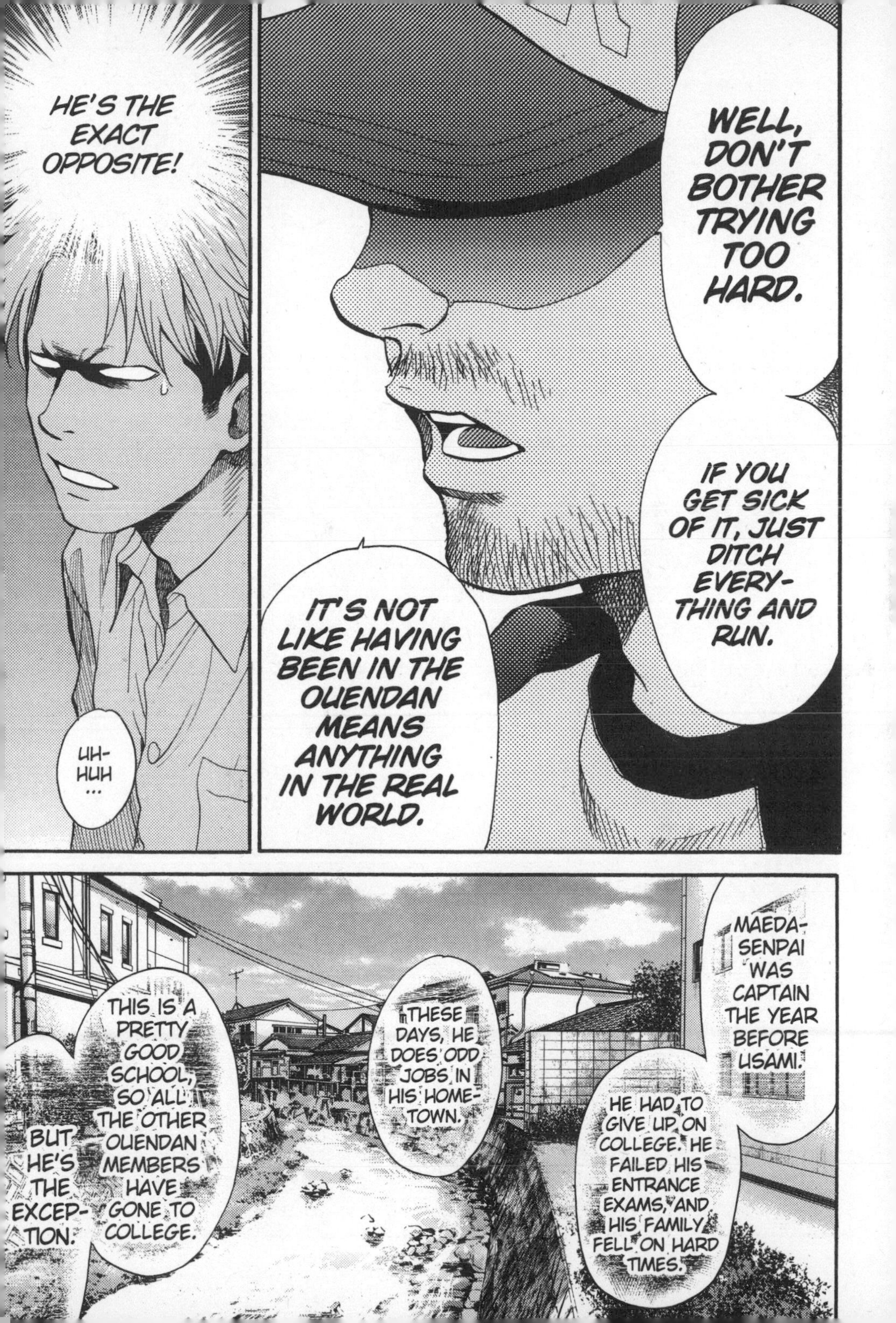
WELL, DON'T BOTHER TRYING TOO HARD.
IF YOU GET SICK OF IT, JUST DITCH EVERYTHING AND RUN.
IT'S NOT LIKE HAVING BEEN IN THE OUENDAN MEANS ANYTHING IN THE REAL WORLD.
HE'S THE EXACT OPPOSITE!
UH-HUH...
MAEDA-SENPAI WAS CAPTAIN THE YEAR BEFORE USAMI.
HE HAD TO GIVE UP ON COLLEGE. HE FAILED HIS ENTRANCE EXAMS, AND HIS FAMILY FELL ON HARD TIMES.
THESE DAYS, HE DOES ODD JOBS IN HIS HOMETOWN.
THIS IS A PRETTY GOOD SCHOOL, SO ALL THE OTHER OUENDAN MEMBERS HAVE GONE TO COLLEGE.
BUT HE'S THE EXCEPTION.

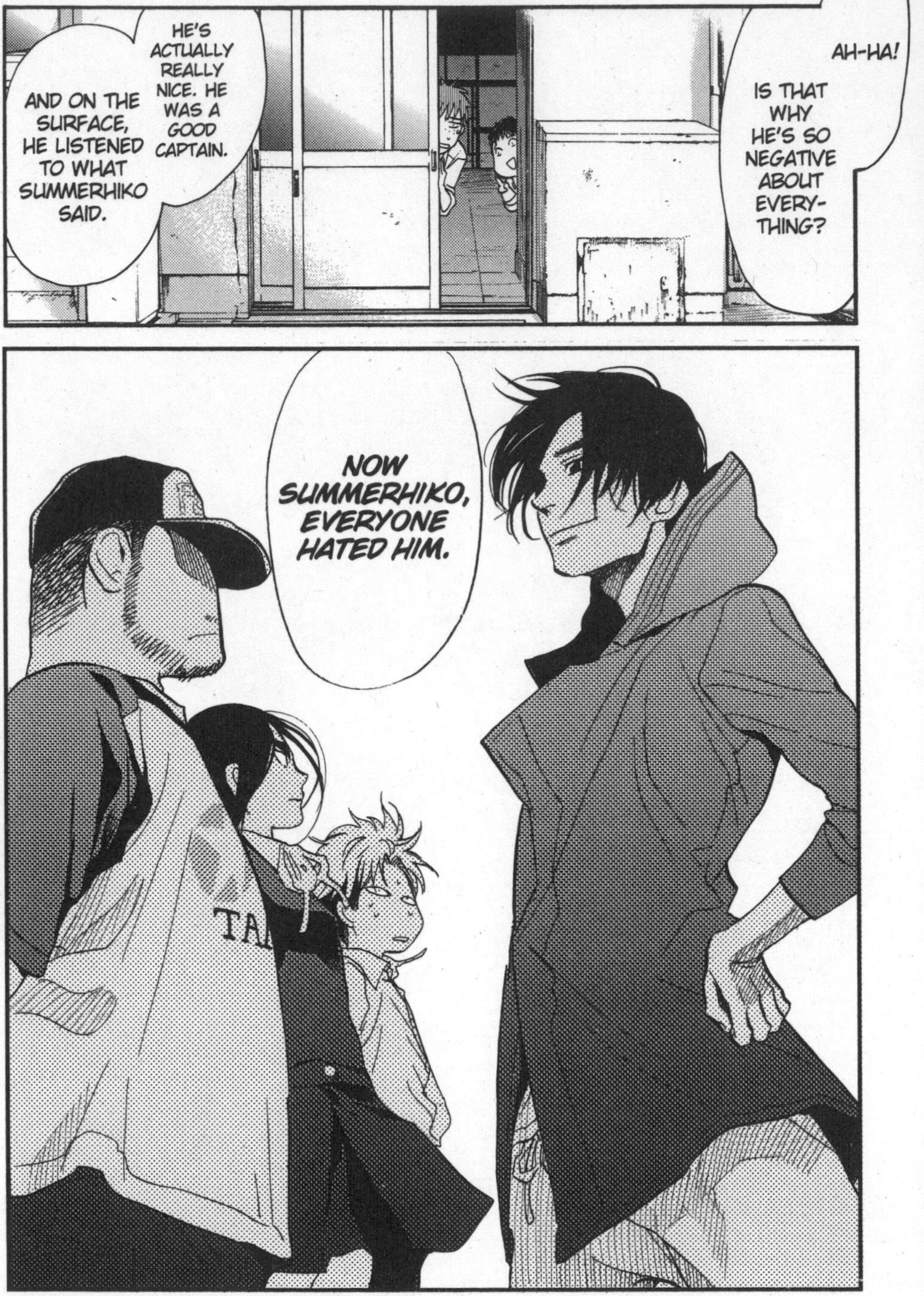
AH-HA!
IS THAT WHY HE'S SO NEGATIVE ABOUT EVERY-THING?
HE'S ACTUALLY REALLY NICE. HE WAS A GOOD CAPTAIN.
AND ON THE SURFACE, HE LISTENED TO WHAT SUMMERHIKO SAID.
NOW SUMMERHIKO, EVERYONE HATED HIM.

Again!!

アゲイン!!

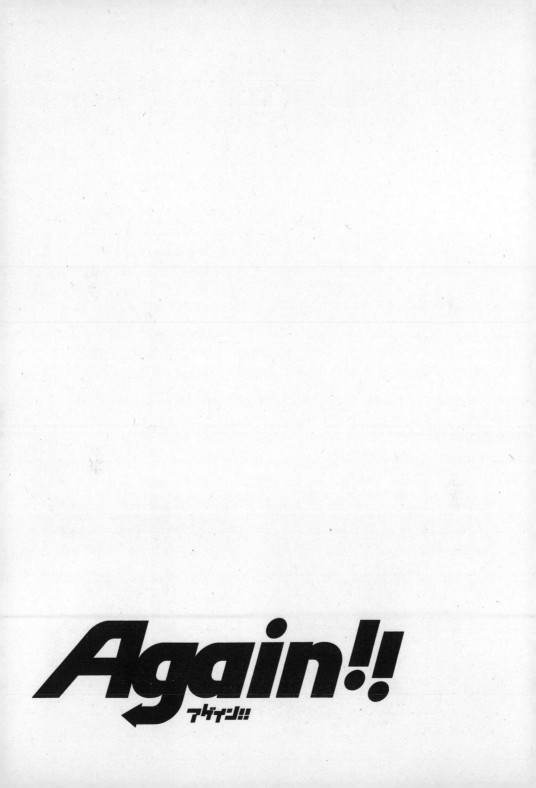

Again!!

アゲイン!!

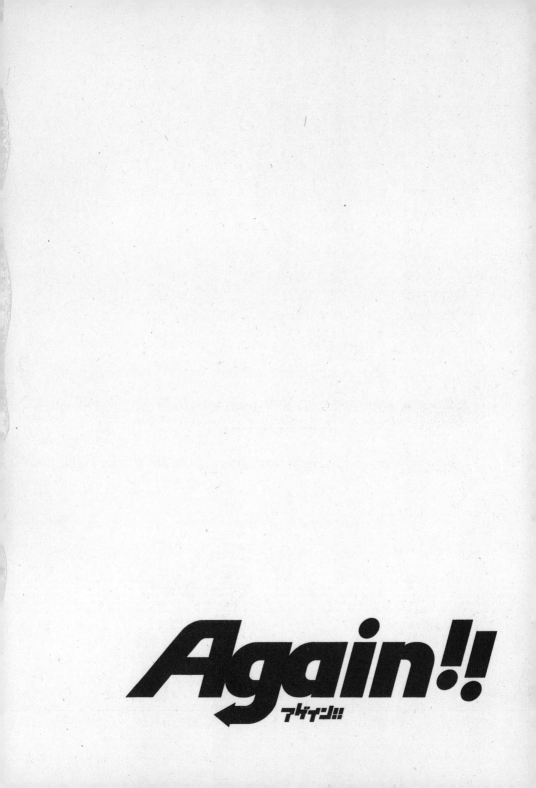

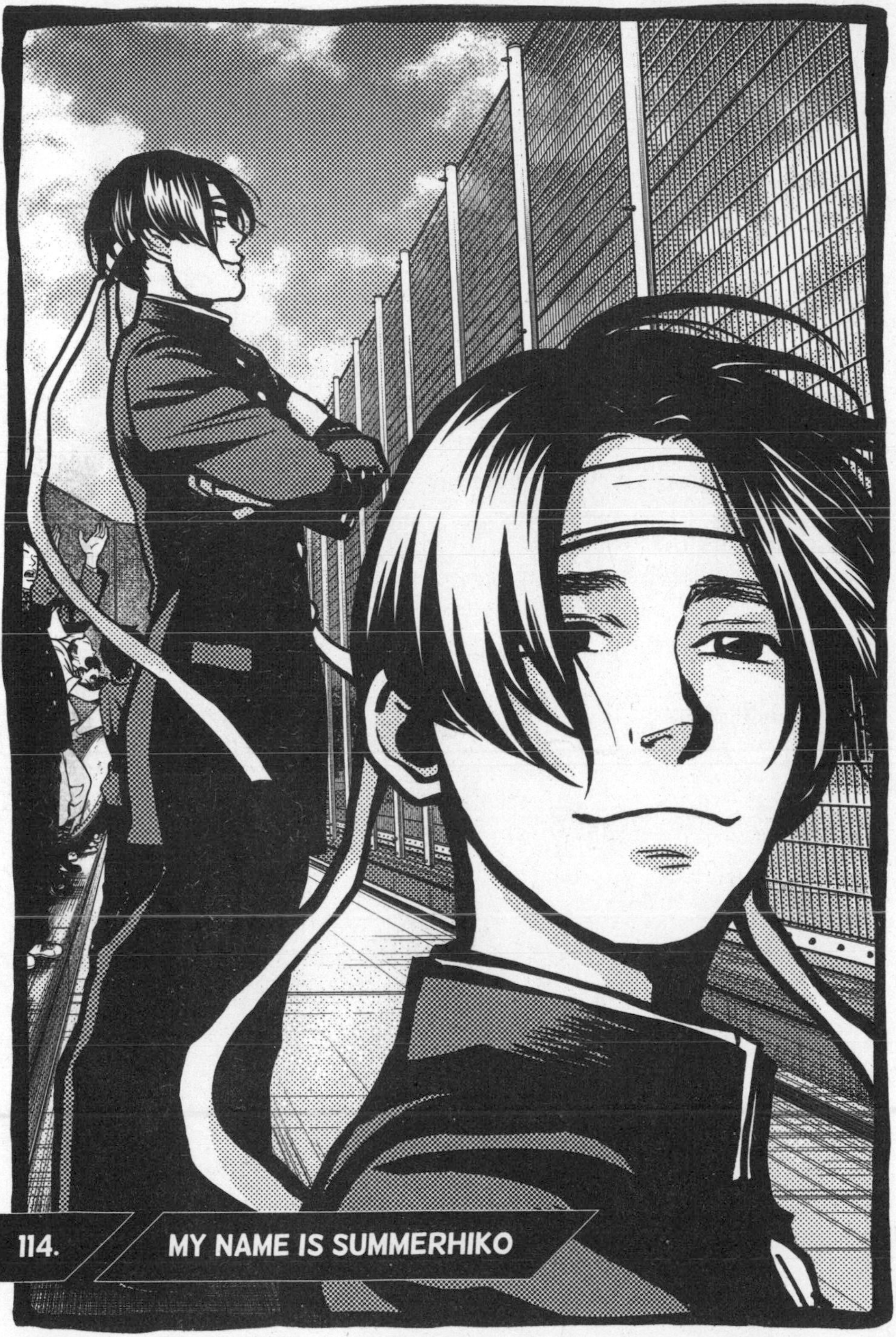
114.
MY NAME IS SUMMERHIKO

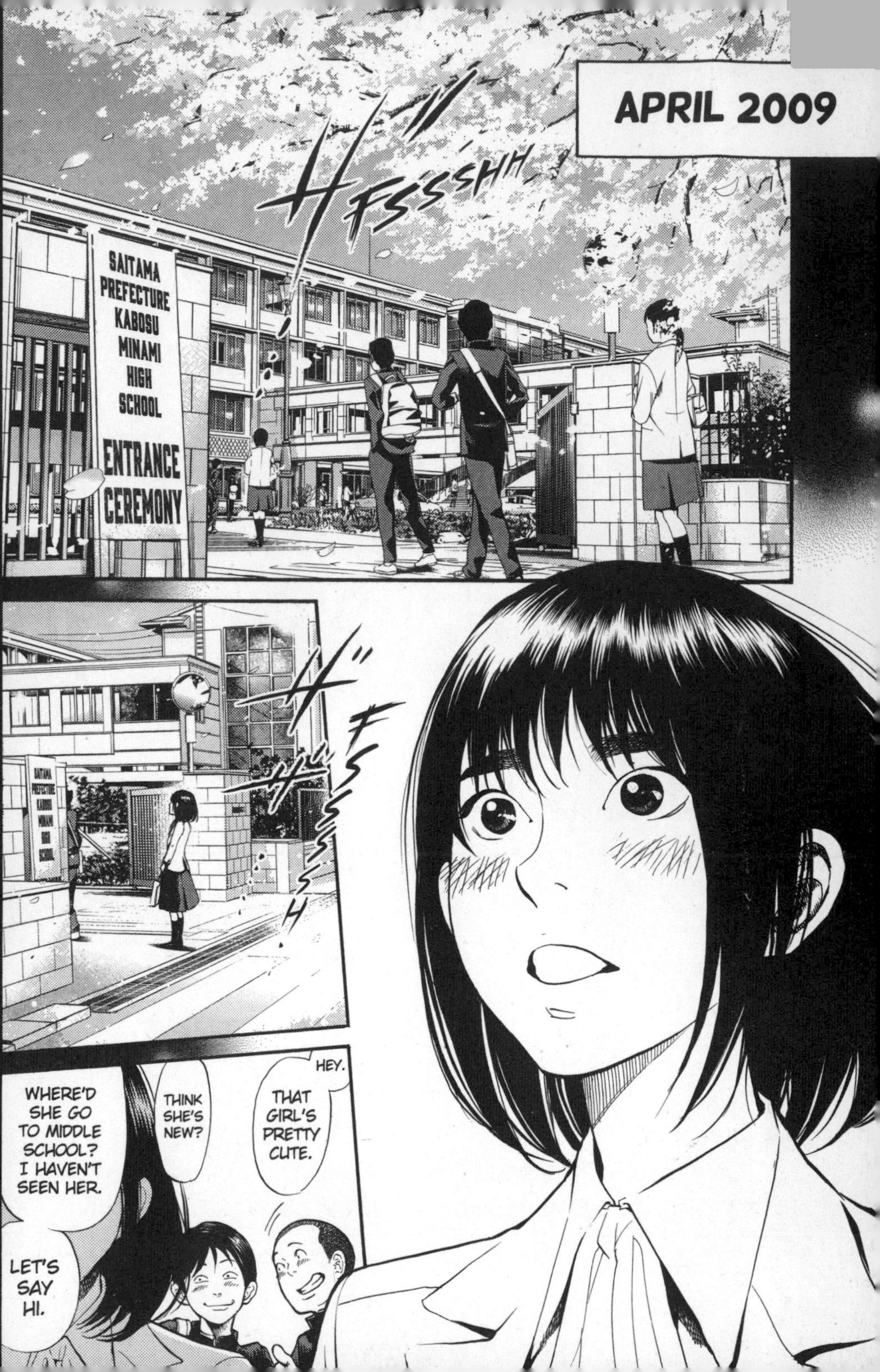
APRIL 2009
FSSSHH
SAITAMA PREFECTURE KABOSU MINAMI HIGH SCHOOL ENTRANCE CEREMONY
FSSSSSH
SAITAMA PREFECTURE KABOSU MINAMI HIGH SCHOOL
HEY.
THAT GIRL'S PRETTY CUTE.
THINK SHE'S NEW?
WHERE'D SHE GO TO MIDDLE SCHOOL? I HAVEN'T SEEN HER.
LET'S SAY HI.

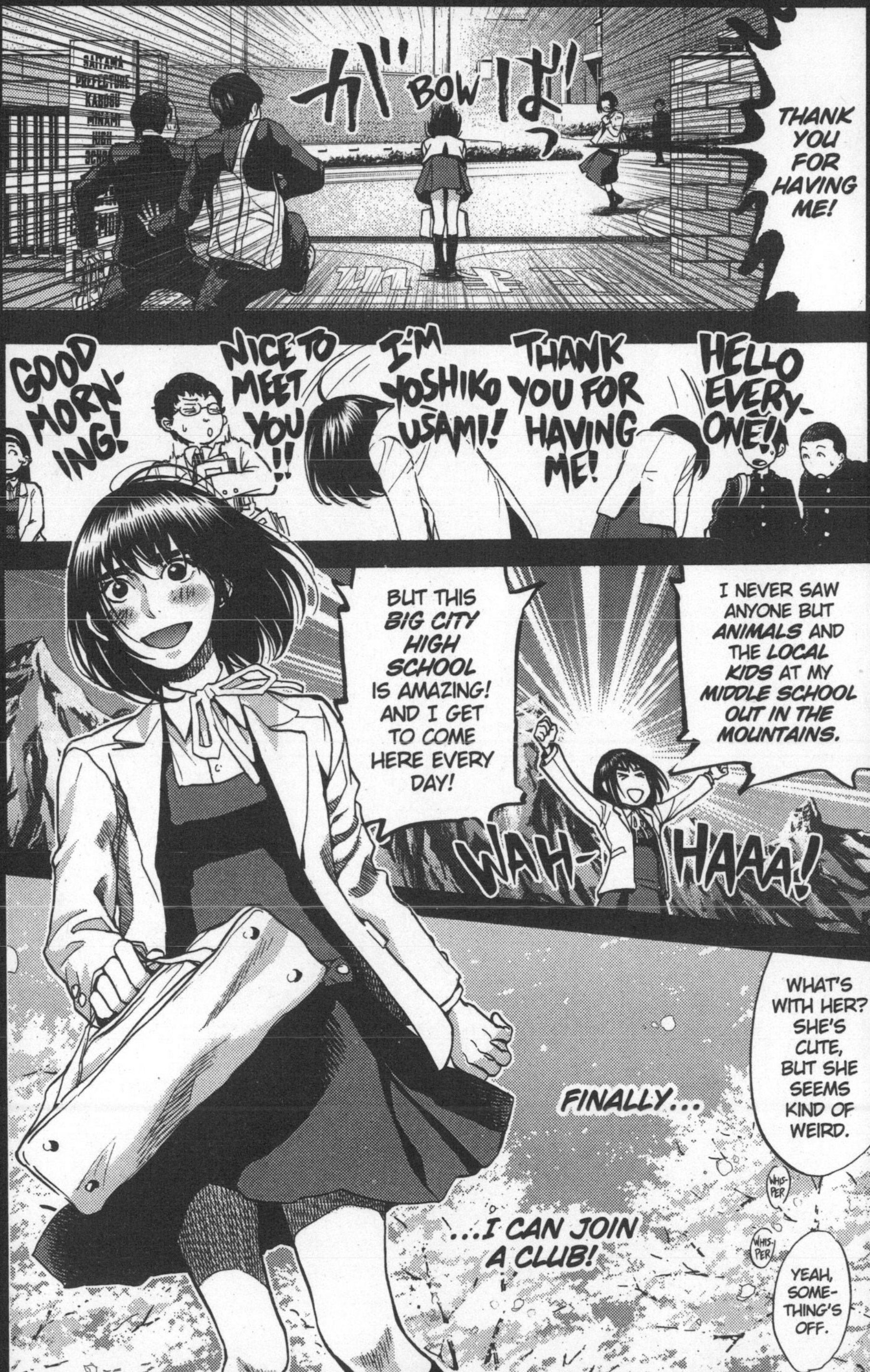
THANK YOU FOR HAVING ME!
ガばっ
BOW
HELLO EVERY-ONE!!
THANK YOU FOR HAVING ME!
I'M YOSHIKO USAMI!
NICE TO MEET YOU!!
GOOD MORN-ING!
I NEVER SAW ANYONE BUT ANIMALS AND THE LOCAL KIDS AT MY MIDDLE SCHOOL OUT IN THE MOUNTAINS.
BUT THIS BIG CITY HIGH SCHOOL IS AMAZING! AND I GET TO COME HERE EVERY DAY!
WAH-HAAA!
WHAT'S WITH HER? SHE'S CUTE, BUT SHE SEEMS KIND OF WEIRD.
WHISPER
WHISPER
YEAH, SOMETHING'S OFF.
FINALLY...
...I CAN JOIN A CLUB!

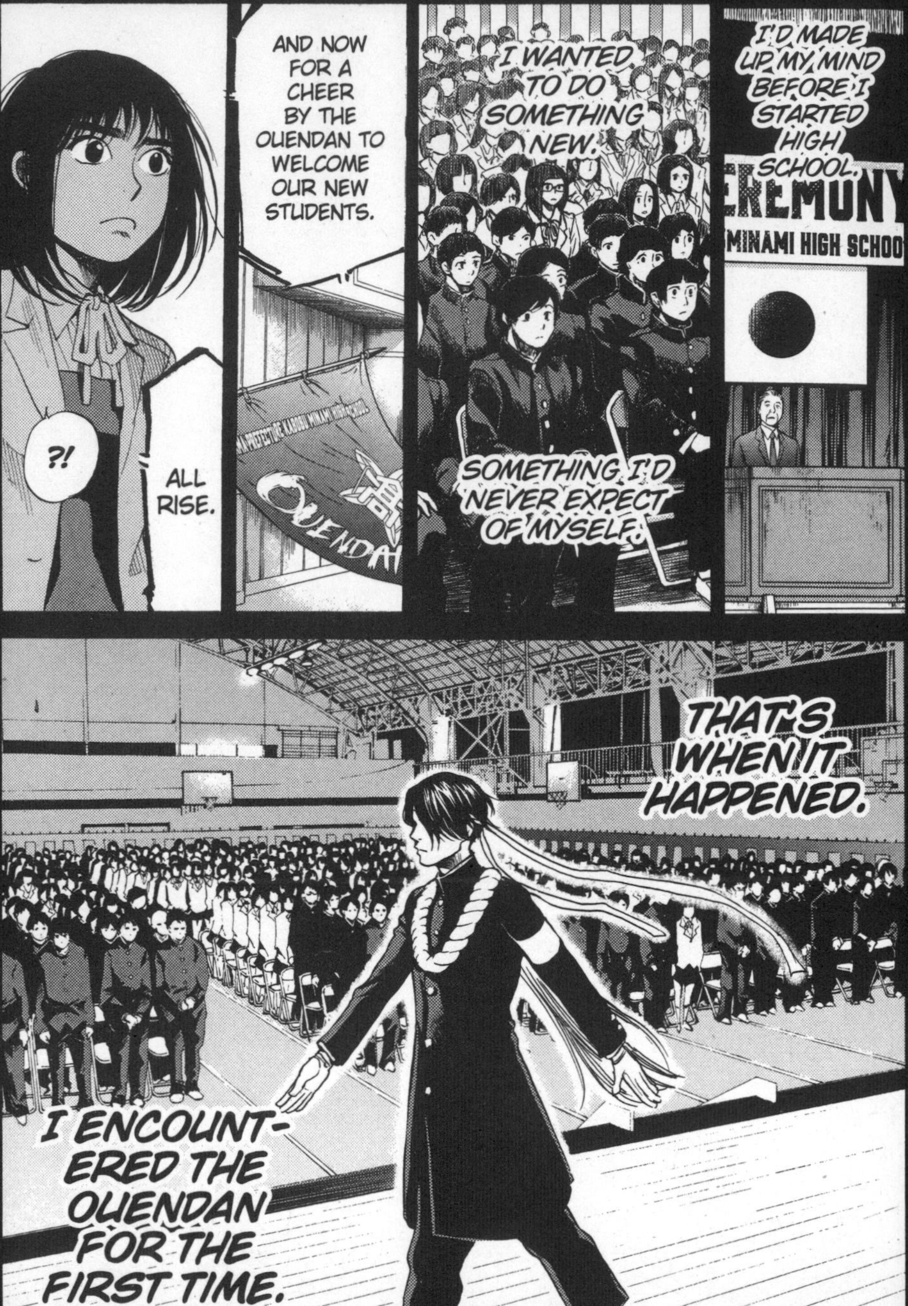
I'D MADE UP MY MIND BEFORE I STARTED HIGH SCHOOL.
EREMONY
MINAMI HIGH SCHOO
I WANTED TO DO SOMETHING NEW.
SOMETHING I'D NEVER EXPECT OF MYSELF.
AND NOW FOR A CHEER BY THE OUENDAN TO WELCOME OUR NEW STUDENTS.
ALL RISE.
?!
THAT'S WHEN IT HAPPENED.
I ENCOUNT-
ERED THE OUENDAN FOR THE FIRST TIME.

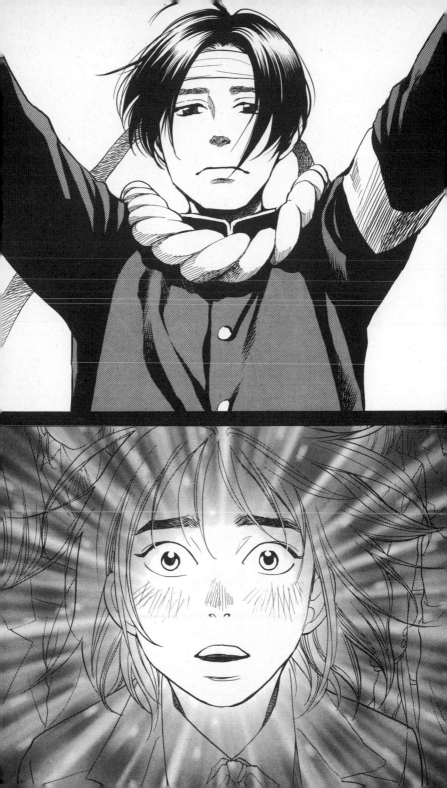

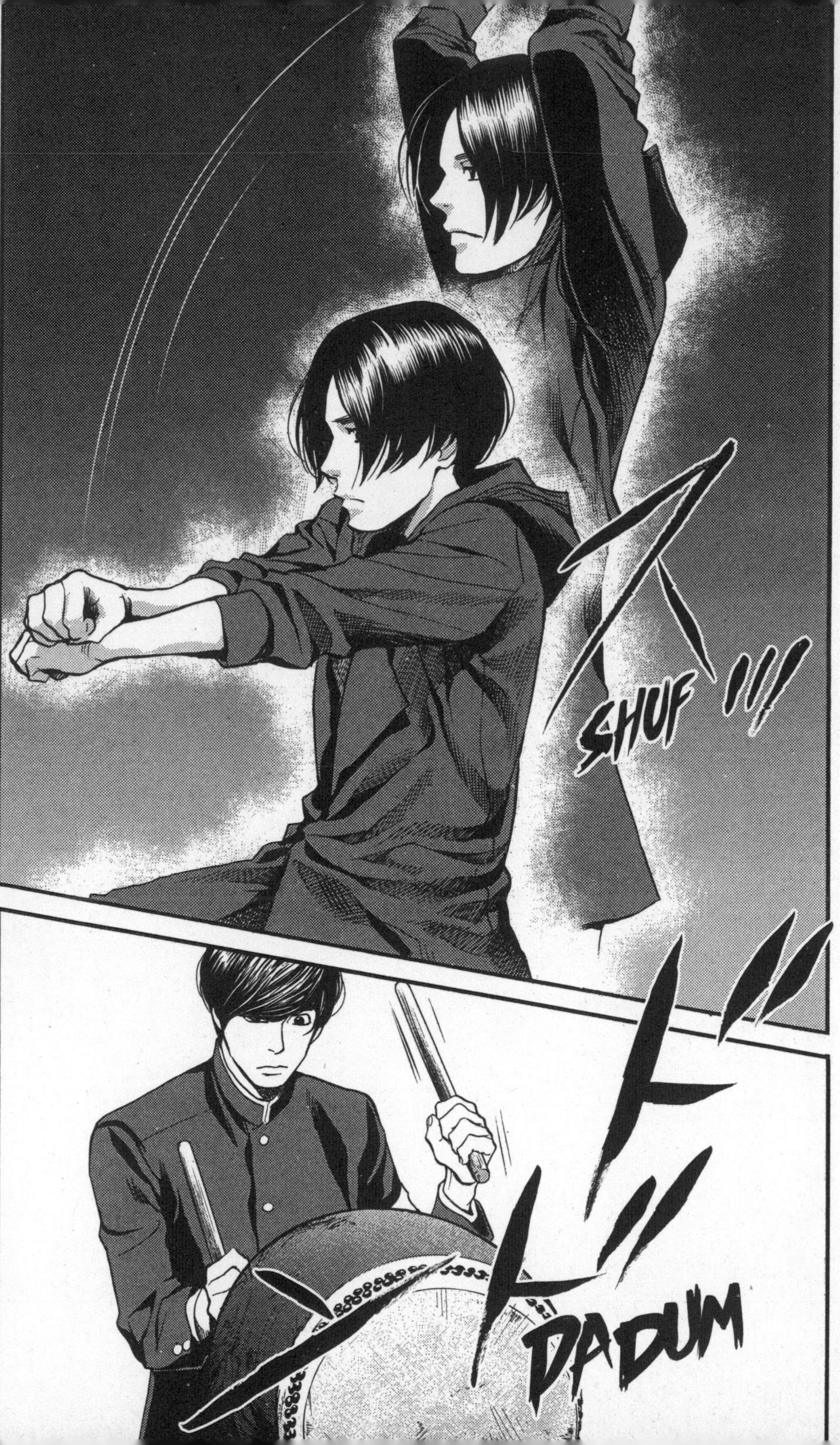
SHUF
DADUM

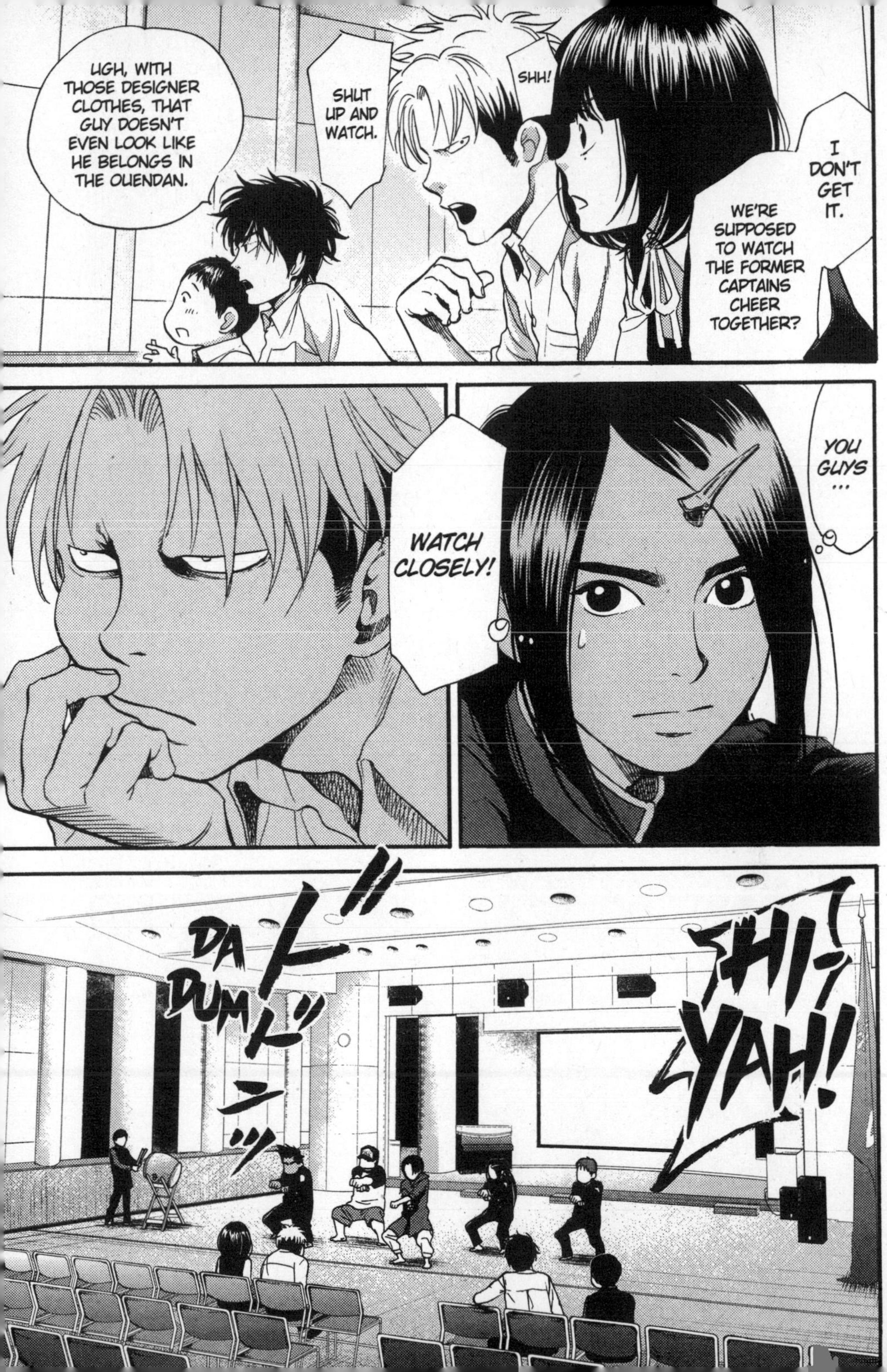

I DON'T GET IT.
WE'RE SUPPOSED TO WATCH THE FORMER CAPTAINS CHEER TOGETHER?
SHH!
SHUT UP AND WATCH.
UGH, WITH THOSE DESIGNER CLOTHES, THAT GUY DOESN'T EVEN LOOK LIKE HE BELONGS IN THE OUENDAN.
YOU GUYS ...
WATCH CLOSELY!
SHI-YAH!
DA DUM

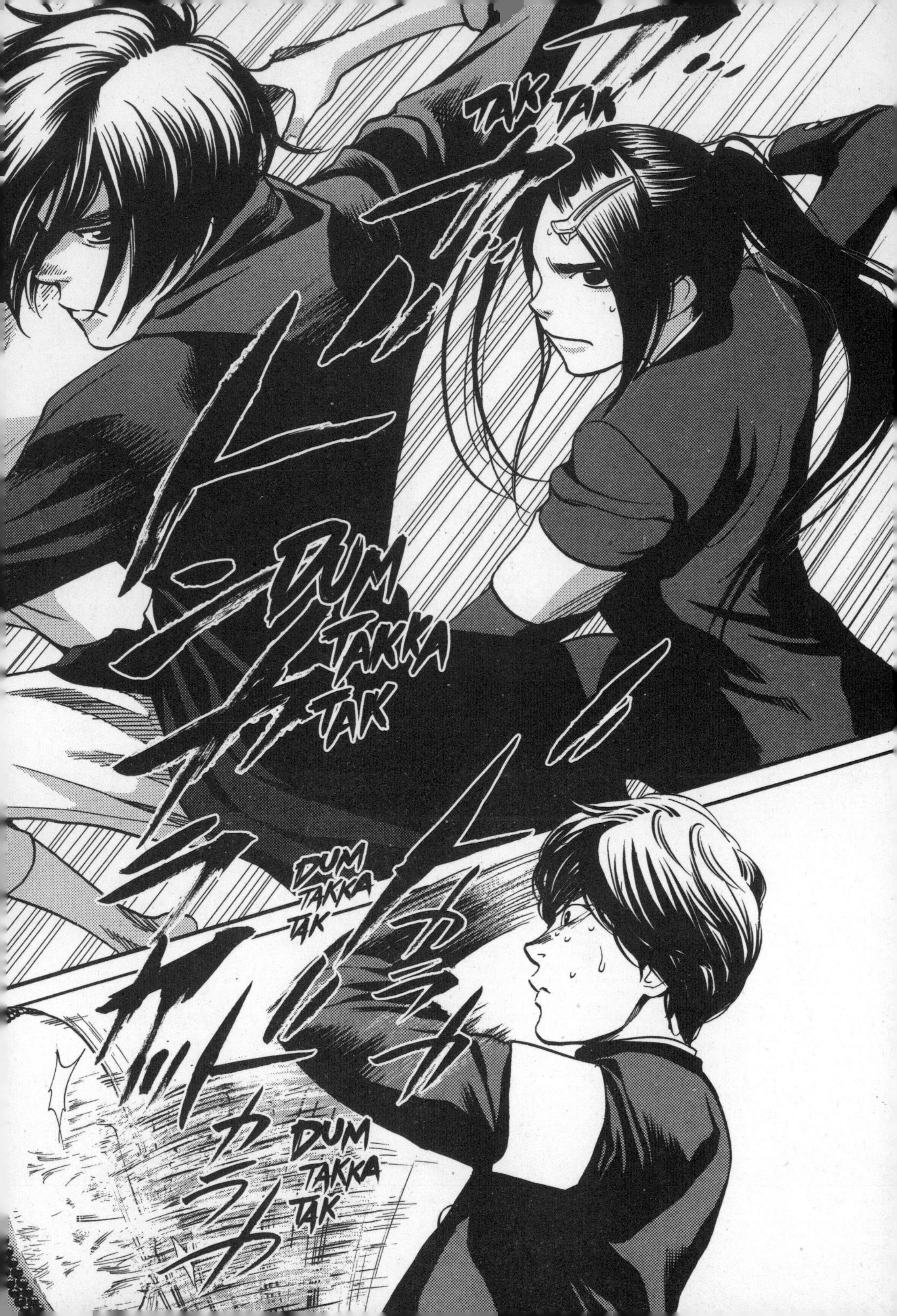
TAK TAK
DUM TAKKA TAK
DUM TAKKA TAK
DUM TAKKA TAK

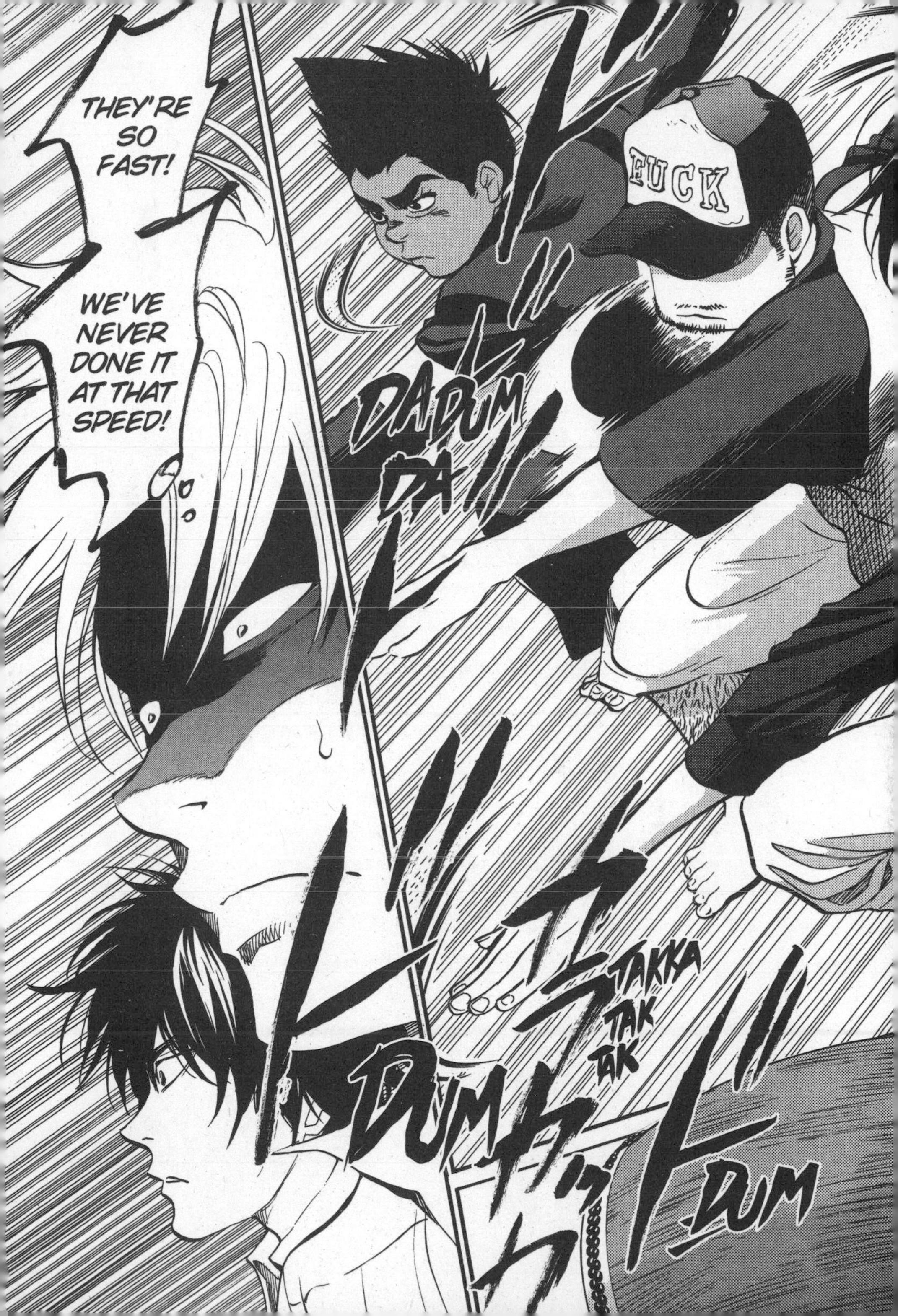
THEY'RE SO FAST!
WE'VE NEVER DONE IT AT THAT SPEED!
FUCK
DADUM DA
TAKKA TAK TAK
DUM
DUM

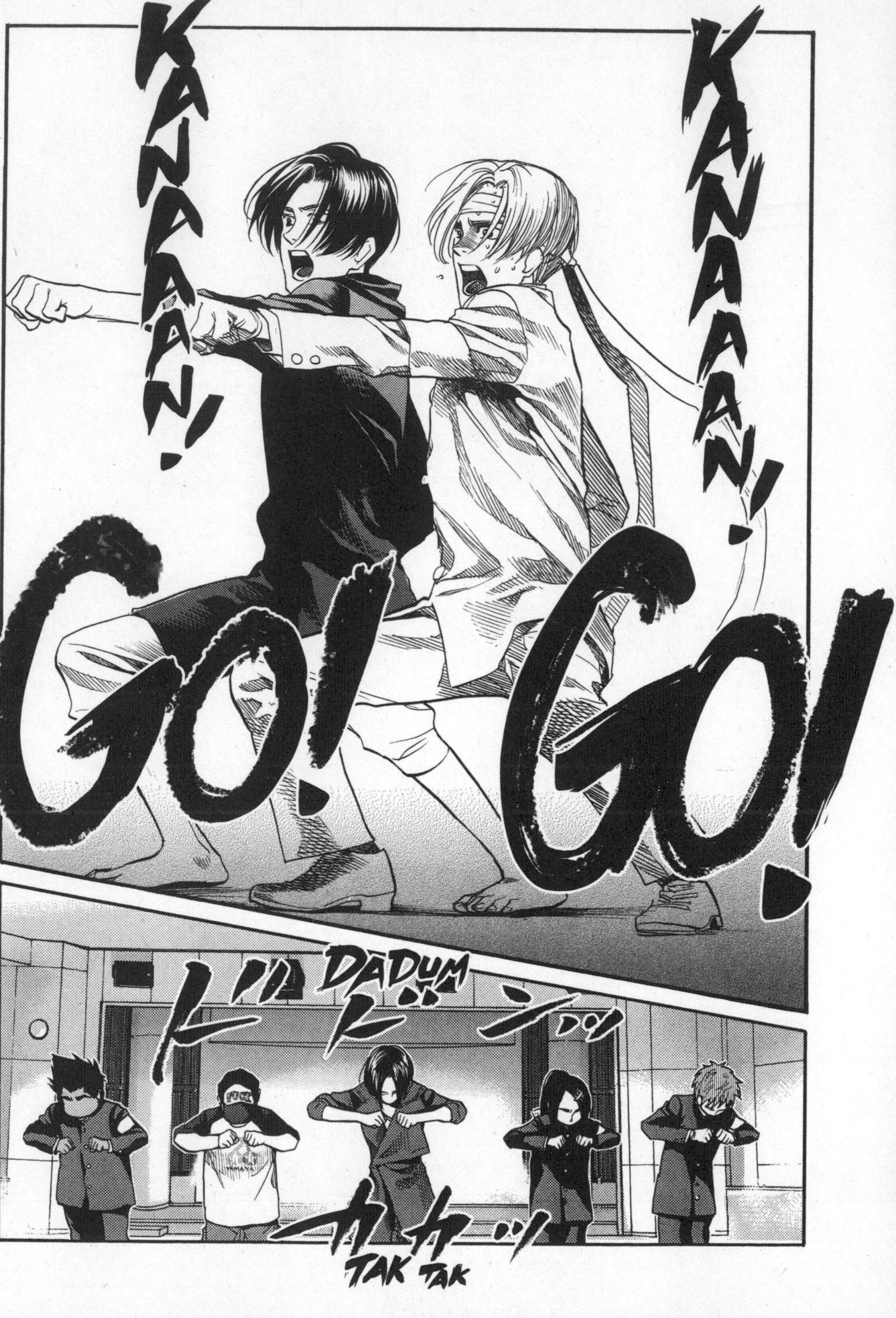
KANAAAN!
KANAAAN!
GO! GO!
DADUM
TAK TAK

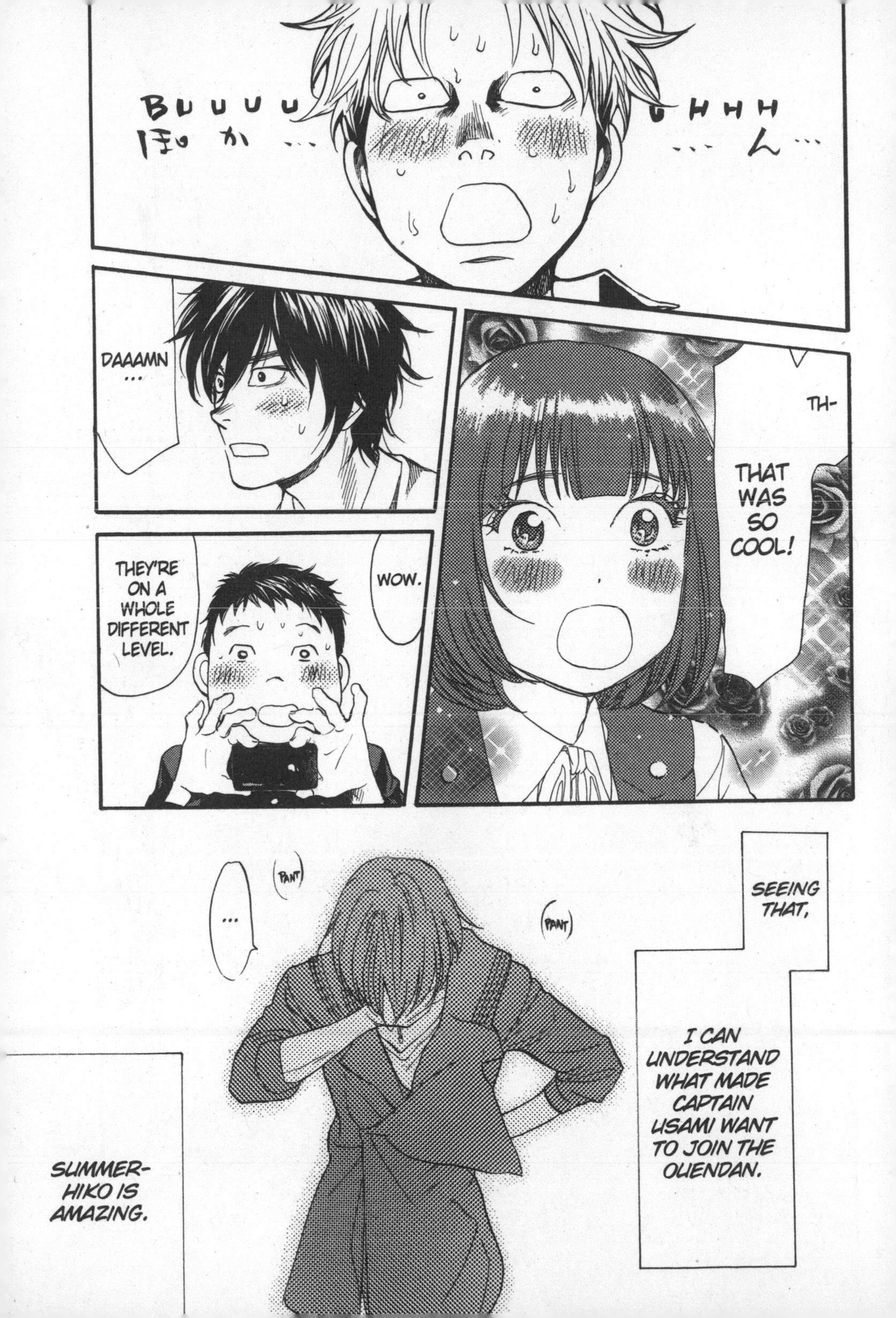
BUUUUUHHH
ほか……ん…
TH-
THAT WAS SO COOL!
DAAAMN ...
WOW.
THEY'RE ON A WHOLE DIFFERENT LEVEL.
SEEING THAT,
I CAN UNDERSTAND WHAT MADE CAPTAIN USAMI WANT TO JOIN THE OUENDAN.
(PANT)
(PANT)
...
SUMMER-HIKO IS AMAZING.

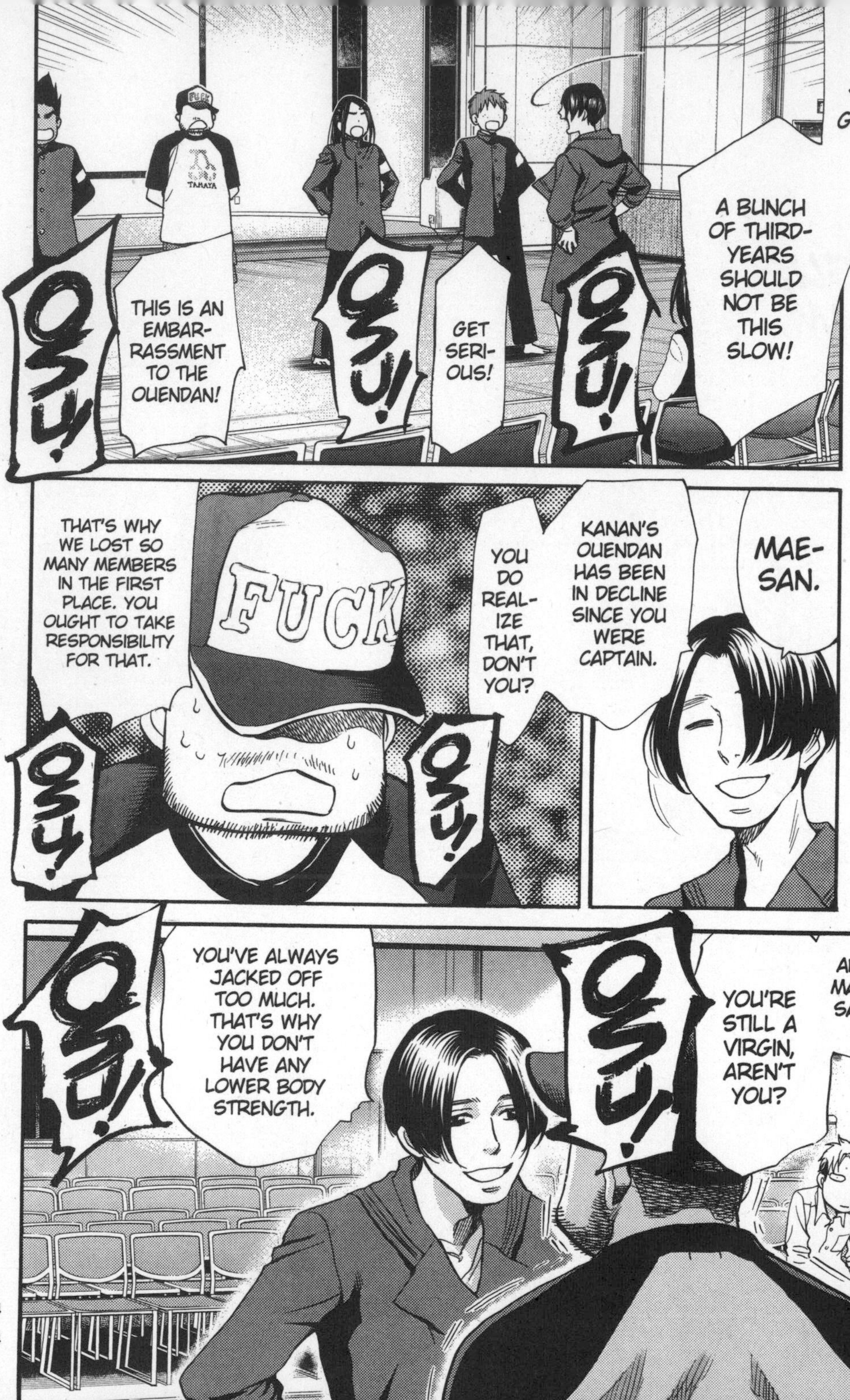
YOU GUYS!
A BUNCH OF THIRD-YEARS SHOULD NOT BE THIS SLOW!
OSU!
GET SERIOUS!
OSU!
THIS IS AN EMBARRASSMENT TO THE OUENDAN!
OSU!
MAE-SAN.
KANAN'S OUENDAN HAS BEEN IN DECLINE SINCE YOU WERE CAPTAIN.
YOU DO REALIZE THAT, DON'T YOU?
OSU!
FUCK
THAT'S WHY WE LOST SO MANY MEMBERS IN THE FIRST PLACE. YOU OUGHT TO TAKE RESPONSIBILITY FOR THAT.
OSU!
AND MAE-SAN,
YOU'RE STILL A VIRGIN, AREN'T YOU?
OSU!
YOU'VE ALWAYS JACKED OFF TOO MUCH. THAT'S WHY YOU DON'T HAVE ANY LOWER BODY STRENGTH.
OSU!

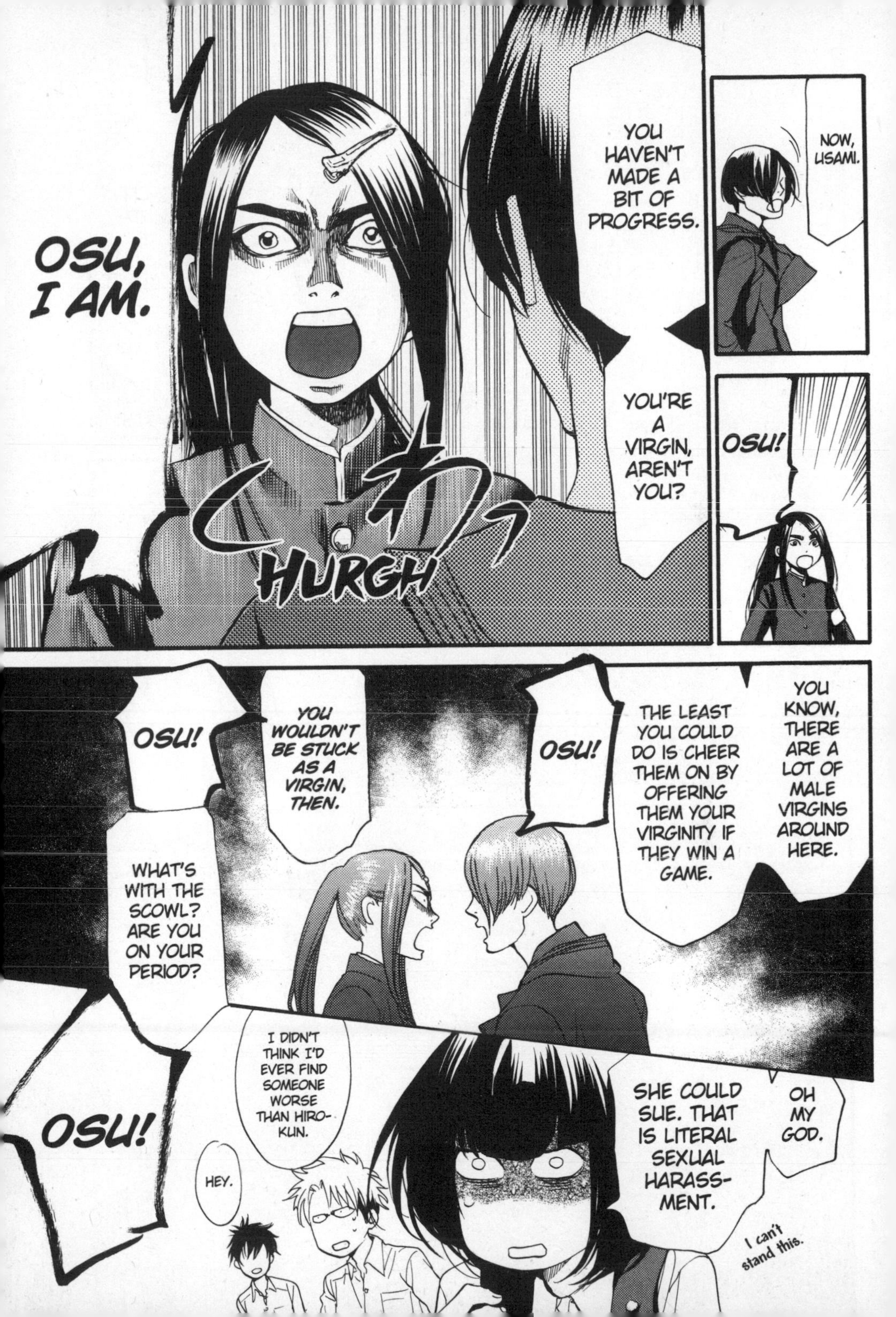
NOW, USAMI.
OSU!
YOU HAVEN'T MADE A BIT OF PROGRESS.
YOU'RE A VIRGIN, AREN'T YOU?
HURGH
OSU, I AM.
YOU KNOW, THERE ARE A LOT OF MALE VIRGINS AROUND HERE.
THE LEAST YOU COULD DO IS CHEER THEM ON BY OFFERING THEM YOUR VIRGINITY IF THEY WIN A GAME.
OSU!
YOU WOULDN'T BE STUCK AS A VIRGIN, THEN.
OSU!
WHAT'S WITH THE SCOWL? ARE YOU ON YOUR PERIOD?
OH MY GOD.
SHE COULD SUE. THAT IS LITERAL SEXUAL HARASS-MENT.
I can't stand this.
I DIDN'T THINK I'D EVER FIND SOMEONE WORSE THAN HIRO-KUN.
HEY.
OSU!

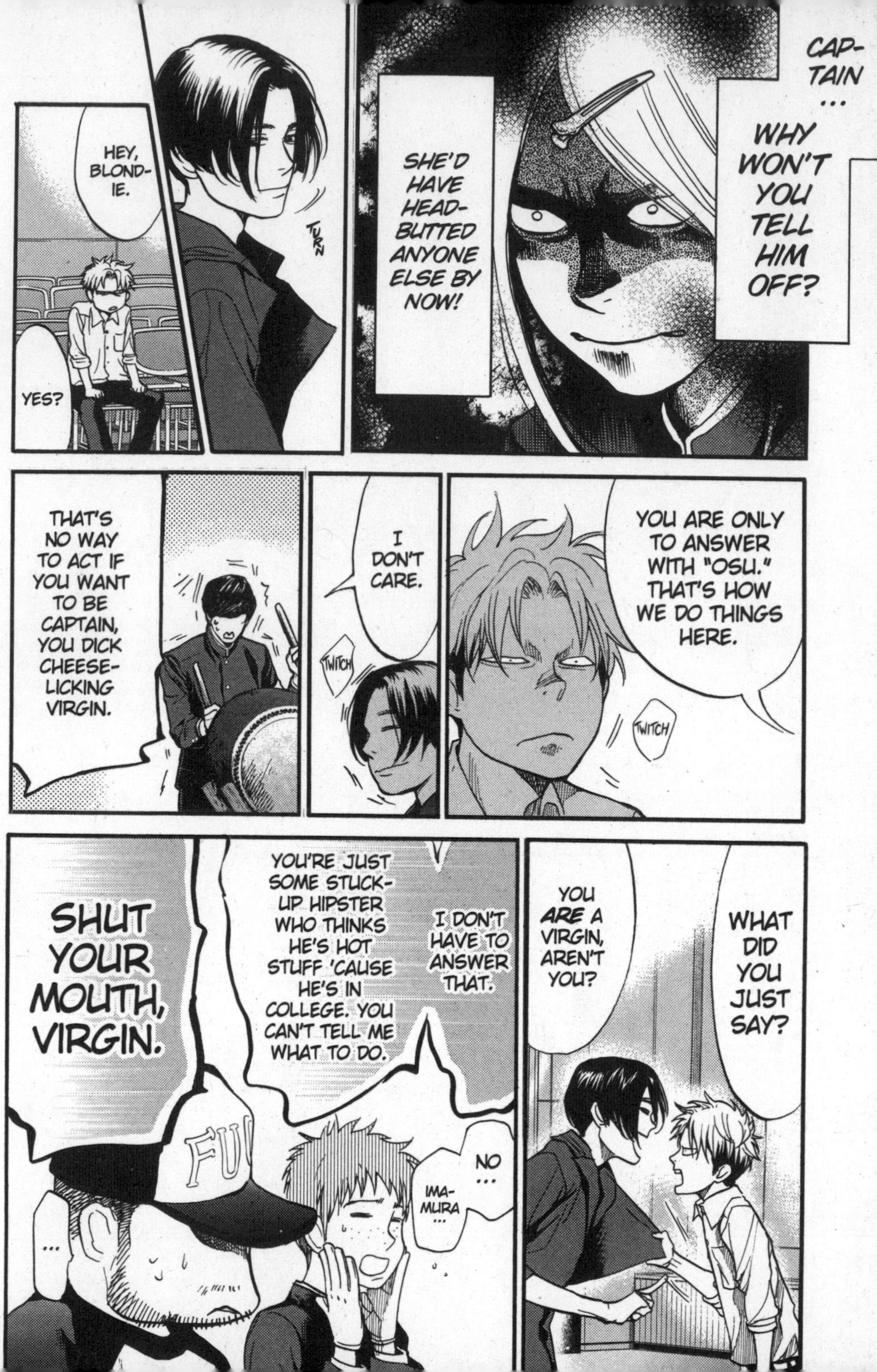
CAPTAIN... WHY WON'T YOU TELL HIM OFF?
SHE'D HAVE HEAD-BUTTED ANYONE ELSE BY NOW!
HEY, BLONDIE.
TURN
YES?
YOU ARE ONLY TO ANSWER WITH "OSU." THAT'S HOW WE DO THINGS HERE.
TWITCH
TWITCH
I DON'T CARE.
THAT'S NO WAY TO ACT IF YOU WANT TO BE CAPTAIN, YOU DICK CHEESE-LICKING VIRGIN.
WHAT DID YOU JUST SAY?
YOU ARE A VIRGIN, AREN'T YOU?
I DON'T HAVE TO ANSWER THAT.
YOU'RE JUST SOME STUCK-UP HIPSTER WHO THINKS HE'S HOT STUFF 'CAUSE HE'S IN COLLEGE. YOU CAN'T TELL ME WHAT TO DO.
SHUT YOUR MOUTH, VIRGIN.
NO...
IMAMURA...
...
FU

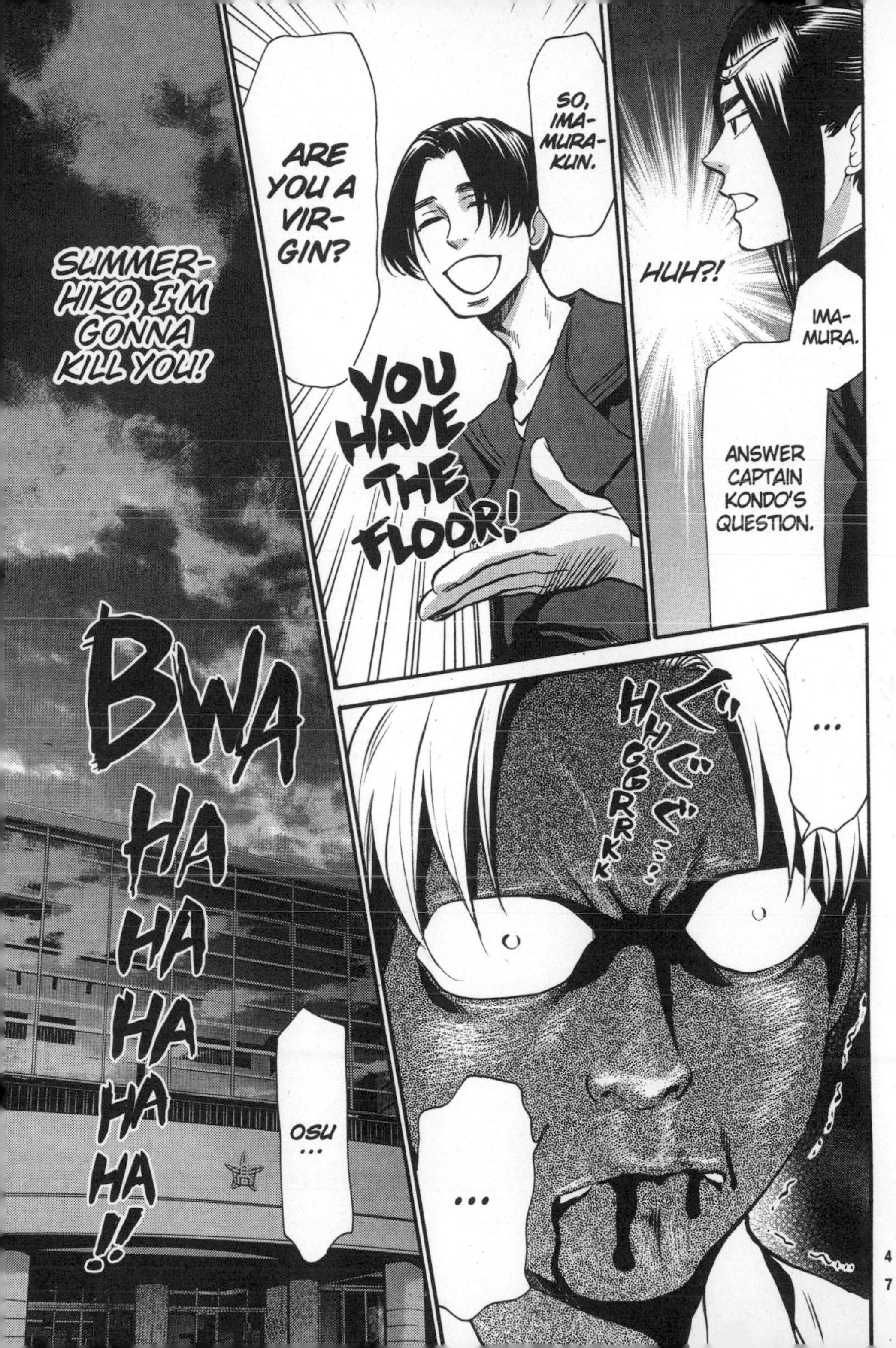
HUH?!
IMA-MURA.
ANSWER CAPTAIN KONDO'S QUESTION.
SO, IMA-MURA-KUN.
ARE YOU A VIR-GIN?
YOU HAVE THE FLOOR!
HNGGRRRK
...
OSU ...
...
SUMMER-HIKO, I'M GONNA KILL YOU!
BWA HA HA HA HA HA HA HA!!

Again!!
アゲイン!!

115. DON'T LOSE HOPE!

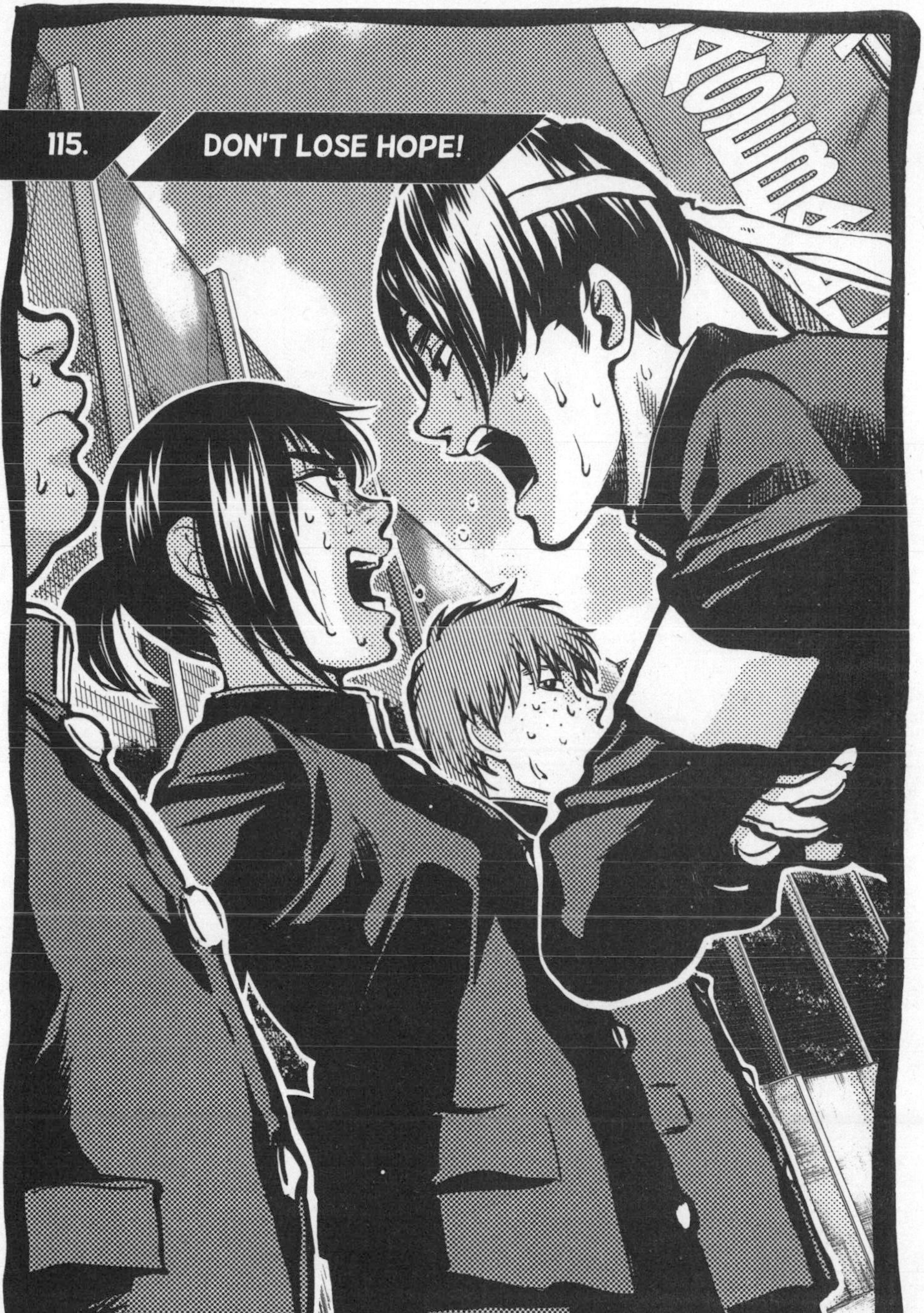

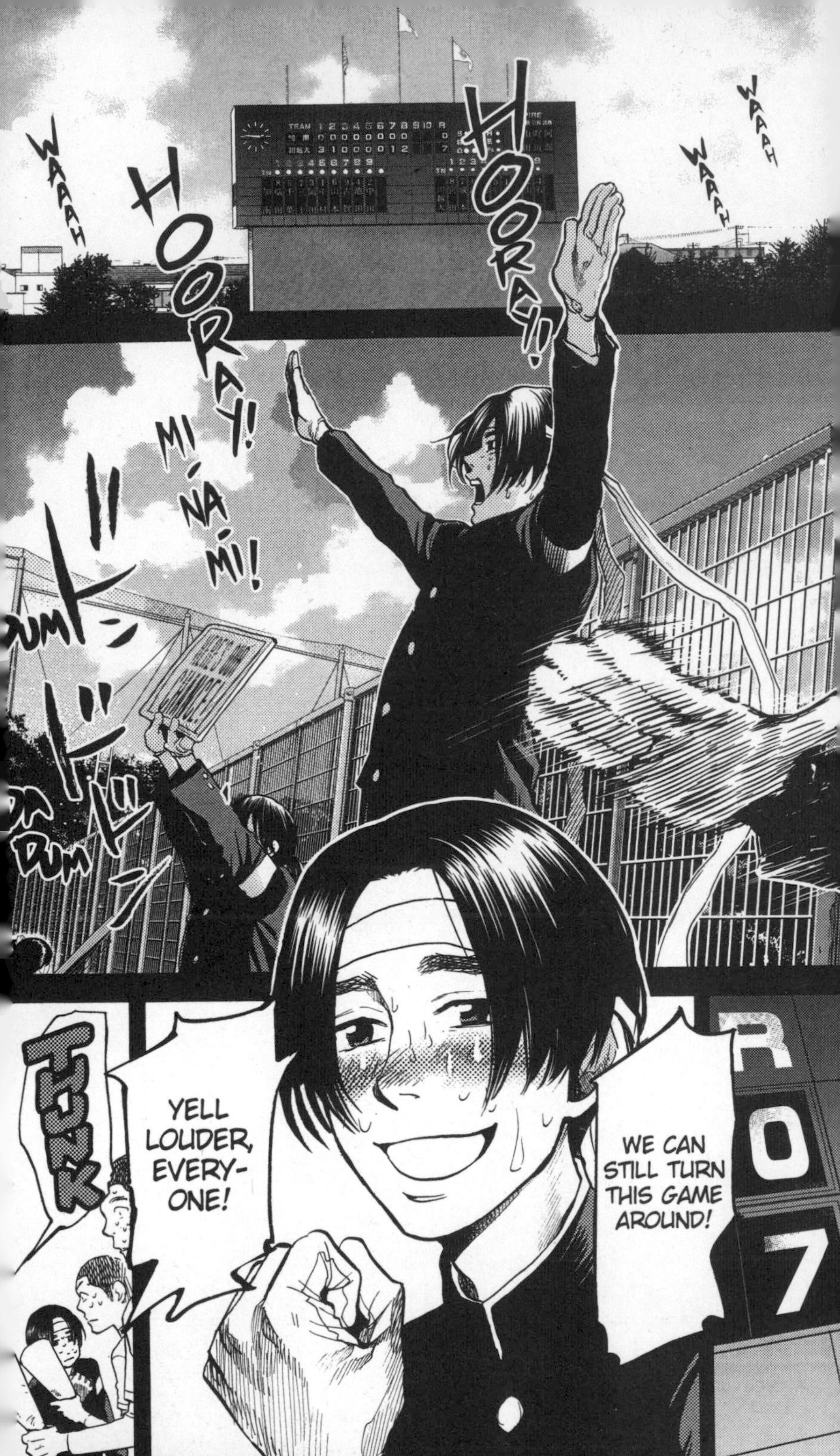
WAAAH
WAAAH
HOORAY!!
HOORAY!
WAAAAH
MI NA MI!
DUM
DA DUM
WE CAN STILL TURN THIS GAME AROUND!
YELL LOUDER, EVERY-ONE!
THUNK

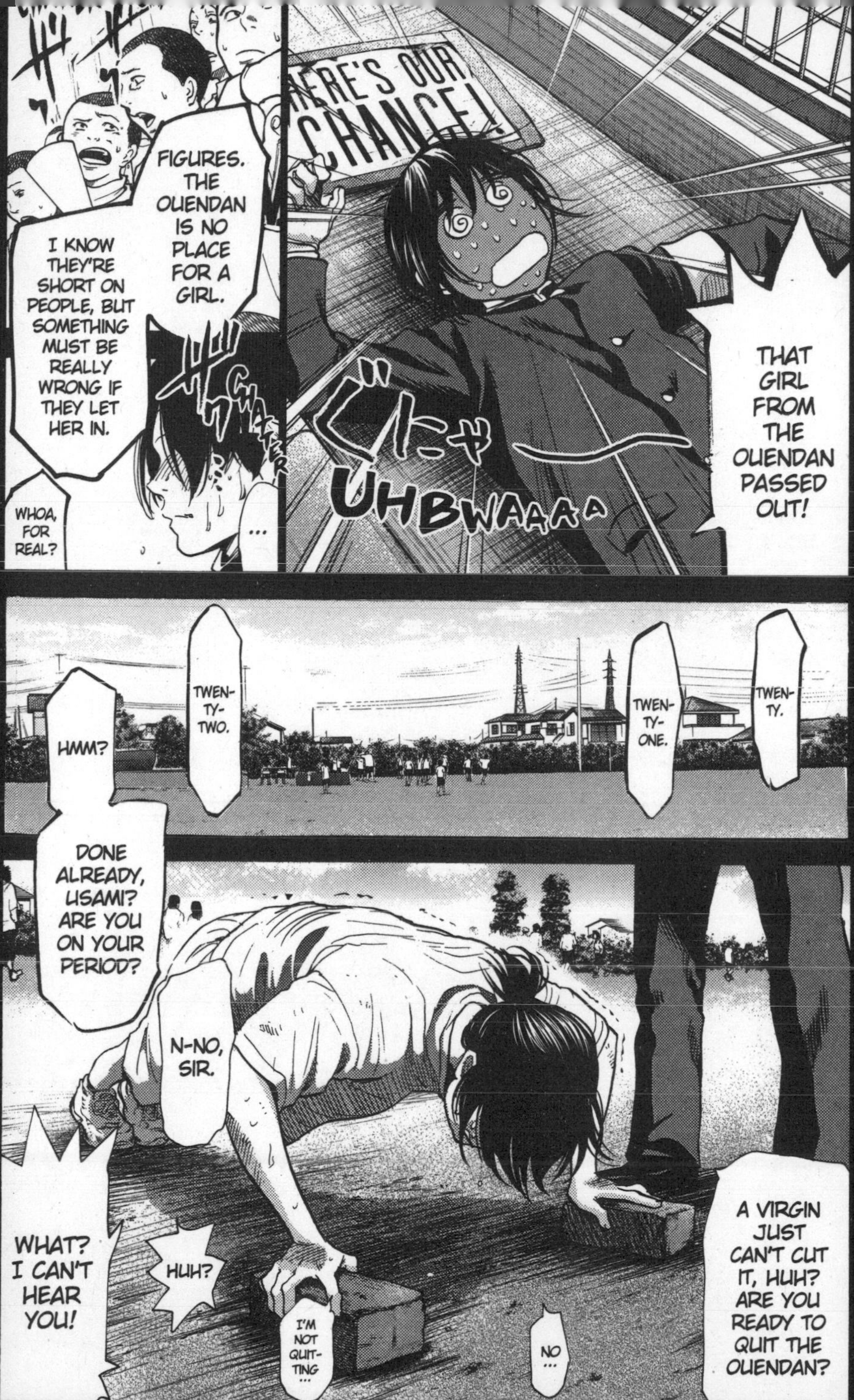

ERE'S OUR CHANCE!
THAT GIRL FROM THE OUENDAN PASSED OUT!
ぐにゃ
UHBWAAAAA
FIGURES. THE OUENDAN IS NO PLACE FOR A GIRL.
I KNOW THEY'RE SHORT ON PEOPLE, BUT SOMETHING MUST BE REALLY WRONG IF THEY LET HER IN.
CHATTER
WHOA, FOR REAL?
...
TWEN-TY.
TWEN-TY-ONE.
TWEN-TY-TWO.
HMM?
DONE ALREADY, USAMI? ARE YOU ON YOUR PERIOD?
N-NO, SIR.
A VIRGIN JUST CAN'T CUT IT, HUH? ARE YOU READY TO QUIT THE OUENDAN?
NO ...
I'M NOT QUIT-TING ...
HUH?
WHAT? I CAN'T HEAR YOU!

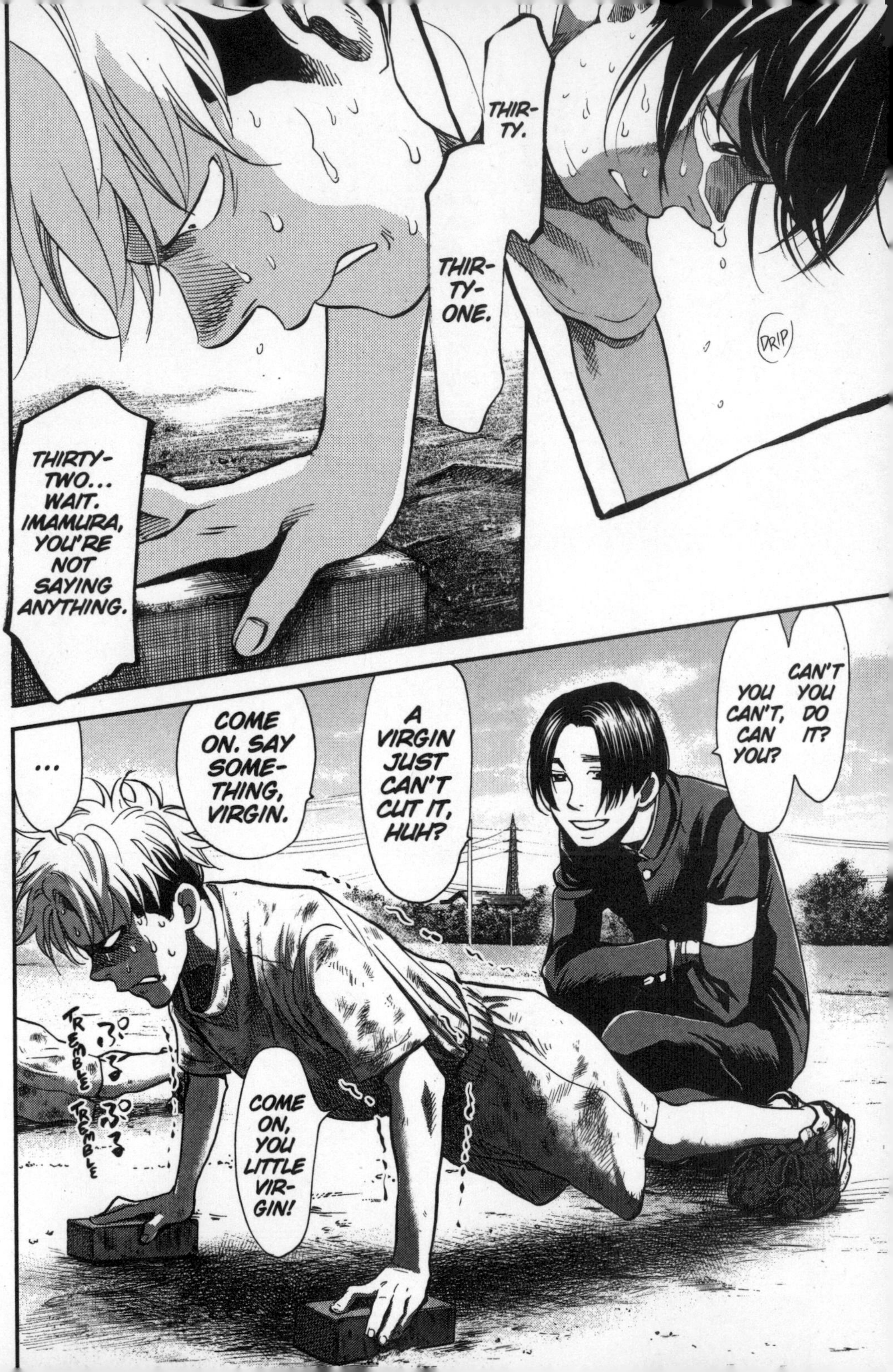
THIR-TY.
THIR-TY-ONE.
DRIP
THIRTY-TWO... WAIT. IMAMURA, YOU'RE NOT SAYING ANYTHING.
CAN'T YOU DO IT?
YOU CAN'T, CAN YOU?
A VIRGIN JUST CAN'T CUT IT, HUH?
COME ON. SAY SOME-THING, VIRGIN.
...
COME ON, YOU LITTLE VIR-GIN!
TREMBLE TREMBLE

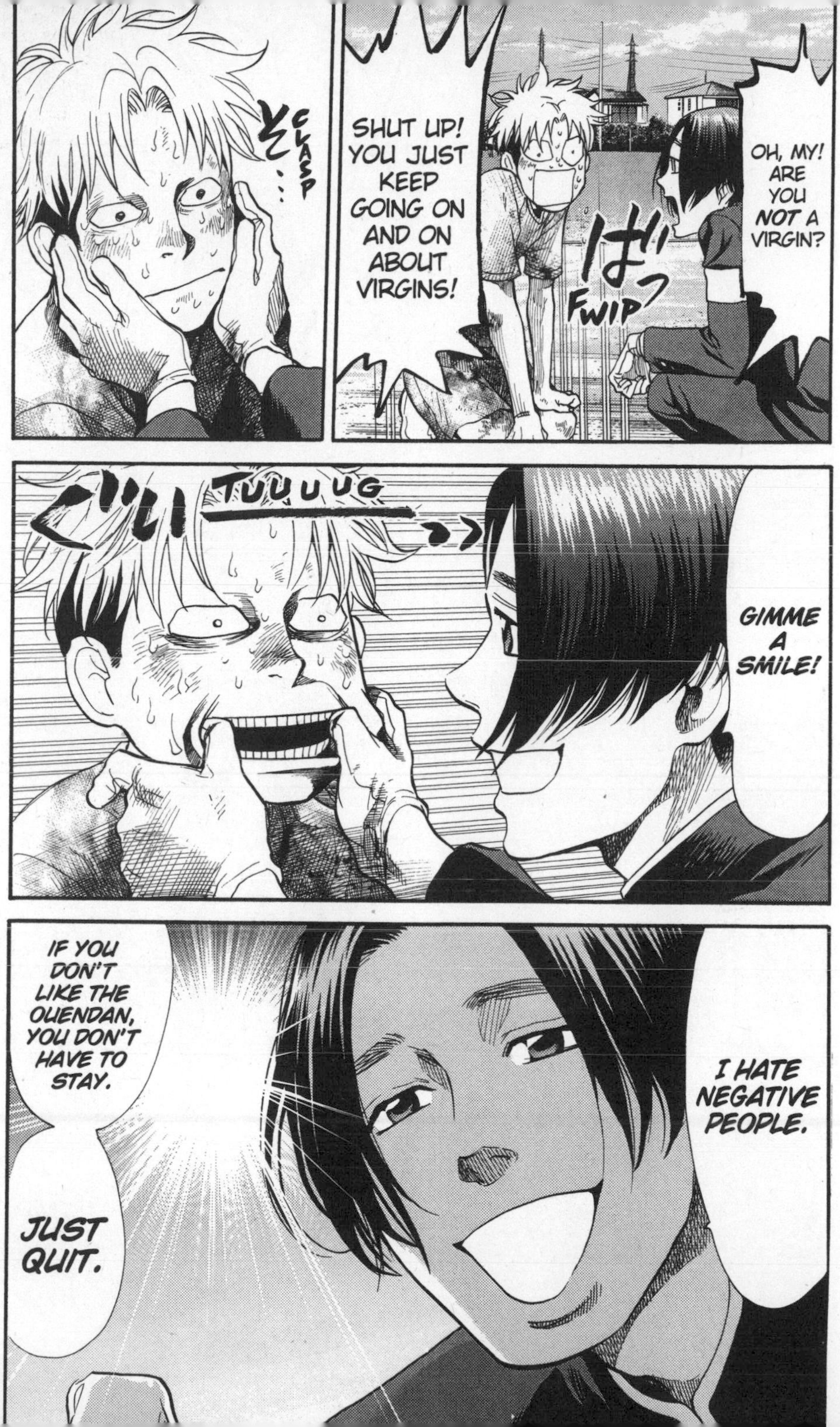
OH, MY! ARE YOU NOT A VIRGIN?
SHUT UP! YOU JUST KEEP GOING ON AND ON ABOUT VIRGINS!
ばっ
FWIP
CLASP
GIMME A SMILE!
TUUUUG
I HATE NEGATIVE PEOPLE.
IF YOU DON'T LIKE THE OUENDAN, YOU DON'T HAVE TO STAY.
JUST QUIT.

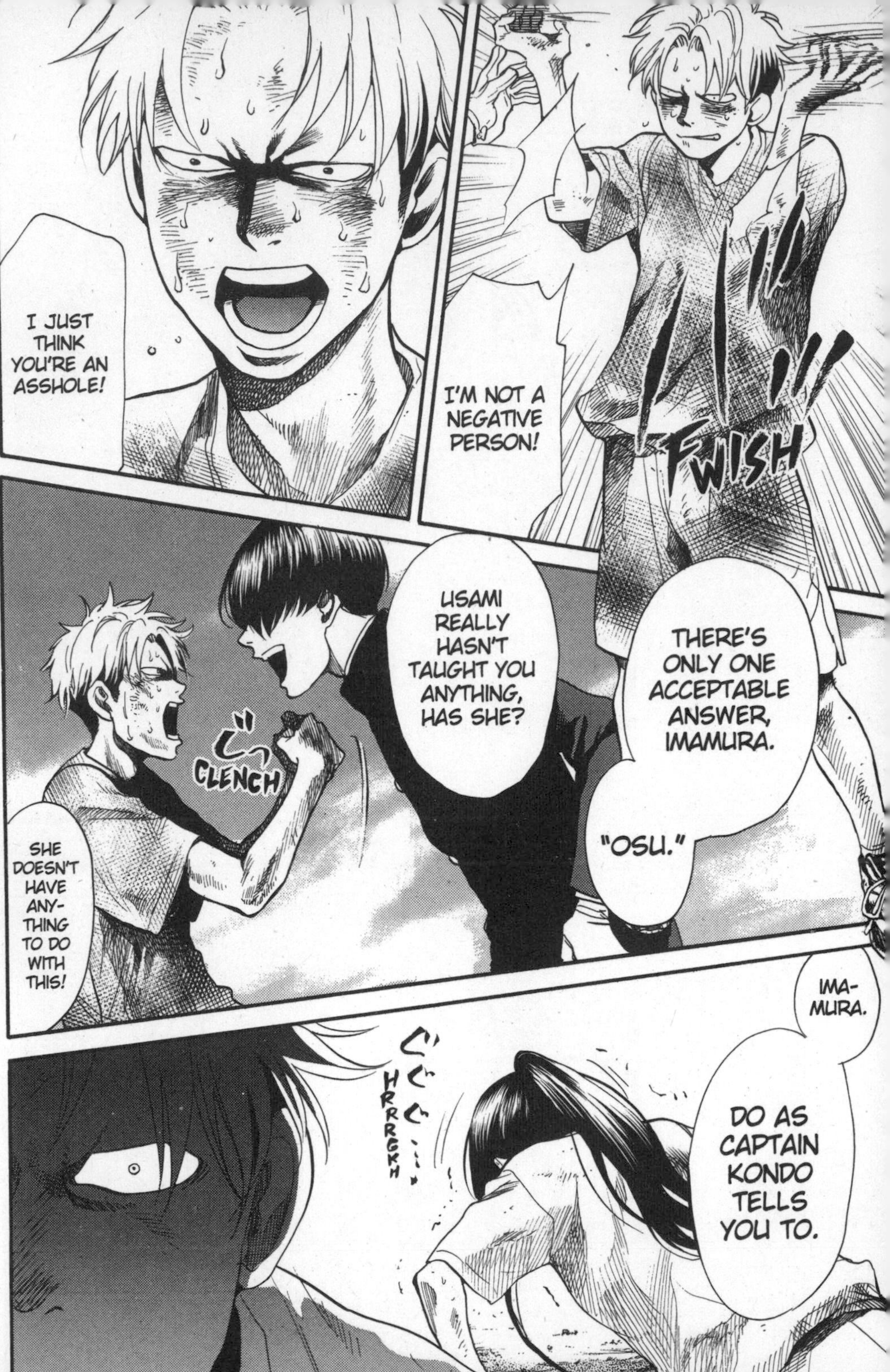
FWISH
I'M NOT A NEGATIVE PERSON!
I JUST THINK YOU'RE AN ASSHOLE!
THERE'S ONLY ONE ACCEPTABLE ANSWER, IMAMURA.
"OSU."
USAMI REALLY HASN'T TAUGHT YOU ANYTHING, HAS SHE?
CLENCH
SHE DOESN'T HAVE ANY-THING TO DO WITH THIS!
IMA-MURA.
DO AS CAPTAIN KONDO TELLS YOU TO.
HRRRGKH

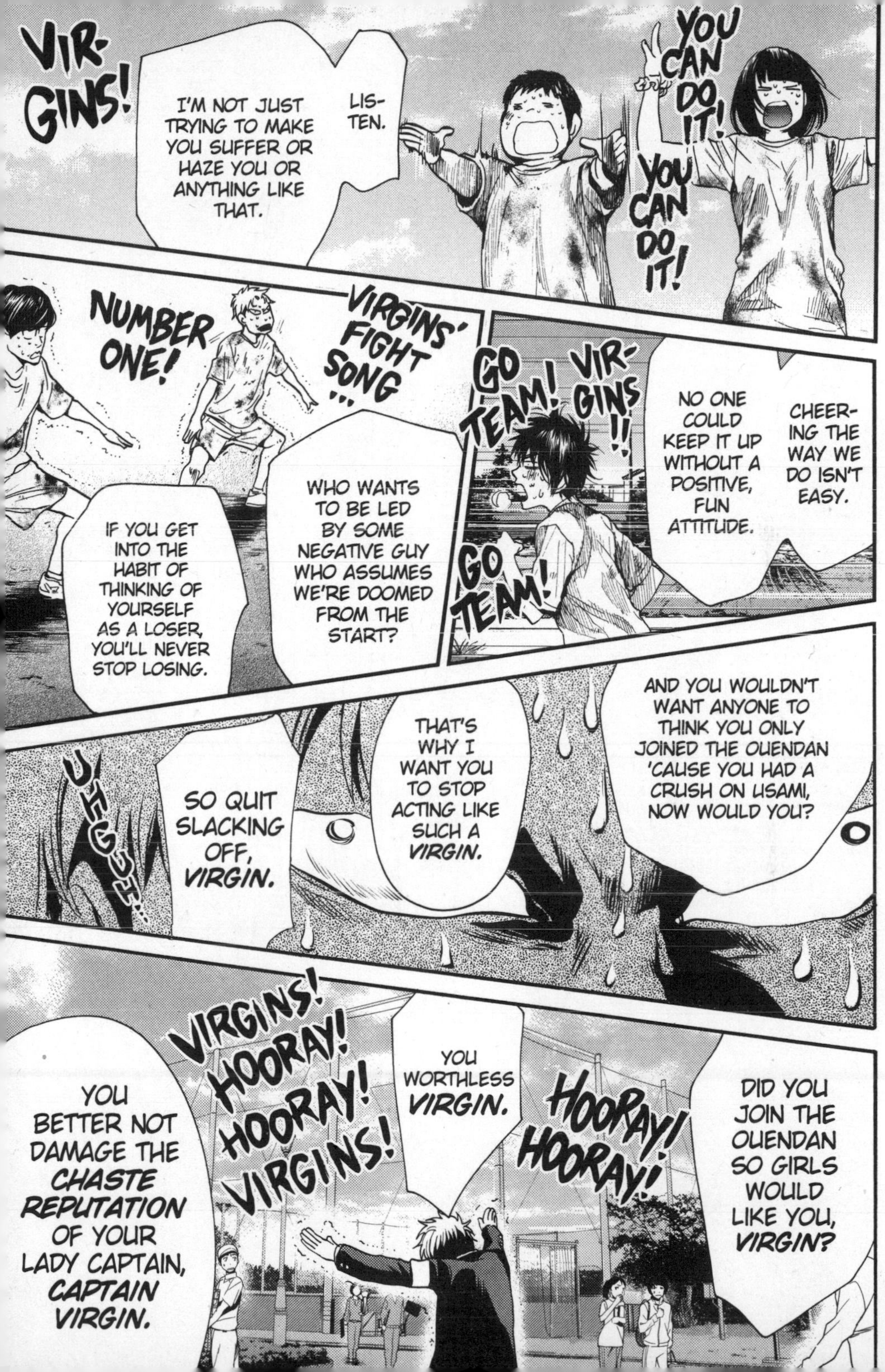
YOU CAN DO IT! YOU CAN DO IT!
LIS-TEN.
I'M NOT JUST TRYING TO MAKE YOU SUFFER OR HAZE YOU OR ANYTHING LIKE THAT.
VIR-GINS!
CHEER-ING THE WAY WE DO ISN'T EASY.
NO ONE COULD KEEP IT UP WITHOUT A POSITIVE, FUN ATTITUDE.
VIR-GINS!!
GO TEAM!
GO TEAM!
VIRGINS' FIGHT SONG...
NUMBER ONE!
WHO WANTS TO BE LED BY SOME NEGATIVE GUY WHO ASSUMES WE'RE DOOMED FROM THE START?
IF YOU GET INTO THE HABIT OF THINKING OF YOURSELF AS A LOSER, YOU'LL NEVER STOP LOSING.
AND YOU WOULDN'T WANT ANYONE TO THINK YOU ONLY JOINED THE OUENDAN 'CAUSE YOU HAD A CRUSH ON USAMI, NOW WOULD YOU?
THAT'S WHY I WANT YOU TO STOP ACTING LIKE SUCH A *VIRGIN*.
SO QUIT SLACKING OFF, *VIRGIN*.
UHGUH...
DID YOU JOIN THE OUENDAN SO GIRLS WOULD LIKE YOU, *VIRGIN*?
HOORAY! HOORAY!
YOU WORTHLESS *VIRGIN*.
VIRGINS! HOORAY! HOORAY! VIRGINS!
YOU BETTER NOT DAMAGE THE *CHASTE REPUTATION* OF YOUR LADY CAPTAIN, *CAPTAIN VIRGIN*.

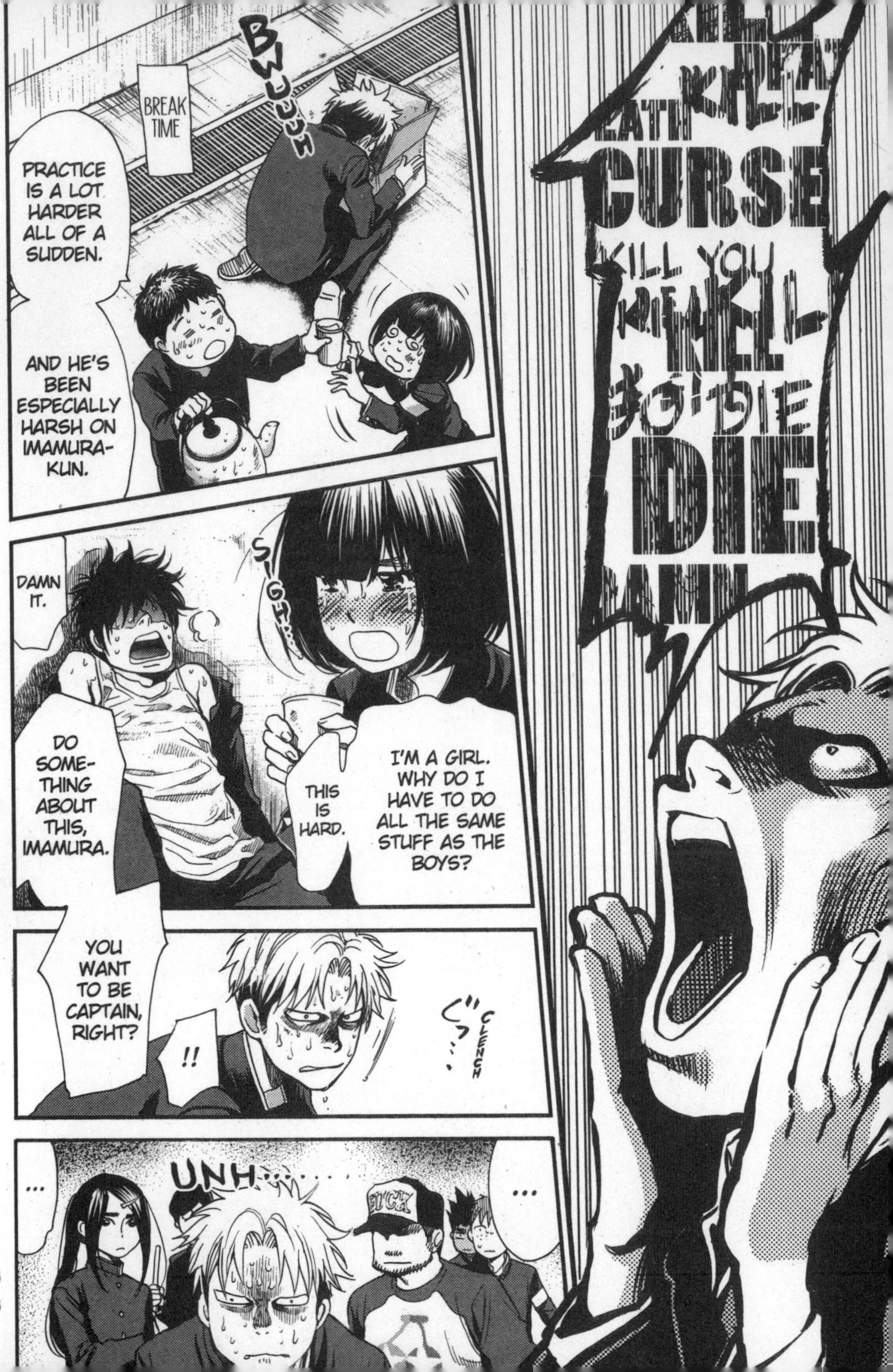
CURSE
KILL YOU
KILL
DIE
BWUUUH
BREAK TIME
PRACTICE IS A LOT HARDER ALL OF A SUDDEN.
AND HE'S BEEN ESPECIALLY HARSH ON IMAMURA-KUN.
SIGH...
I'M A GIRL. WHY DO I HAVE TO DO ALL THE SAME STUFF AS THE BOYS?
THIS IS HARD.
DAMN IT.
DO SOMETHING ABOUT THIS, IMAMURA.
CLENCH
!!
YOU WANT TO BE CAPTAIN, RIGHT?
...
UNH......
...

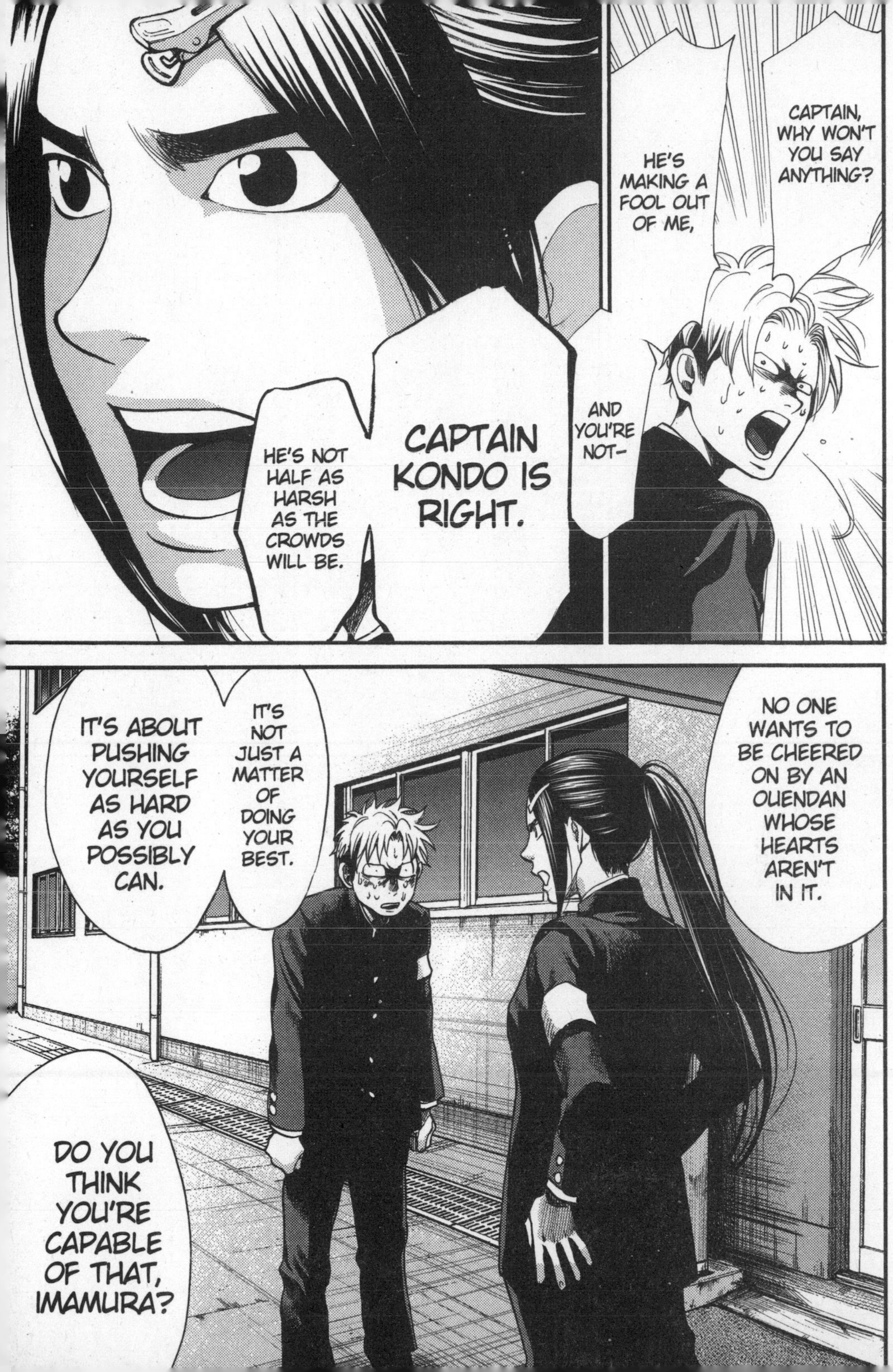
CAPTAIN, WHY WON'T YOU SAY ANYTHING?
HE'S MAKING A FOOL OUT OF ME,
AND YOU'RE NOT-
CAPTAIN KONDO IS RIGHT.
HE'S NOT HALF AS HARSH AS THE CROWDS WILL BE.
NO ONE WANTS TO BE CHEERED ON BY AN OUENDAN WHOSE HEARTS AREN'T IN IT.
IT'S NOT JUST A MATTER OF DOING YOUR BEST.
IT'S ABOUT PUSHING YOURSELF AS HARD AS YOU POSSIBLY CAN.
DO YOU THINK YOU'RE CAPABLE OF THAT, IMAMURA?

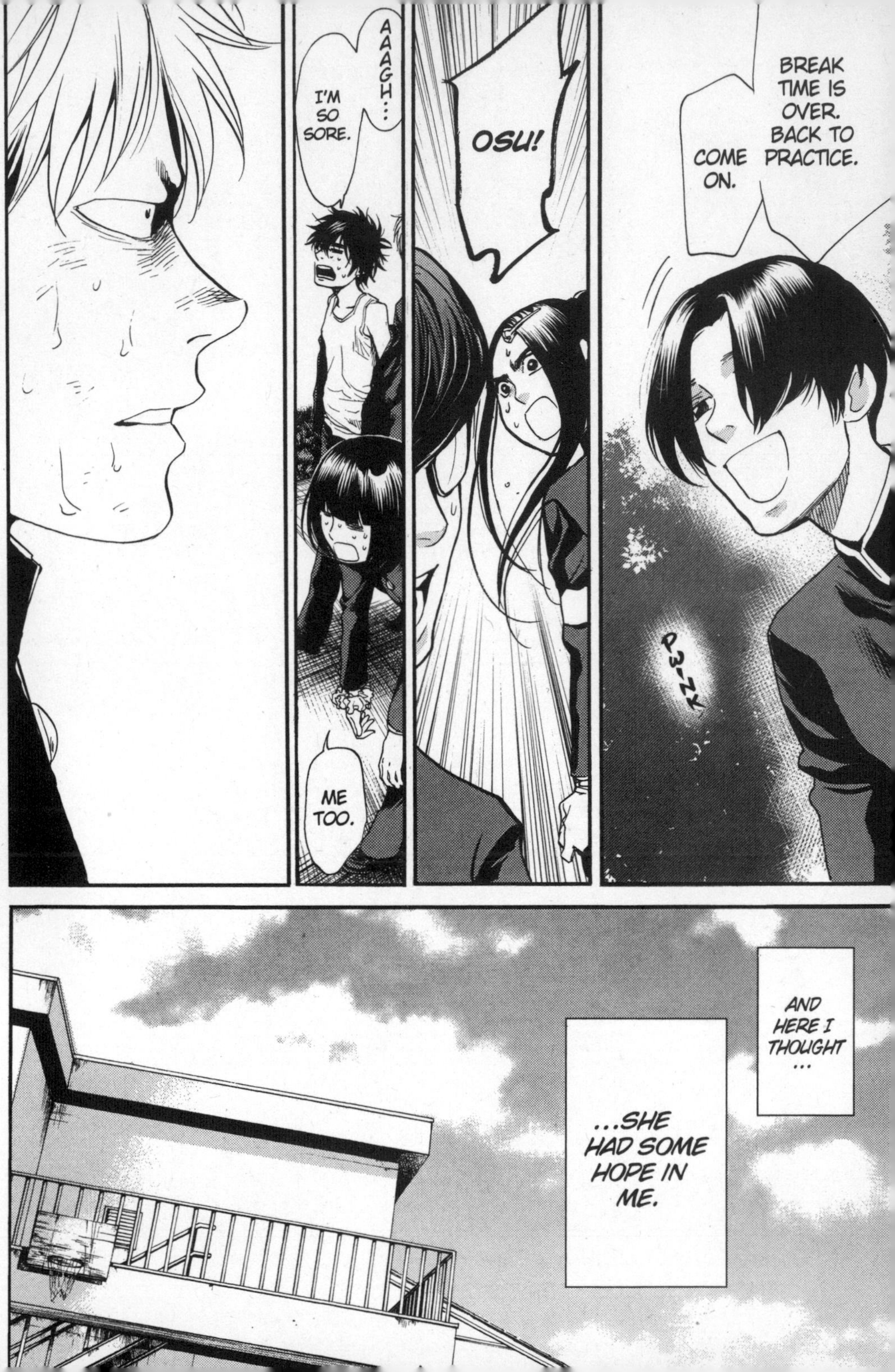
BREAK TIME IS OVER. BACK TO PRACTICE.
COME ON.
OSU!
AAAGH...
I'M SO SORE.
ME TOO.
AND HERE I THOUGHT...
...SHE HAD SOME HOPE IN ME.

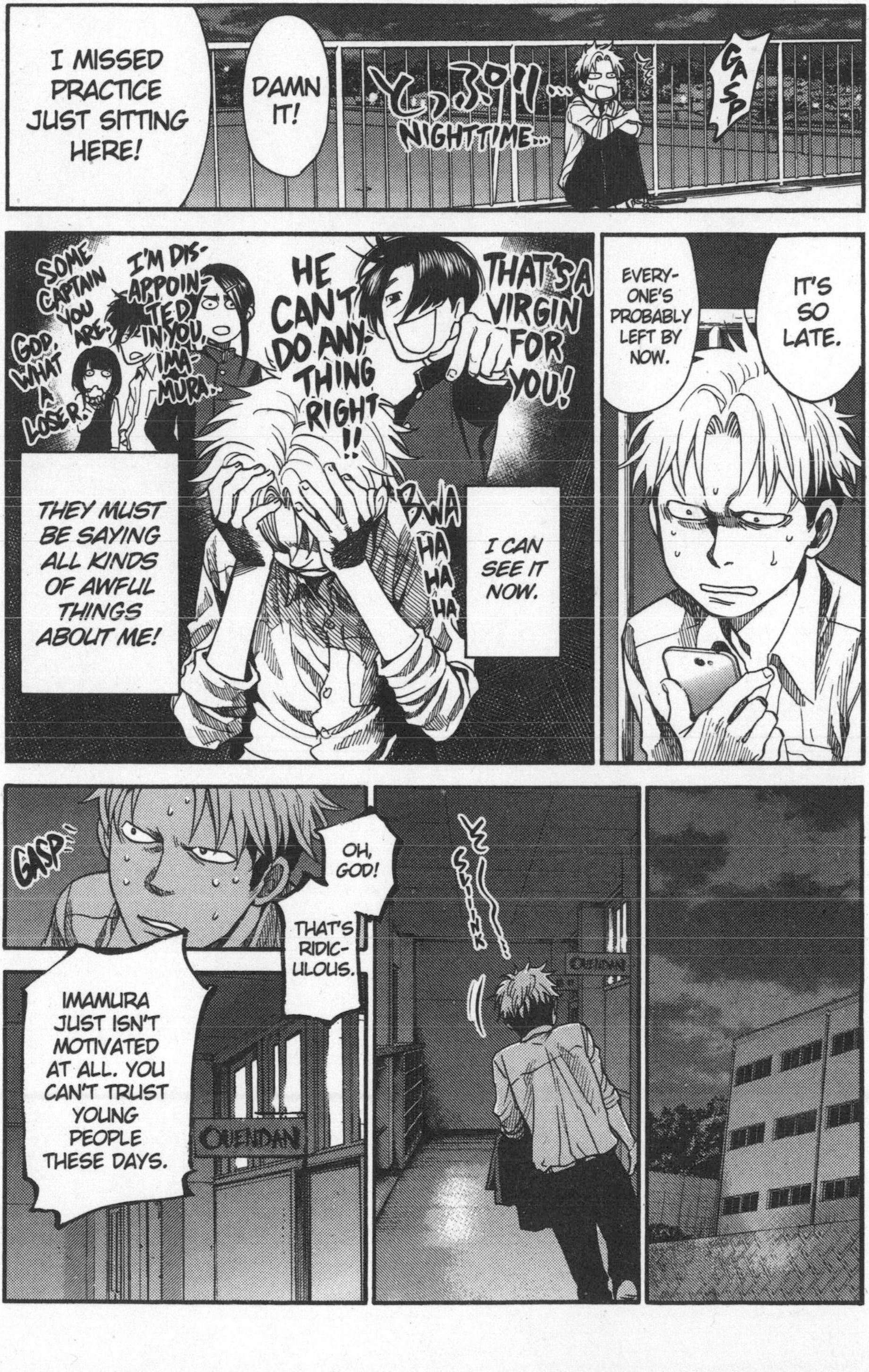
GASP
NIGHTTIME...
DAMN IT!
I MISSED PRACTICE JUST SITTING HERE!
IT'S SO LATE.
EVERYONE'S PROBABLY LEFT BY NOW.
THAT'S A VIRGIN FOR YOU!
HE CAN'T DO ANYTHING RIGHT!!
I'M DISAPPOINTED IN YOU, IMAMURA.
SOME CAPTAIN YOU ARE.
GOD, WHAT A LOSER.
I CAN SEE IT NOW.
BWA HA HA HA HA
THEY MUST BE SAYING ALL KINDS OF AWFUL THINGS ABOUT ME!
SLINK...
OUENDAN
OH, GOD!
GASP
THAT'S RIDICULOUS.
IMAMURA JUST ISN'T MOTIVATED AT ALL. YOU CAN'T TRUST YOUNG PEOPLE THESE DAYS.
OUENDAN

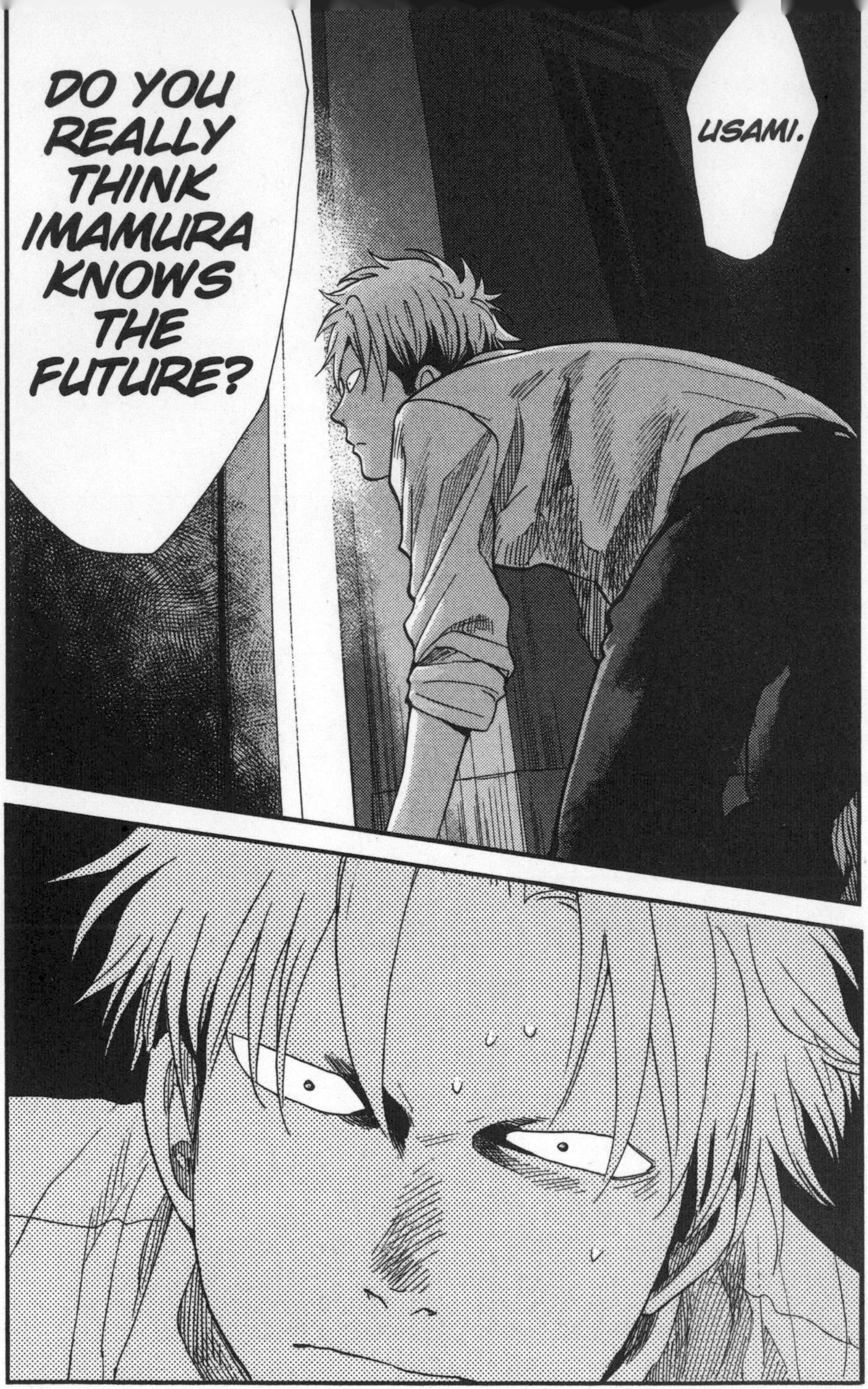
USAMI.
DO YOU REALLY THINK IMAMURA KNOWS THE FUTURE?

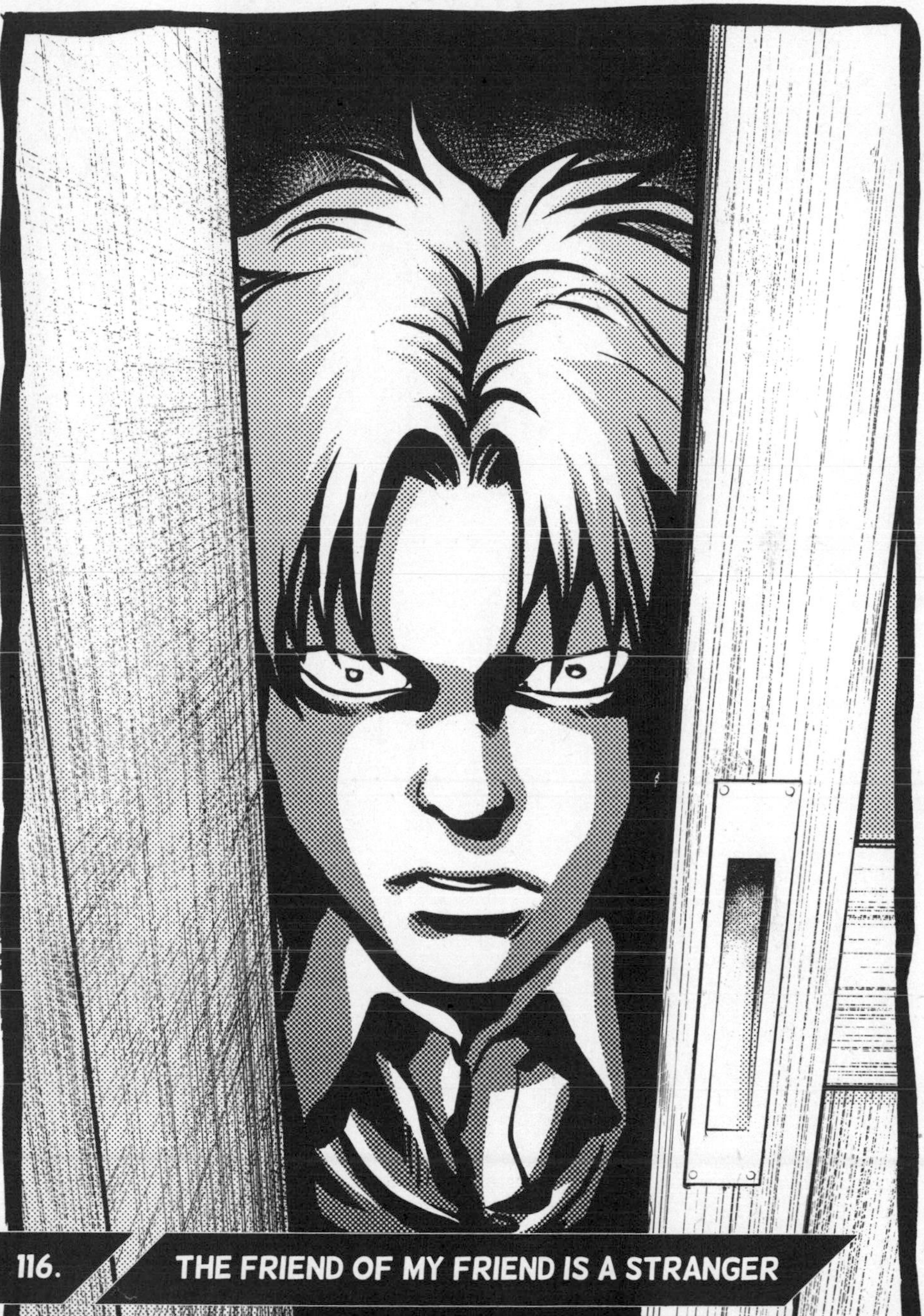

116. THE FRIEND OF MY FRIEND IS A STRANGER

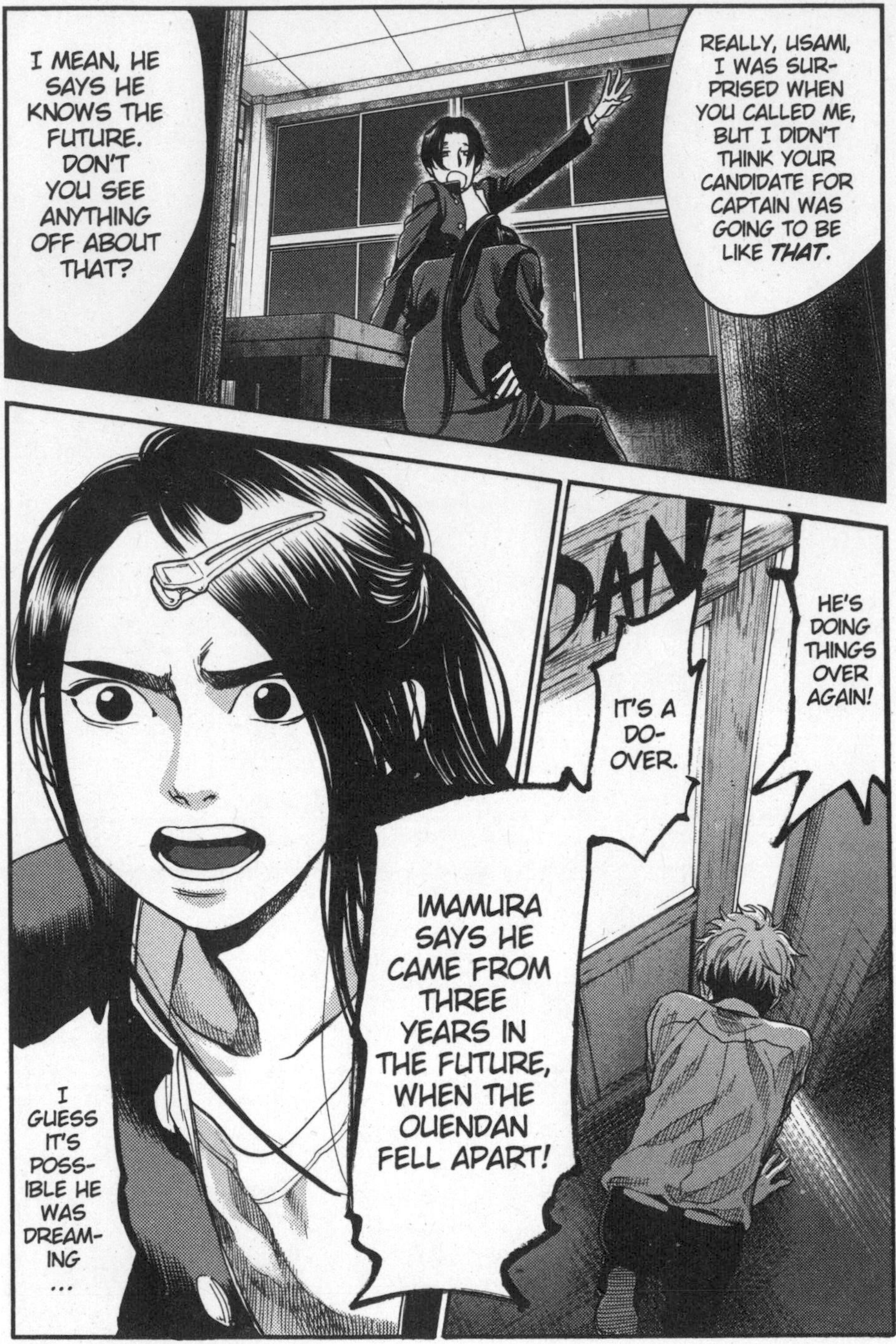
REALLY, USAMI, I WAS SURPRISED WHEN YOU CALLED ME, BUT I DIDN'T THINK YOUR CANDIDATE FOR CAPTAIN WAS GOING TO BE LIKE *THAT*.
I MEAN, HE SAYS HE KNOWS THE FUTURE. DON'T YOU SEE ANYTHING OFF ABOUT THAT?
DAN
HE'S DOING THINGS OVER AGAIN!
IT'S A DO-OVER.
IMAMURA SAYS HE CAME FROM THREE YEARS IN THE FUTURE, WHEN THE OUENDAN FELL APART!
I GUESS IT'S POSSIBLE HE WAS DREAMING...

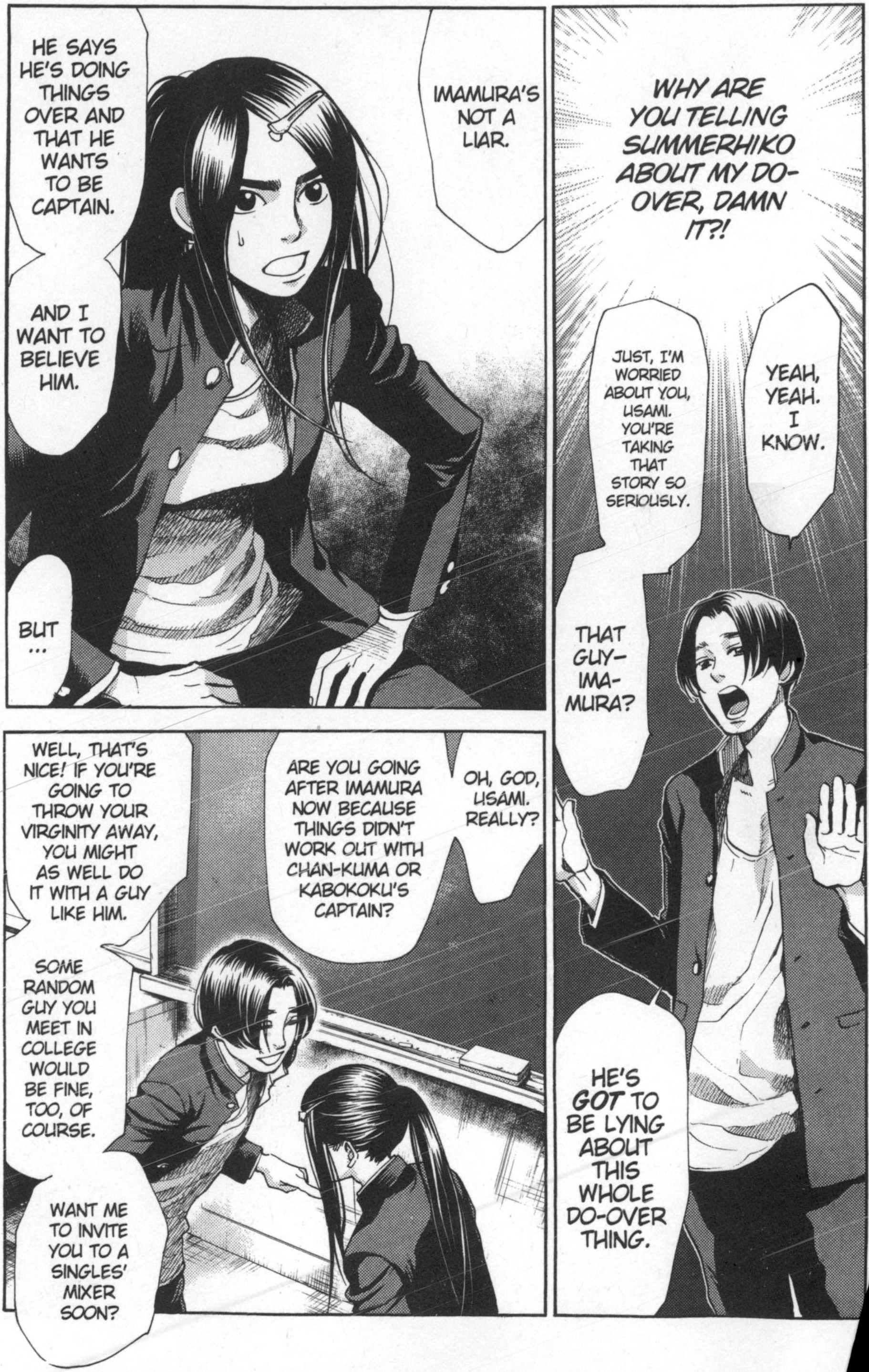
WHY ARE YOU TELLING SUMMERHIKO ABOUT MY DO-OVER, DAMN IT?!
YEAH, YEAH. I KNOW.
JUST, I'M WORRIED ABOUT YOU, USAMI. YOU'RE TAKING THAT STORY SO SERIOUSLY.
THAT GUY—IMAMURA?
HE'S ***GOT*** TO BE LYING ABOUT THIS WHOLE DO-OVER THING.
IMAMURA'S NOT A LIAR.
HE SAYS HE'S DOING THINGS OVER AND THAT HE WANTS TO BE CAPTAIN.
AND I WANT TO BELIEVE HIM.
BUT ...
OH, GOD, USAMI. REALLY?
ARE YOU GOING AFTER IMAMURA NOW BECAUSE THINGS DIDN'T WORK OUT WITH CHAN-KUMA OR KABOKOKU'S CAPTAIN?
WELL, THAT'S NICE! IF YOU'RE GOING TO THROW YOUR VIRGINITY AWAY, YOU MIGHT AS WELL DO IT WITH A GUY LIKE HIM.
SOME RANDOM GUY YOU MEET IN COLLEGE WOULD BE FINE, TOO, OF COURSE.
WANT ME TO INVITE YOU TO A SINGLES' MIXER SOON?

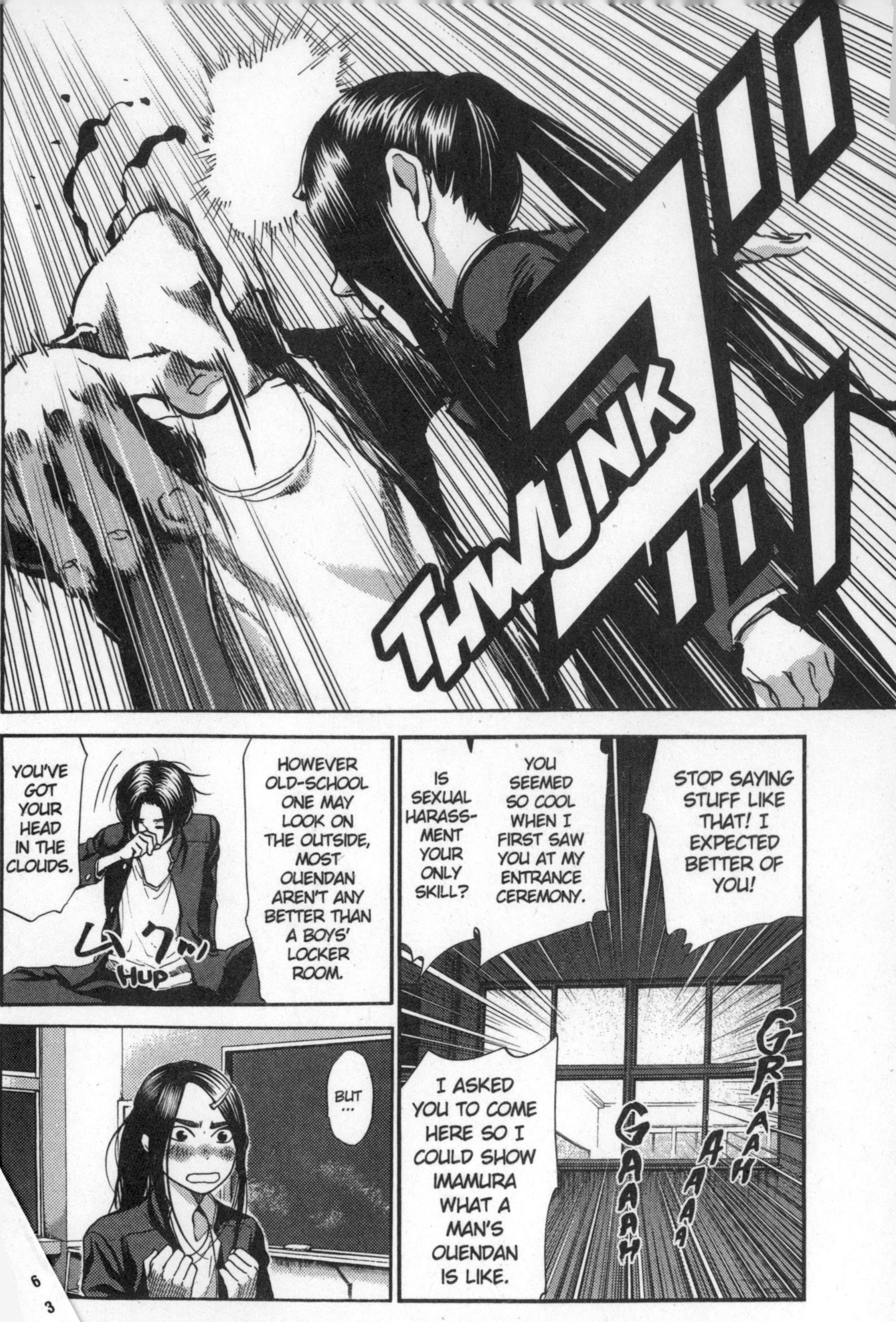
THWUNK
STOP SAYING STUFF LIKE THAT! I EXPECTED BETTER OF YOU!
YOU SEEMED SO COOL WHEN I FIRST SAW YOU AT MY ENTRANCE CEREMONY.
IS SEXUAL HARASS-MENT YOUR ONLY SKILL?
I ASKED YOU TO COME HERE SO I COULD SHOW IMAMURA WHAT A MAN'S OUENDAN IS LIKE.
GRAAAH
GAAAAAH
HOWEVER OLD-SCHOOL ONE MAY LOOK ON THE OUTSIDE, MOST OUENDAN AREN'T ANY BETTER THAN A BOYS' LOCKER ROOM.
YOU'VE GOT YOUR HEAD IN THE CLOUDS.
HUP
BUT ...

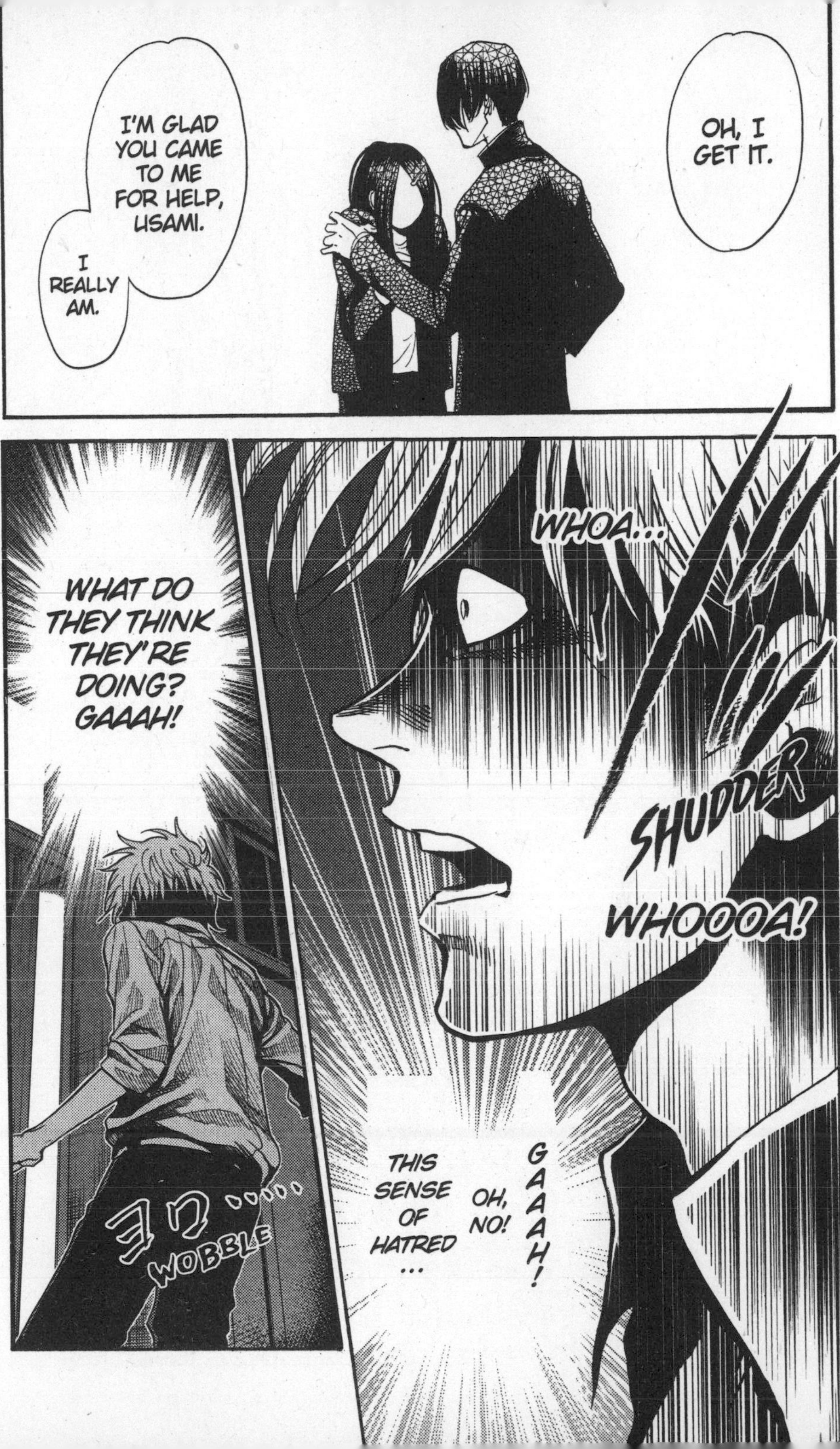

OH, I GET IT.
I'M GLAD YOU CAME TO ME FOR HELP, USAMI.
I REALLY AM.
WHOA...
SHUDDER
WHOOOA!
GAAAAH!
OH, NO!
THIS SENSE OF HATRED...
WHAT DO THEY THINK THEY'RE DOING? GAAAH!
ヨワ......
WOBBLE

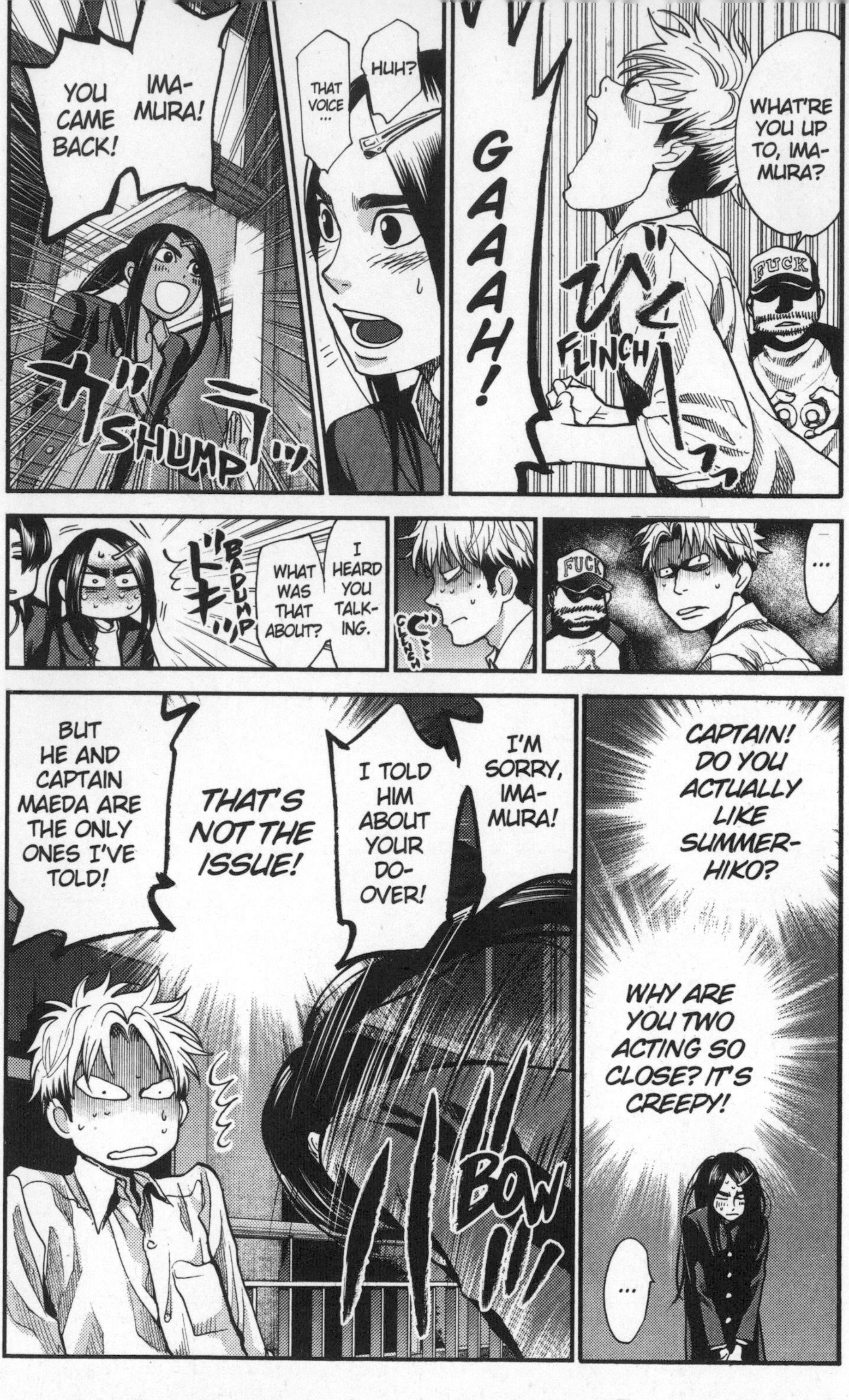
WHAT'RE YOU UP TO, IMA-MURA?
GAAAAH!
FLINCH
HUH?
THAT VOICE ...
IMA-MURA!
YOU CAME BACK!
SHUMP
...
CLENCH
I HEARD YOU TALK-ING.
WHAT WAS THAT ABOUT?
BADUMP
CAPTAIN! DO YOU ACTUALLY LIKE SUMMER-HIKO?
WHY ARE YOU TWO ACTING SO CLOSE? IT'S CREEPY!
...
I'M SORRY, IMA-MURA!
I TOLD HIM ABOUT YOUR DO-OVER!
THAT'S NOT THE ISSUE!
BUT HE AND CAPTAIN MAEDA ARE THE ONLY ONES I'VE TOLD!
BOW!!

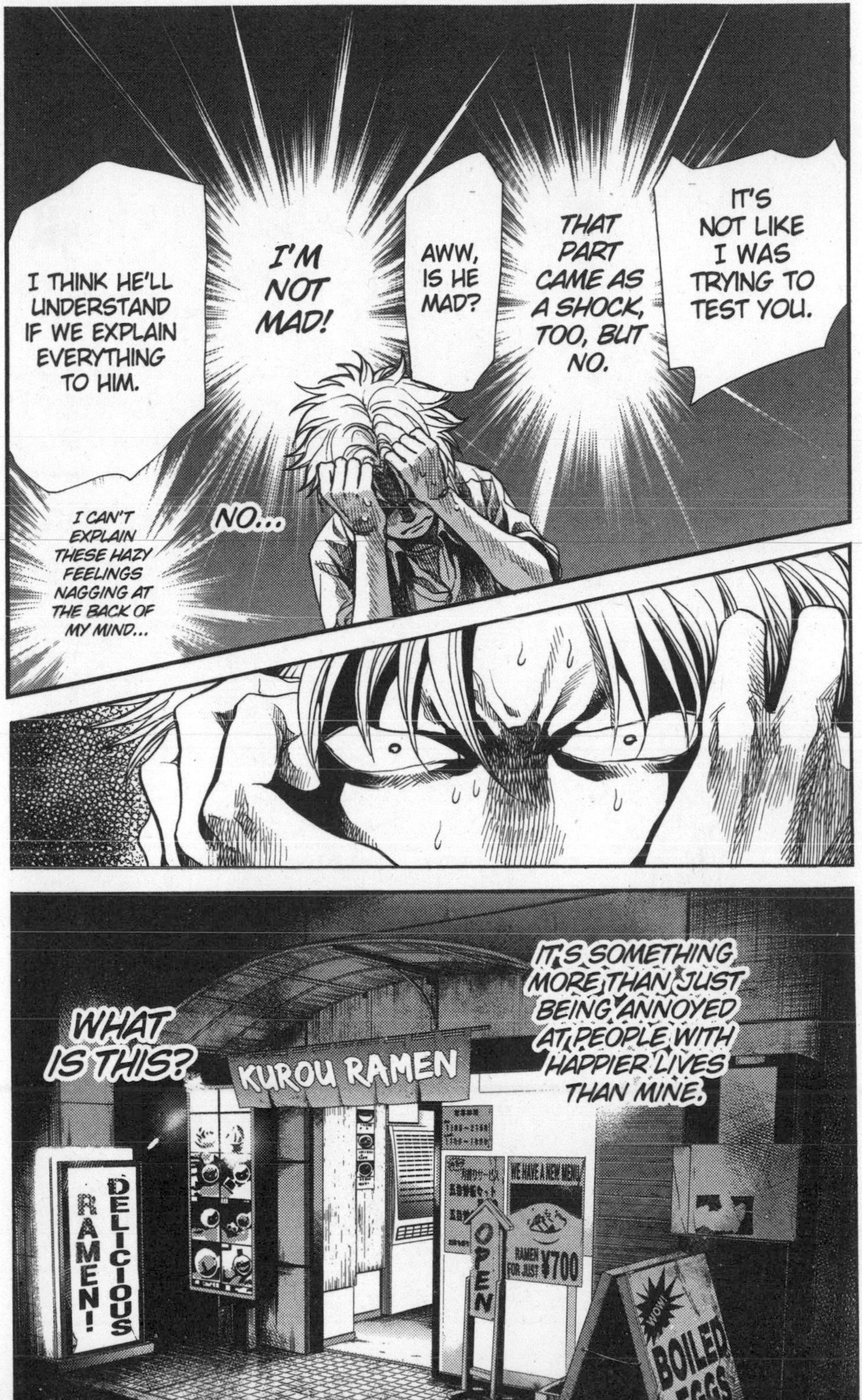
IT'S NOT LIKE I WAS TRYING TO TEST YOU.
THAT PART CAME AS A SHOCK, TOO, BUT NO.
AWW, IS HE MAD?
I'M NOT MAD!
I THINK HE'LL UNDERSTAND IF WE EXPLAIN EVERYTHING TO HIM.
NO...
I CAN'T EXPLAIN THESE HAZY FEELINGS NAGGING AT THE BACK OF MY MIND...
IT'S SOMETHING MORE THAN JUST BEING ANNOYED AT PEOPLE WITH HAPPIER LIVES THAN MINE.
WHAT IS THIS?
KUROU RAMEN
WE HAVE A NEW MENU!
RAMEN FOR JUST ¥700
OPEN
DELICIOUS
RAMEN!
WOW!
BOILED

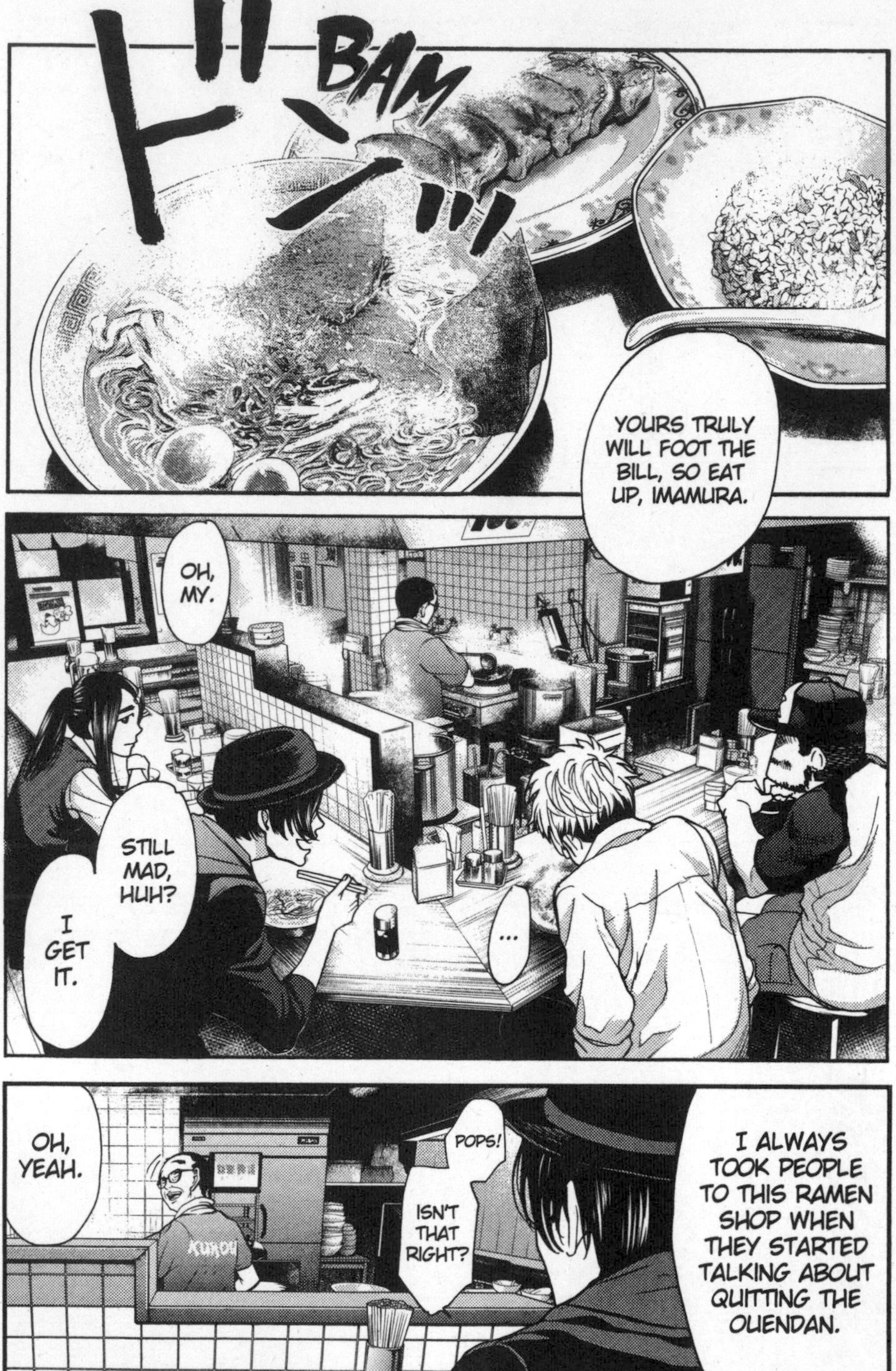
BAM
YOURS TRULY WILL FOOT THE BILL, SO EAT UP, IMAMURA.
...
OH, MY.
STILL MAD, HUH?
I GET IT.
I ALWAYS TOOK PEOPLE TO THIS RAMEN SHOP WHEN THEY STARTED TALKING ABOUT QUITTING THE OUENDAN.
POPS!
ISN'T THAT RIGHT?
OH, YEAH.

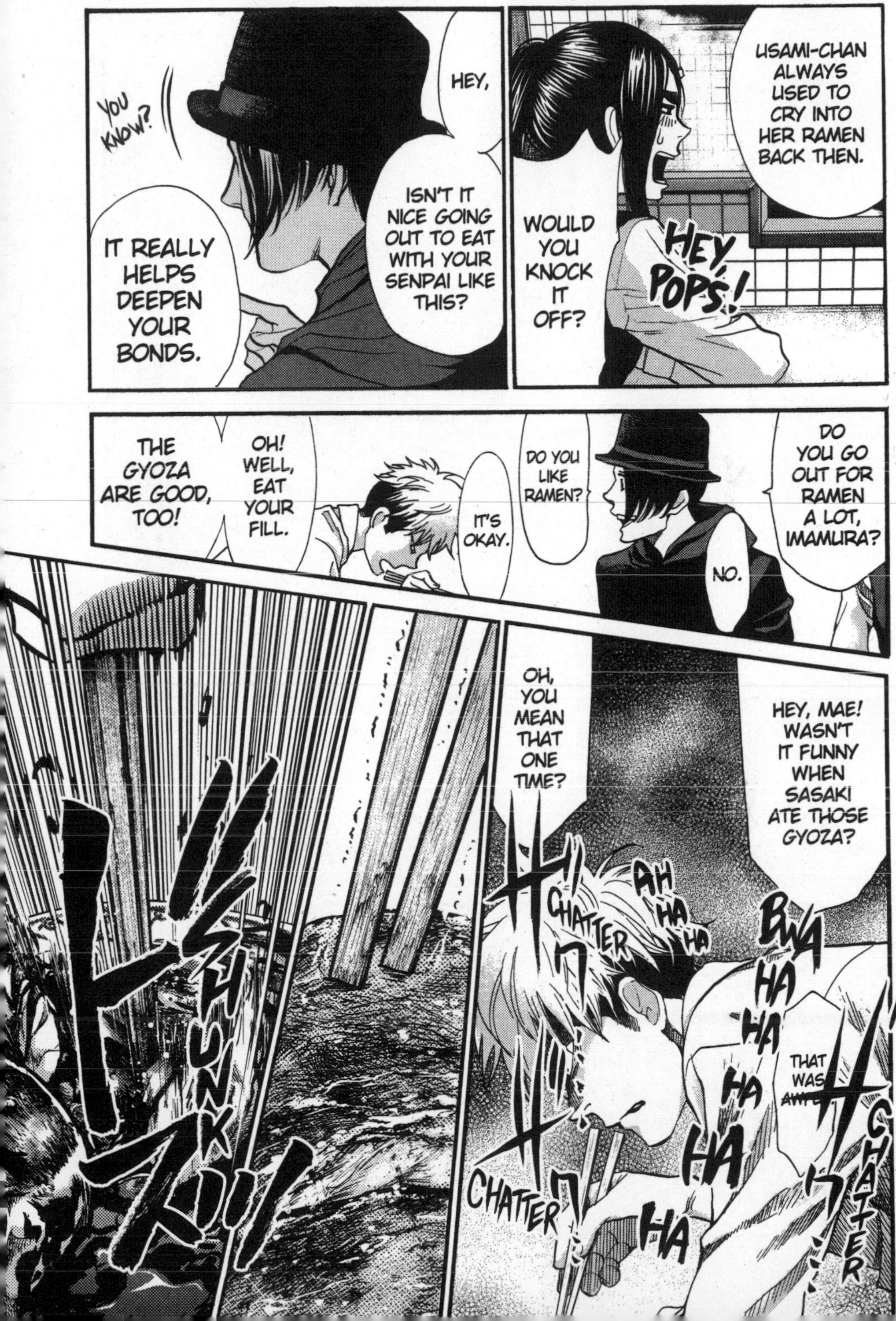

USAMI-CHAN ALWAYS USED TO CRY INTO HER RAMEN BACK THEN.
HEY, POPS!
WOULD YOU KNOCK IT OFF?
HEY,
ISN'T IT NICE GOING OUT TO EAT WITH YOUR SENPAI LIKE THIS?
YOU KNOW?
IT REALLY HELPS DEEPEN YOUR BONDS.
DO YOU GO OUT FOR RAMEN A LOT, IMAMURA?
NO.
DO YOU LIKE RAMEN?
IT'S OKAY.
OH! WELL, EAT YOUR FILL.
THE GYOZA ARE GOOD, TOO!
HEY, MAE! WASN'T IT FUNNY WHEN SASAKI ATE THOSE GYOZA?
OH, YOU MEAN THAT ONE TIME?
BWA HA HA HA HA HA HA
THAT WAS
CHATTER
AH HA HA
CHATTER
CHATTER
SHUNK

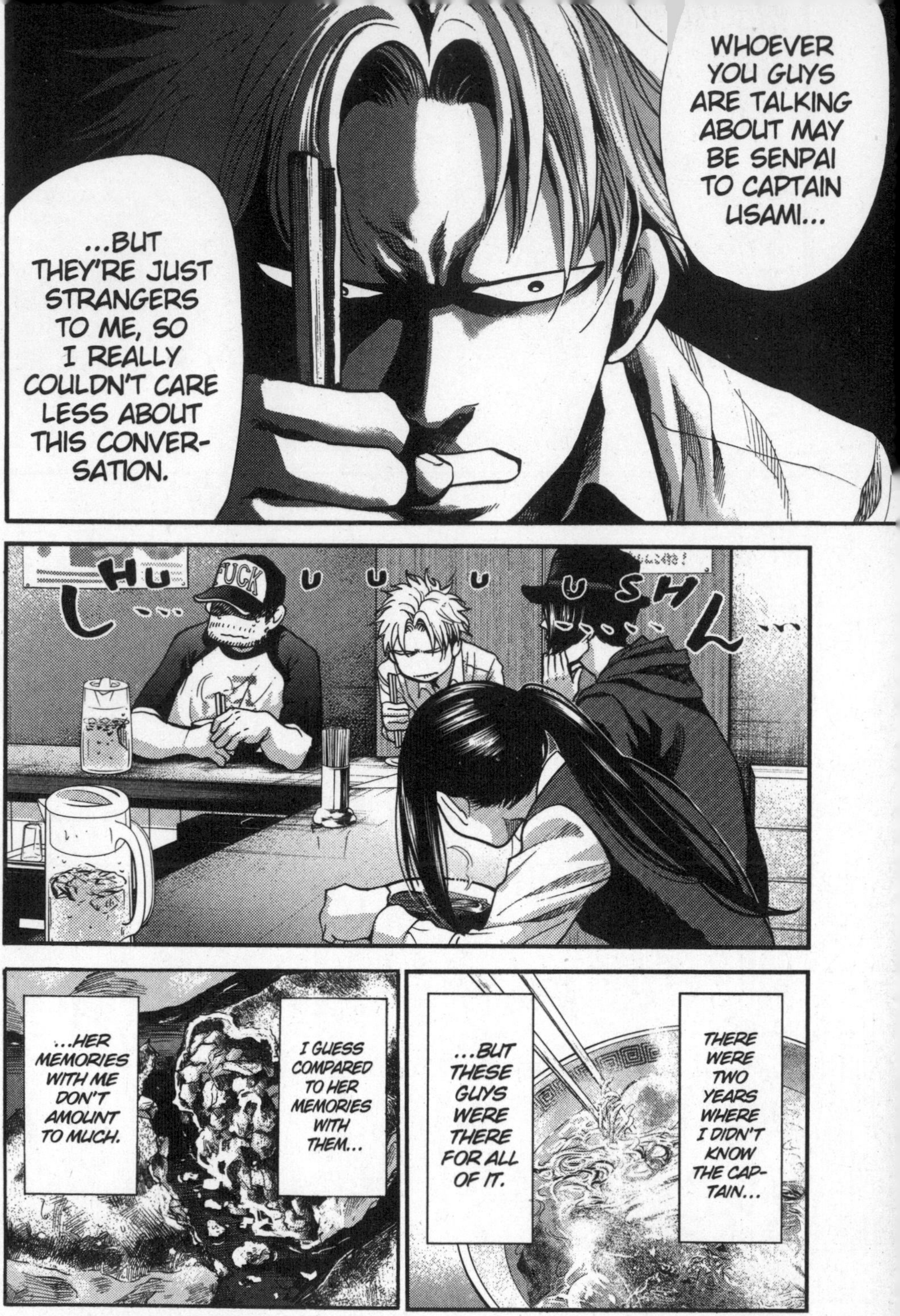
WHOEVER YOU GUYS ARE TALKING ABOUT MAY BE SENPAI TO CAPTAIN USAMI...
...BUT THEY'RE JUST STRANGERS TO ME, SO I REALLY COULDN'T CARE LESS ABOUT THIS CONVERSATION.
LHUUUUUSHL
THERE WERE TWO YEARS WHERE I DIDN'T KNOW THE CAPTAIN...
...BUT THESE GUYS WERE THERE FOR ALL OF IT.
I GUESS COMPARED TO HER MEMORIES WITH THEM...
...HER MEMORIES WITH ME DON'T AMOUNT TO MUCH.

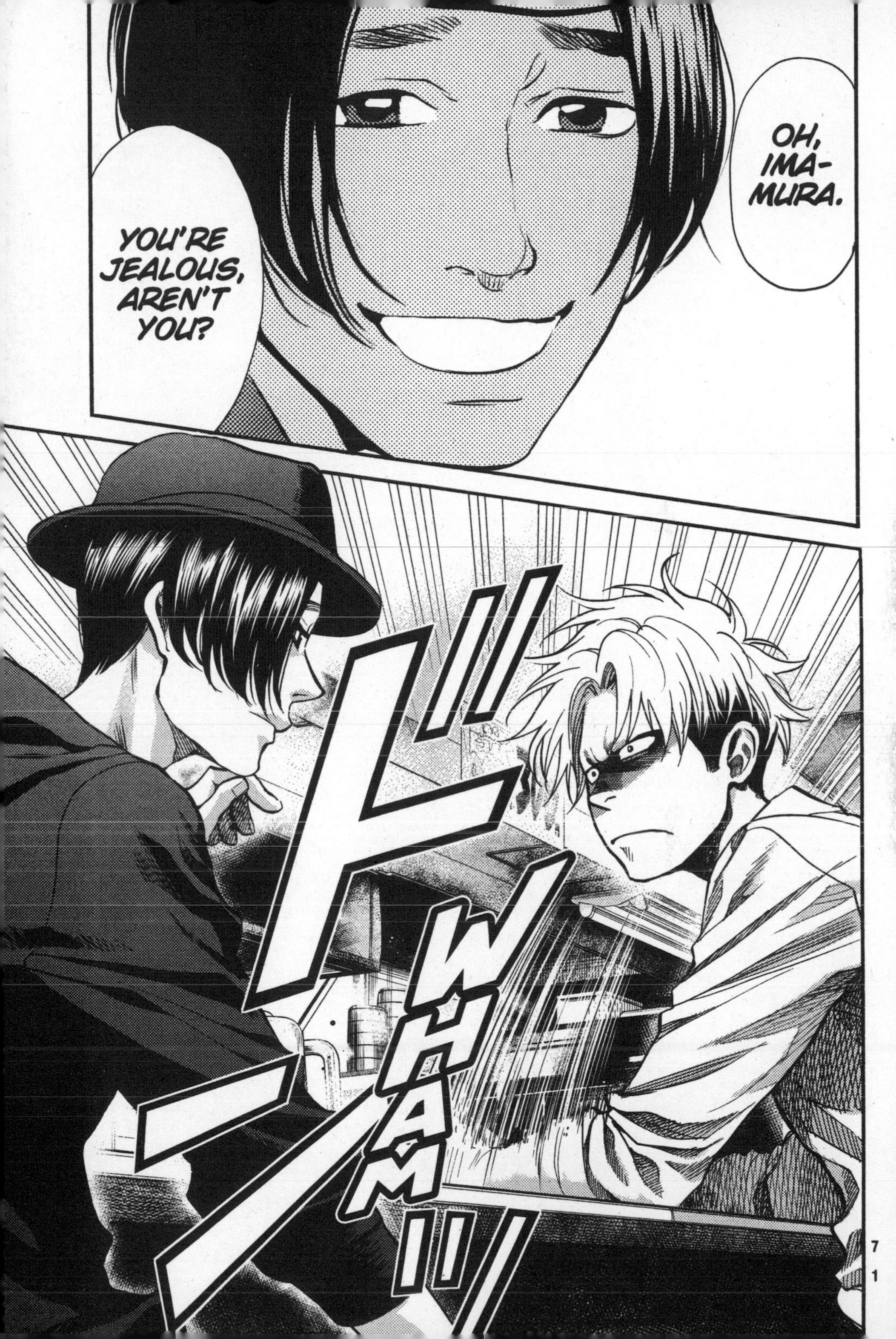
OH, IMA-MURA.
YOU'RE JEALOUS, AREN'T YOU?
WHAM!!

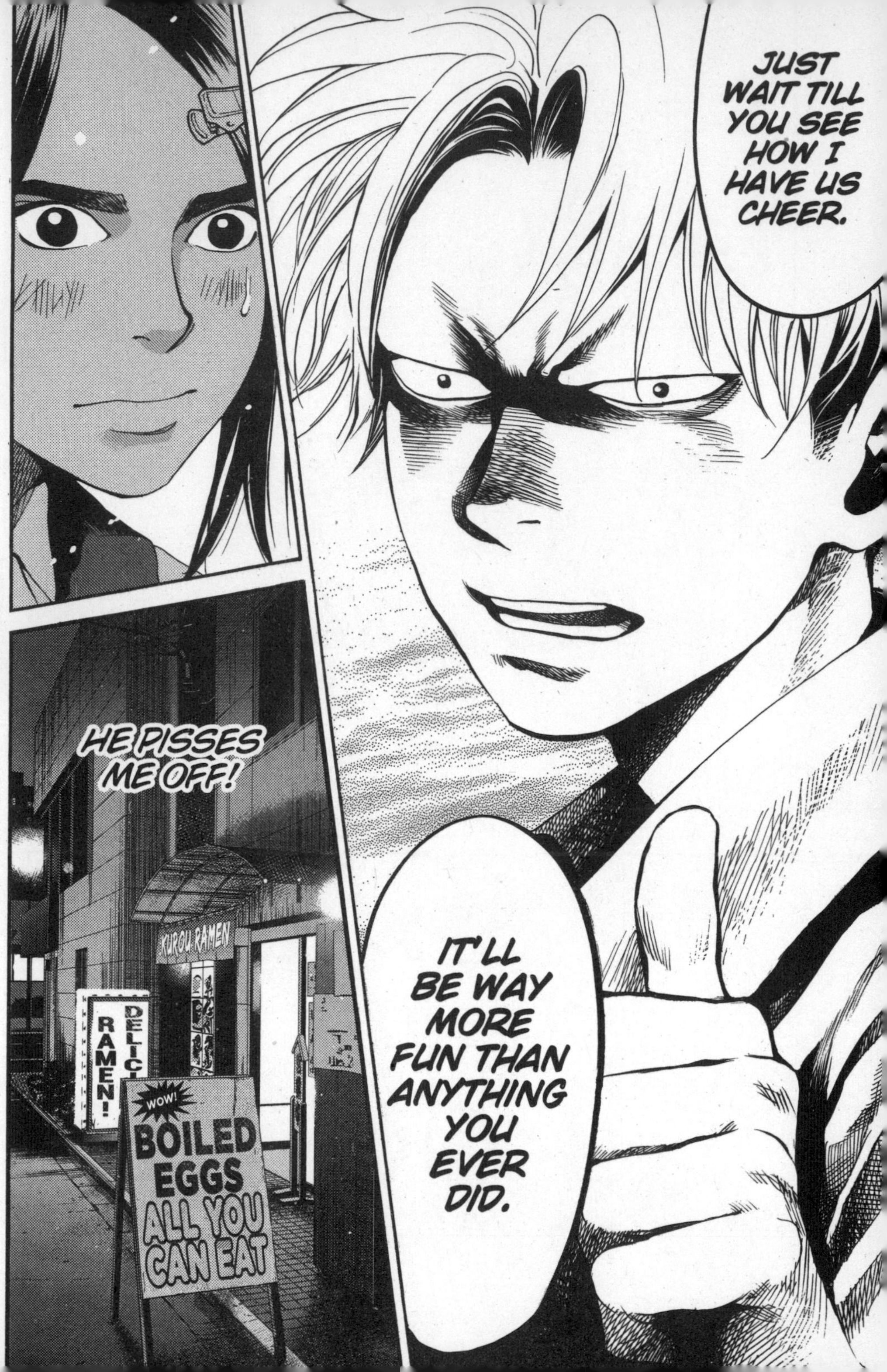
JUST WAIT TILL YOU SEE HOW I HAVE US CHEER.
IT'LL BE WAY MORE FUN THAN ANYTHING YOU EVER DID.
HE PISSES ME OFF!
KUROU RAMEN
RAMEN!
WOW!
BOILED EGGS ALL YOU CAN EAT

Again!!
アゲイン!!

Again!!

アゲイン!!

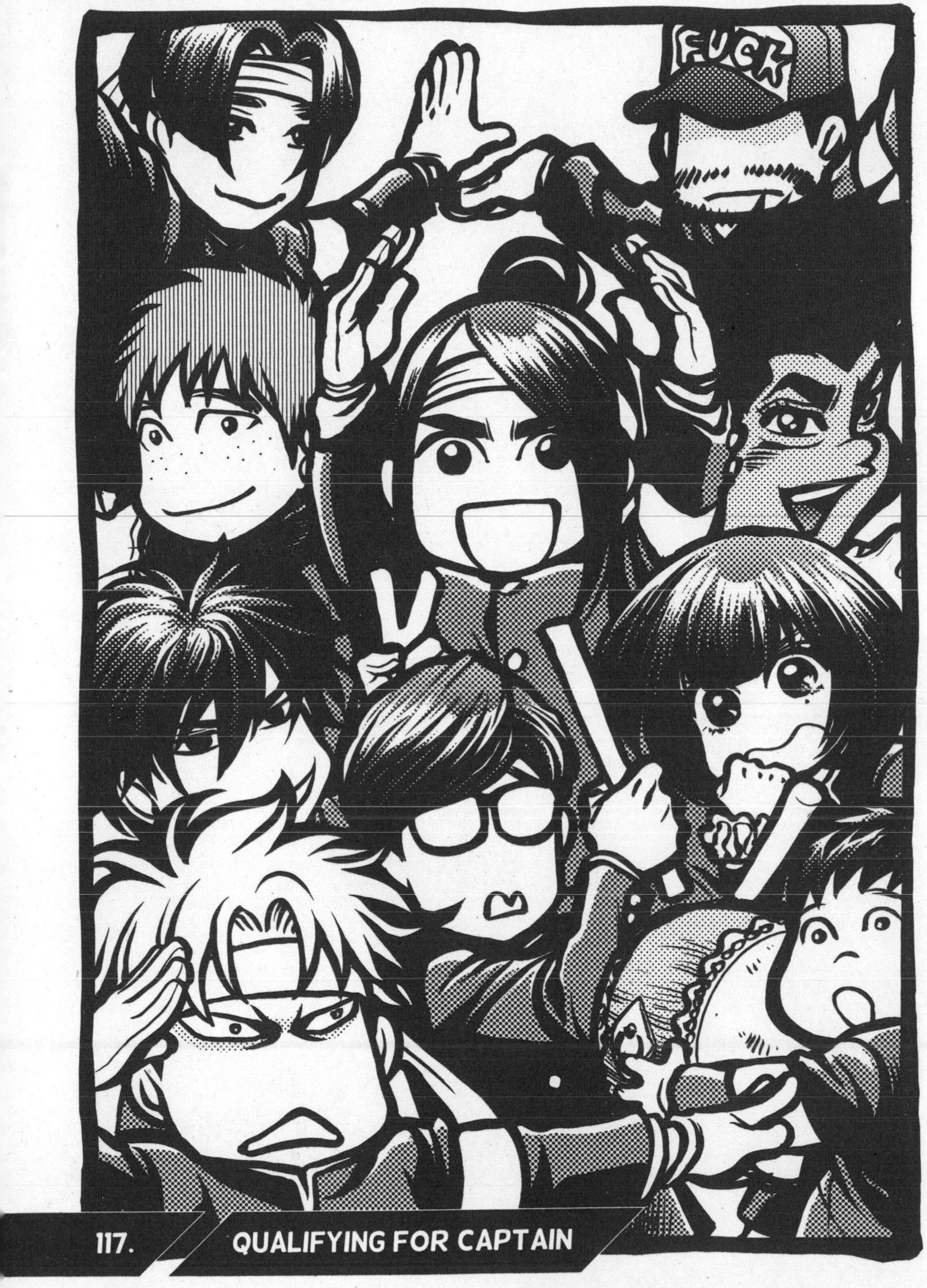
FUCK

117. QUALIFYING FOR CAPTAIN

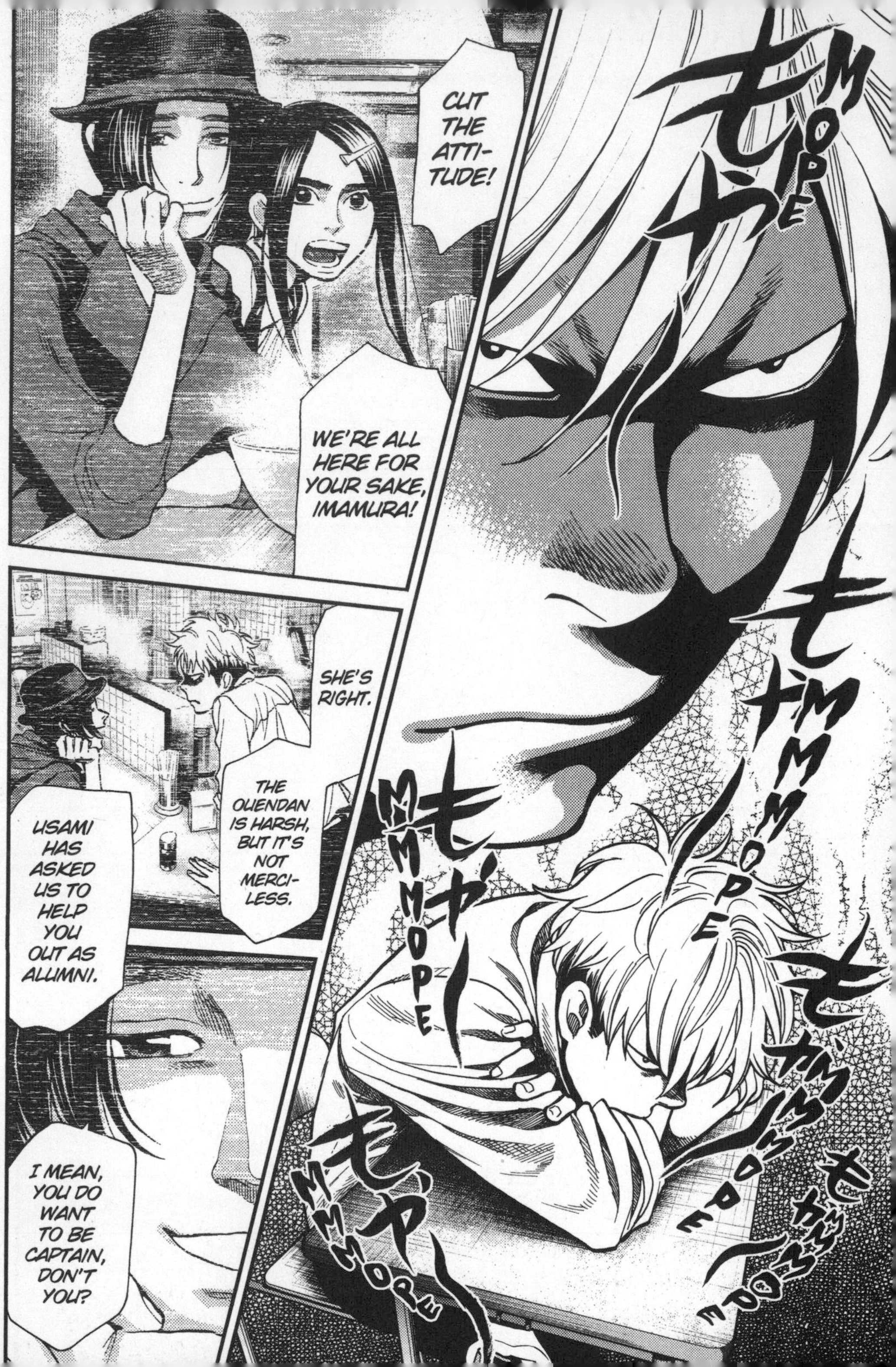
MOPE
MMMMOPE
MMMMOPE
CUT THE ATTI-TUDE!
WE'RE ALL HERE FOR YOUR SAKE, IMAMURA!
SHE'S RIGHT.
THE OUENDAN IS HARSH, BUT IT'S NOT MERCI-LESS.
USAMI HAS ASKED US TO HELP YOU OUT AS ALUMNI.
I MEAN, YOU DO WANT TO BE CAPTAIN, DON'T YOU?

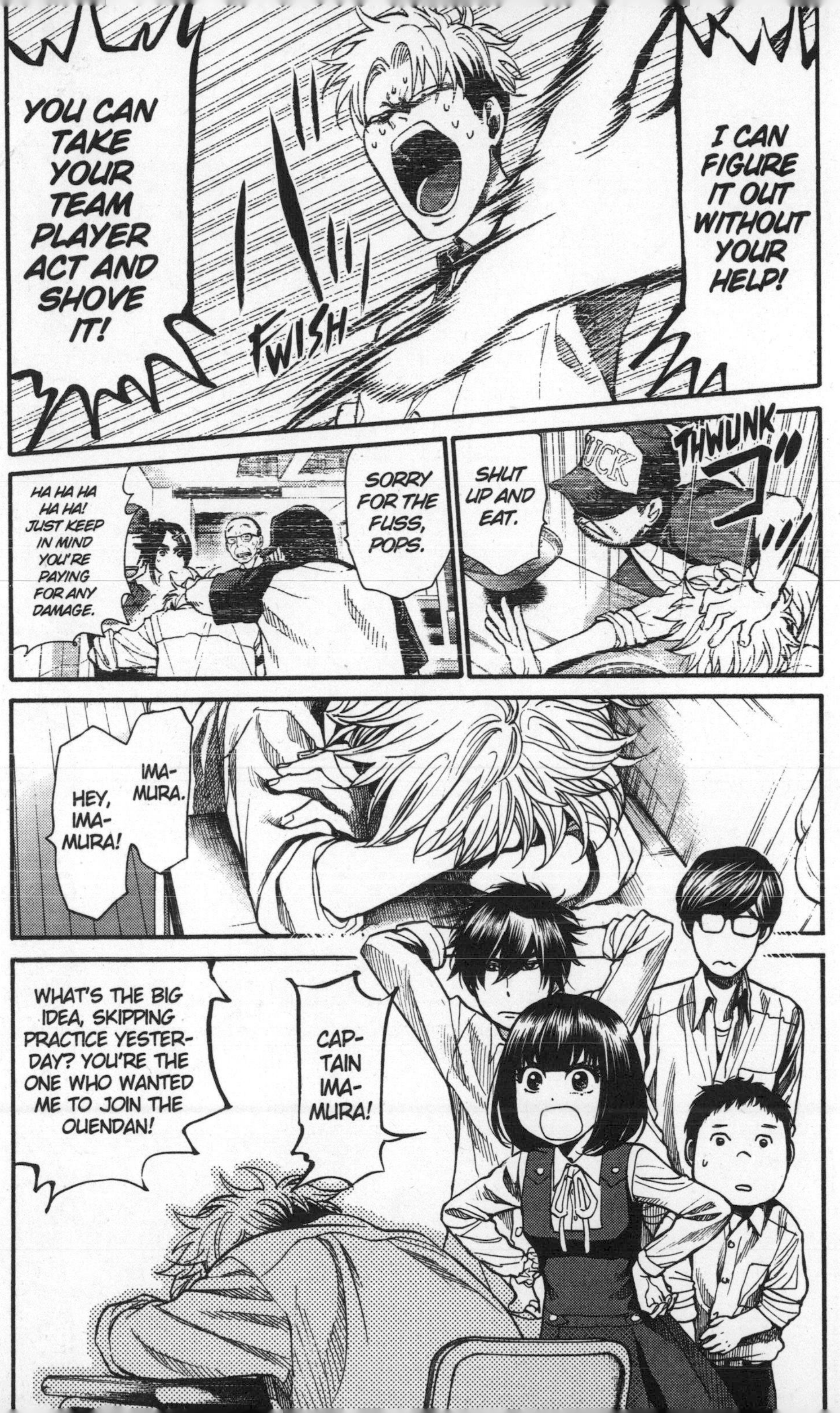
I CAN FIGURE IT OUT WITHOUT YOUR HELP!
YOU CAN TAKE YOUR TEAM PLAYER ACT AND SHOVE IT!
FWISH
THWUNK
SHUT UP AND EAT.
SORRY FOR THE FUSS, POPS.
HA HA HA HA HA! JUST KEEP IN MIND YOU'RE PAYING FOR ANY DAMAGE.
IMA-MURA.
HEY, IMA-MURA!
CAP-TAIN IMA-MURA!
WHAT'S THE BIG IDEA, SKIPPING PRACTICE YESTER-DAY? YOU'RE THE ONE WHO WANTED ME TO JOIN THE OUENDAN!

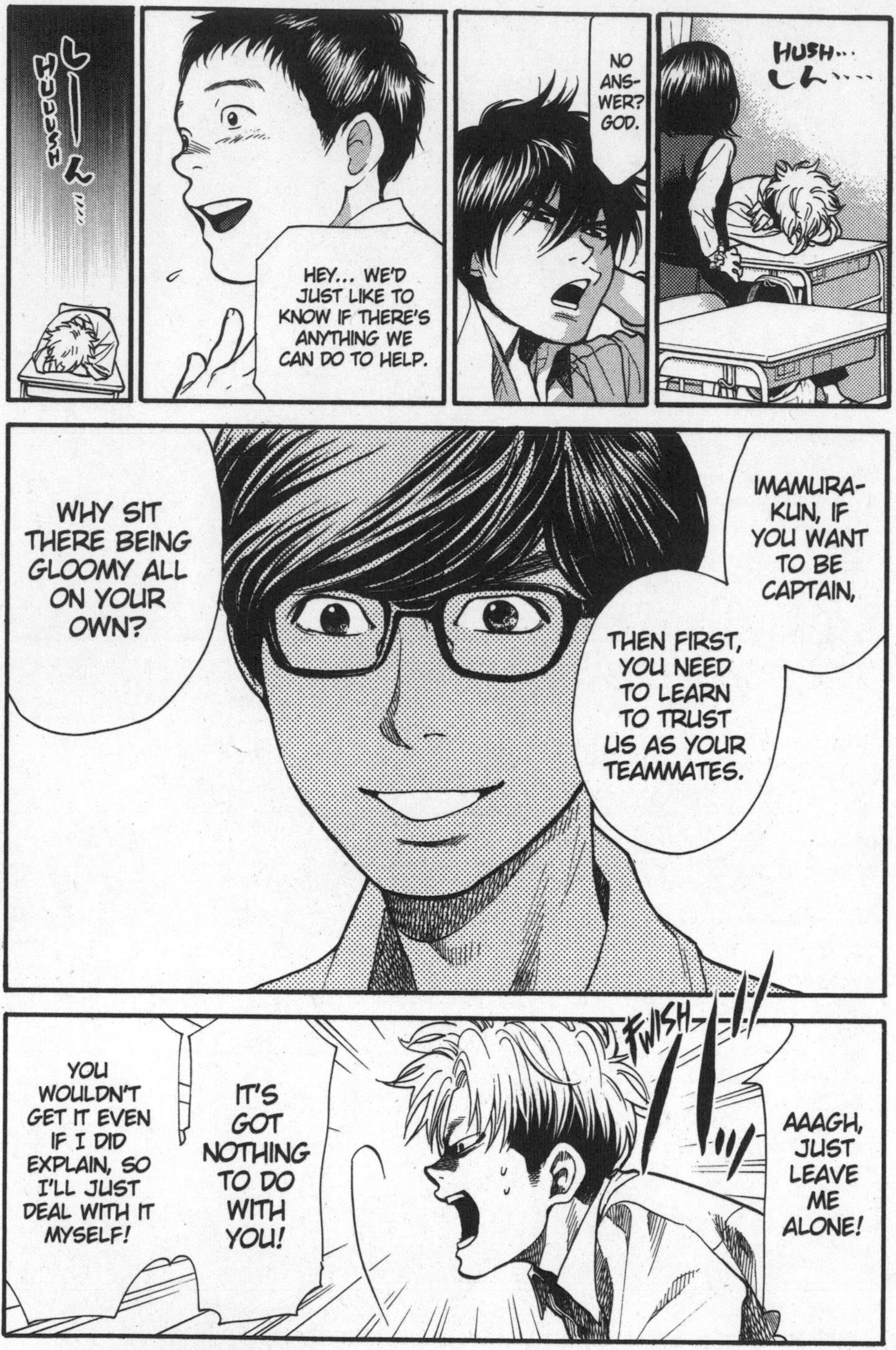
HUSH...
しん……
NO ANS-WER? GOD.
HEY... WE'D JUST LIKE TO KNOW IF THERE'S ANYTHING WE CAN DO TO HELP.
しーーん……
HUUUSH
IMAMURA-KUN, IF YOU WANT TO BE CAPTAIN,
THEN FIRST, YOU NEED TO LEARN TO TRUST US AS YOUR TEAMMATES.
WHY SIT THERE BEING GLOOMY ALL ON YOUR OWN?
FWISH
AAAGH, JUST LEAVE ME ALONE!
IT'S GOT NOTHING TO DO WITH YOU!
YOU WOULDN'T GET IT EVEN IF I DID EXPLAIN, SO I'LL JUST DEAL WITH IT MYSELF!

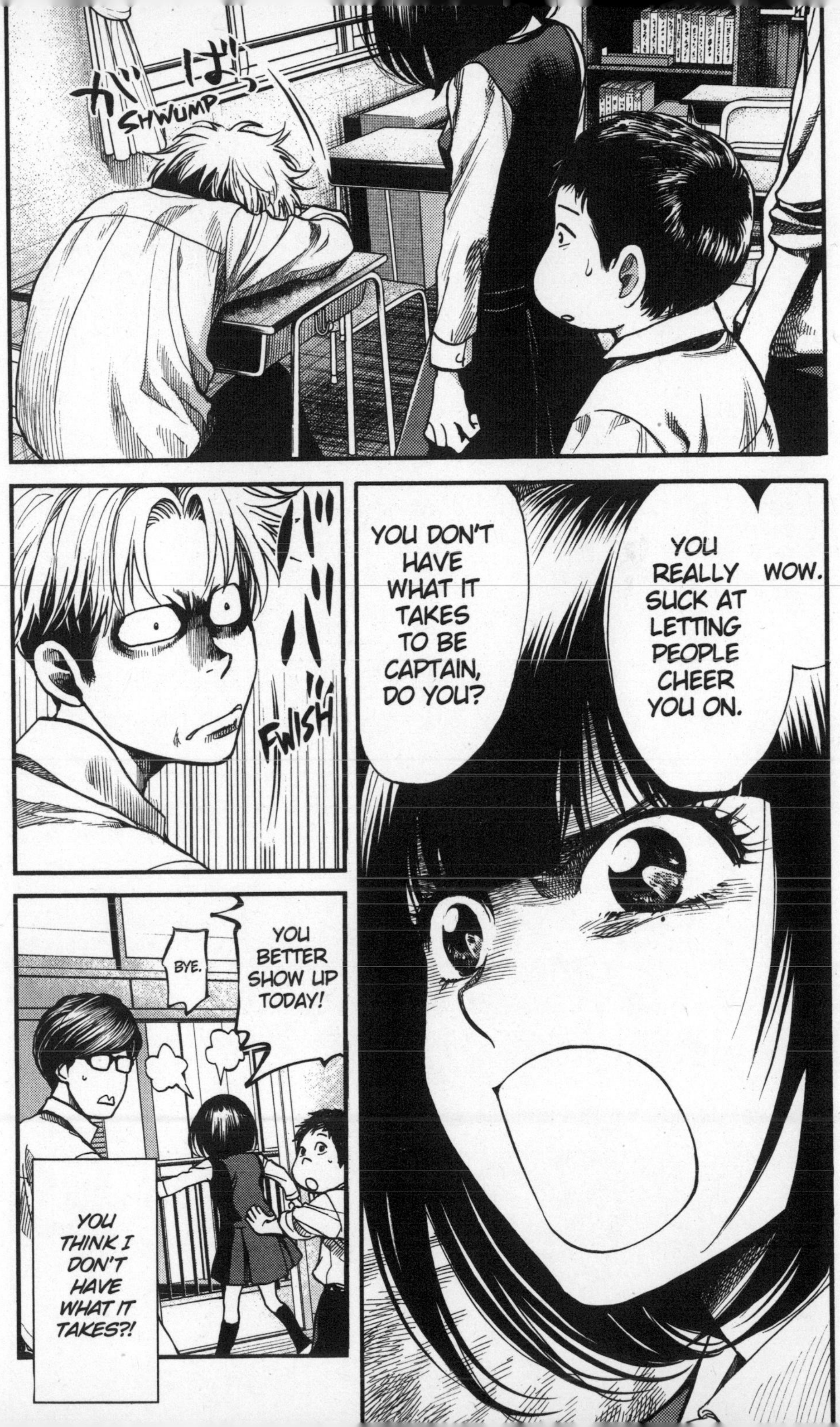
がばっ
SHWUMP
WOW.
YOU REALLY SUCK AT LETTING PEOPLE CHEER YOU ON.
YOU DON'T HAVE WHAT IT TAKES TO BE CAPTAIN, DO YOU?
FWISH
YOU BETTER SHOW UP TODAY!
BYE.
YOU THINK I DON'T HAVE WHAT IT TAKES?!

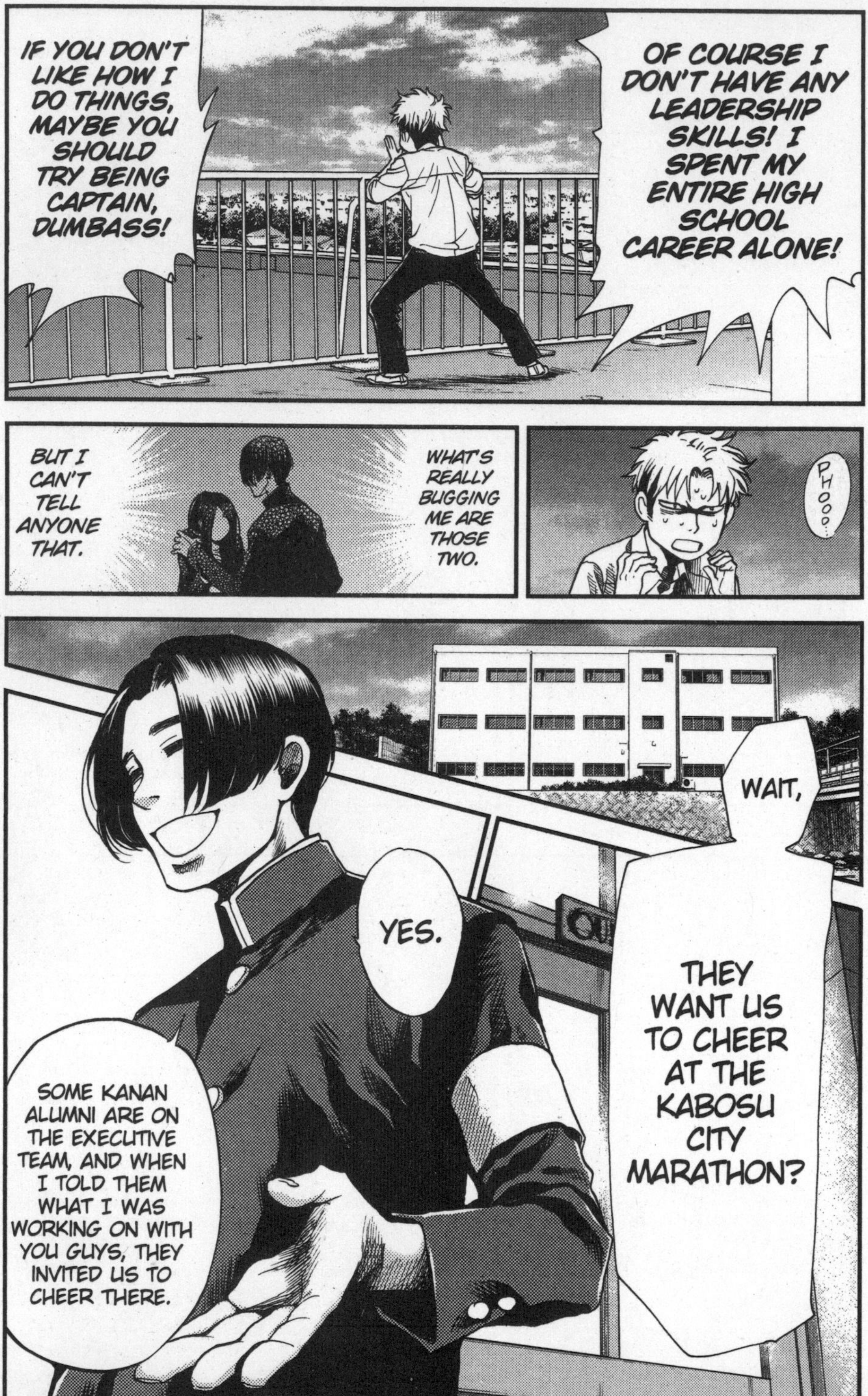
OF COURSE I DON'T HAVE ANY LEADERSHIP SKILLS! I SPENT MY ENTIRE HIGH SCHOOL CAREER ALONE!
IF YOU DON'T LIKE HOW I DO THINGS, MAYBE YOU SHOULD TRY BEING CAPTAIN, DUMBASS!
PHOOO...
WHAT'S REALLY BUGGING ME ARE THOSE TWO.
BUT I CAN'T TELL ANYONE THAT.
WAIT,
THEY WANT US TO CHEER AT THE KABOSU CITY MARATHON?
YES.
SOME KANAN ALUMNI ARE ON THE EXECUTIVE TEAM, AND WHEN I TOLD THEM WHAT I WAS WORKING ON WITH YOU GUYS, THEY INVITED US TO CHEER THERE.

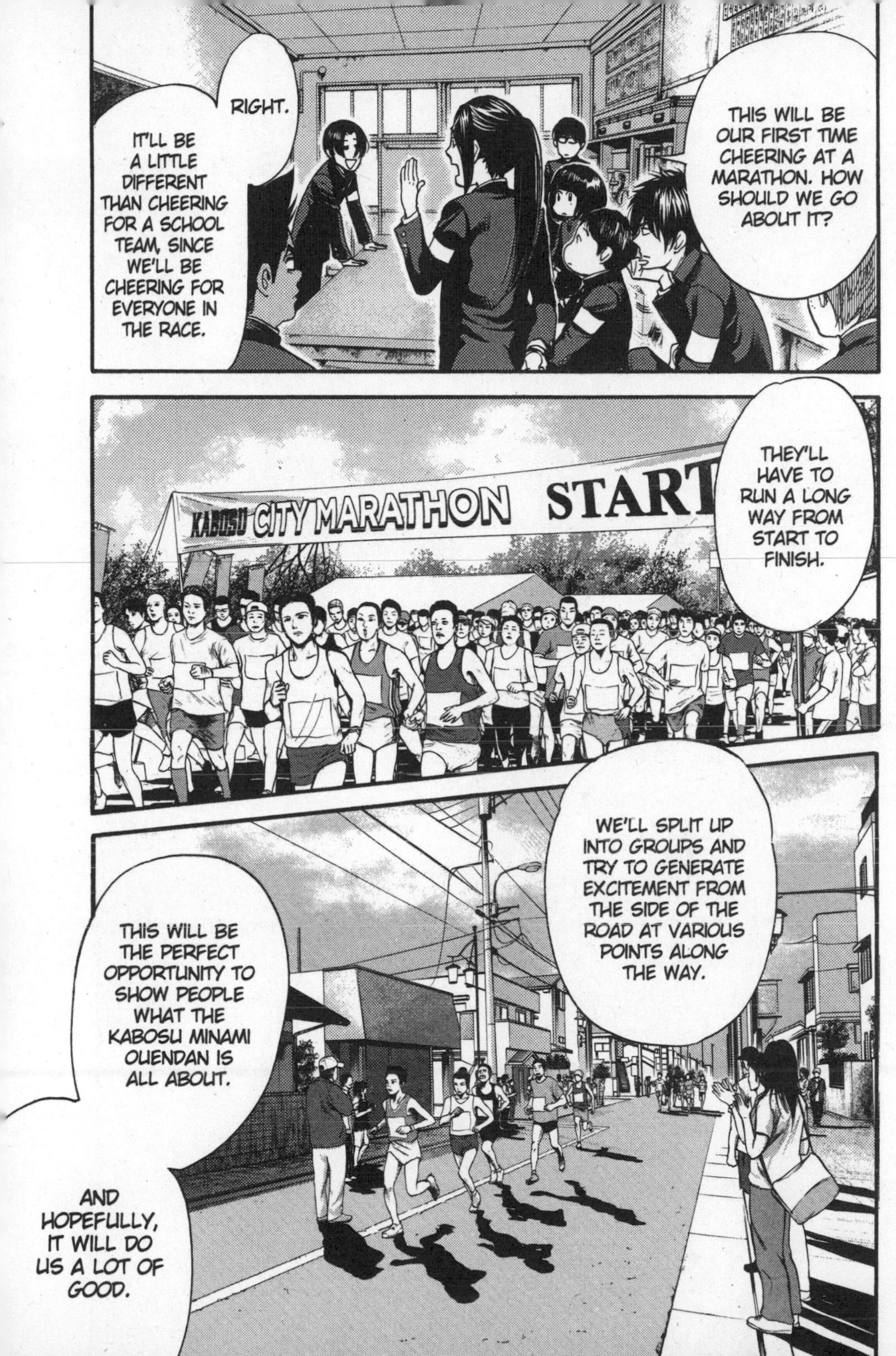
THIS WILL BE OUR FIRST TIME CHEERING AT A MARATHON. HOW SHOULD WE GO ABOUT IT?
RIGHT.
IT'LL BE A LITTLE DIFFERENT THAN CHEERING FOR A SCHOOL TEAM, SINCE WE'LL BE CHEERING FOR EVERYONE IN THE RACE.
KABOSU CITY MARATHON START
THEY'LL HAVE TO RUN A LONG WAY FROM START TO FINISH.
WE'LL SPLIT UP INTO GROUPS AND TRY TO GENERATE EXCITEMENT FROM THE SIDE OF THE ROAD AT VARIOUS POINTS ALONG THE WAY.
THIS WILL BE THE PERFECT OPPORTUNITY TO SHOW PEOPLE WHAT THE KABOSU MINAMI OUENDAN IS ALL ABOUT.
AND HOPEFULLY, IT WILL DO US A LOT OF GOOD.

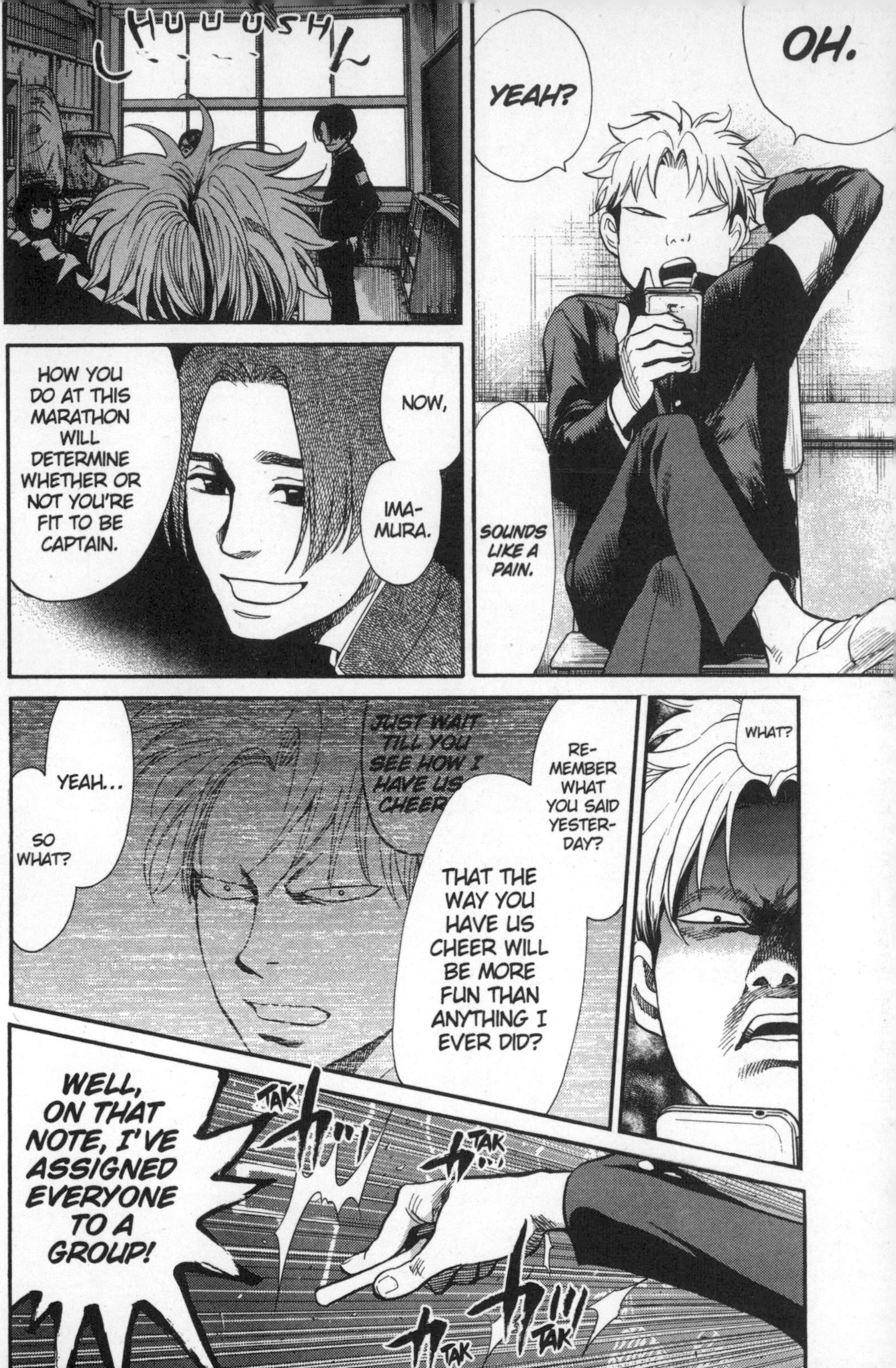
OH.
YEAH?
SOUNDS LIKE A PAIN.
HUUUUSH
NOW, IMA-MURA.
HOW YOU DO AT THIS MARATHON WILL DETERMINE WHETHER OR NOT YOU'RE FIT TO BE CAPTAIN.
WHAT?
RE-MEMBER WHAT YOU SAID YESTER-DAY?
THAT THE WAY YOU HAVE US CHEER WILL BE MORE FUN THAN ANYTHING I EVER DID?
JUST WAIT TILL YOU SEE HOW I HAVE US CHEER
YEAH...
SO WHAT?
WELL, ON THAT NOTE, I'VE ASSIGNED EVERYONE TO A GROUP!
TAK
TAK
TAK
TAK

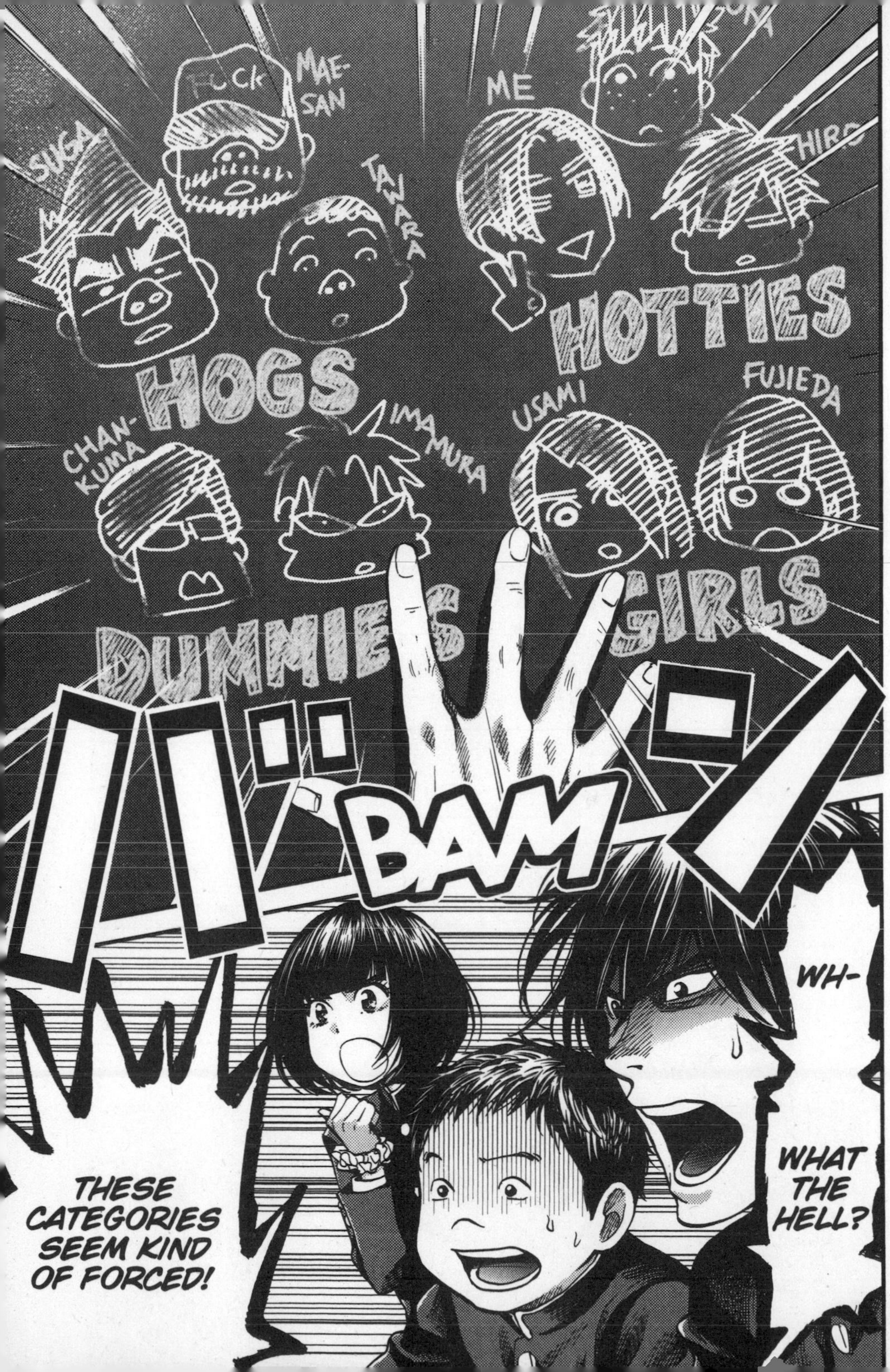
ME
HIRO
HOTTIES
MAE-SAN
FUCK
TAWARA
SUGA
HOGS
FUJIEDA
USAMI
GIRLS
IMAMURA
CHAN-KUMA
DUMMIES
BAM
WH-
WHAT THE HELL?
THESE CATEGORIES SEEM KIND OF FORCED!

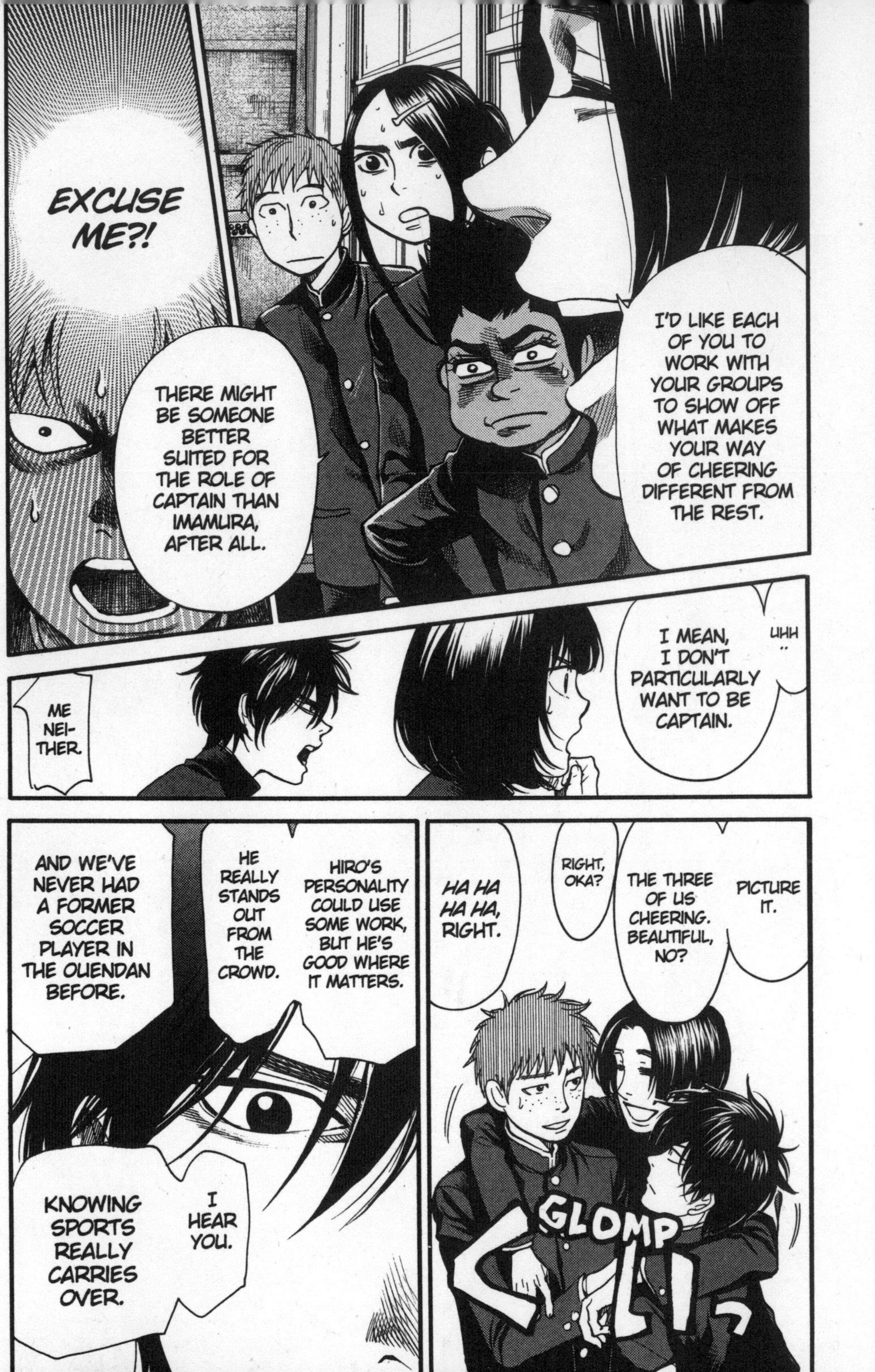
I'D LIKE EACH OF YOU TO WORK WITH YOUR GROUPS TO SHOW OFF WHAT MAKES YOUR WAY OF CHEERING DIFFERENT FROM THE REST.
THERE MIGHT BE SOMEONE BETTER SUITED FOR THE ROLE OF CAPTAIN THAN IMAMURA, AFTER ALL.
EXCUSE ME?!
UHH..
I MEAN, I DON'T PARTICULARLY WANT TO BE CAPTAIN.
ME NEI-THER.
PICTURE IT.
THE THREE OF US CHEERING. BEAUTIFUL, NO?
RIGHT, OKA?
HA HA HA HA, RIGHT.
GLOMP
HIRO'S PERSONALITY COULD USE SOME WORK, BUT HE'S GOOD WHERE IT MATTERS.
HE REALLY STANDS OUT FROM THE CROWD.
AND WE'VE NEVER HAD A FORMER SOCCER PLAYER IN THE OUENDAN BEFORE.
KNOWING SPORTS REALLY CARRIES OVER.
I HEAR YOU.

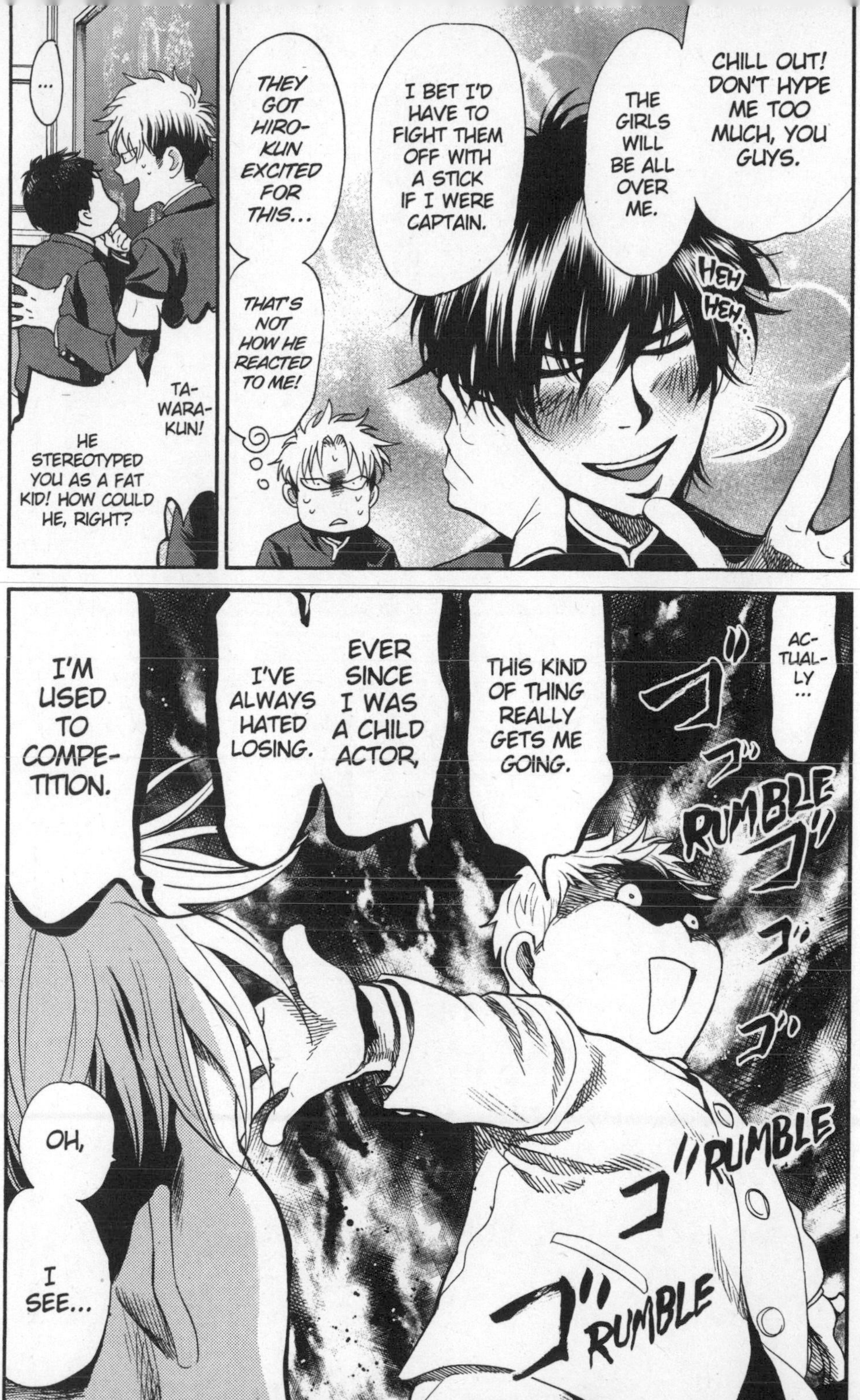
CHILL OUT! DON'T HYPE ME TOO MUCH, YOU GUYS.
THE GIRLS WILL BE ALL OVER ME.
HEH HEH...
I BET I'D HAVE TO FIGHT THEM OFF WITH A STICK IF I WERE CAPTAIN.
THEY GOT HIRO-KUN EXCITED FOR THIS...
THAT'S NOT HOW HE REACTED TO ME!
...
TA-WARA-KUN!
HE STEREOTYPED YOU AS A FAT KID! HOW COULD HE, RIGHT?
ACTUALLY...
THIS KIND OF THING REALLY GETS ME GOING.
EVER SINCE I WAS A CHILD ACTOR,
I'VE ALWAYS HATED LOSING.
I'M USED TO COMPETITION.
RUMBLE
RUMBLE
RUMBLE
OH,
I SEE...

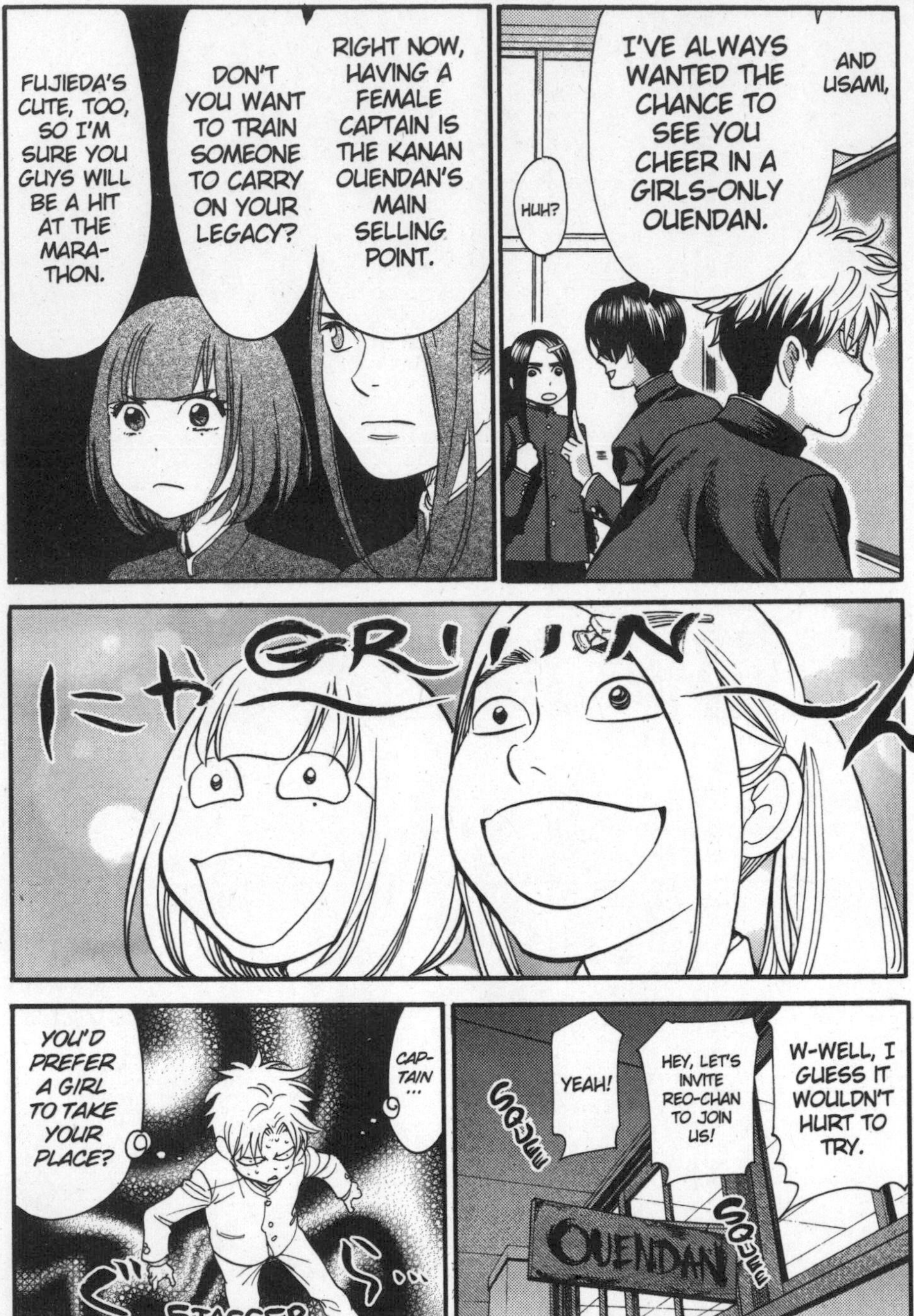
AND USAMI,
I'VE ALWAYS WANTED THE CHANCE TO SEE YOU CHEER IN A GIRLS-ONLY OUENDAN.
HUH?
RIGHT NOW, HAVING A FEMALE CAPTAIN IS THE KANAN OUENDAN'S MAIN SELLING POINT.
DON'T YOU WANT TO TRAIN SOMEONE TO CARRY ON YOUR LEGACY?
FUJIEDA'S CUTE, TOO, SO I'M SURE YOU GUYS WILL BE A HIT AT THE MARA-THON.
GRIIIN
W-WELL, I GUESS IT WOULDN'T HURT TO TRY.
HEY, LET'S INVITE REO-CHAN TO JOIN US!
YEAH!
SQUEE
SQUEE
OUENDAN
CAP-TAIN...
YOU'D PREFER A GIRL TO TAKE YOUR PLACE?
STAGGER

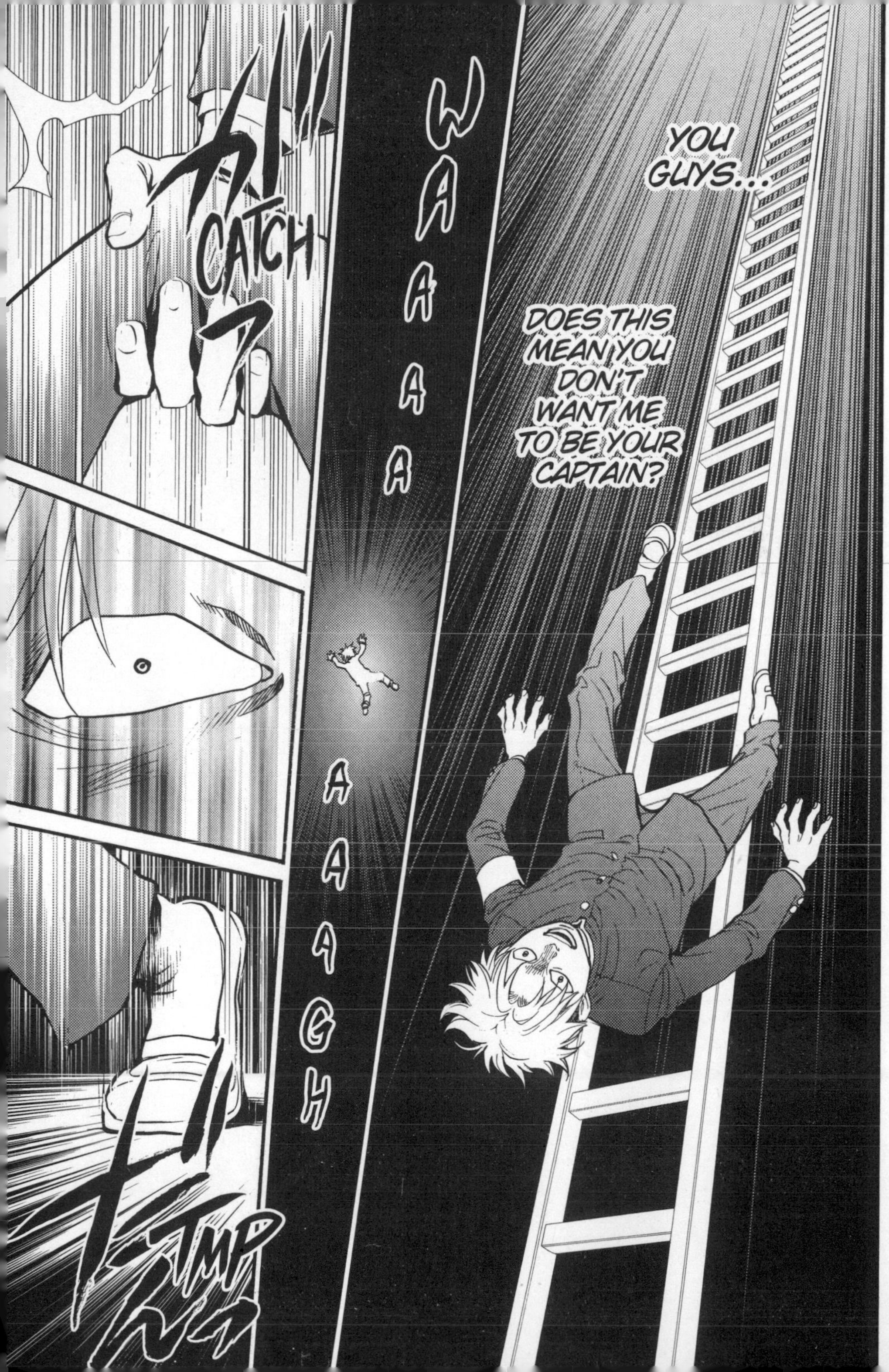
YOU GUYS...
DOES THIS MEAN YOU DON'T WANT ME TO BE YOUR CAPTAIN?
WAAAAAAAAGH
CATCH
TMP

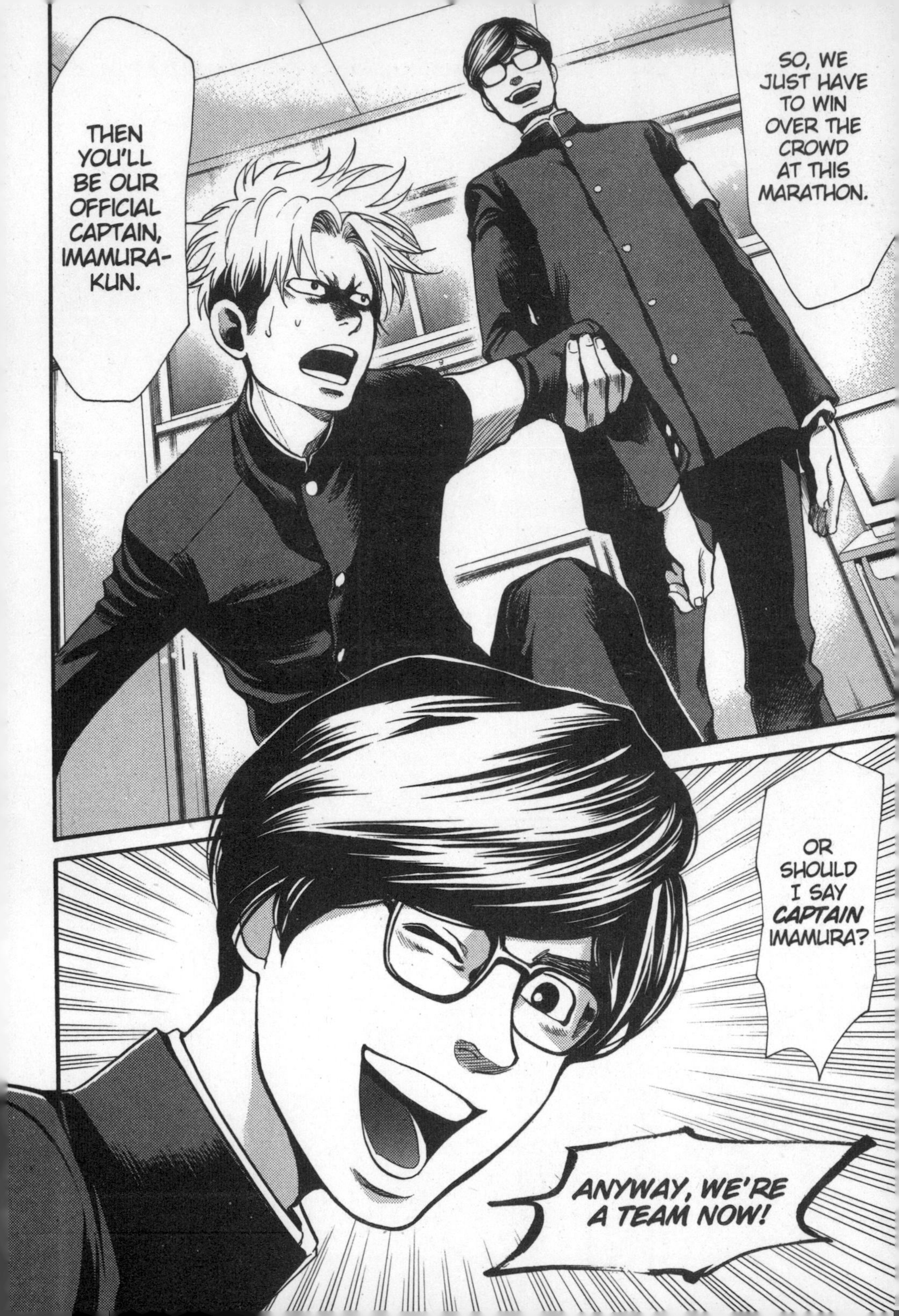
SO, WE JUST HAVE TO WIN OVER THE CROWD AT THIS MARATHON.
THEN YOU'LL BE OUR OFFICIAL CAPTAIN, IMAMURA-KUN.
OR SHOULD I SAY *CAPTAIN* IMAMURA?
ANYWAY, WE'RE A TEAM NOW!

118. DIVIDE AND SELF-OWN

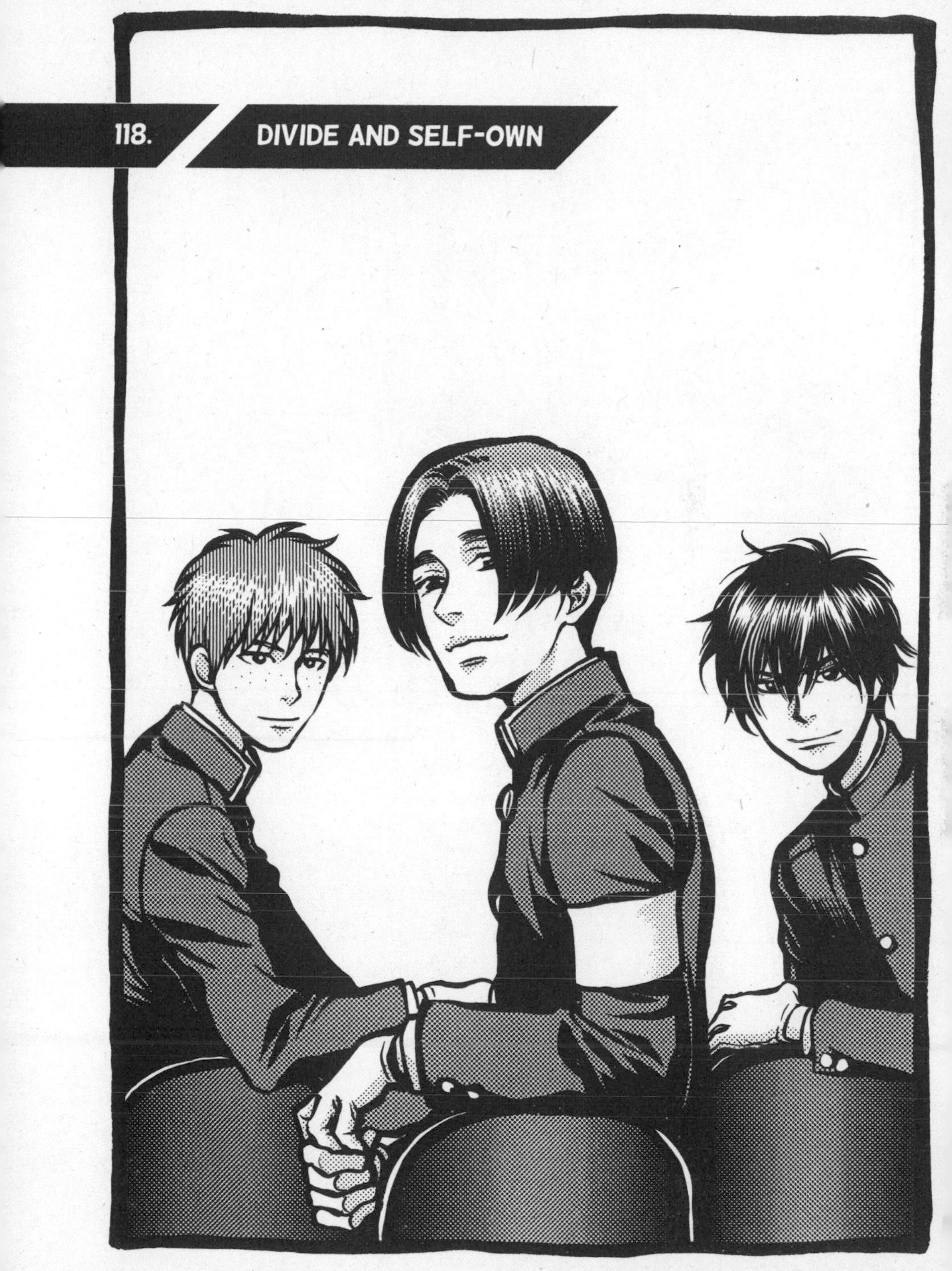

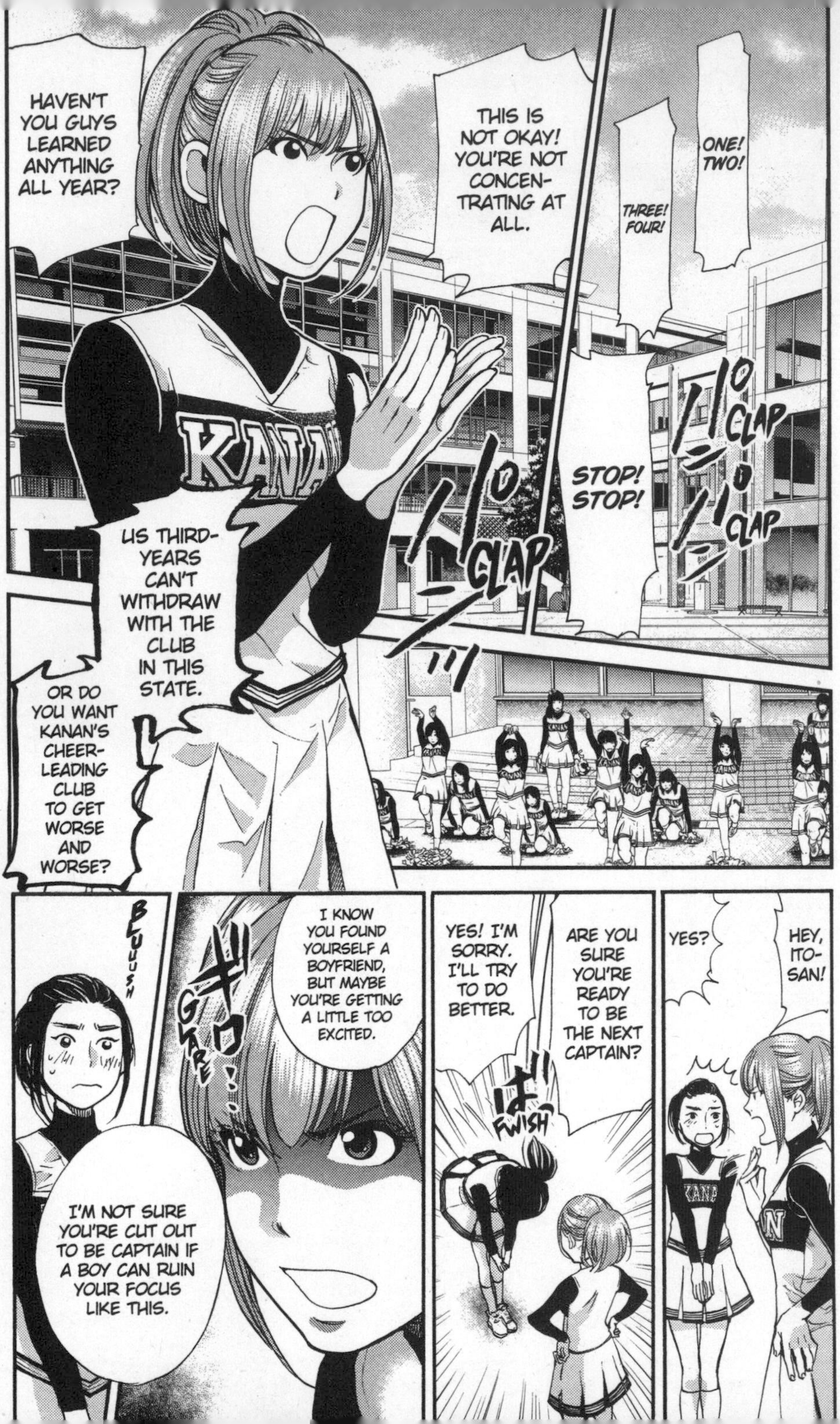
ONE! TWO!
THREE! FOUR!
CLAP CLAP CLAP
STOP! STOP!
CLAP
THIS IS NOT OKAY! YOU'RE NOT CONCEN-TRATING AT ALL.
HAVEN'T YOU GUYS LEARNED ANYTHING ALL YEAR?
US THIRD-YEARS CAN'T WITHDRAW WITH THE CLUB IN THIS STATE.
OR DO YOU WANT KANAN'S CHEER-LEADING CLUB TO GET WORSE AND WORSE?
HEY, ITO-SAN!
YES?
ARE YOU SURE YOU'RE READY TO BE THE NEXT CAPTAIN?
YES! I'M SORRY. I'LL TRY TO DO BETTER.
FWISH
I KNOW YOU FOUND YOURSELF A BOYFRIEND, BUT MAYBE YOU'RE GETTING A LITTLE TOO EXCITED.
GLARE
BLUUUSH
I'M NOT SURE YOU'RE CUT OUT TO BE CAPTAIN IF A BOY CAN RUIN YOUR FOCUS LIKE THIS.

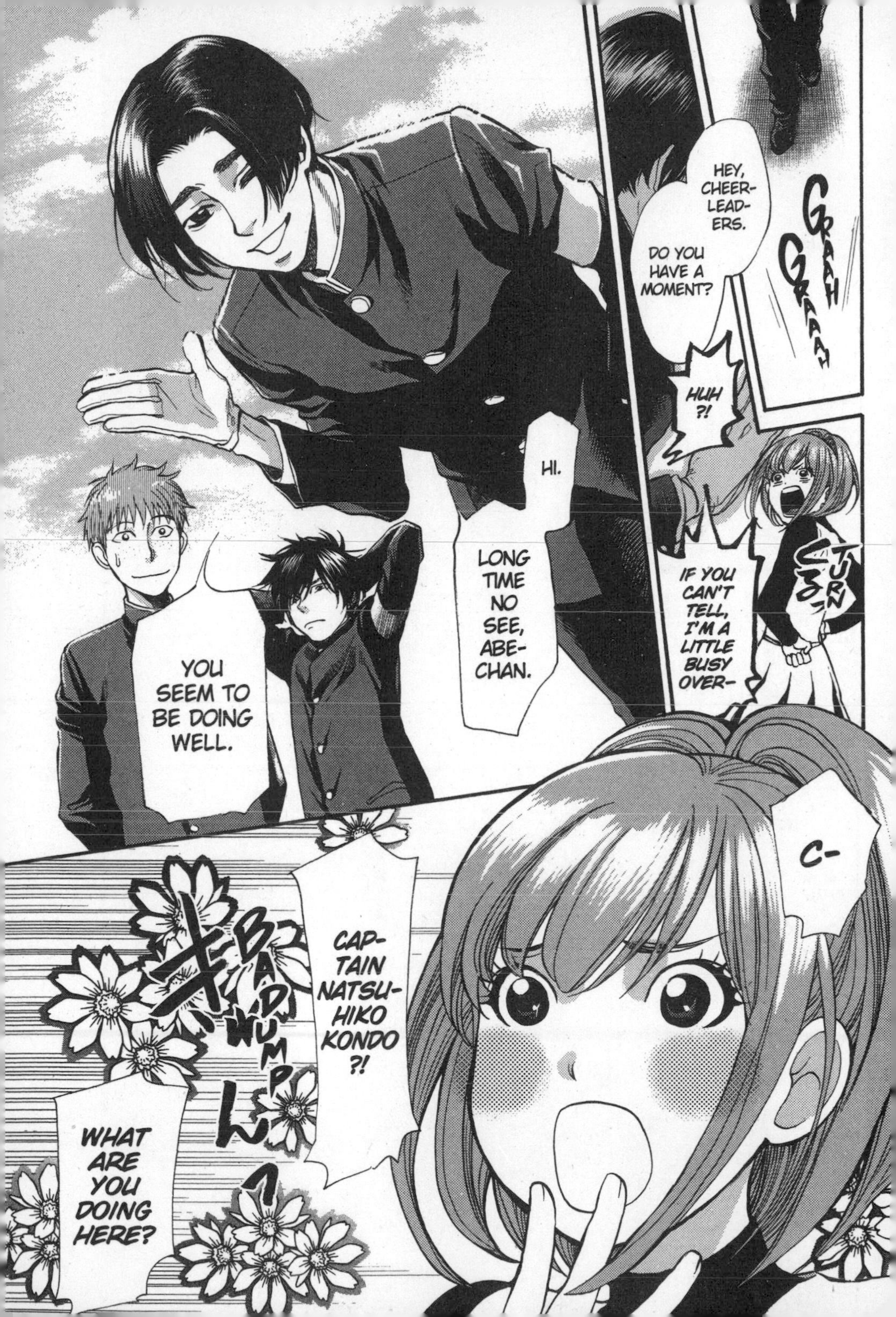

HEY, CHEER-LEADERS.
DO YOU HAVE A MOMENT?
GRAAAH GRAAAH
HUH?!
TURN
IF YOU CAN'T TELL, I'M A LITTLE BUSY OVER-
HI.
LONG TIME NO SEE, ABE-CHAN.
YOU SEEM TO BE DOING WELL.
C-
CAP-TAIN NATSU-HIKO KONDO?!
BADUMP
WHAT ARE YOU DOING HERE?

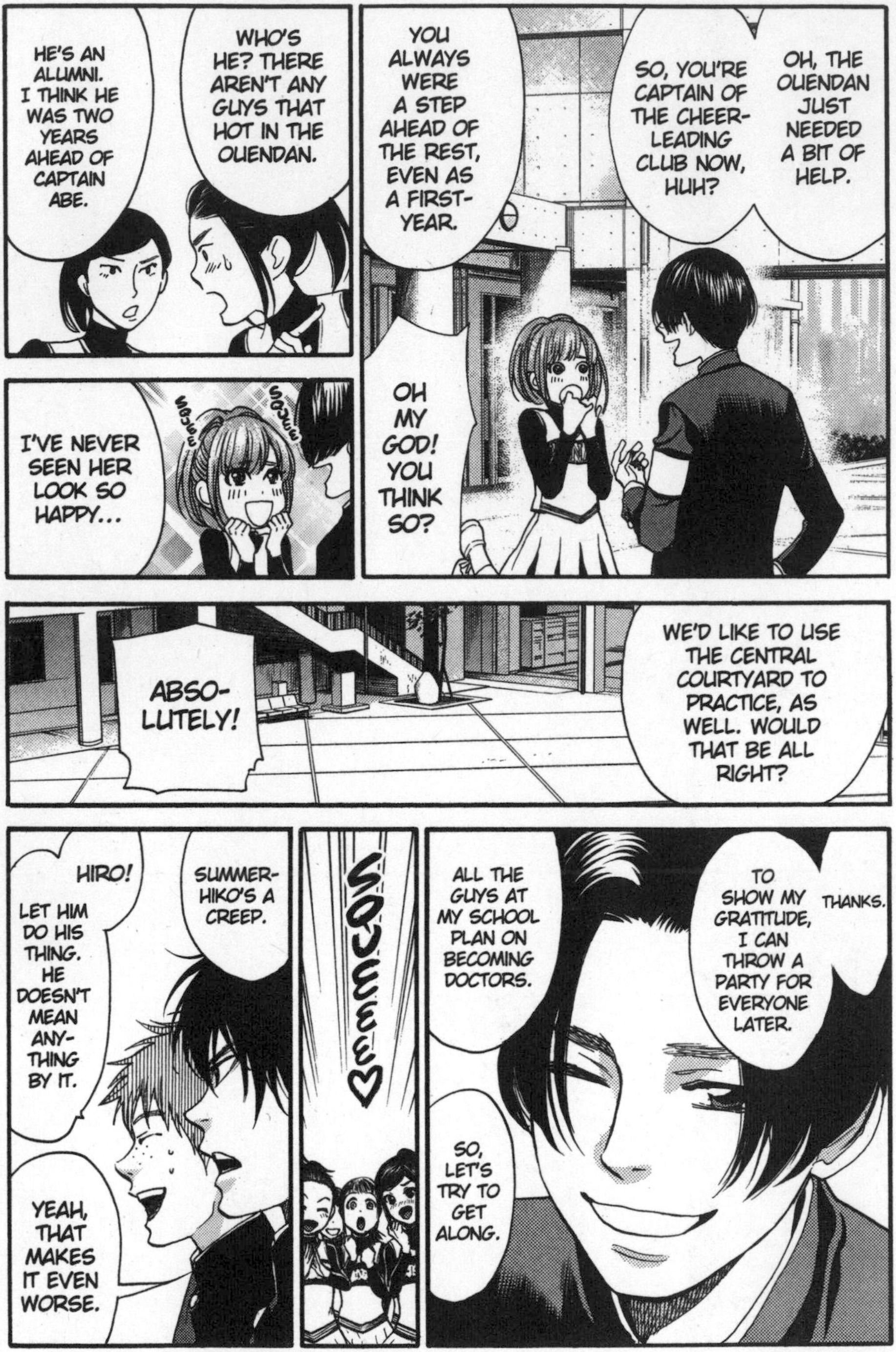
OH, THE OUENDAN JUST NEEDED A BIT OF HELP.
SO, YOU'RE CAPTAIN OF THE CHEER-LEADING CLUB NOW, HUH?
YOU ALWAYS WERE A STEP AHEAD OF THE REST, EVEN AS A FIRST-YEAR.
OH MY GOD! YOU THINK SO?
WHO'S HE? THERE AREN'T ANY GUYS THAT HOT IN THE OUENDAN.
HE'S AN ALUMNI. I THINK HE WAS TWO YEARS AHEAD OF CAPTAIN ABE.
SQUEE
SQUEE
I'VE NEVER SEEN HER LOOK SO HAPPY...
WE'D LIKE TO USE THE CENTRAL COURTYARD TO PRACTICE, AS WELL. WOULD THAT BE ALL RIGHT?
ABSO-LUTELY!
THANKS.
TO SHOW MY GRATITUDE, I CAN THROW A PARTY FOR EVERYONE LATER.
ALL THE GUYS AT MY SCHOOL PLAN ON BECOMING DOCTORS.
SO, LET'S TRY TO GET ALONG.
SQUEEEE♥
SUMMER-HIKO'S A CREEP.
HIRO!
LET HIM DO HIS THING. HE DOESN'T MEAN ANY-THING BY IT.
YEAH, THAT MAKES IT EVEN WORSE.

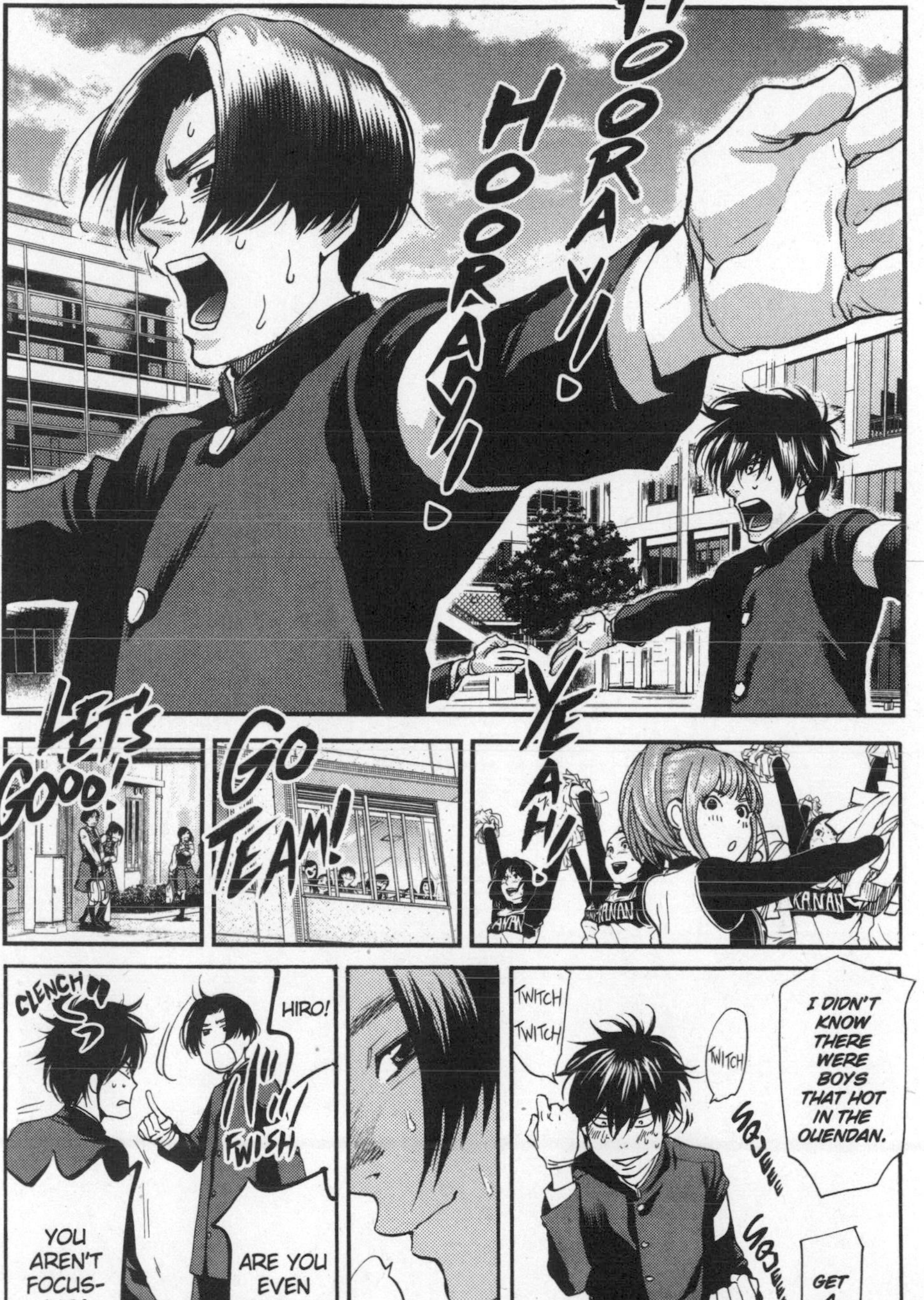
HOORAY!
HOORAY!
YEAH!
GO TEAM!
LET'S GOOO!
I DIDN'T KNOW THERE WERE BOYS THAT HOT IN THE OUENDAN.
TWITCH
TWITCH
TWITCH
SQUEEE
SQUEEE
GET A PIC-TURE!
...
HIRO!
CLENCH
FWISH
ARE YOU EVEN TRYING?
YOU AREN'T FOCUS-ING!

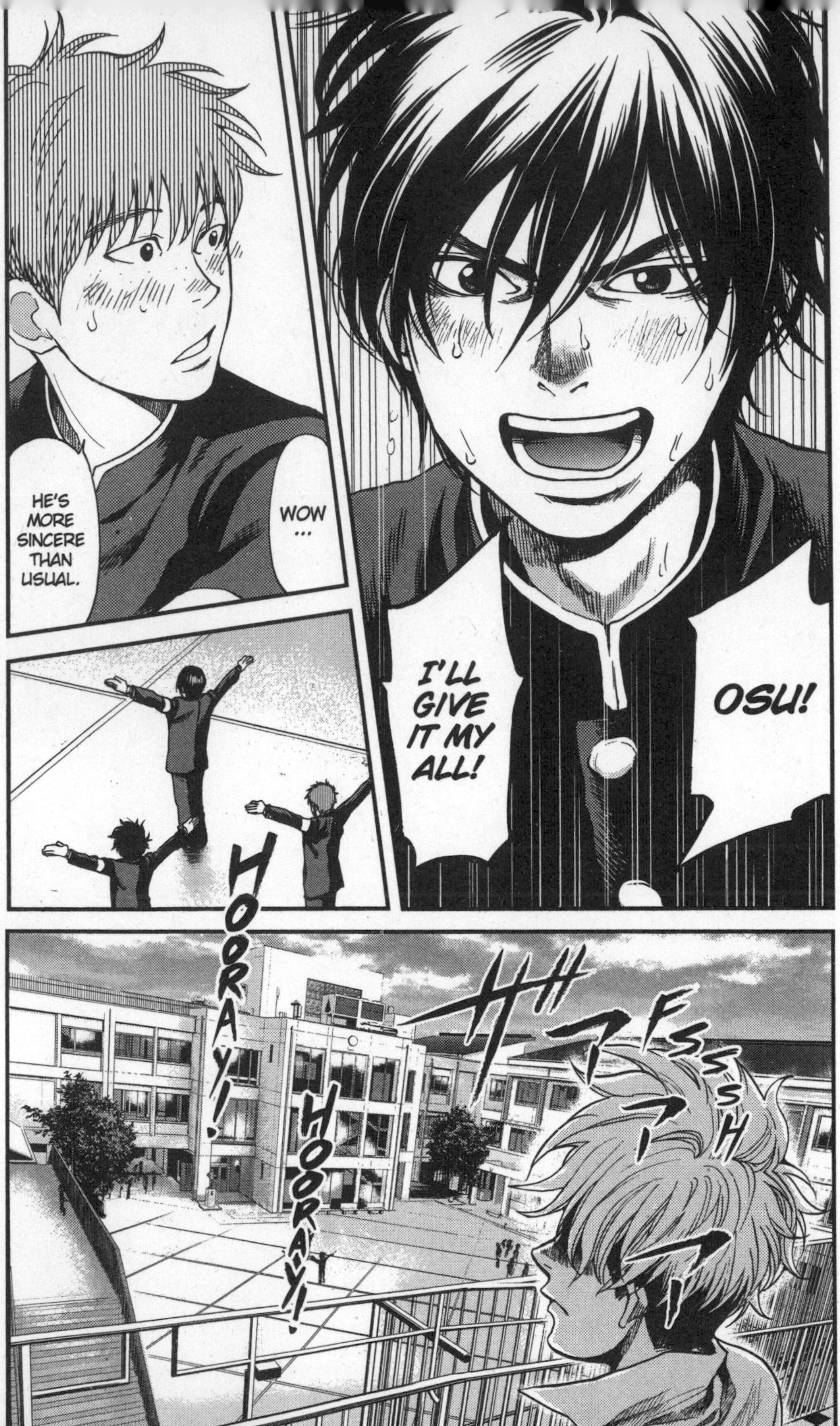
OSU!
I'LL GIVE IT MY ALL!
WOW ...
HE'S MORE SINCERE THAN USUAL.
HOORAY!
FSSSH
HOORAY!

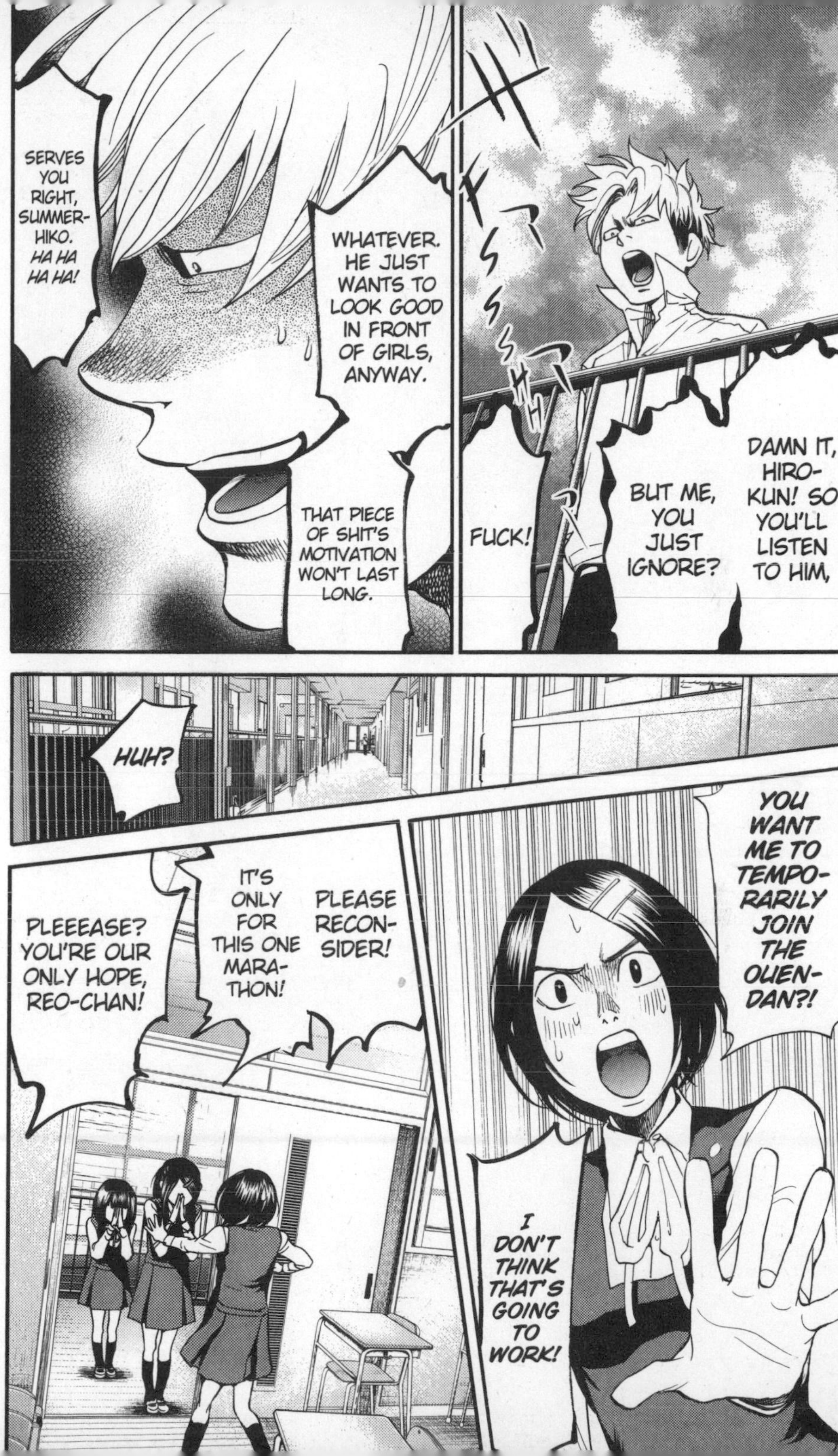
DAMN IT, HIRO-KUN! SO YOU'LL LISTEN TO HIM,
BUT ME, YOU JUST IGNORE?
FUCK!
WHATEVER. HE JUST WANTS TO LOOK GOOD IN FRONT OF GIRLS, ANYWAY.
SERVES YOU RIGHT, SUMMER-HIKO. HA HA HA HA!
THAT PIECE OF SHIT'S MOTIVATION WON'T LAST LONG.
HUH?
YOU WANT ME TO TEMPORARILY JOIN THE OUEN-DAN?!
I DON'T THINK THAT'S GOING TO WORK!
PLEASE RECONSIDER!
IT'S ONLY FOR THIS ONE MARATHON!
PLEEEASE? YOU'RE OUR ONLY HOPE, REO-CHAN!

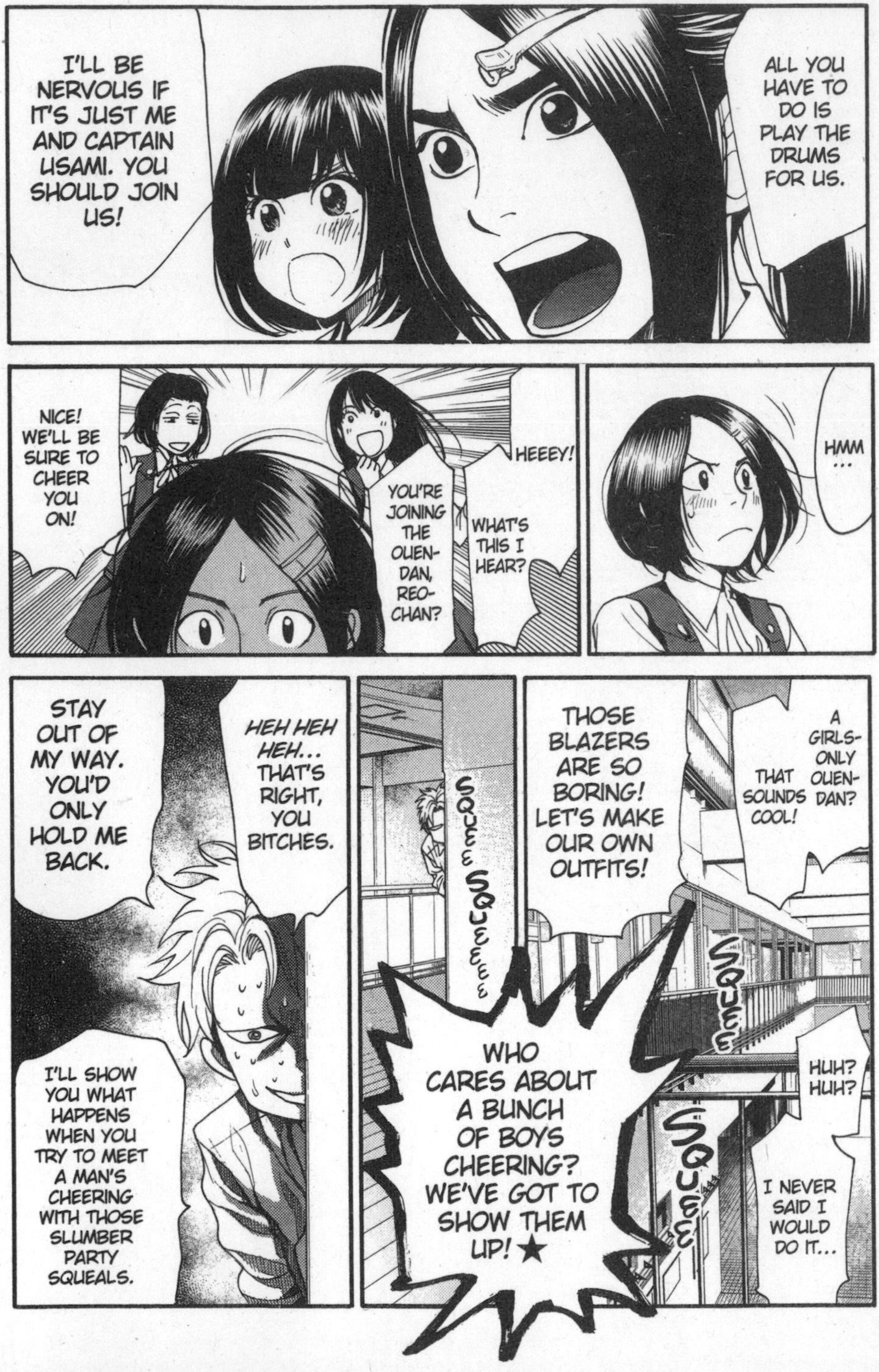
ALL YOU HAVE TO DO IS PLAY THE DRUMS FOR US.
I'LL BE NERVOUS IF IT'S JUST ME AND CAPTAIN USAMI. YOU SHOULD JOIN US!
HMM...
HEEEY!
WHAT'S THIS I HEAR?
YOU'RE JOINING THE OUEN-DAN, REO-CHAN?
NICE! WE'LL BE SURE TO CHEER YOU ON!
A GIRLS-ONLY OUEN-DAN?
THAT SOUNDS COOL!
THOSE BLAZERS ARE SO BORING! LET'S MAKE OUR OWN OUTFITS!
SQUEE
HUH? HUH?
WHO CARES ABOUT A BUNCH OF BOYS CHEERING? WE'VE GOT TO SHOW THEM UP! ★
SQUEE
I NEVER SAID I WOULD DO IT...
SQUEE SQUEE SQUEEEEE
HEH HEH HEH... THAT'S RIGHT, YOU BITCHES.
STAY OUT OF MY WAY. YOU'D ONLY HOLD ME BACK.
I'LL SHOW YOU WHAT HAPPENS WHEN YOU TRY TO MEET A MAN'S CHEERING WITH THOSE SLUMBER PARTY SQUEALS.

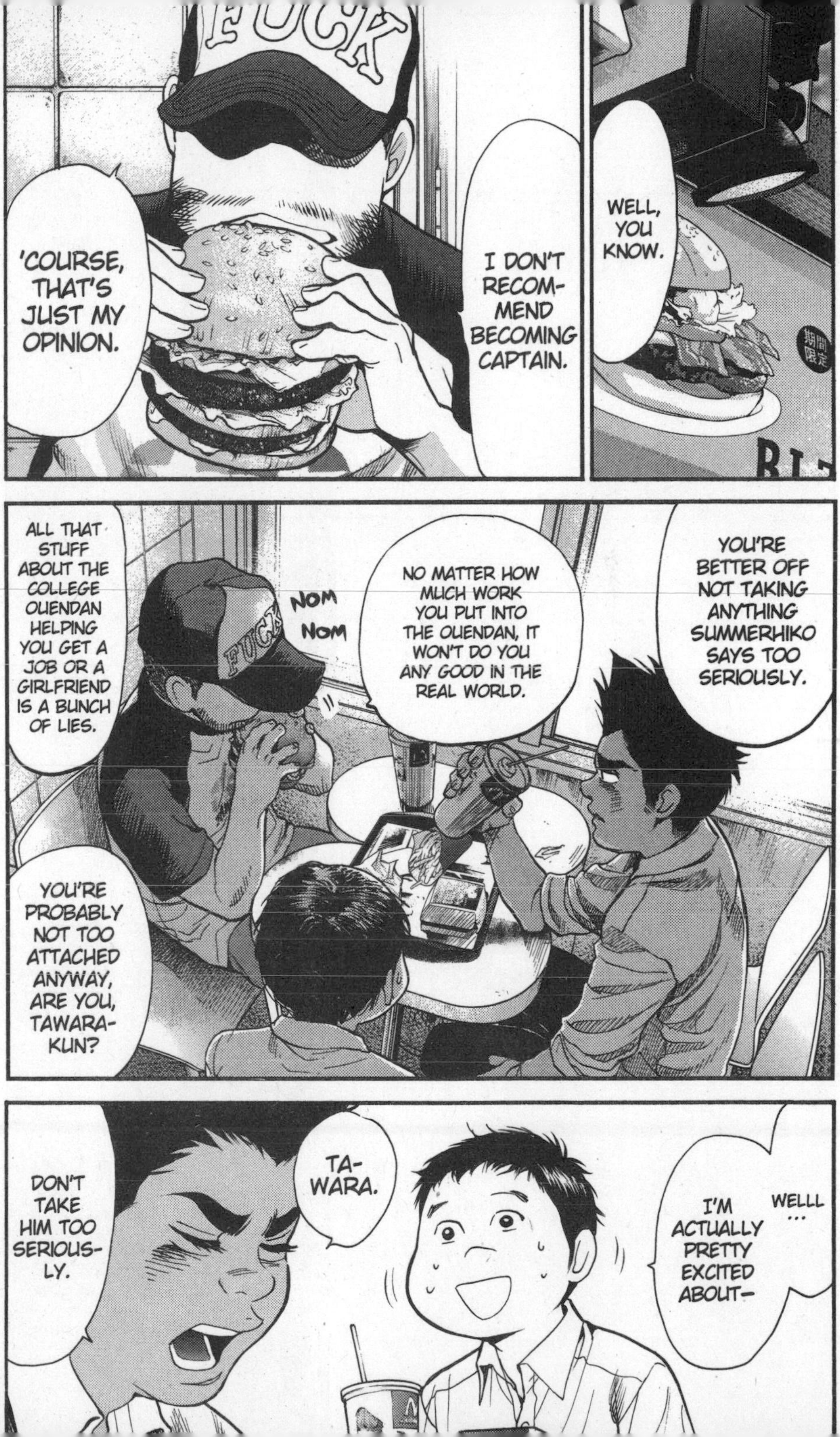
WELL, YOU KNOW.
期間限定
I DON'T RECOMMEND BECOMING CAPTAIN.
FUCK
'COURSE, THAT'S JUST MY OPINION.
YOU'RE BETTER OFF NOT TAKING ANYTHING SUMMERHIKO SAYS TOO SERIOUSLY.
NO MATTER HOW MUCH WORK YOU PUT INTO THE OUENDAN, IT WON'T DO YOU ANY GOOD IN THE REAL WORLD.
NOM NOM
FUCK
ALL THAT STUFF ABOUT THE COLLEGE OUENDAN HELPING YOU GET A JOB OR A GIRLFRIEND IS A BUNCH OF LIES.
YOU'RE PROBABLY NOT TOO ATTACHED ANYWAY, ARE YOU, TAWARA-KUN?
WELLL ...
I'M ACTUALLY PRETTY EXCITED ABOUT—
TA-WARA.
DON'T TAKE HIM TOO SERIOUS-LY.

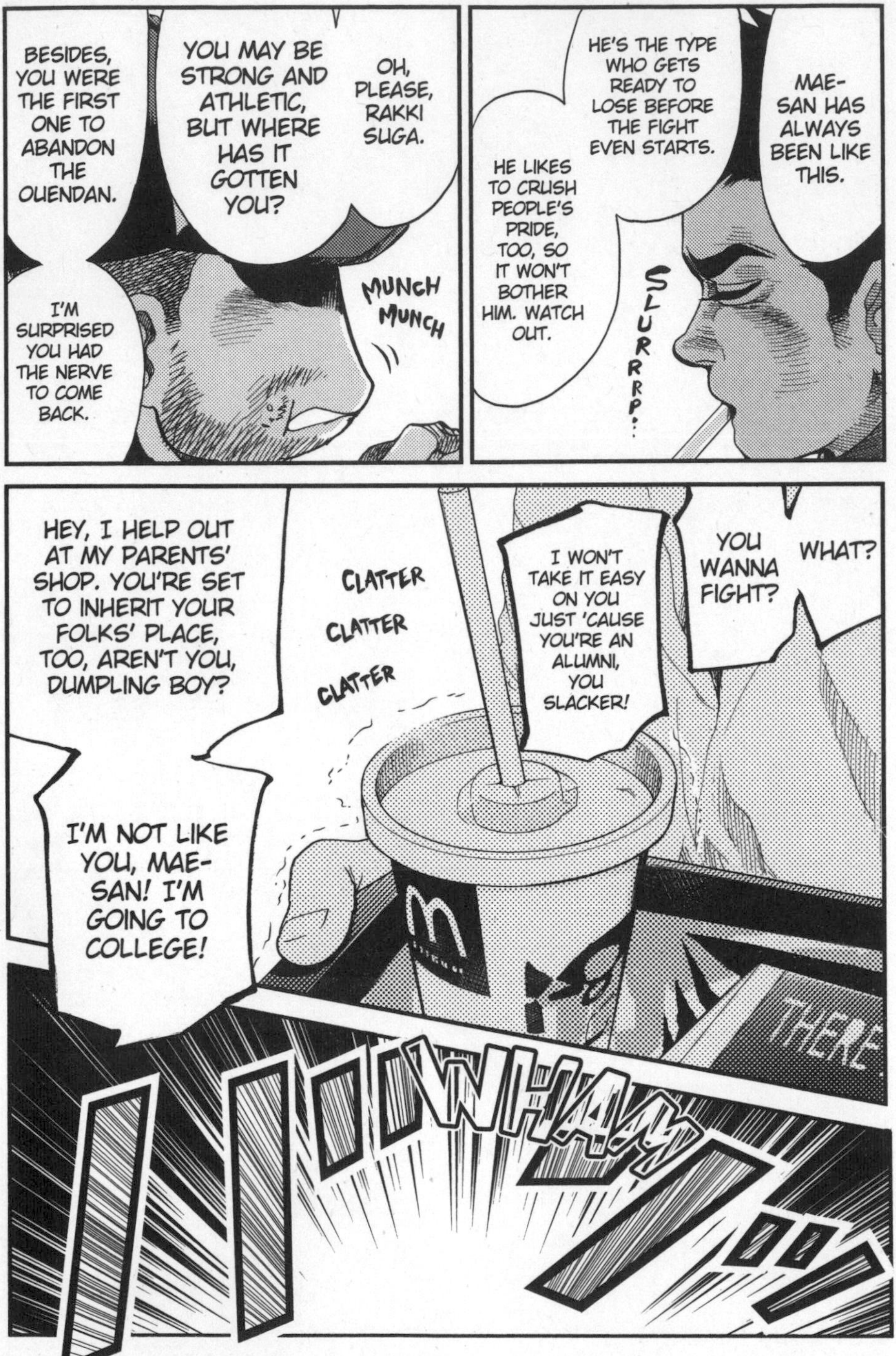
MAE-SAN HAS ALWAYS BEEN LIKE THIS.
HE'S THE TYPE WHO GETS READY TO LOSE BEFORE THE FIGHT EVEN STARTS.
HE LIKES TO CRUSH PEOPLE'S PRIDE, TOO, SO IT WON'T BOTHER HIM. WATCH OUT.
SLURRRP
OH, PLEASE, RAKKI SUGA.
YOU MAY BE STRONG AND ATHLETIC, BUT WHERE HAS IT GOTTEN YOU?
BESIDES, YOU WERE THE FIRST ONE TO ABANDON THE OUENDAN.
MUNCH MUNCH
I'M SURPRISED YOU HAD THE NERVE TO COME BACK.
WHAT?
YOU WANNA FIGHT?
I WON'T TAKE IT EASY ON YOU JUST 'CAUSE YOU'RE AN ALUMNI, YOU SLACKER!
CLATTER
CLATTER
CLATTER
HEY, I HELP OUT AT MY PARENTS' SHOP. YOU'RE SET TO INHERIT YOUR FOLKS' PLACE, TOO, AREN'T YOU, DUMPLING BOY?
I'M NOT LIKE YOU, MAE-SAN! I'M GOING TO COLLEGE!
THERE
WHAAM

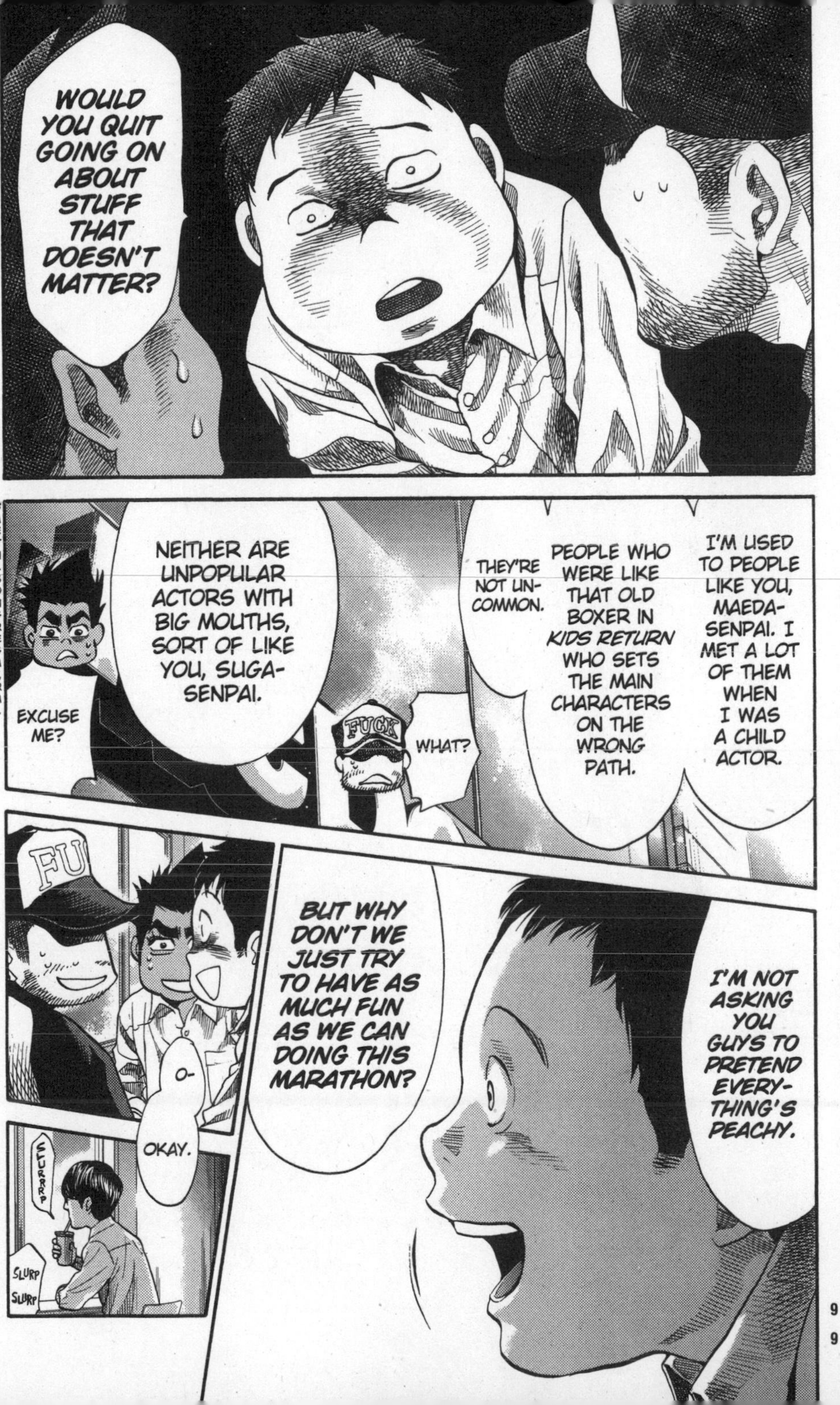
WOULD YOU QUIT GOING ON ABOUT STUFF THAT DOESN'T MATTER?
I'M USED TO PEOPLE LIKE YOU, MAEDA-SENPAI. I MET A LOT OF THEM WHEN I WAS A CHILD ACTOR.
PEOPLE WHO WERE LIKE THAT OLD BOXER IN *KIDS RETURN* WHO SETS THE MAIN CHARACTERS ON THE WRONG PATH.
THEY'RE NOT UN-COMMON.
FUCK
WHAT?
NEITHER ARE UNPOPULAR ACTORS WITH BIG MOUTHS, SORT OF LIKE YOU, SUGA-SENPAI.
EXCUSE ME?
I'M NOT ASKING YOU GUYS TO PRETEND EVERY-THING'S PEACHY.
BUT WHY DON'T WE JUST TRY TO HAVE AS MUCH FUN AS WE CAN DOING THIS MARATHON?
FU
O-
OKAY.
SLURRRP
SLURP
SLURP

NOTE: *KIDS RETURN* IS A 1996 JAPANESE FILM ABOUT TWO HIGH SCHOOL DROPOUTS WHO TRY TO FIND DIRECTION AND MEANING IN THEIR LIVES–ONE BY BECOMING A YAKUZA LIEUTENANT, AND THE OTHER BY BECOMING A BOXER.

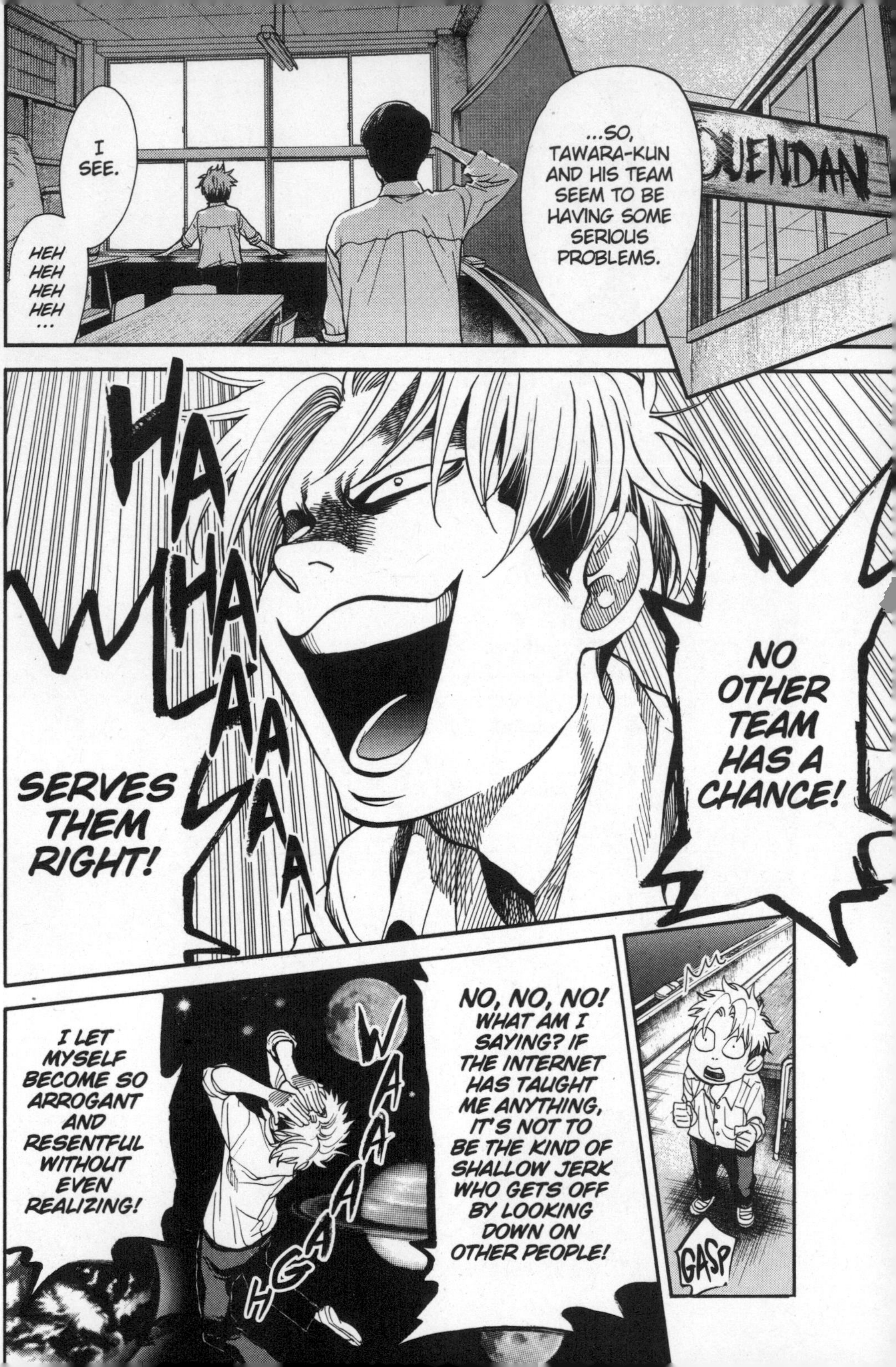
OUENDAN
...SO, TAWARA-KUN AND HIS TEAM SEEM TO BE HAVING SOME SERIOUS PROBLEMS.
I SEE.
HEH HEH HEH HEH ...
NO OTHER TEAM HAS A CHANCE!
SERVES THEM RIGHT!
GASP
NO, NO, NO! WHAT AM I SAYING? IF THE INTERNET HAS TAUGHT ME ANYTHING, IT'S NOT TO BE THE KIND OF SHALLOW JERK WHO GETS OFF BY LOOKING DOWN ON OTHER PEOPLE!
I LET MYSELF BECOME SO ARROGANT AND RESENTFUL WITHOUT EVEN REALIZING!

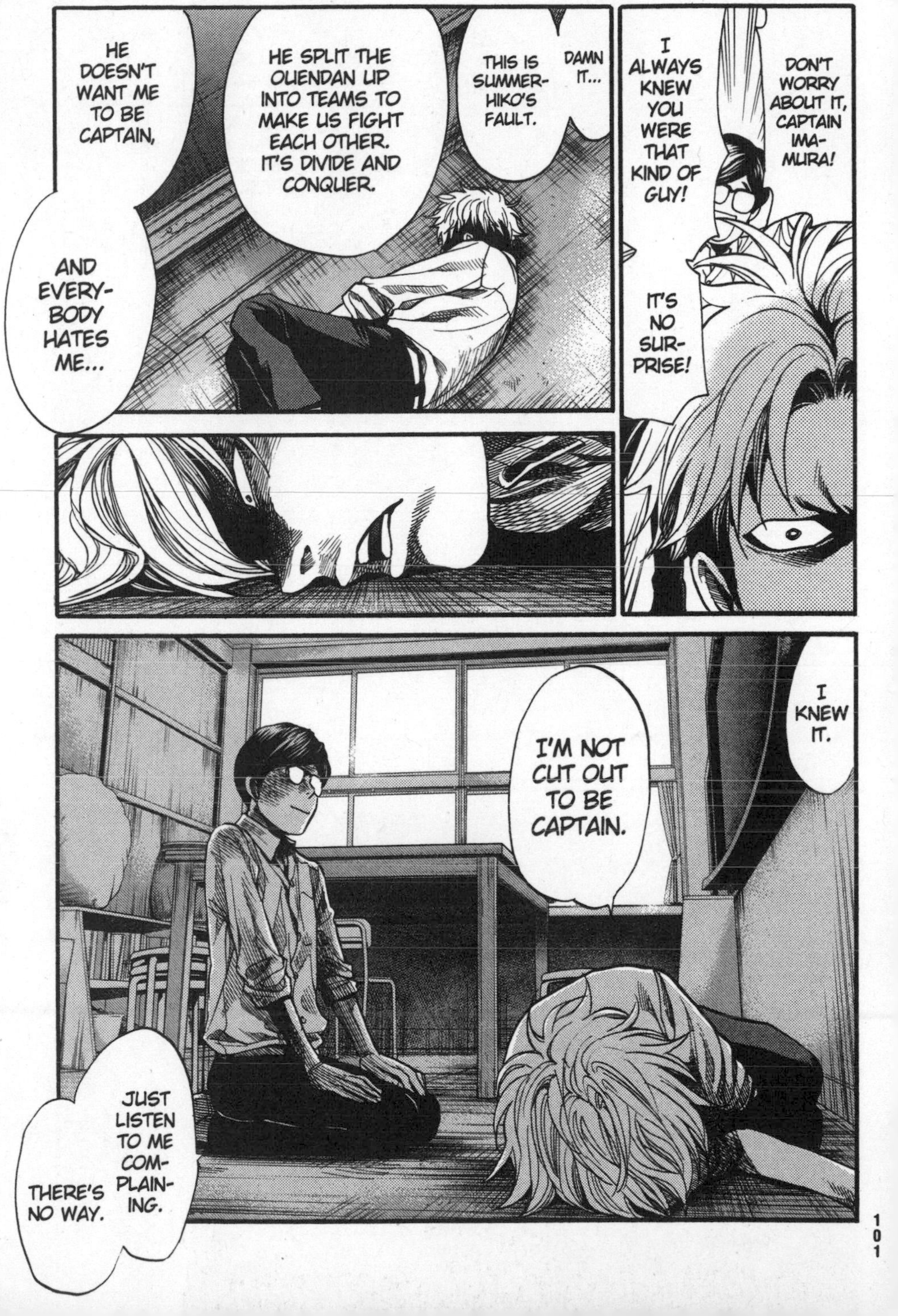
DON'T WORRY ABOUT IT, CAPTAIN IMAMURA!
I ALWAYS KNEW YOU WERE THAT KIND OF GUY!
IT'S NO SURPRISE!
DAMN IT...
THIS IS SUMMERHIKO'S FAULT.
HE SPLIT THE OUENDAN UP INTO TEAMS TO MAKE US FIGHT EACH OTHER. IT'S DIVIDE AND CONQUER.
HE DOESN'T WANT ME TO BE CAPTAIN,
AND EVERYBODY HATES ME...
I KNEW IT.
I'M NOT CUT OUT TO BE CAPTAIN.
JUST LISTEN TO ME COMPLAINING.
THERE'S NO WAY.

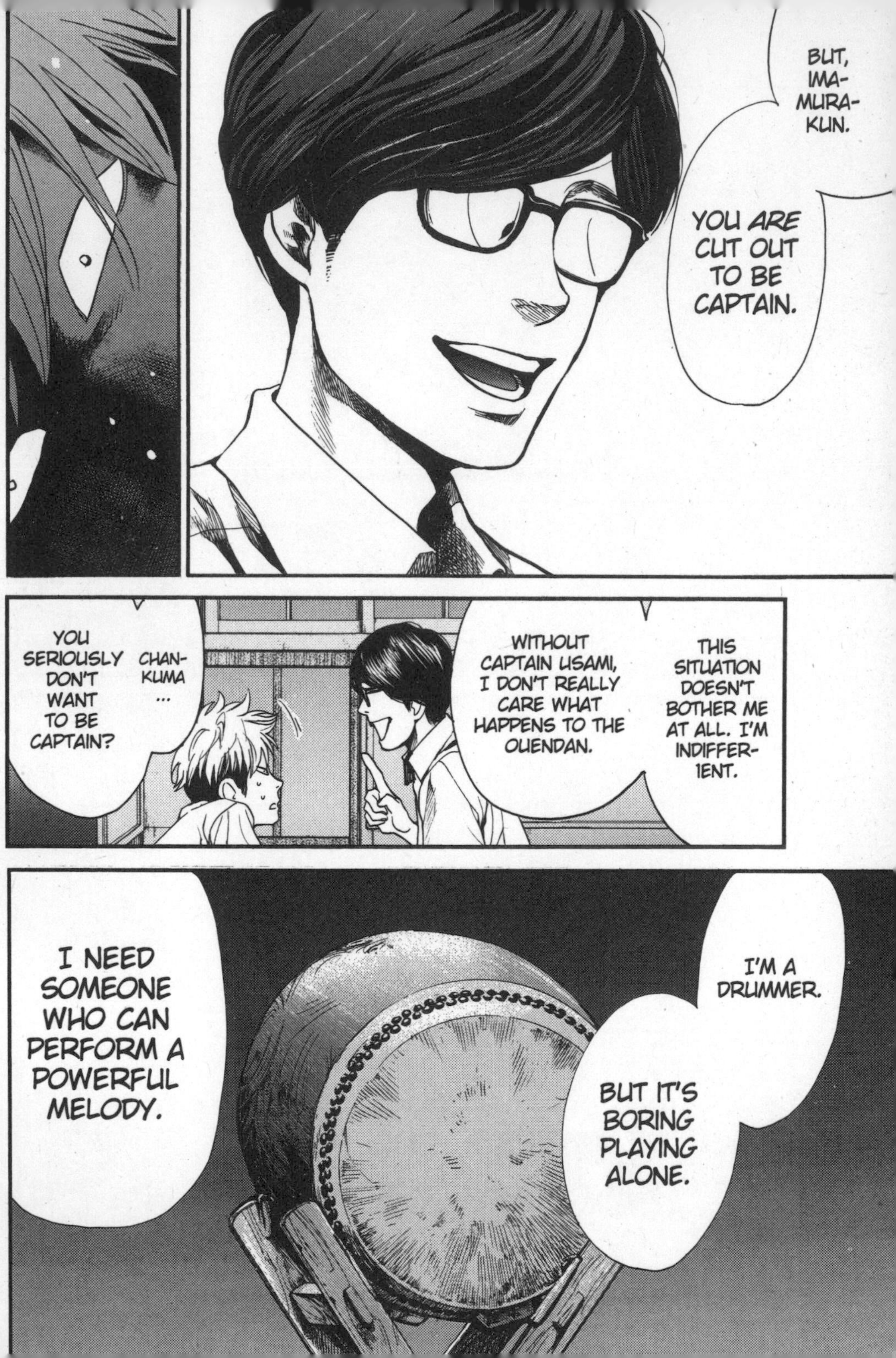
BUT, IMAMURA-KUN.
YOU ARE CUT OUT TO BE CAPTAIN.
THIS SITUATION DOESN'T BOTHER ME AT ALL. I'M INDIFFERENT.
WITHOUT CAPTAIN USAMI, I DON'T REALLY CARE WHAT HAPPENS TO THE OUENDAN.
CHANKUMA...
YOU SERIOUSLY DON'T WANT TO BE CAPTAIN?
I'M A DRUMMER.
BUT IT'S BORING PLAYING ALONE.
I NEED SOMEONE WHO CAN PERFORM A POWERFUL MELODY.

Again!!

アゲイン!!

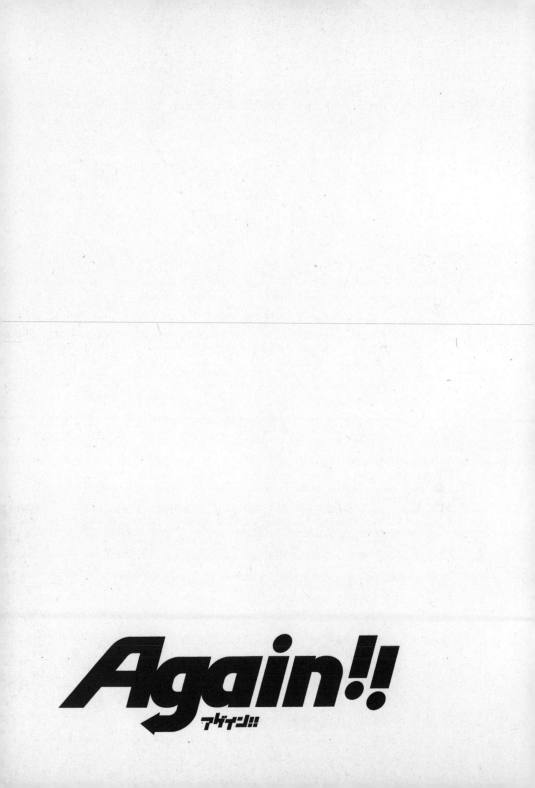

Again!!

アゲイン!!

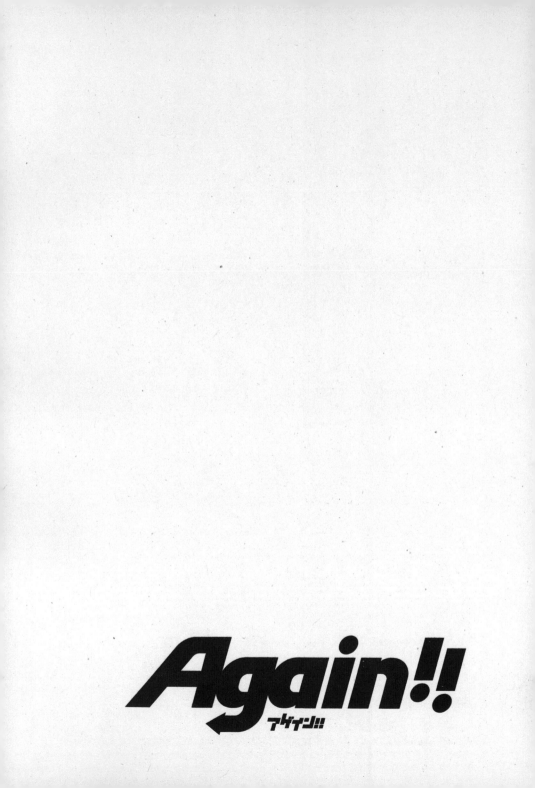

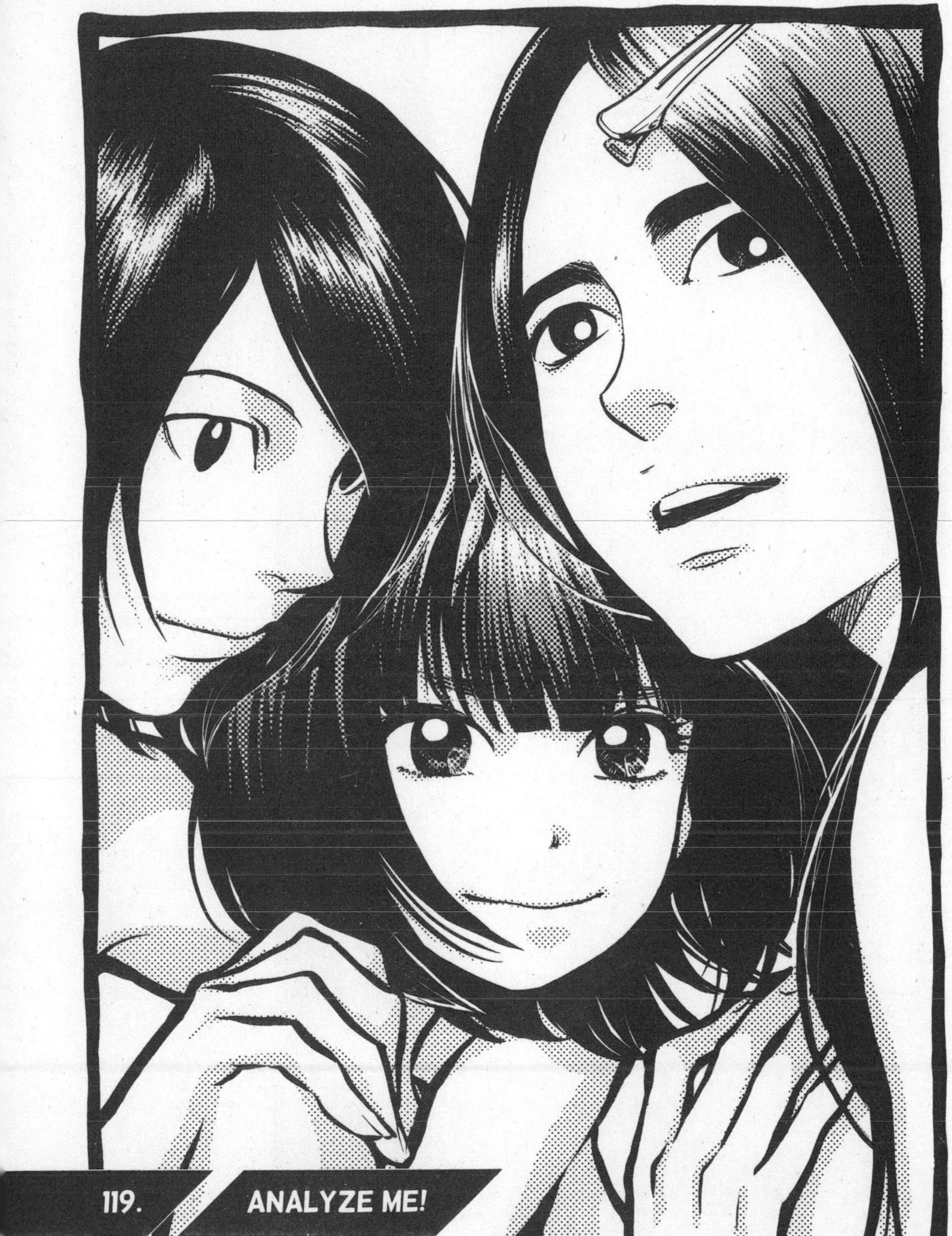
119.
ANALYZE ME!

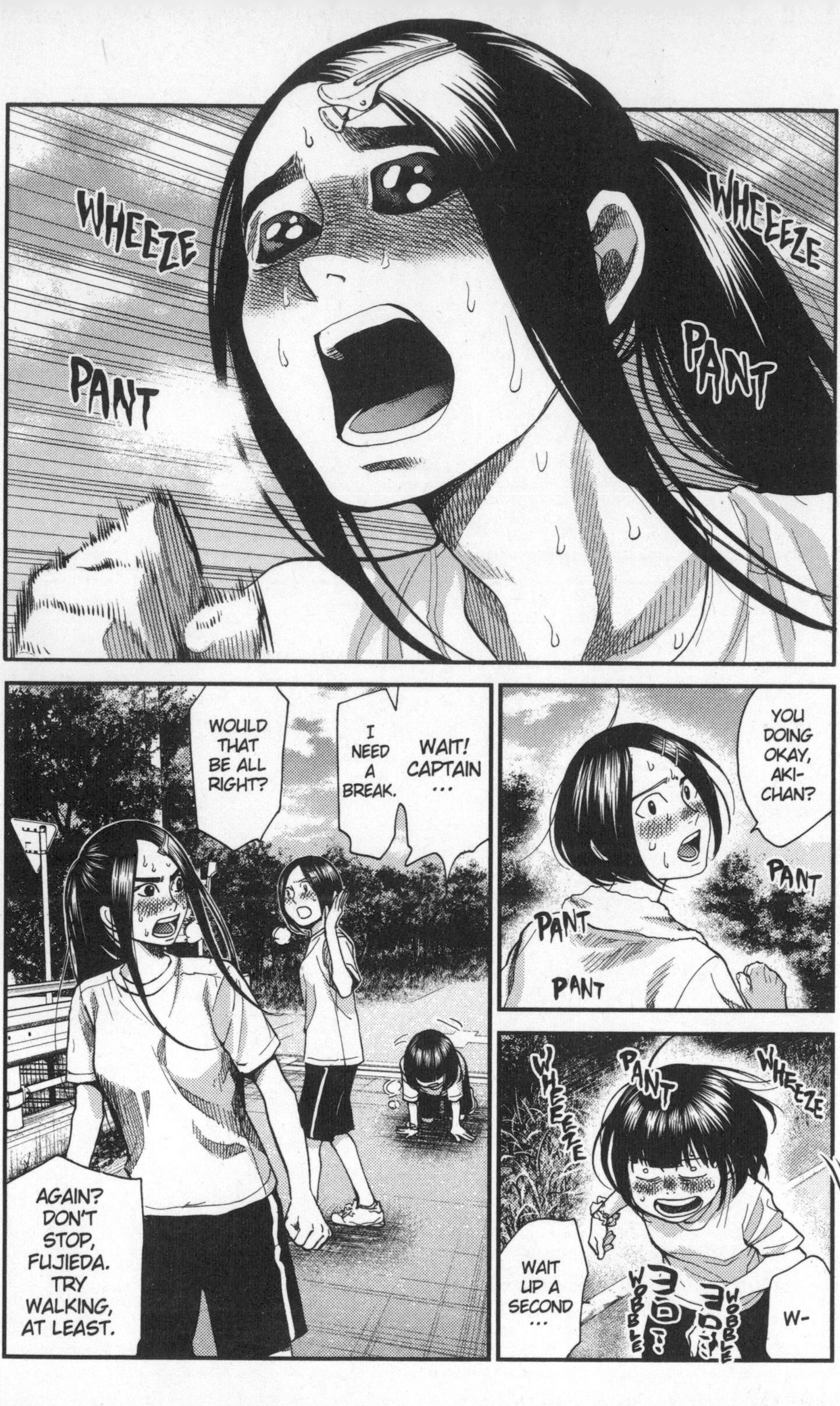
WHEEEZE
PANT
WHEEZE
PANT
YOU DOING OKAY, AKI-CHAN?
PANT
PANT
PANT
WHEEZE
PANT
WHEEZE
W-
WOBBLE
WOBBLE
WAIT UP A SECOND…
WAIT! CAPTAIN…
I NEED A BREAK.
WOULD THAT BE ALL RIGHT?
AGAIN? DON'T STOP, FUJIEDA. TRY WALKING, AT LEAST.

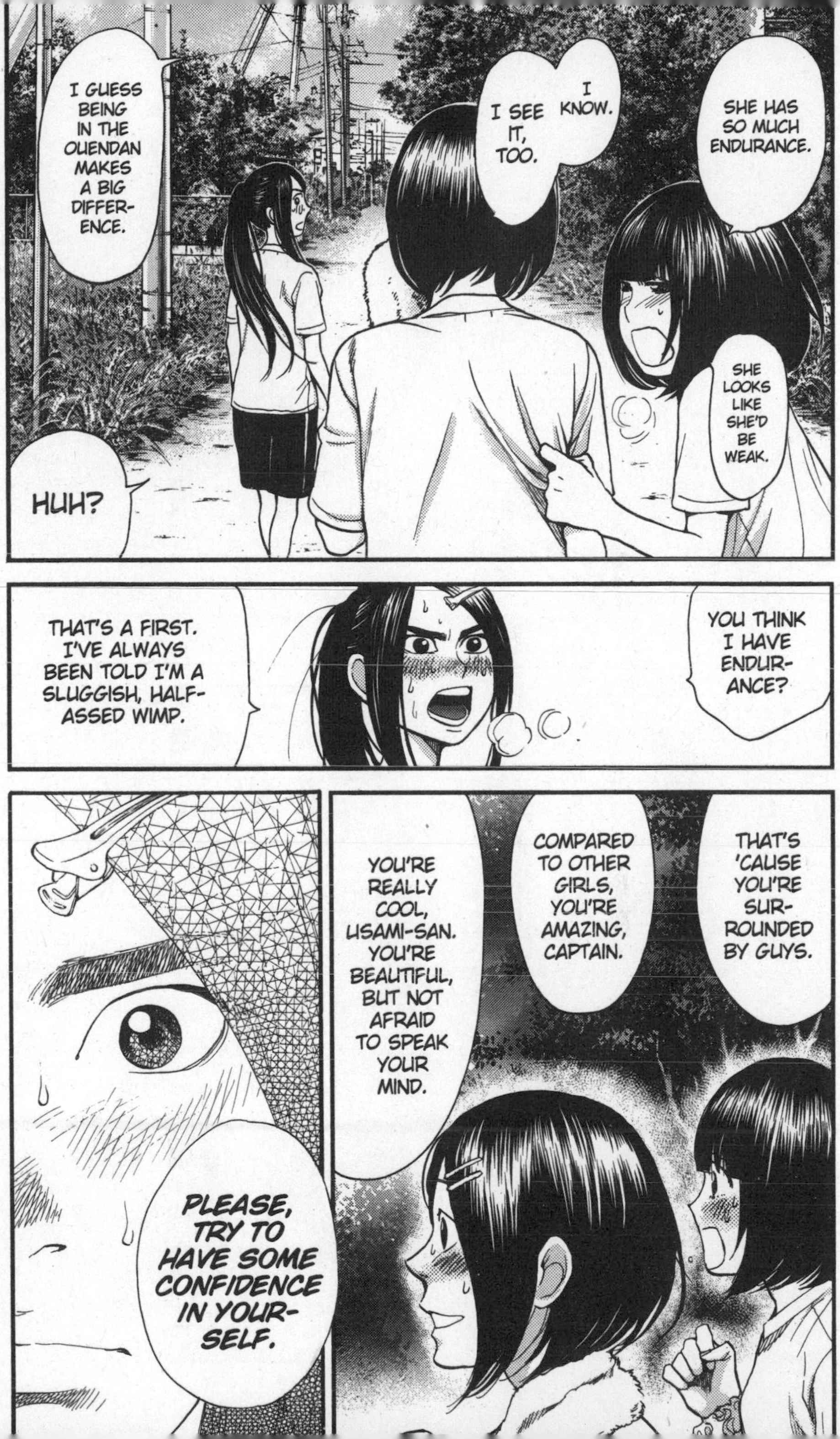
SHE HAS SO MUCH ENDURANCE.
SHE LOOKS LIKE SHE'D BE WEAK.
I KNOW.
I SEE IT, TOO.
I GUESS BEING IN THE OUENDAN MAKES A BIG DIFFERENCE.
HUH?
YOU THINK I HAVE ENDURANCE?
THAT'S A FIRST. I'VE ALWAYS BEEN TOLD I'M A SLUGGISH, HALF-ASSED WIMP.
THAT'S 'CAUSE YOU'RE SURROUNDED BY GUYS.
COMPARED TO OTHER GIRLS, YOU'RE AMAZING, CAPTAIN.
YOU'RE REALLY COOL, USAMI-SAN. YOU'RE BEAUTIFUL, BUT NOT AFRAID TO SPEAK YOUR MIND.
PLEASE, TRY TO HAVE SOME CONFIDENCE IN YOURSELF.

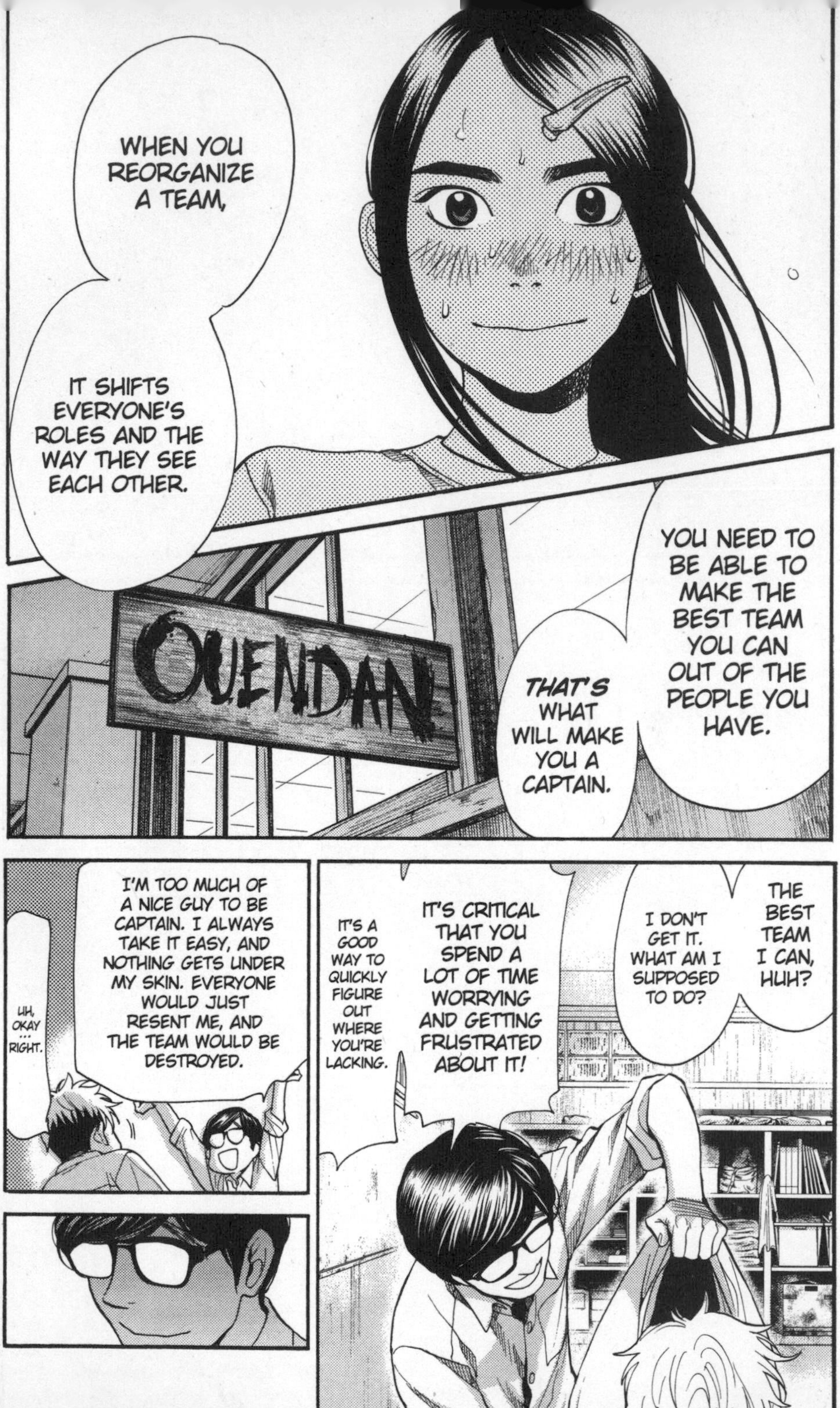
WHEN YOU REORGANIZE A TEAM,
IT SHIFTS EVERYONE'S ROLES AND THE WAY THEY SEE EACH OTHER.
OUENDAN
YOU NEED TO BE ABLE TO MAKE THE BEST TEAM YOU CAN OUT OF THE PEOPLE YOU HAVE.
THAT'S WHAT WILL MAKE YOU A CAPTAIN.
THE BEST TEAM I CAN, HUH?
I DON'T GET IT. WHAT AM I SUPPOSED TO DO?
IT'S CRITICAL THAT YOU SPEND A LOT OF TIME WORRYING AND GETTING FRUSTRATED ABOUT IT!
IT'S A GOOD WAY TO QUICKLY FIGURE OUT WHERE YOU'RE LACKING.
I'M TOO MUCH OF A NICE GUY TO BE CAPTAIN. I ALWAYS TAKE IT EASY, AND NOTHING GETS UNDER MY SKIN. EVERYONE WOULD JUST RESENT ME, AND THE TEAM WOULD BE DESTROYED.
UH, OKAY ... RIGHT.

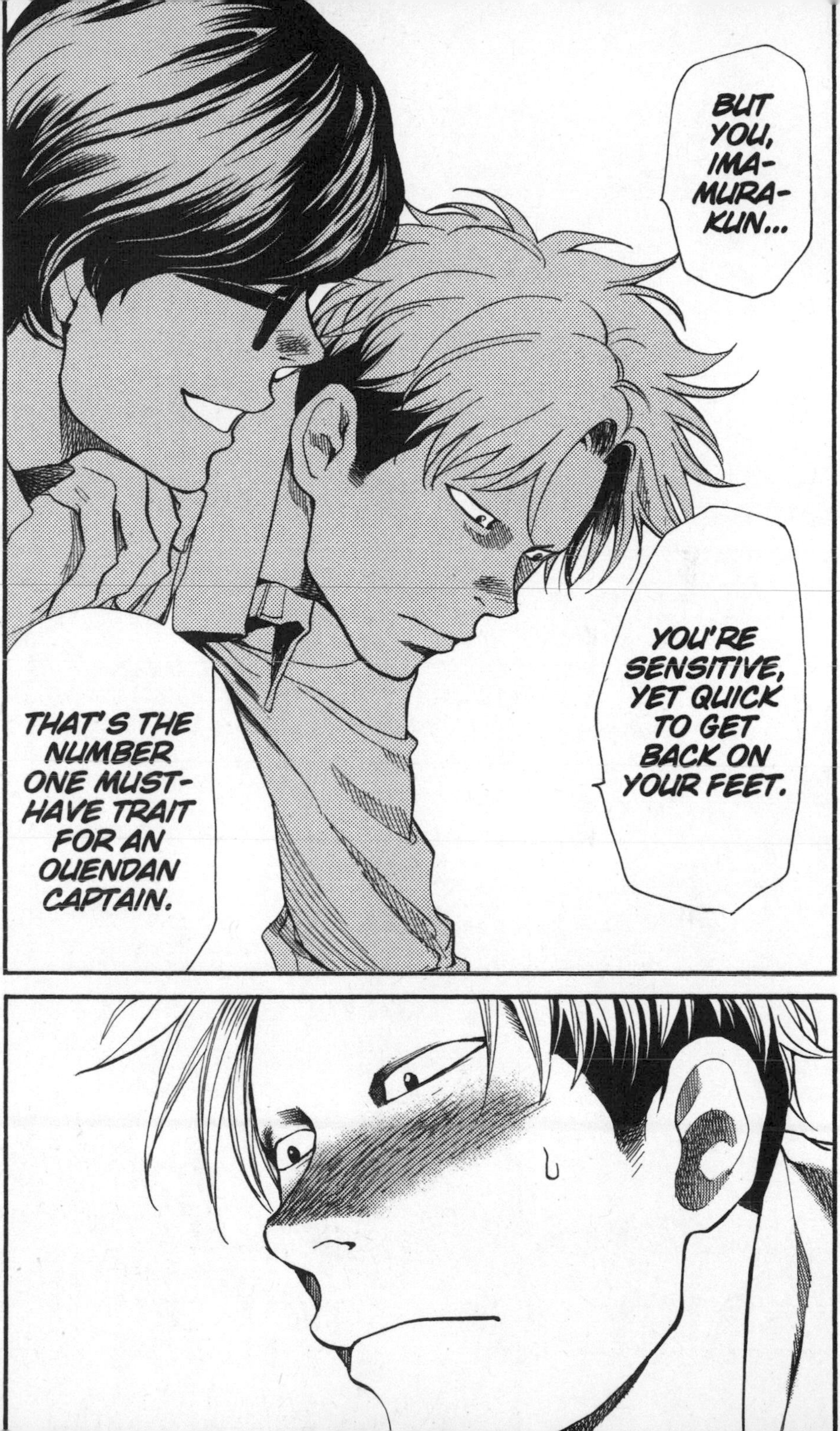
BUT YOU, IMAMURA-KUN...
YOU'RE SENSITIVE, YET QUICK TO GET BACK ON YOUR FEET.
THAT'S THE NUMBER ONE MUST-HAVE TRAIT FOR AN OUENDAN CAPTAIN.

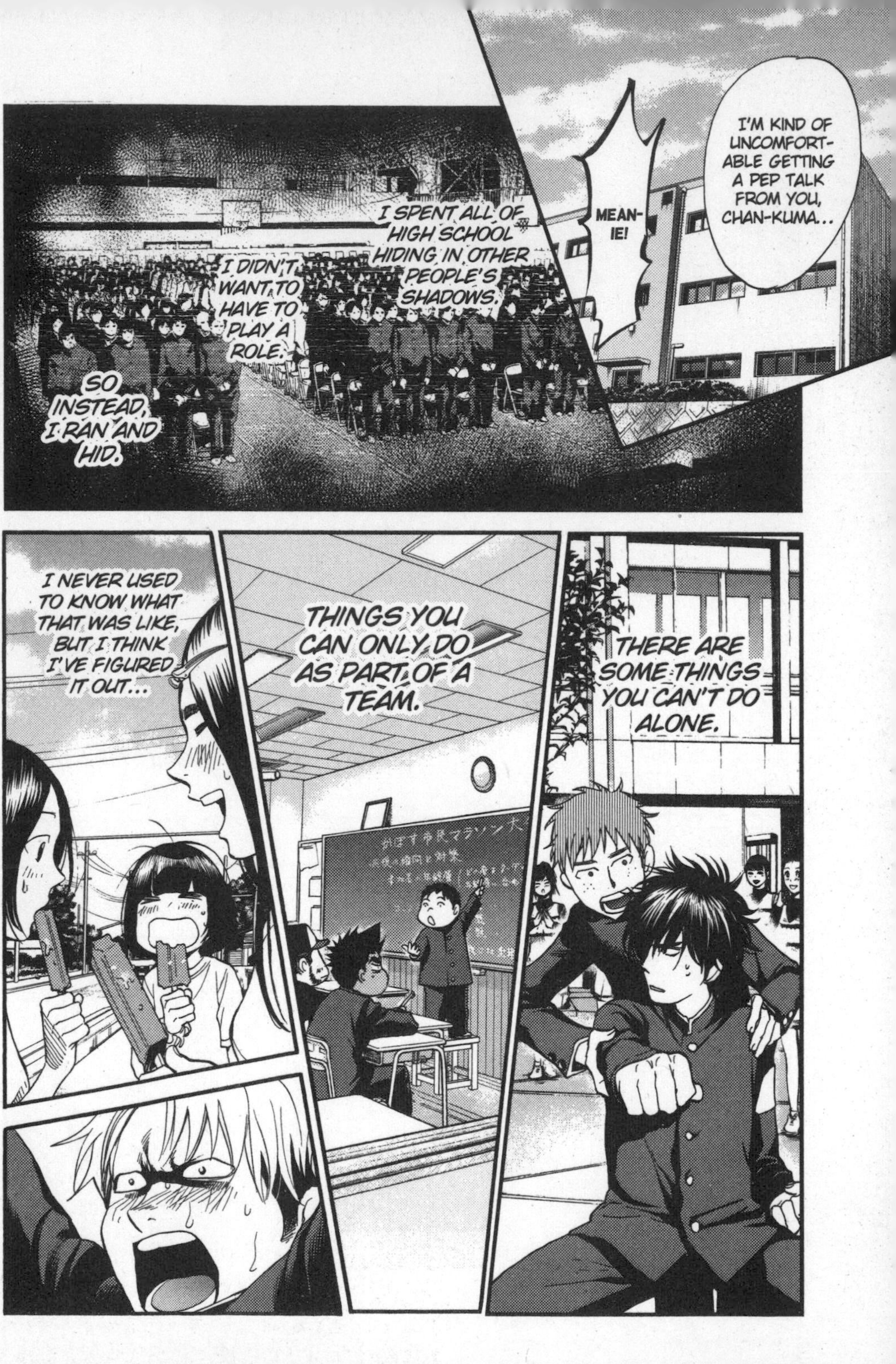
I'M KIND OF UNCOMFORTABLE GETTING A PEP TALK FROM YOU, CHAN-KUMA...
MEANIE!
I SPENT ALL OF HIGH SCHOOL HIDING IN OTHER PEOPLE'S SHADOWS.
I DIDN'T WANT TO HAVE TO PLAY A ROLE.
SO INSTEAD, I RAN AND HID.
THERE ARE SOME THINGS YOU CAN'T DO ALONE.
THINGS YOU CAN ONLY DO AS PART OF A TEAM.
I NEVER USED TO KNOW WHAT THAT WAS LIKE, BUT I THINK I'VE FIGURED IT OUT...

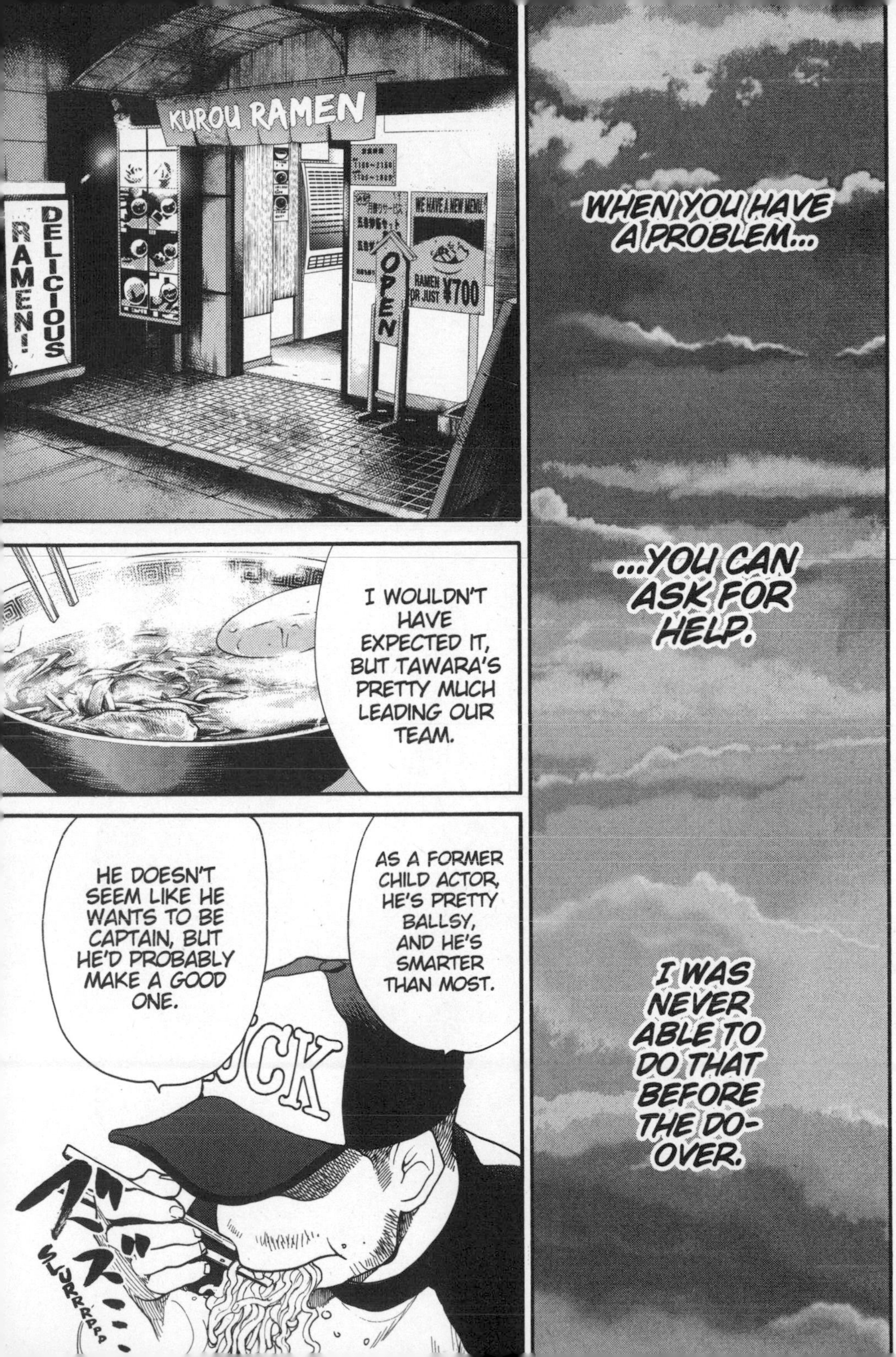
WHEN YOU HAVE A PROBLEM...
...YOU CAN ASK FOR HELP.
I WAS NEVER ABLE TO DO THAT BEFORE THE DO-OVER.
KUROU RAMEN
DELICIOUS RAMEN!
WE HAVE A NEW MENU
RAMEN FOR JUST ¥700
OPEN
I WOULDN'T HAVE EXPECTED IT, BUT TAWARA'S PRETTY MUCH LEADING OUR TEAM.
AS A FORMER CHILD ACTOR, HE'S PRETTY BALLSY, AND HE'S SMARTER THAN MOST.
HE DOESN'T SEEM LIKE HE WANTS TO BE CAPTAIN, BUT HE'D PROBABLY MAKE A GOOD ONE.
SLURRRPPP

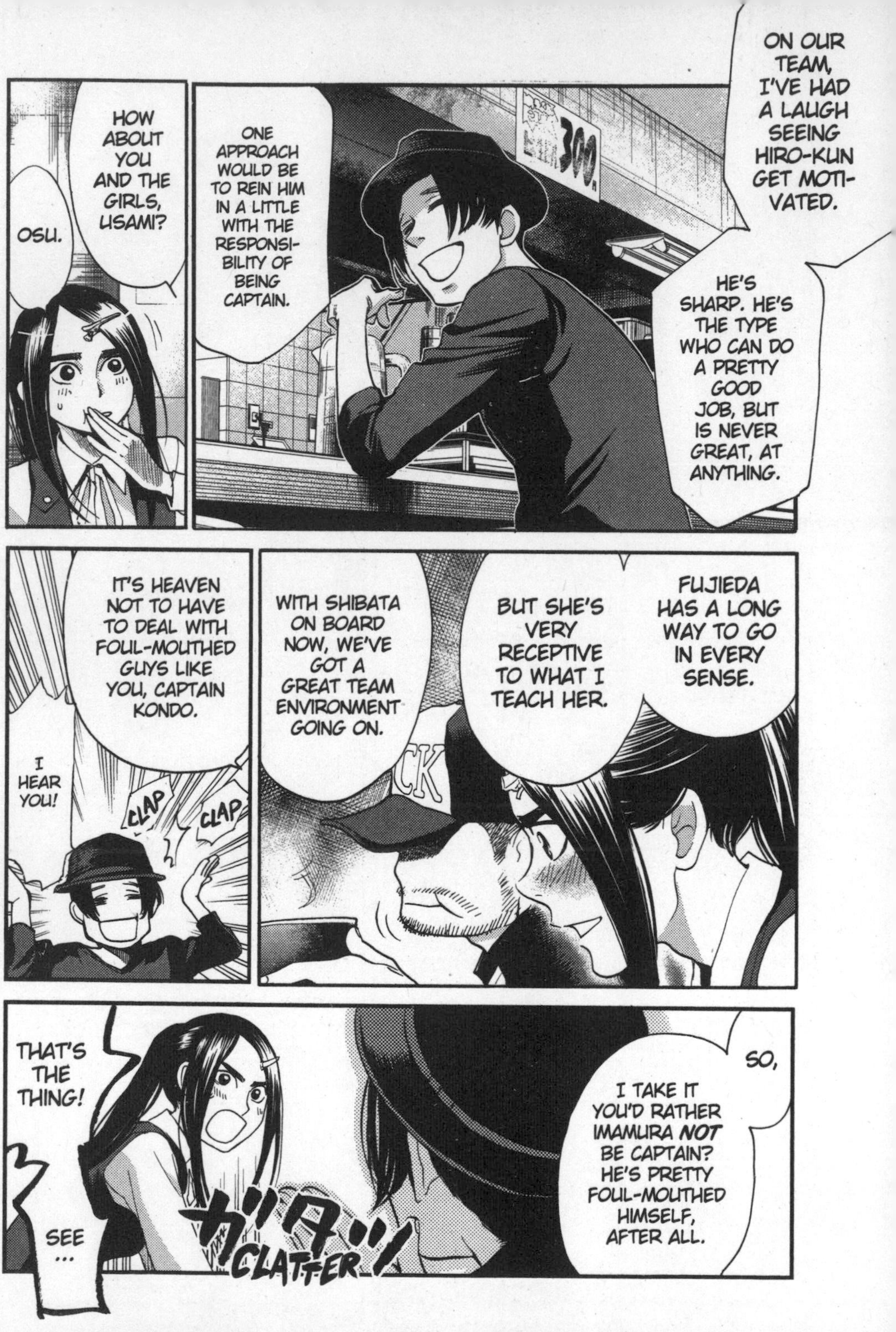
ON OUR TEAM, I'VE HAD A LAUGH SEEING HIRO-KUN GET MOTI-VATED.
HE'S SHARP. HE'S THE TYPE WHO CAN DO A PRETTY GOOD JOB, BUT IS NEVER GREAT, AT ANYTHING.
ONE APPROACH WOULD BE TO REIN HIM IN A LITTLE WITH THE RESPONSI-BILITY OF BEING CAPTAIN.
HOW ABOUT YOU AND THE GIRLS, USAMI?
OSU.
FUJIEDA HAS A LONG WAY TO GO IN EVERY SENSE.
BUT SHE'S VERY RECEPTIVE TO WHAT I TEACH HER.
WITH SHIBATA ON BOARD NOW, WE'VE GOT A GREAT TEAM ENVIRONMENT GOING ON.
IT'S HEAVEN NOT TO HAVE TO DEAL WITH FOUL-MOUTHED GUYS LIKE YOU, CAPTAIN KONDO.
I HEAR YOU!
CLAP
CLAP
SO,
I TAKE IT YOU'D RATHER IMAMURA NOT BE CAPTAIN? HE'S PRETTY FOUL-MOUTHED HIMSELF, AFTER ALL.
THAT'S THE THING!
SEE ...
CLATTER

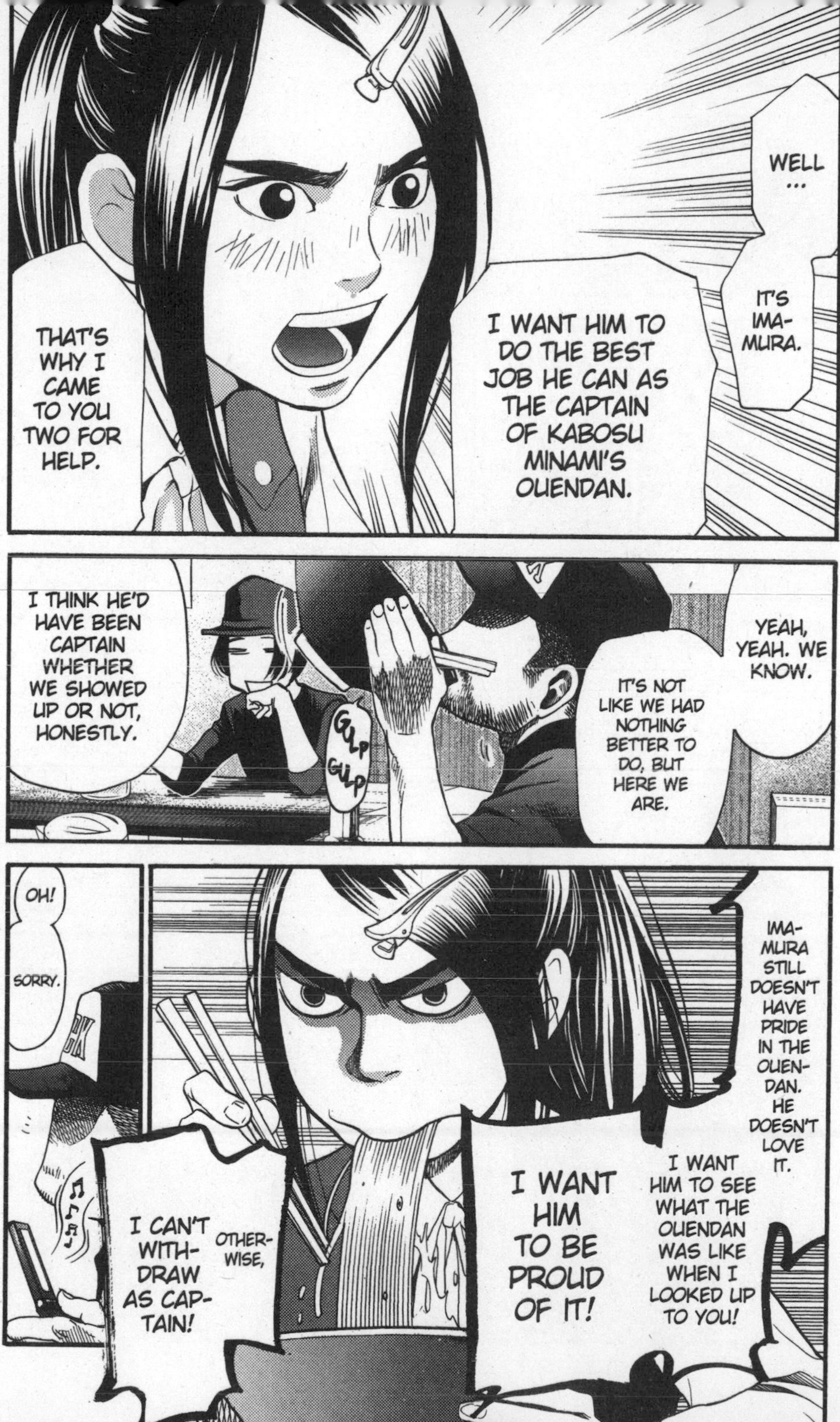
WELL ...
IT'S IMA-MURA.
I WANT HIM TO DO THE BEST JOB HE CAN AS THE CAPTAIN OF KABOSU MINAMI'S OUENDAN.
THAT'S WHY I CAME TO YOU TWO FOR HELP.
YEAH, YEAH. WE KNOW.
IT'S NOT LIKE WE HAD NOTHING BETTER TO DO, BUT HERE WE ARE.
GULP GULP
I THINK HE'D HAVE BEEN CAPTAIN WHETHER WE SHOWED UP OR NOT, HONESTLY.
IMA-MURA STILL DOESN'T HAVE PRIDE IN THE OUEN-DAN. HE DOESN'T LOVE IT.
I WANT HIM TO SEE WHAT THE OUENDAN WAS LIKE WHEN I LOOKED UP TO YOU!
I WANT HIM TO BE PROUD OF IT!
OTHER-WISE,
I CAN'T WITH-DRAW AS CAP-TAIN!
OH!
SORRY.

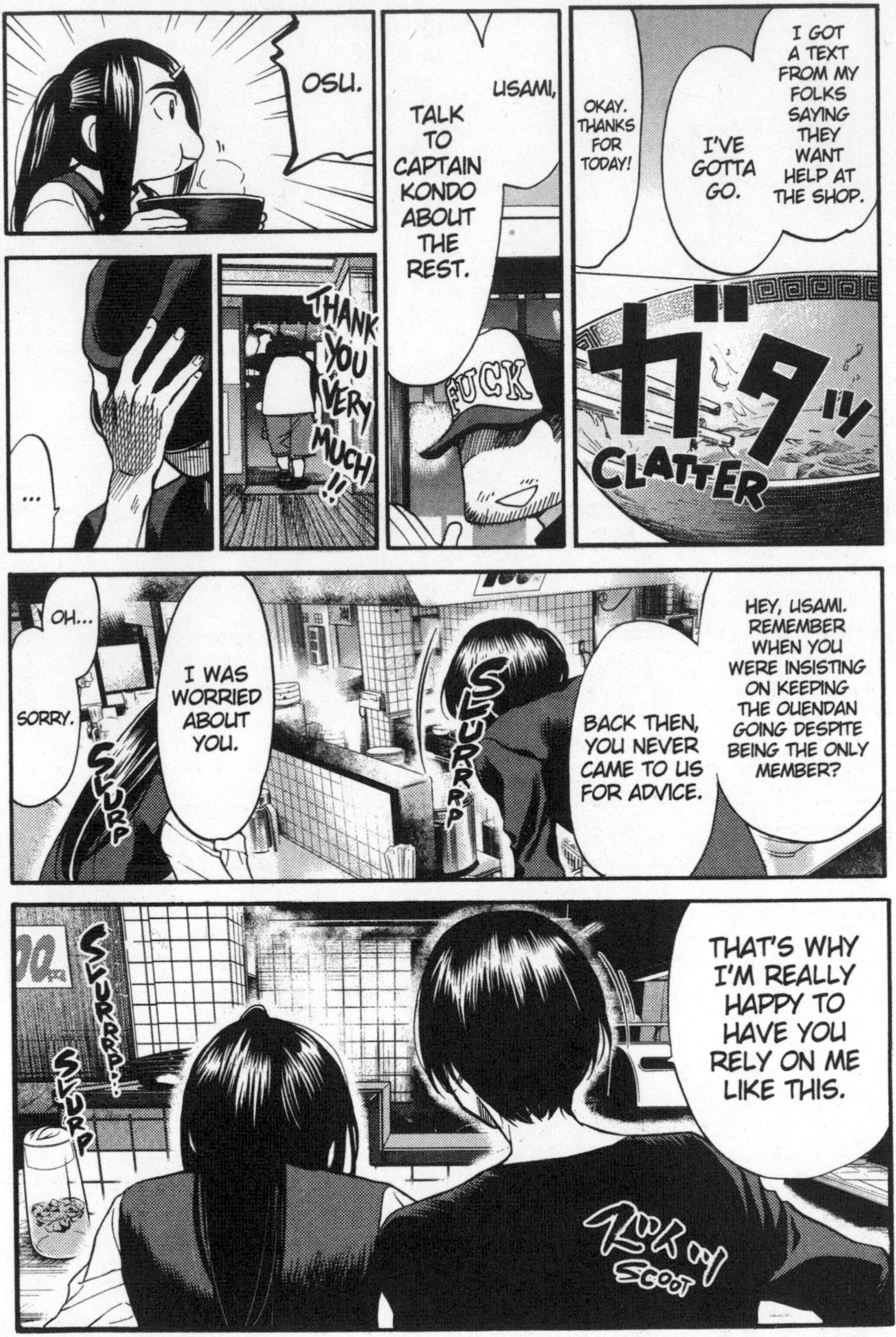
I GOT A TEXT FROM MY FOLKS SAYING THEY WANT HELP AT THE SHOP.
I'VE GOTTA GO.
OKAY. THANKS FOR TODAY!
ガタッ
CLATTER
USAMI,
TALK TO CAPTAIN KONDO ABOUT THE REST.
FUCK
OSU.
THANK YOU VERY MUCH!!
...
HEY, USAMI. REMEMBER WHEN YOU WERE INSISTING ON KEEPING THE OUENDAN GOING DESPITE BEING THE ONLY MEMBER?
BACK THEN, YOU NEVER CAME TO US FOR ADVICE.
SLURRRP
I WAS WORRIED ABOUT YOU.
OH...
SORRY.
SLURP
THAT'S WHY I'M REALLY HAPPY TO HAVE YOU RELY ON ME LIKE THIS.
ズルッ
SCOOT
SLURRRP..
SLURP

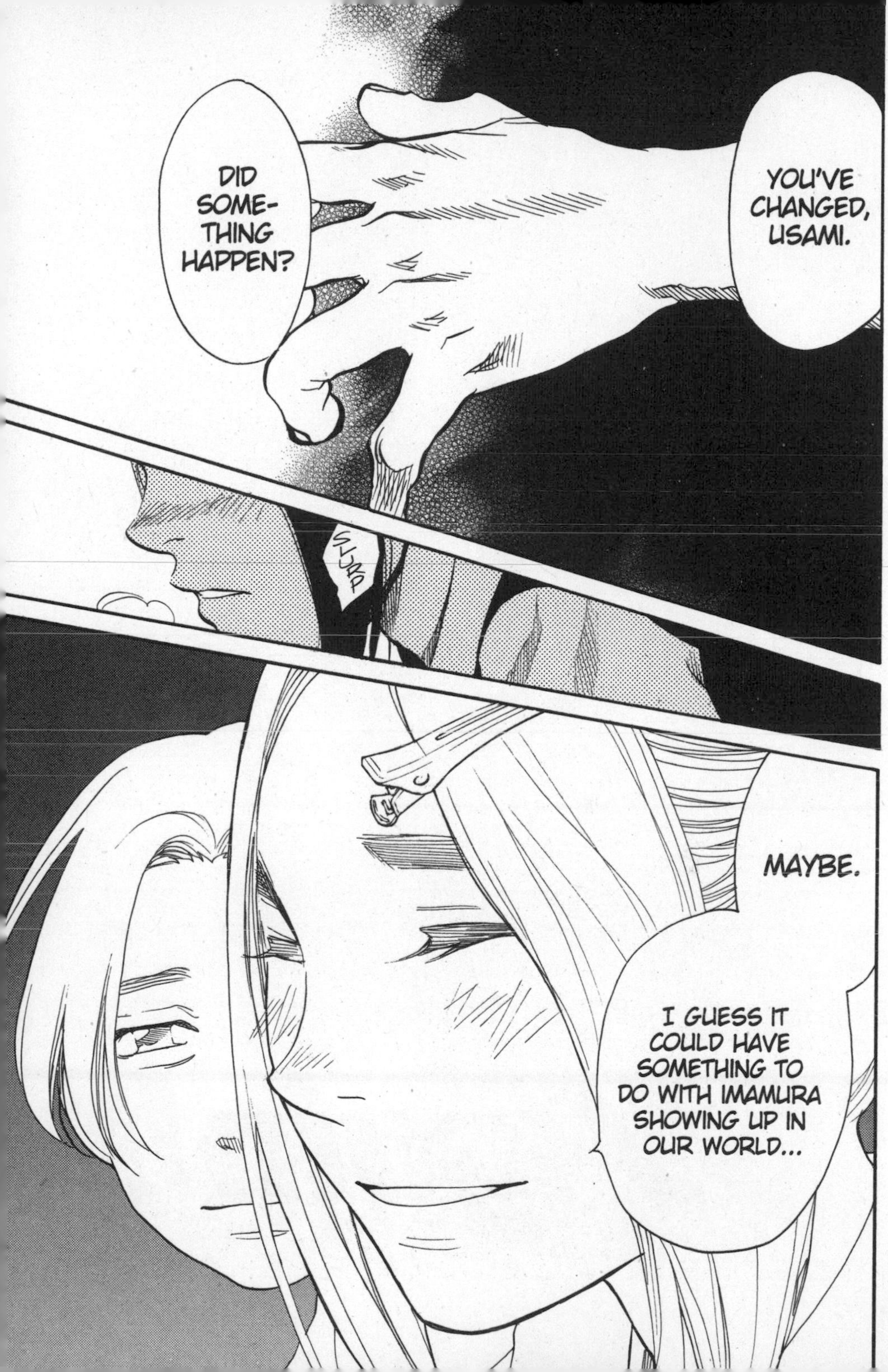
YOU'VE CHANGED, USAMI.
DID SOME-THING HAPPEN?
SLURP
MAYBE.
I GUESS IT COULD HAVE SOMETHING TO DO WITH IMAMURA SHOWING UP IN OUR WORLD...

Again!!

アゲイン!!

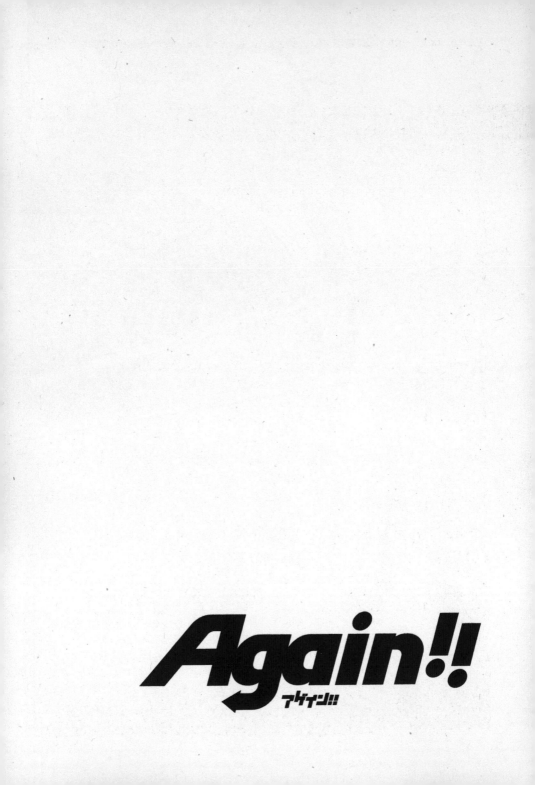

120. LOVE BEYOND THE STREAM

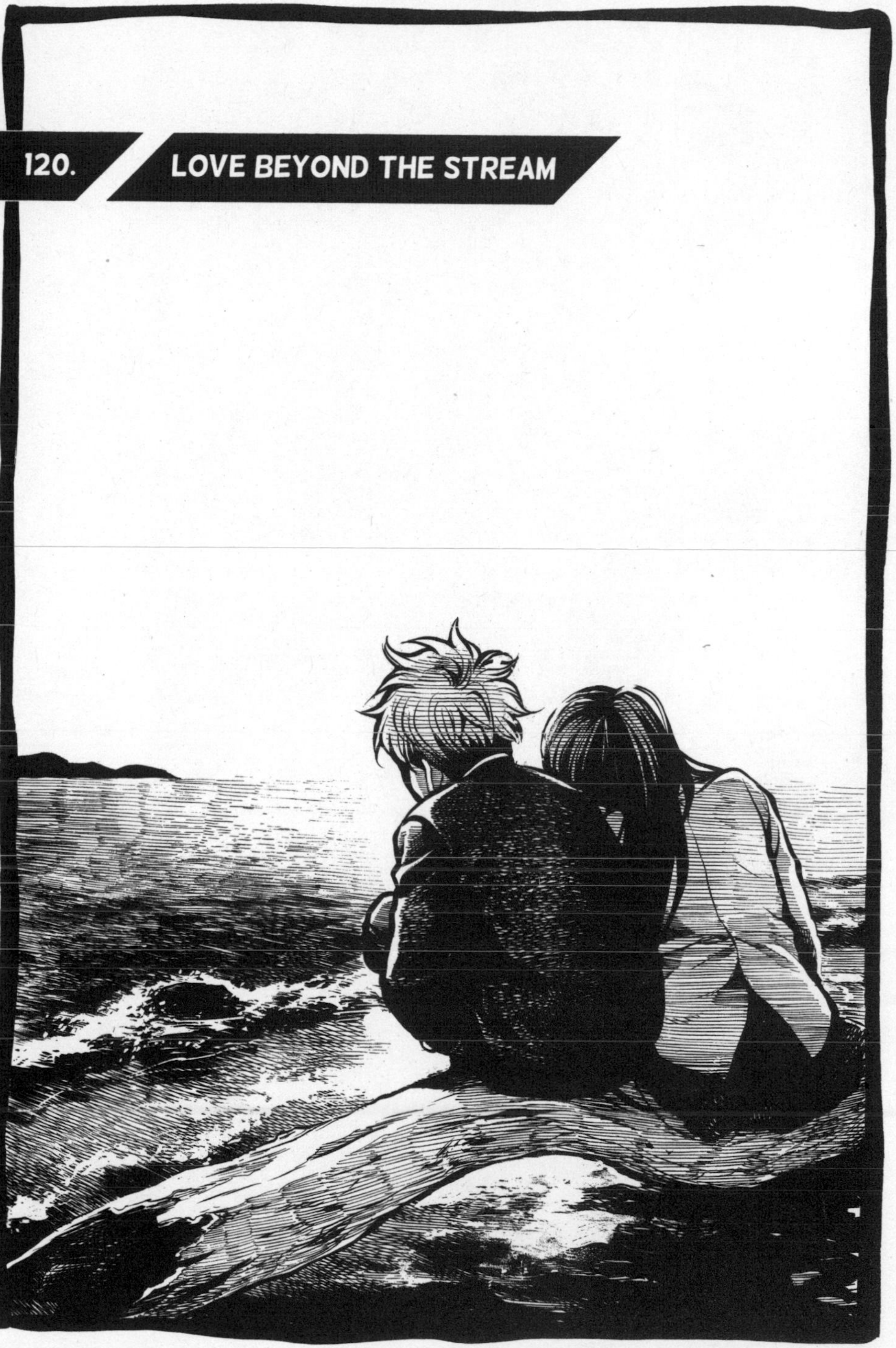

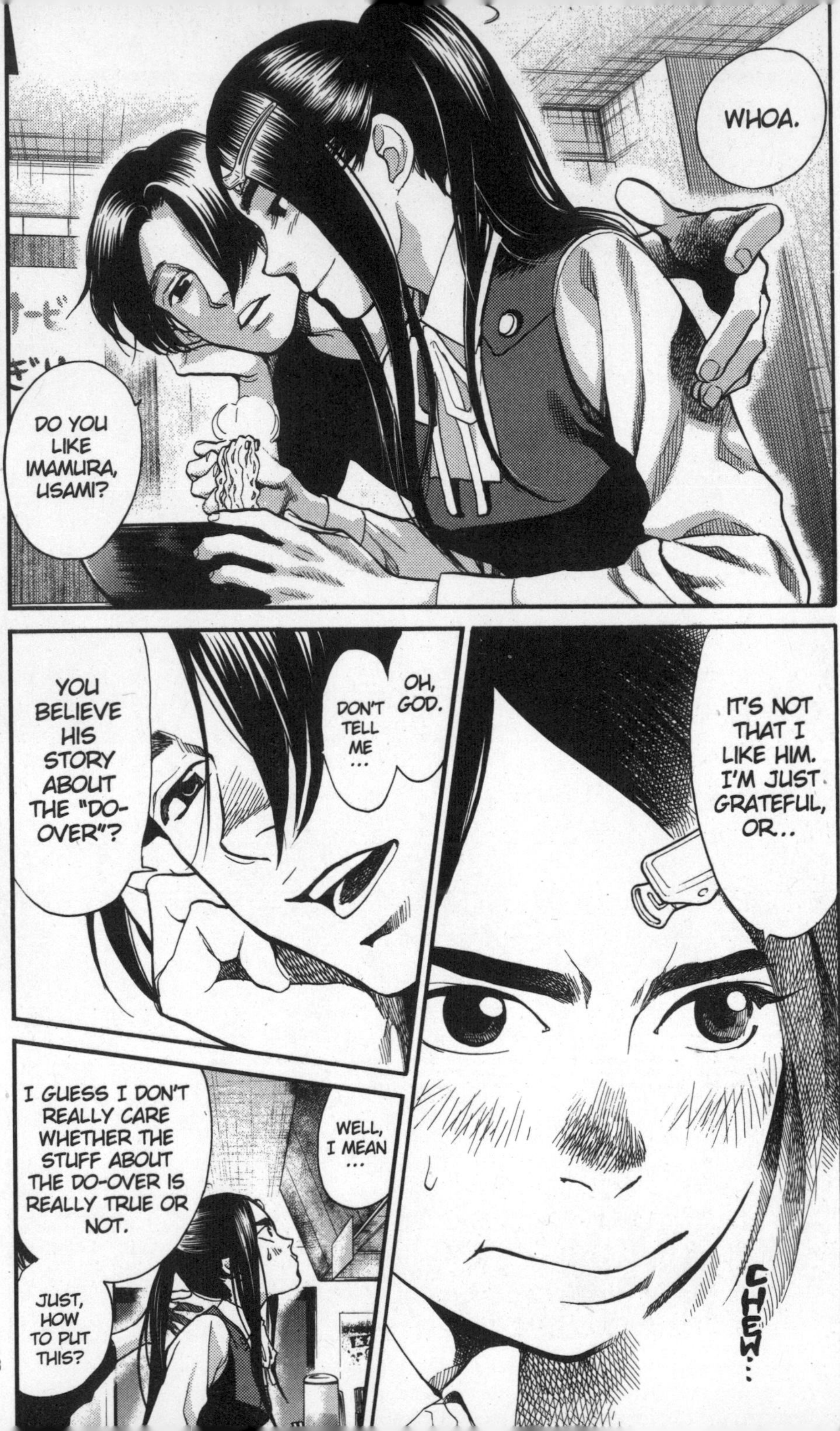
WHOA.
DO YOU LIKE IMAMURA, USAMI?
IT'S NOT THAT I LIKE HIM. I'M JUST GRATEFUL, OR..
CHEW...
OH, GOD.
DON'T TELL ME ...
YOU BELIEVE HIS STORY ABOUT THE "DO-OVER"?
WELL, I MEAN ...
I GUESS I DON'T REALLY CARE WHETHER THE STUFF ABOUT THE DO-OVER IS REALLY TRUE OR NOT.
JUST, HOW TO PUT THIS?

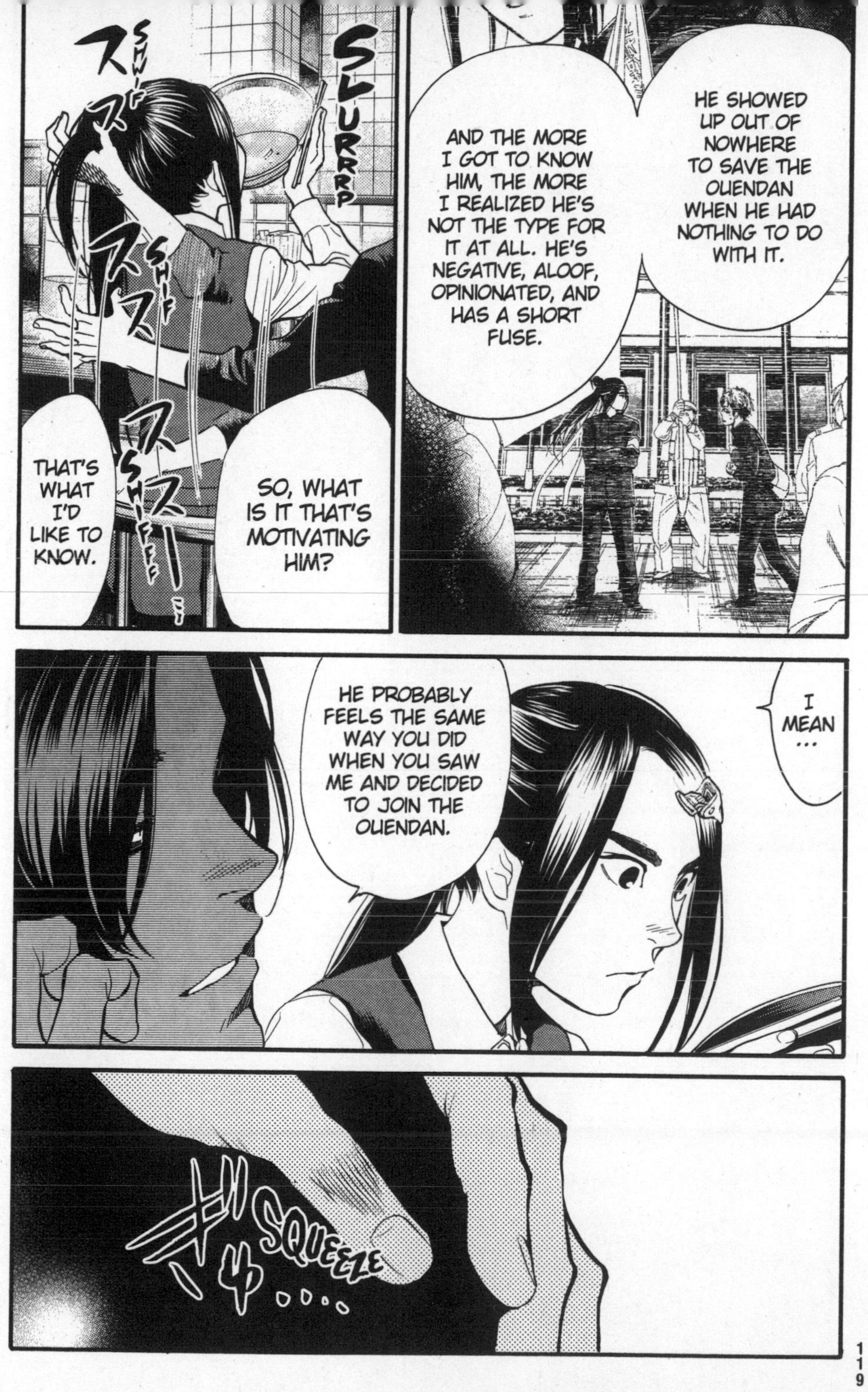
HE SHOWED UP OUT OF NOWHERE TO SAVE THE OUENDAN WHEN HE HAD NOTHING TO DO WITH IT.
AND THE MORE I GOT TO KNOW HIM, THE MORE I REALIZED HE'S NOT THE TYPE FOR IT AT ALL. HE'S NEGATIVE, ALOOF, OPINIONATED, AND HAS A SHORT FUSE.
SLURRRP
SHWIF
SHIF
SHIFFF
SO, WHAT IS IT THAT'S MOTIVATING HIM?
THAT'S WHAT I'D LIKE TO KNOW.
I MEAN...
HE PROBABLY FEELS THE SAME WAY YOU DID WHEN YOU SAW ME AND DECIDED TO JOIN THE OUENDAN.
SQUEEZE

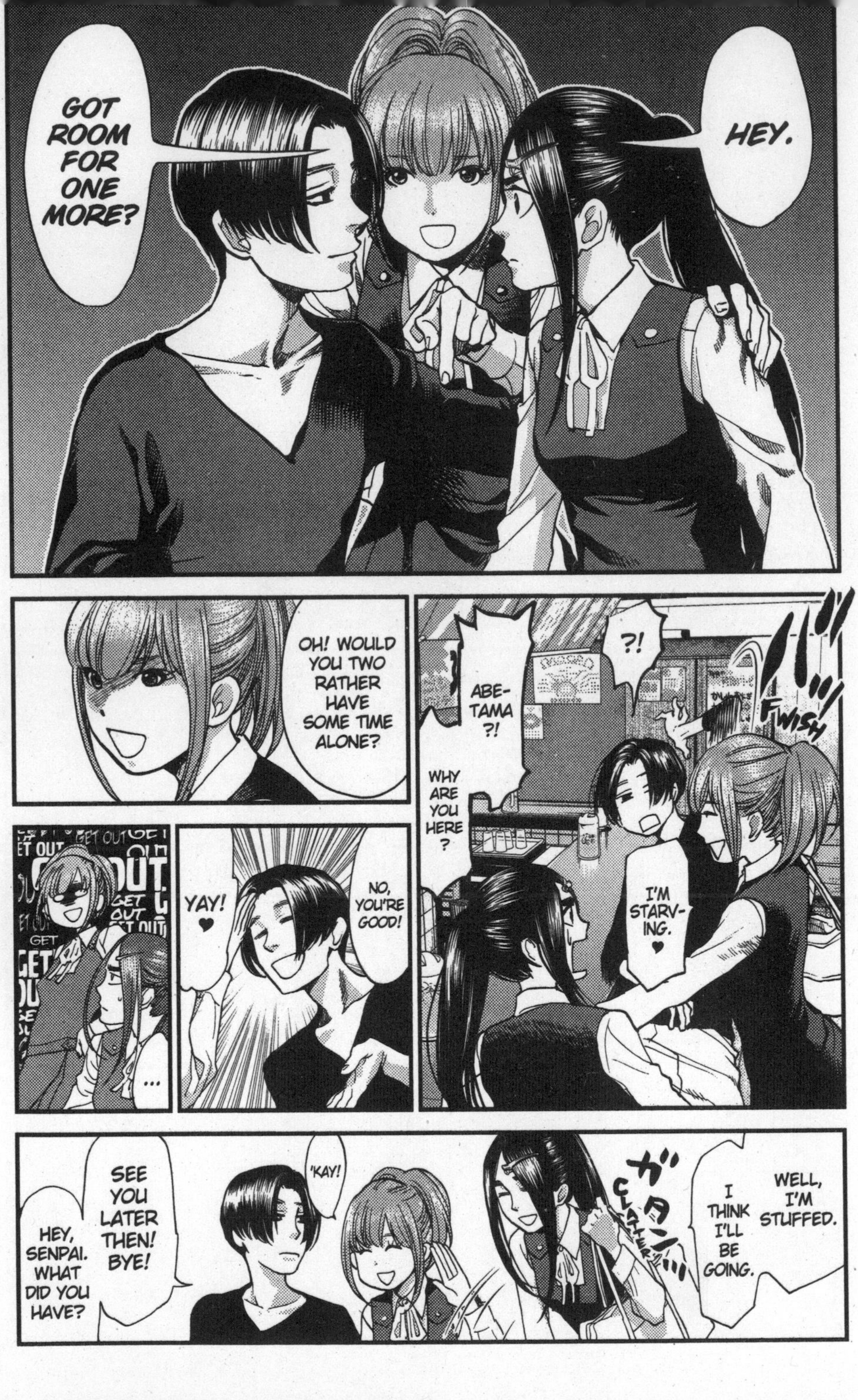
HEY.
GOT ROOM FOR ONE MORE?
?!
ABE-TAMA?!
WHY ARE YOU HERE?
FWISH
I'M STARV-ING. ♥
OH! WOULD YOU TWO RATHER HAVE SOME TIME ALONE?
NO, YOU'RE GOOD!
YAY! ♥
GET OUT
...
WELL, I'M STUFFED.
I THINK I'LL BE GOING.
ガタン
CLATTER
'KAY!
SEE YOU LATER THEN! BYE!
HEY, SENPAI. WHAT DID YOU HAVE?

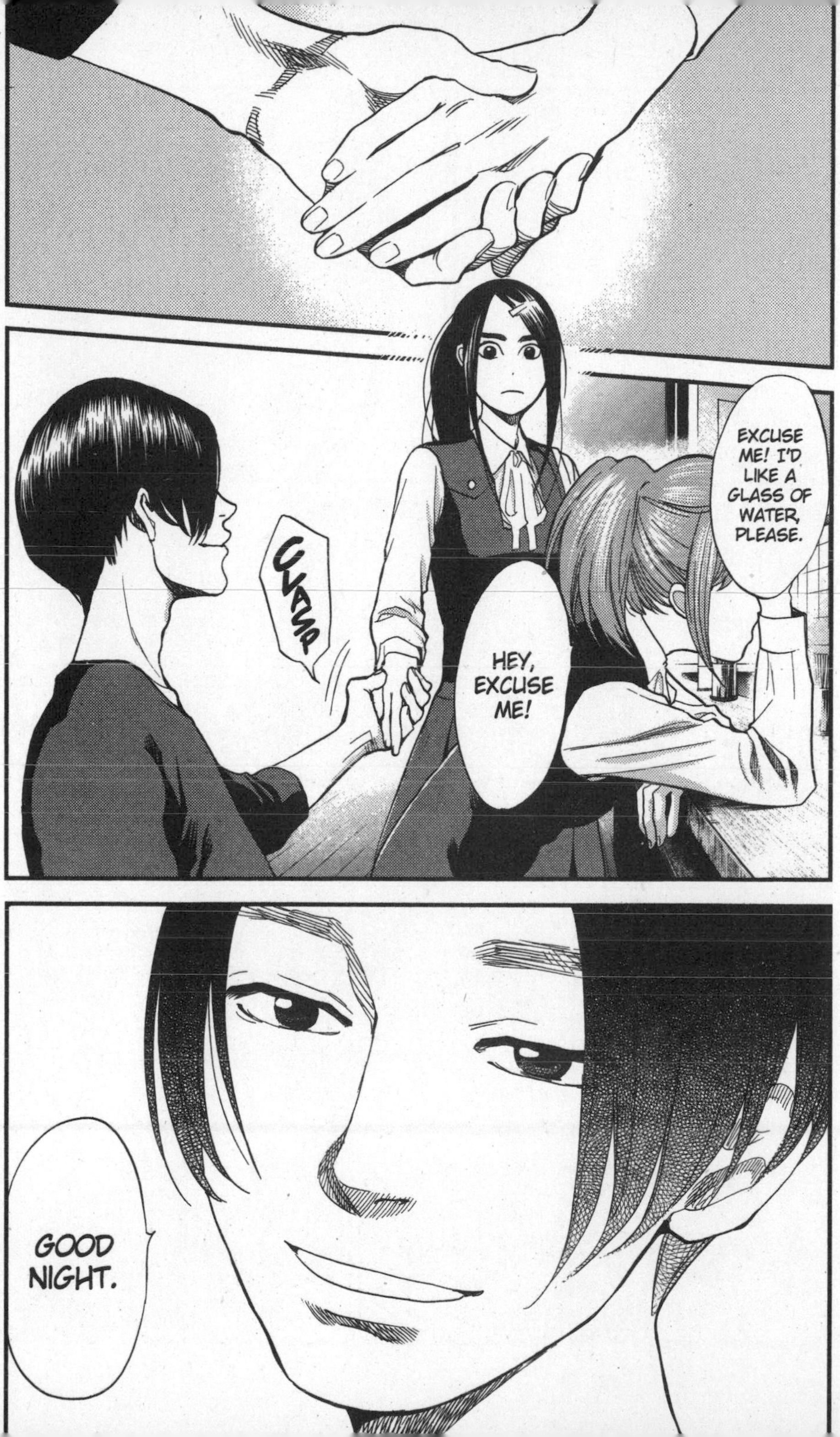
EXCUSE ME! I'D LIKE A GLASS OF WATER, PLEASE.
HEY, EXCUSE ME!
CLASP
GOOD NIGHT.

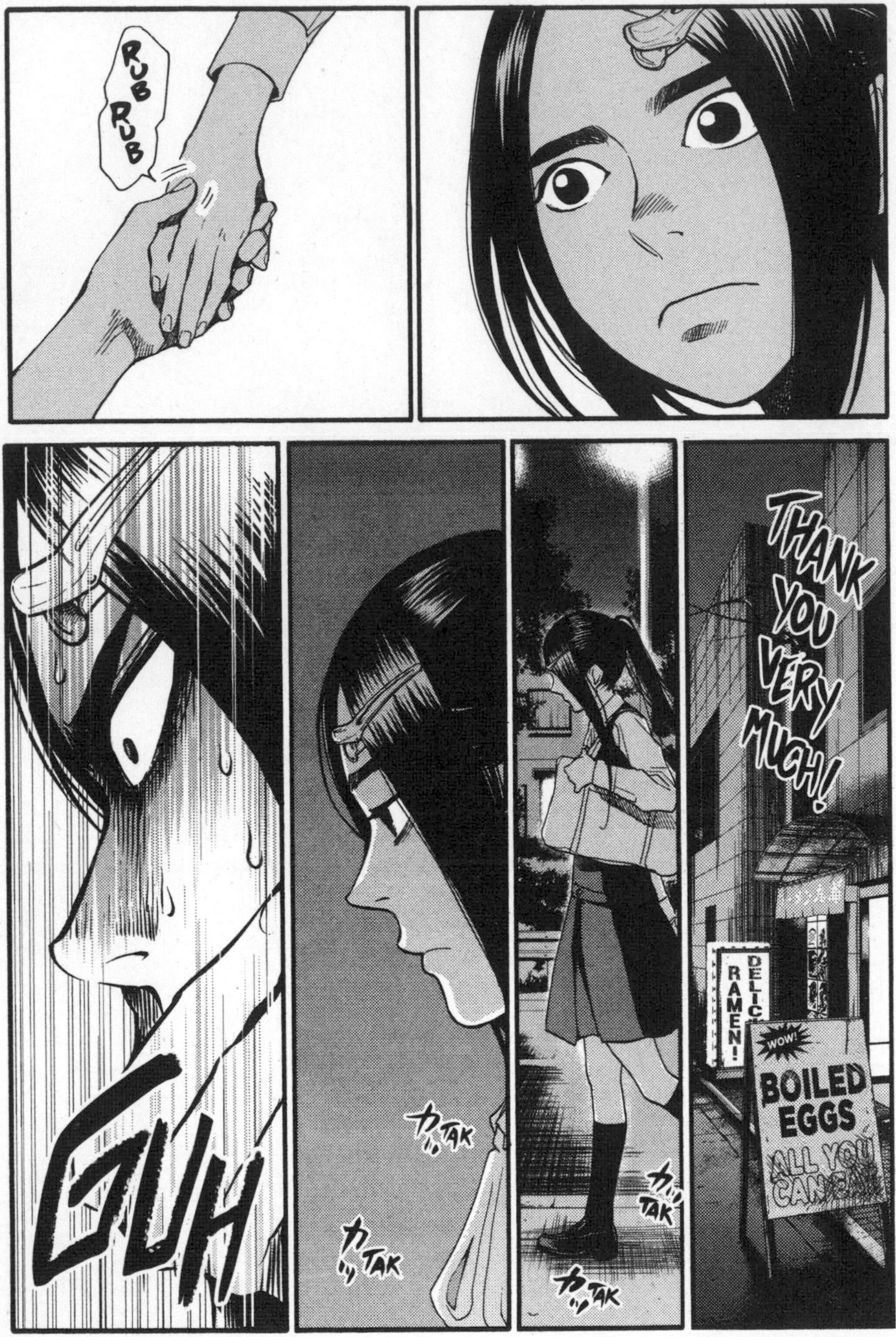
RUB RUB
THANK YOU VERY MUCH!
RAMEN!
DELIC
WOW!
BOILED EGGS
ALL YOU CAN
カッ TAK
カッ TAK
カッ TAK
カッ TAK
カッ TAK
GUH

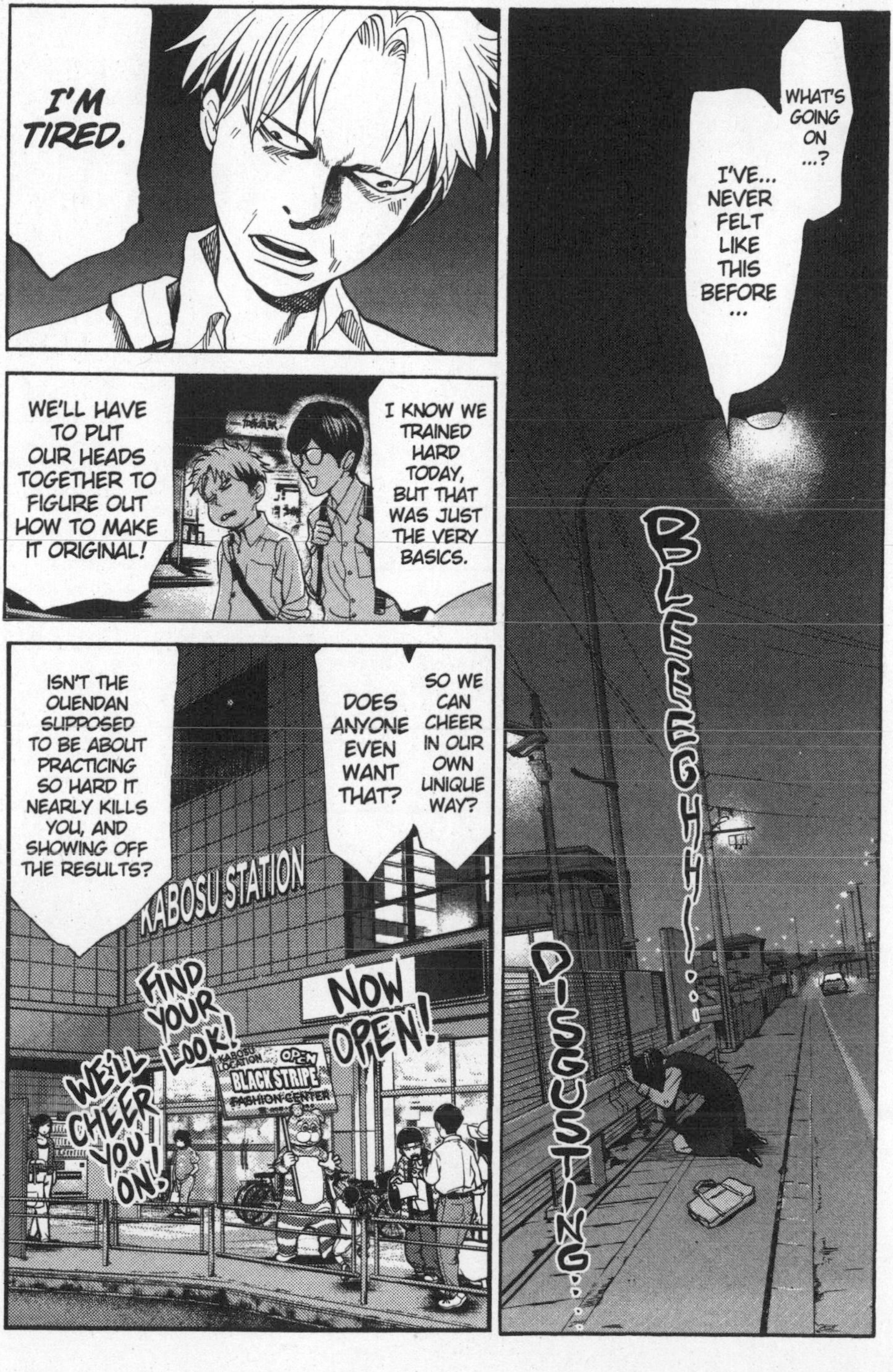
WHAT'S GOING ON ...?
I'VE... NEVER FELT LIKE THIS BEFORE ...
BLEEEEGHH~...
DISGUSTING...
I'M TIRED.
I KNOW WE TRAINED HARD TODAY, BUT THAT WAS JUST THE VERY BASICS.
WE'LL HAVE TO PUT OUR HEADS TOGETHER TO FIGURE OUT HOW TO MAKE IT ORIGINAL!
SO WE CAN CHEER IN OUR OWN UNIQUE WAY?
DOES ANYONE EVEN WANT THAT?
ISN'T THE OUENDAN SUPPOSED TO BE ABOUT PRACTICING SO HARD IT NEARLY KILLS YOU, AND SHOWING OFF THE RESULTS?
KABOSU STATION
NOW OPEN!
FIND YOUR LOOK!
KABOSU LOCATION
OPEN
BLACK STRIPE
FASHION CENTER
WE'LL CHEER YOU ON!

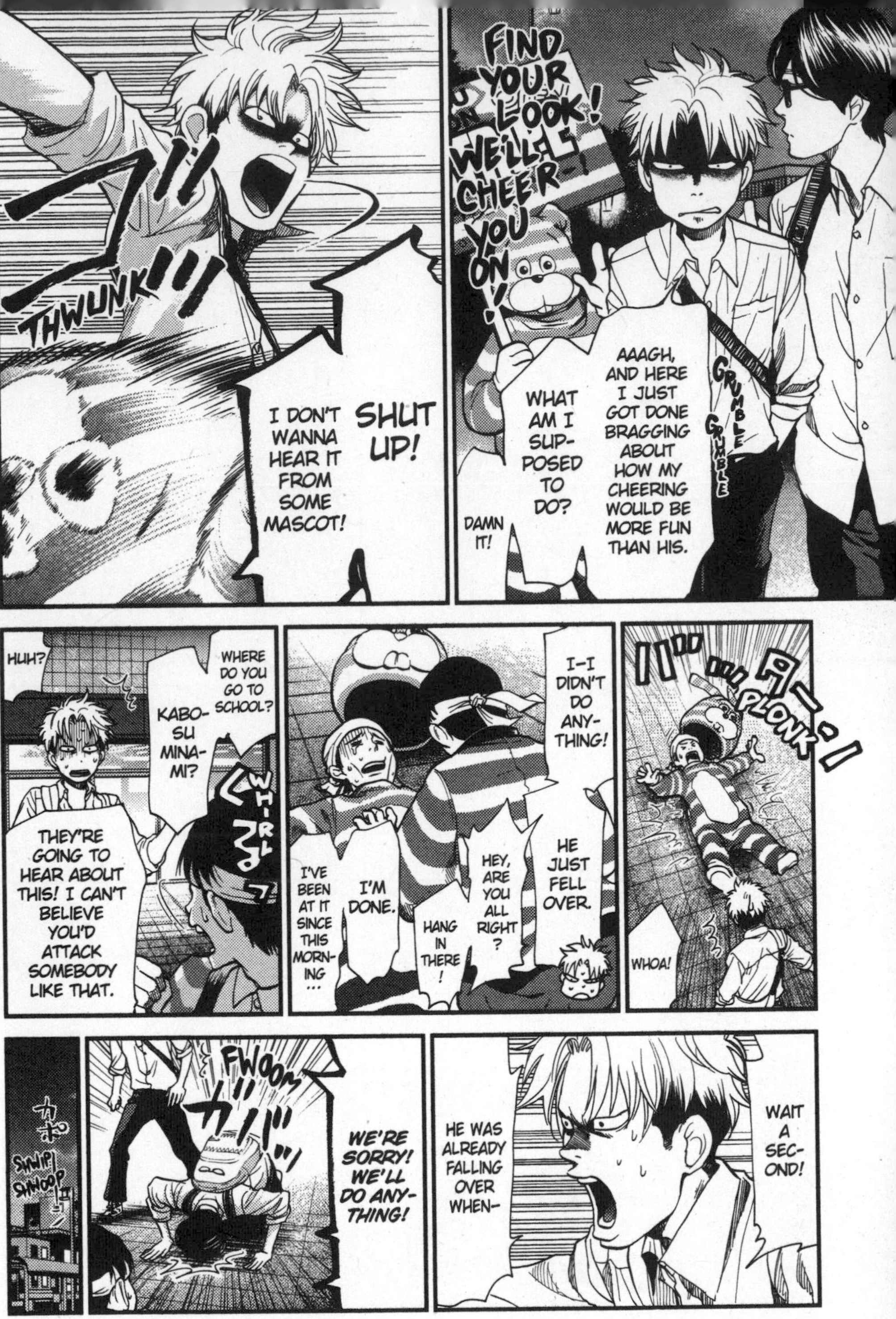
FIND YOUR LOOK! WE'LL CHEER YOU ON!
AAAGH, AND HERE I JUST GOT DONE BRAGGING ABOUT HOW MY CHEERING WOULD BE MORE FUN THAN HIS.
GRUMBLE GRUMBLE
WHAT AM I SUP-POSED TO DO?
DAMN IT!
SHUT UP!
I DON'T WANNA HEAR IT FROM SOME MASCOT!
THWUNK
PLONK
WHOA!
I-I DIDN'T DO ANY-THING!
HE JUST FELL OVER.
HEY, ARE YOU ALL RIGHT?
HANG IN THERE!
I'M DONE.
I'VE BEEN AT IT SINCE THIS MORN-ING...
WHERE DO YOU GO TO SCHOOL?
HUH?
KABO-SU MINA-MI?
WHIRL
THEY'RE GOING TO HEAR ABOUT THIS! I CAN'T BELIEVE YOU'D ATTACK SOMEBODY LIKE THAT.
WAIT A SEC-OND!
HE WAS ALREADY FALLING OVER WHEN-
FWOOM
WE'RE SORRY! WE'LL DO ANY-THING!
SHWIP! SHWOOP

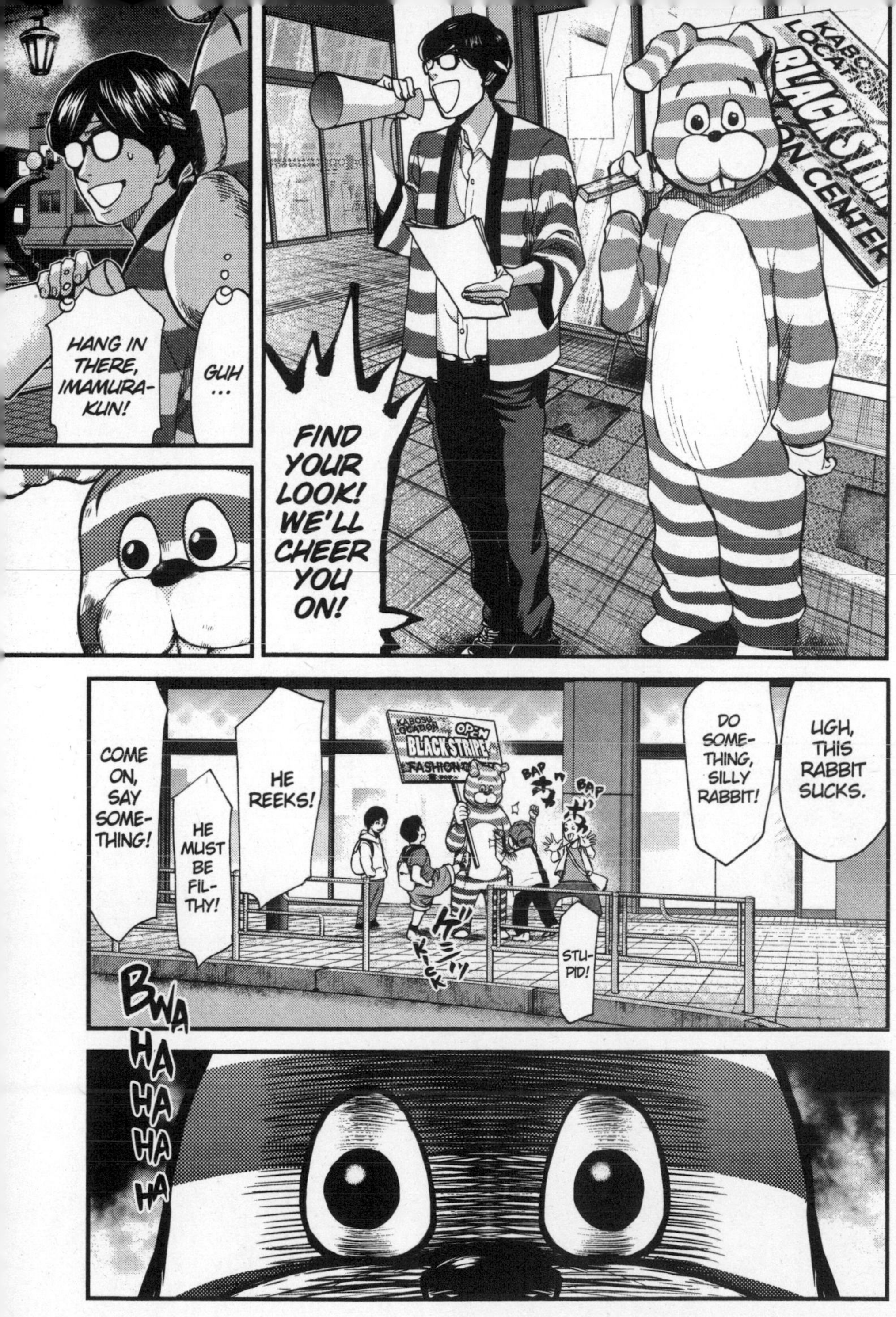
FIND YOUR LOOK! WE'LL CHEER YOU ON!
GUH ...
HANG IN THERE, IMAMURA-KUN!
UGH, THIS RABBIT SUCKS.
DO SOMETHING, SILLY RABBIT!
OPEN
BLACK STRIPE
BAP
BAP
HE REEKS!
COME ON, SAY SOMETHING!
HE MUST BE FILTHY!
KICK
STUPID!
BWAHAHAHAHAHA

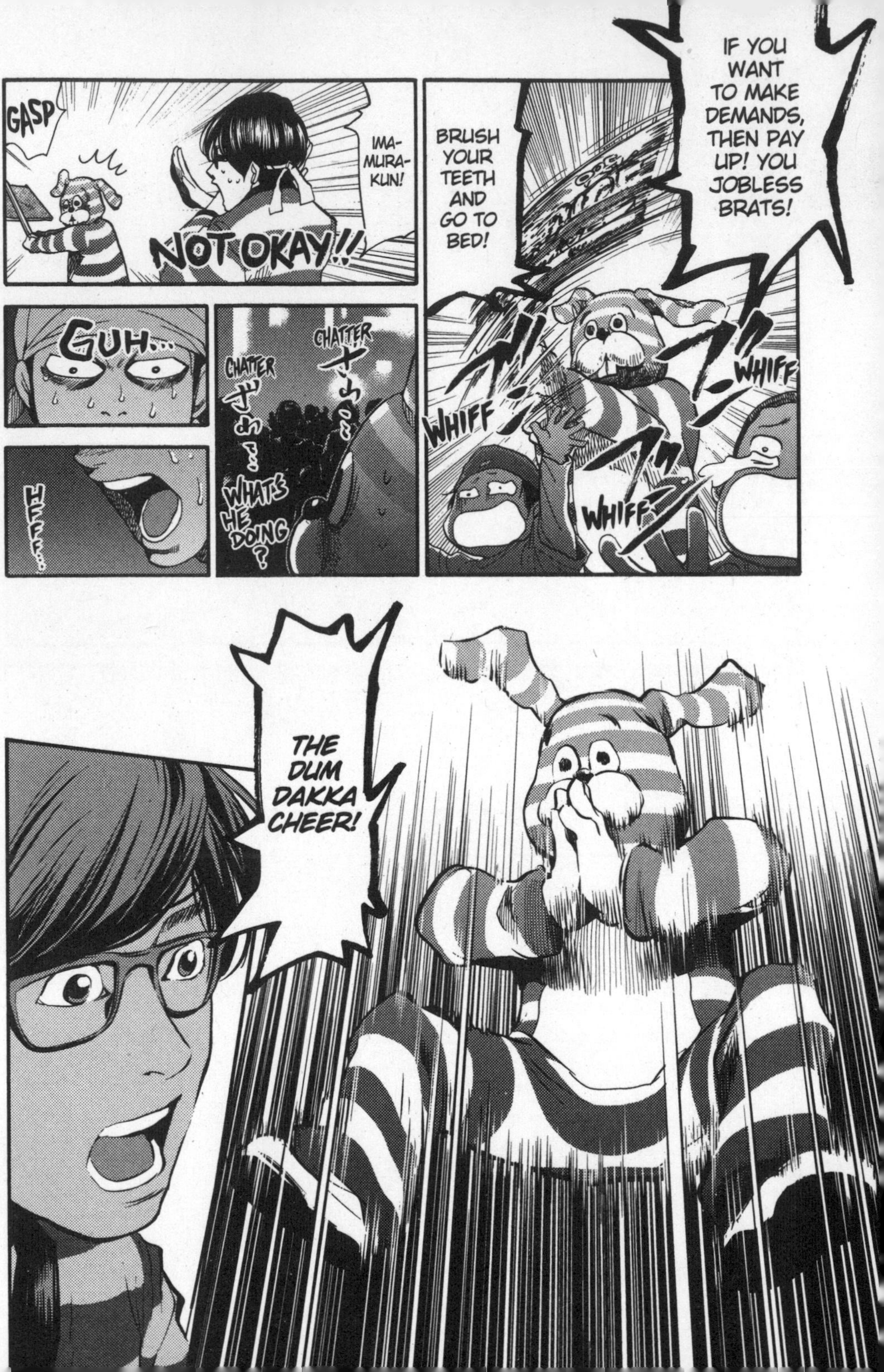
IF YOU WANT TO MAKE DEMANDS, THEN PAY UP! YOU JOBLESS BRATS!
BRUSH YOUR TEETH AND GO TO BED!
WHIFF
WHIFF
WHIFF
IMA-MURA-KUN!
GASP
NOT OKAY!!
CHATTER
CHATTER
WHAT'S HE DOING?
GUH...
HFFF...
THE DUM DAKKA CHEER!

121. STREETSIDE CHEER UP!!

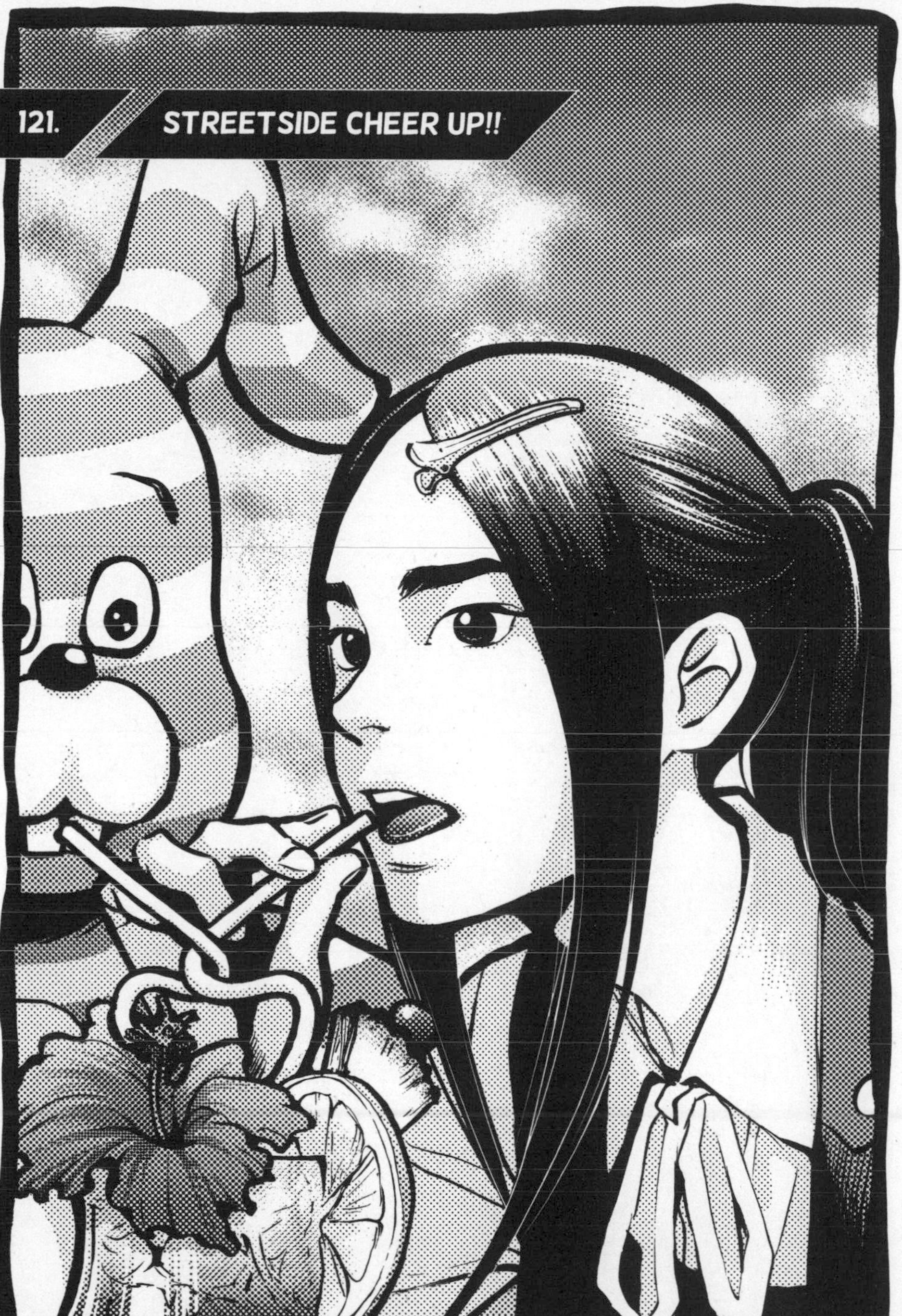

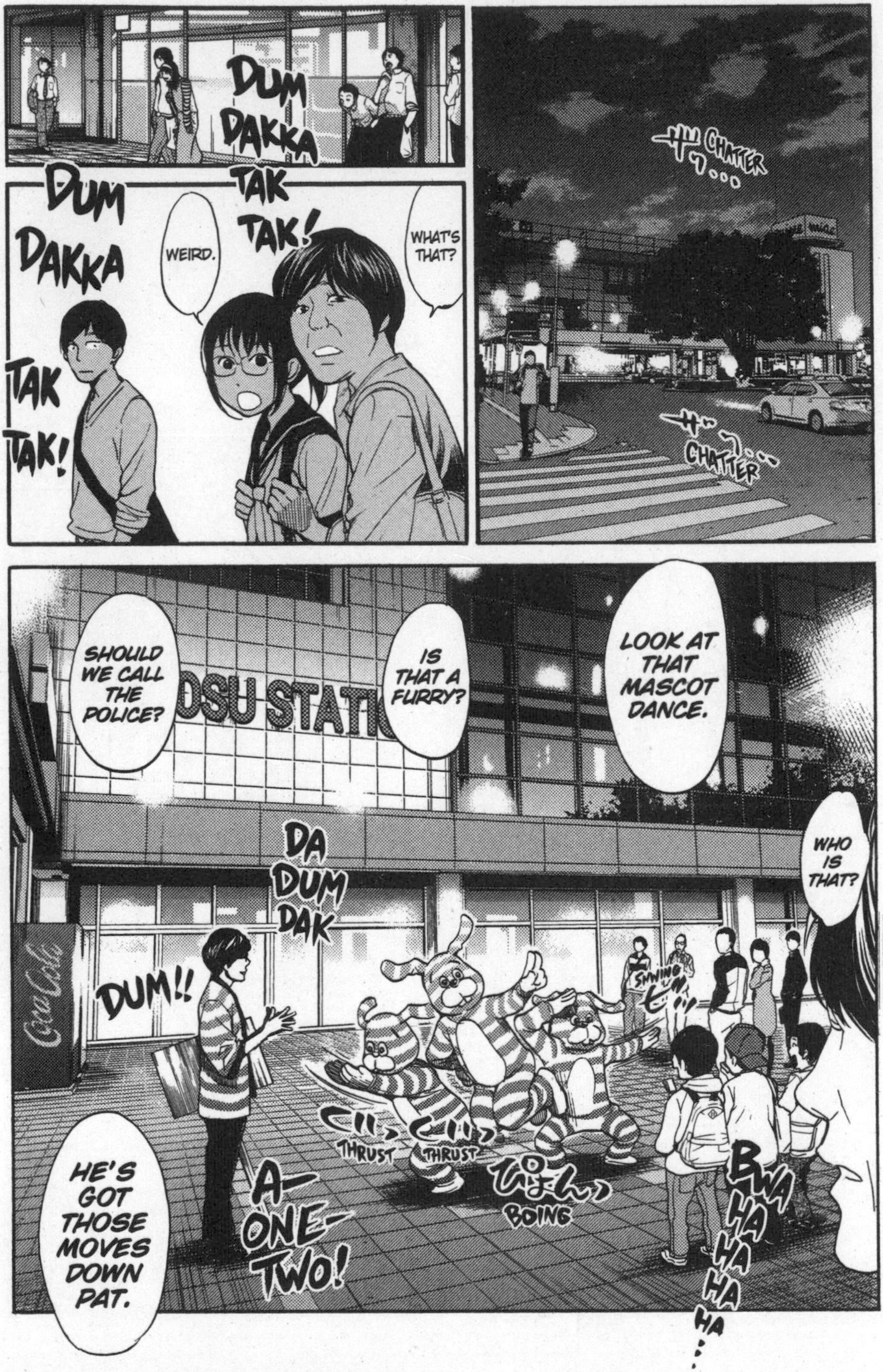
CHATTER
CHATTER
DUM
DAKKA
TAK
TAK!
DUM
DAKKA
TAK
TAK!
WHAT'S THAT?
WEIRD.
WHO IS THAT?
LOOK AT THAT MASCOT DANCE.
IS THAT A FURRY?
SHOULD WE CALL THE POLICE?
OSU STATI
DA DUM DAK
DUM!!
Coca-Cola
SHWING
THRUST
THRUST
BOING
BWA HA HA HA HA HA...
A-ONE-TWO!
HE'S GOT THOSE MOVES DOWN PAT.

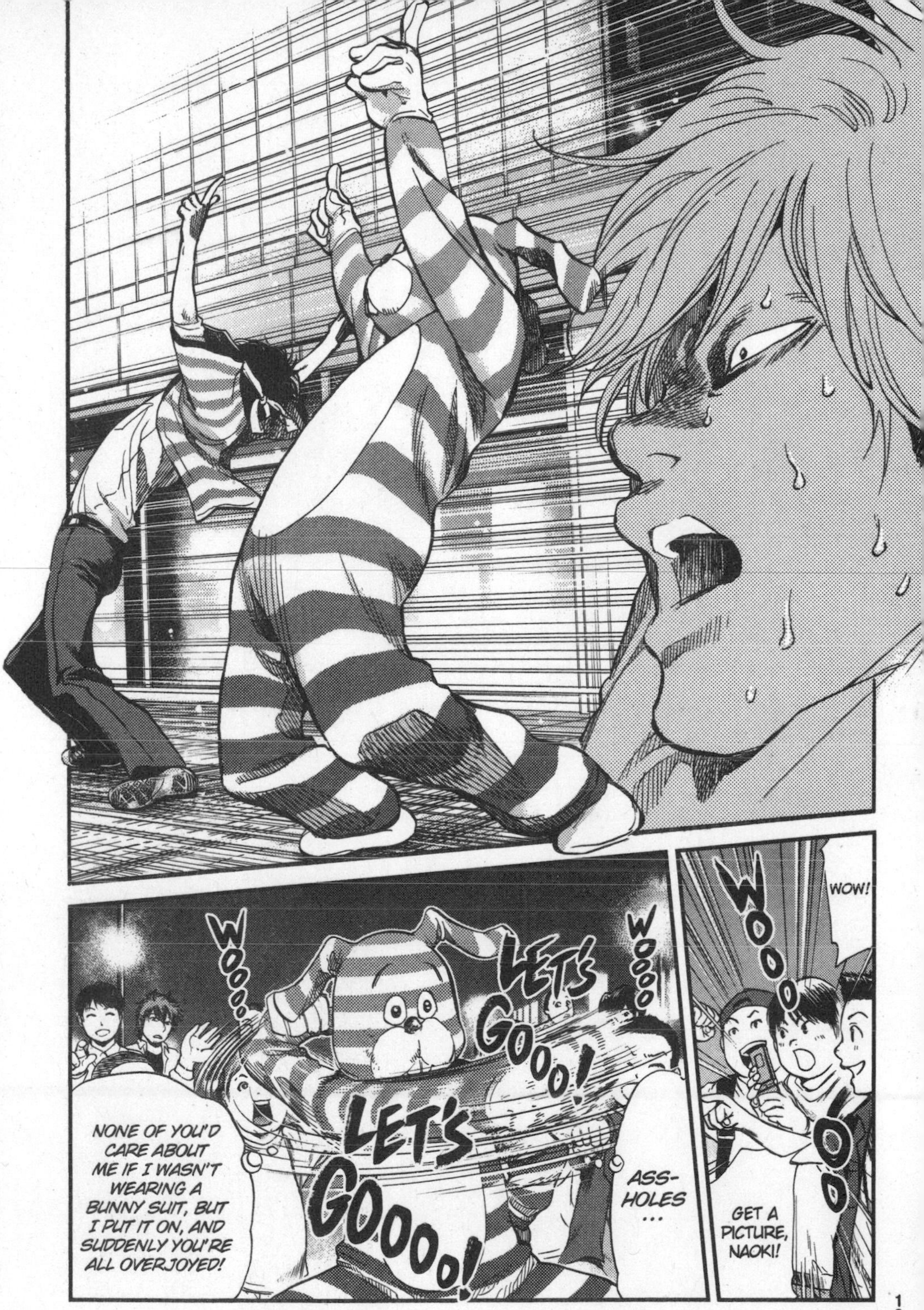
WOW!
WOOOO...
GET A PICTURE, NAOKI!
WOOOOO
LET'S GOOOO!
WOOOO...
ASS-HOLES...
LET'S GOOOO!
NONE OF YOU'D CARE ABOUT ME IF I WASN'T WEARING A BUNNY SUIT, BUT I PUT IT ON, AND SUDDENLY YOU'RE ALL OVERJOYED!

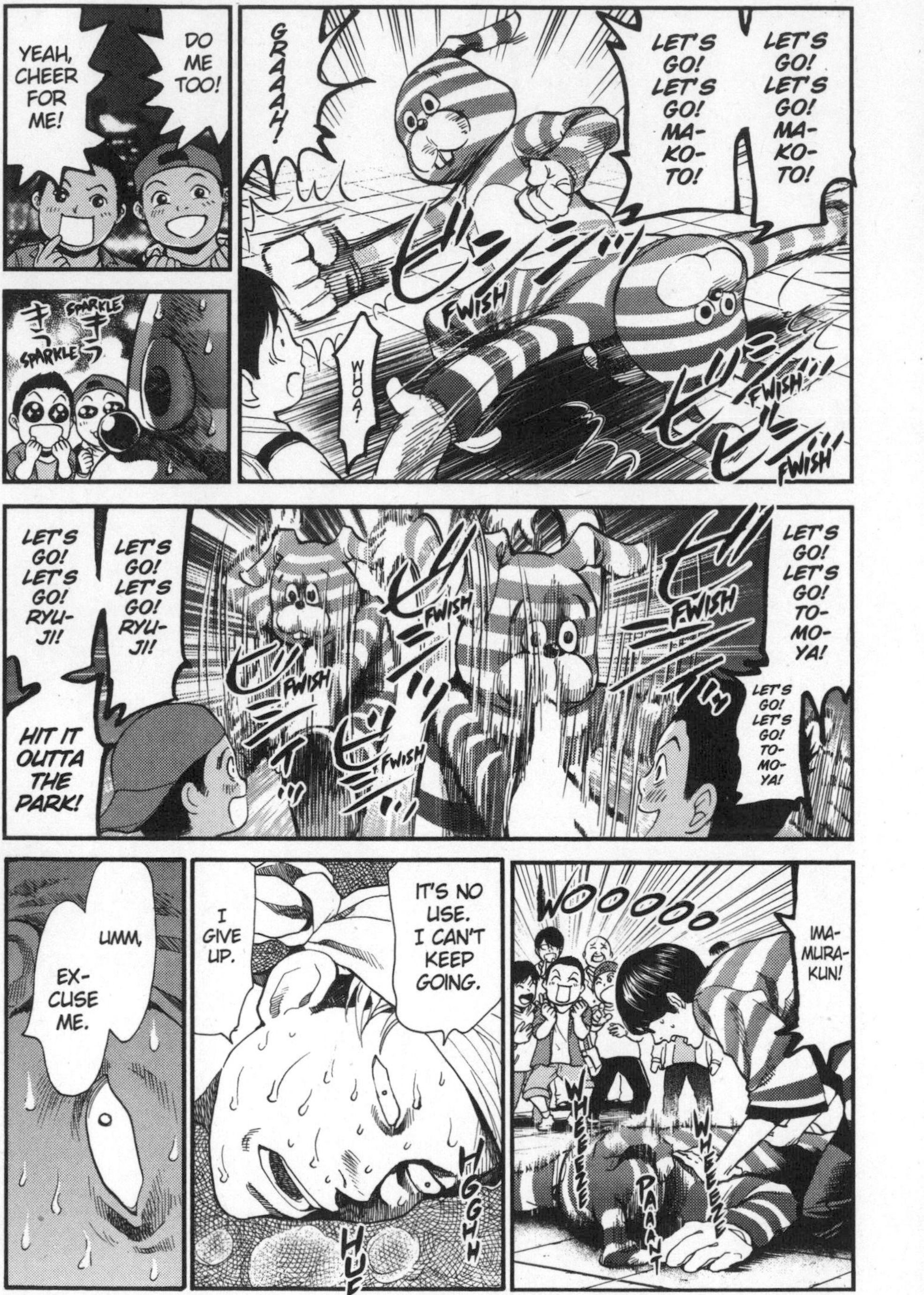
LET'S GO! LET'S GO! MA-KO-TO!
LET'S GO! LET'S GO! MA-KO-TO!
GRAAAAH!
FWISH
WHOA!
FWISH
FWISH
DO ME TOO!
YEAH, CHEER FOR ME!
SPARKLE
SPARKLE
LET'S GO! LET'S GO! TO-MO-YA!
FWISH
LET'S GO! LET'S GO! TO-MO-YA!
FWISH
FWISH
FWISH
LET'S GO! LET'S GO! RYU-JI!
LET'S GO! LET'S GO! RYU-JI!
HIT IT OUTTA THE PARK!
WOOOOO
IMA-MURA-KUN!
WHEEZE
PAAANT
WHEEZE
IT'S NO USE. I CAN'T KEEP GOING.
I GIVE UP.
HGGGH
HUFF
UMM, EXCUSE ME.

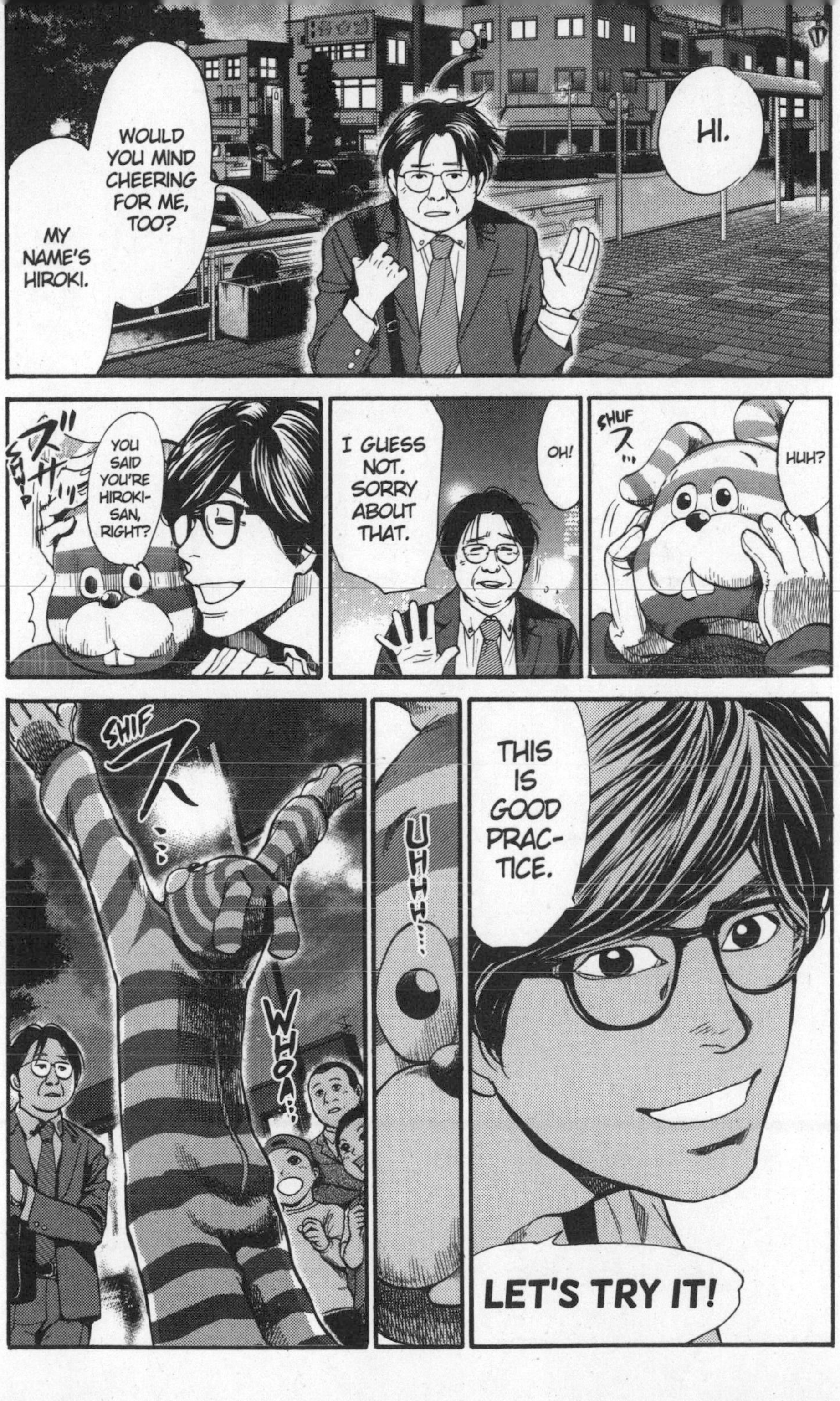
HI.
WOULD YOU MIND CHEERING FOR ME, TOO?
MY NAME'S HIROKI.
SHUF
HUH?
OH!
I GUESS NOT. SORRY ABOUT THAT.
YOU SAID YOU'RE HIROKI-SAN, RIGHT?
THIS IS GOOD PRAC-TICE.
UHHH...
LET'S TRY IT!
SHIF
WHOA...

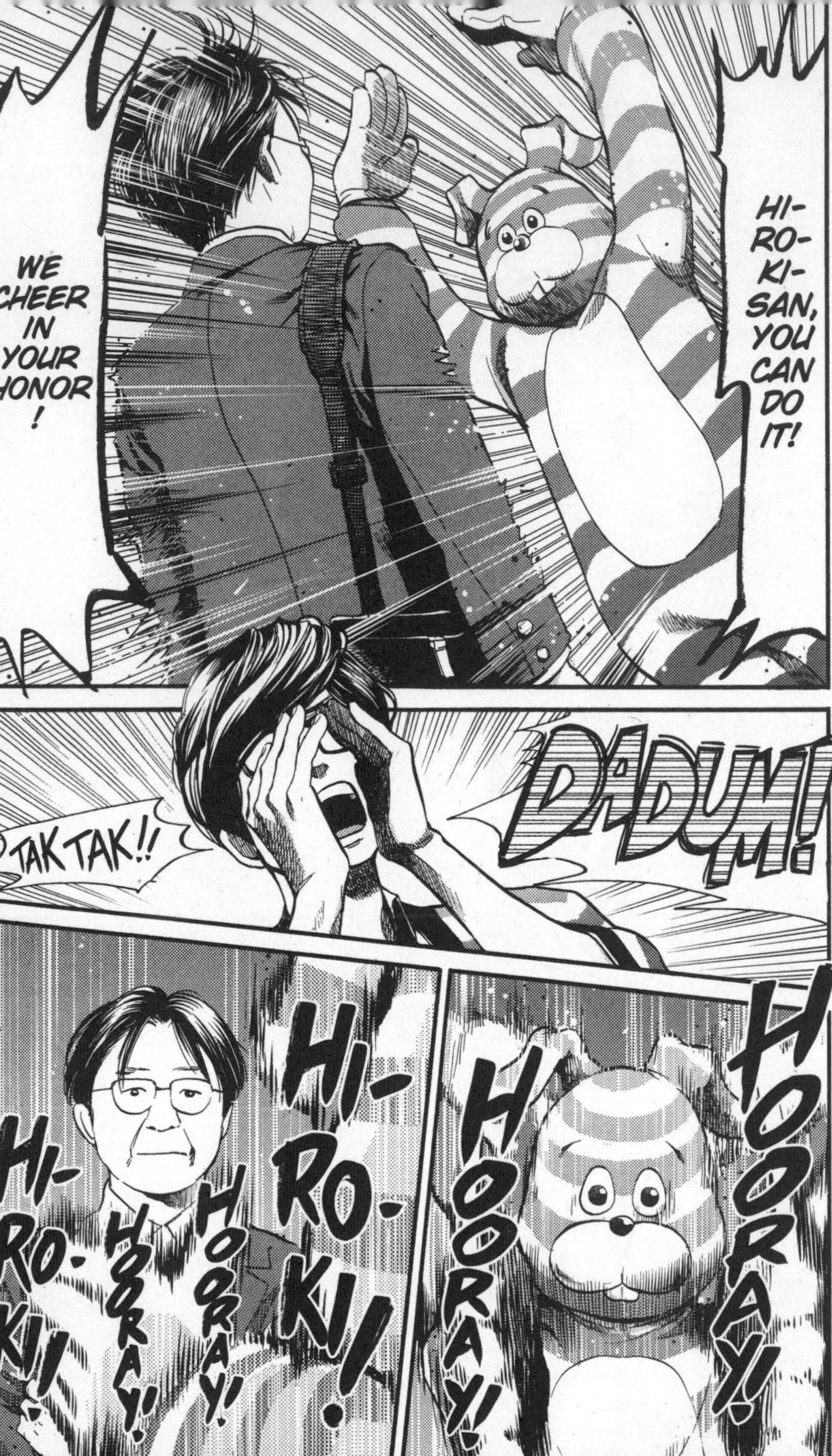
HI-RO-KI-SAN, YOU CAN DO IT!
WE CHEER IN YOUR HONOR!
DADUM!
TAK TAK!!
HOORAY!
HOORAY!
HI-RO-KI!
HOORAY!
HOORAY!
HI-RO-KI!

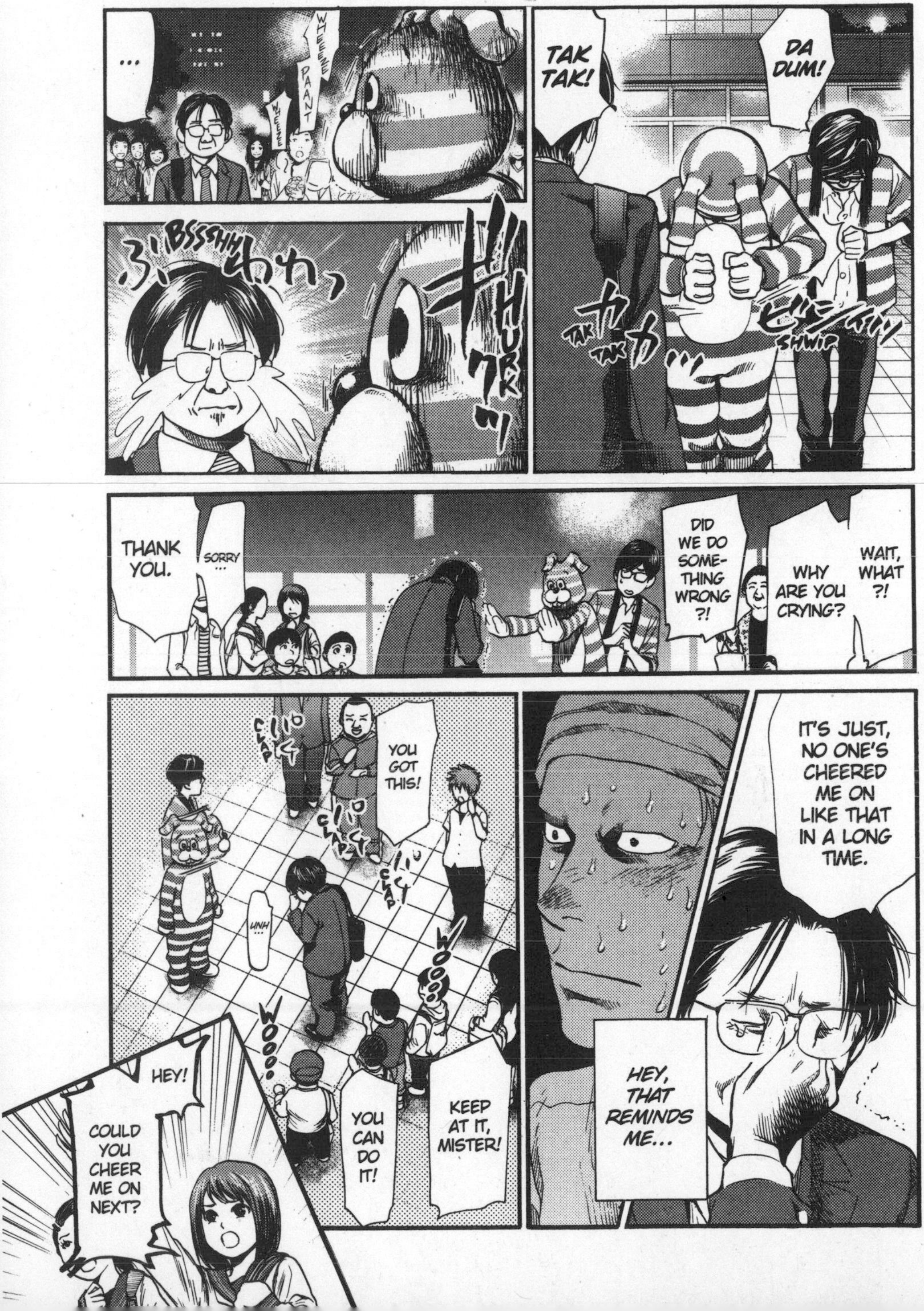
DA DUM!
TAK TAK!
TAK TAK
SHWIP
...
WHEEEZE
PAANT
WHEEZE
BSSSHHH
HURK
WAIT, WHAT?!
WHY ARE YOU CRYING?
DID WE DO SOMETHING WRONG?!
SORRY...
THANK YOU.
IT'S JUST, NO ONE'S CHEERED ME ON LIKE THAT IN A LONG TIME.
HEY, THAT REMINDS ME...
YOU GOT THIS!
CLAP
CLAP
CLAP
UNH...
WOOOO
WOOOO
KEEP AT IT, MISTER!
YOU CAN DO IT!
HEY!
COULD YOU CHEER ME ON NEXT?

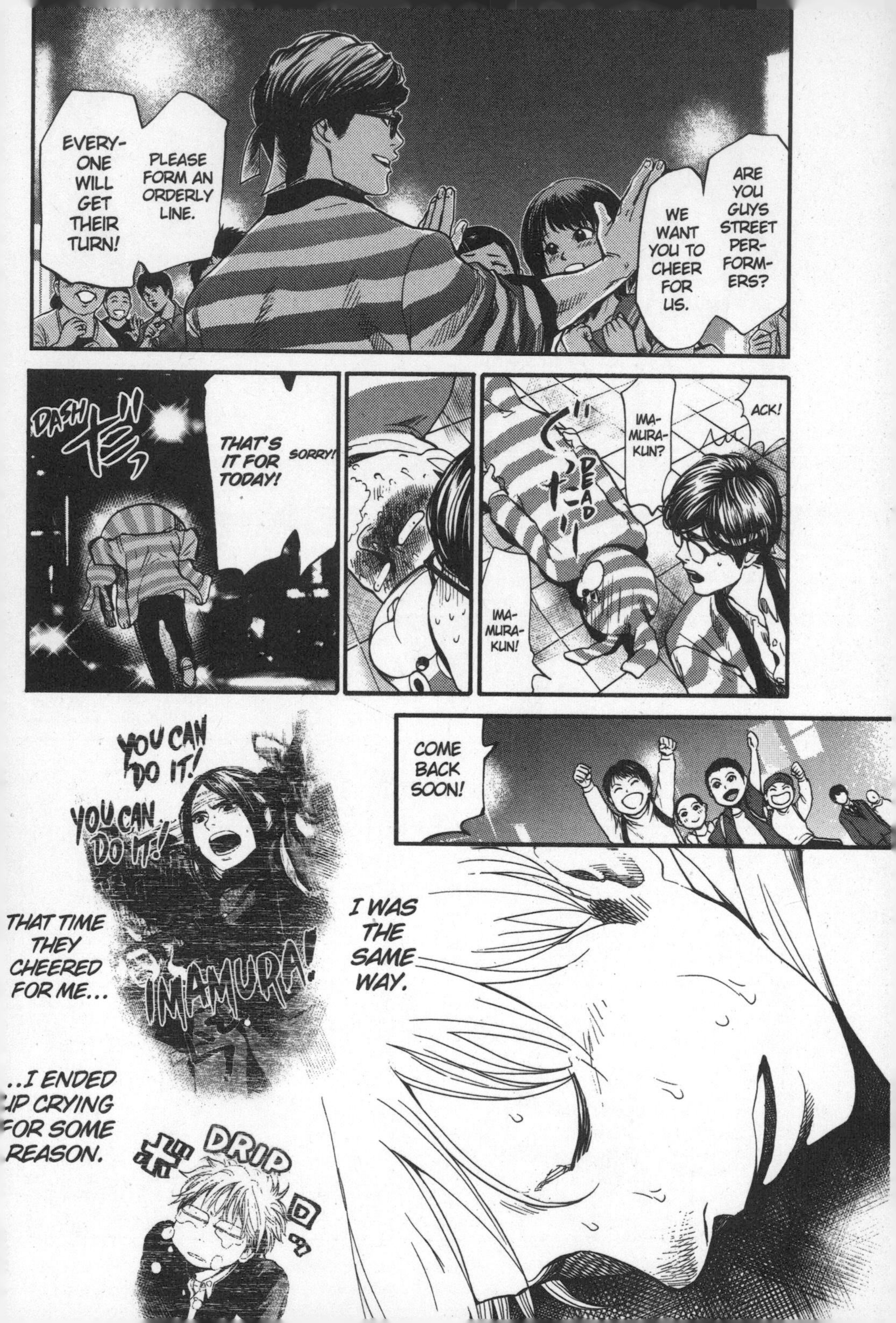
ARE YOU GUYS STREET PERFORMERS?
WE WANT YOU TO CHEER FOR US.
PLEASE FORM AN ORDERLY LINE.
EVERYONE WILL GET THEIR TURN!
ACK!
IMAMURA-KUN?
DEAD
IMAMURA-KUN!
SORRY!
THAT'S IT FOR TODAY!
DASH
COME BACK SOON!
I WAS THE SAME WAY.
YOU CAN DO IT!
YOU CAN DO IT!
THAT TIME THEY CHEERED FOR ME...
IMAMURA!
...I ENDED UP CRYING FOR SOME REASON.
DRIP

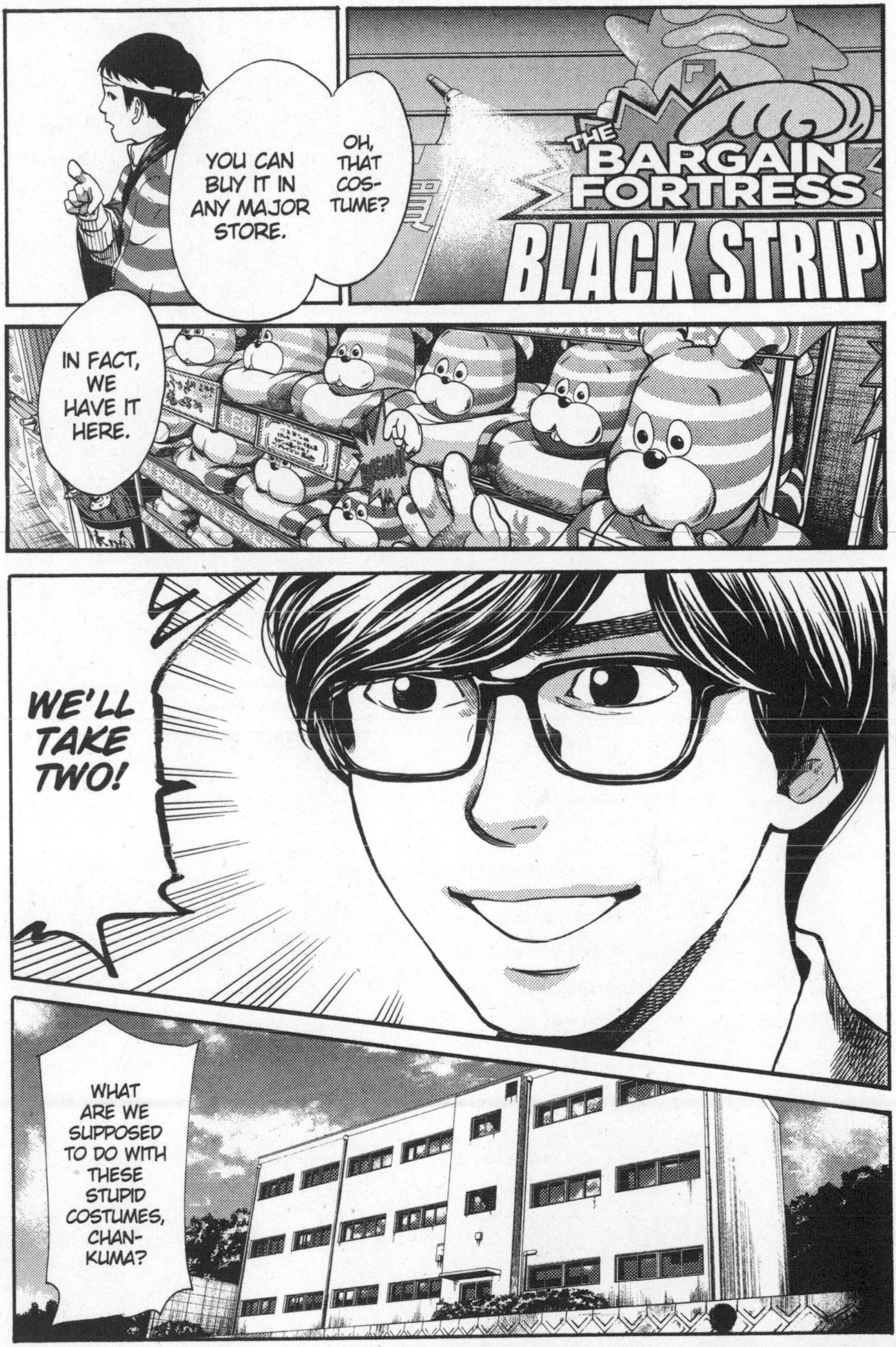
THE BARGAIN FORTRESS
BLACK STRIP
OH, THAT COS-TUME?
YOU CAN BUY IT IN ANY MAJOR STORE.
IN FACT, WE HAVE IT HERE.
WE'LL TAKE TWO!
WHAT ARE WE SUPPOSED TO DO WITH THESE STUPID COSTUMES, CHAN-KUMA?

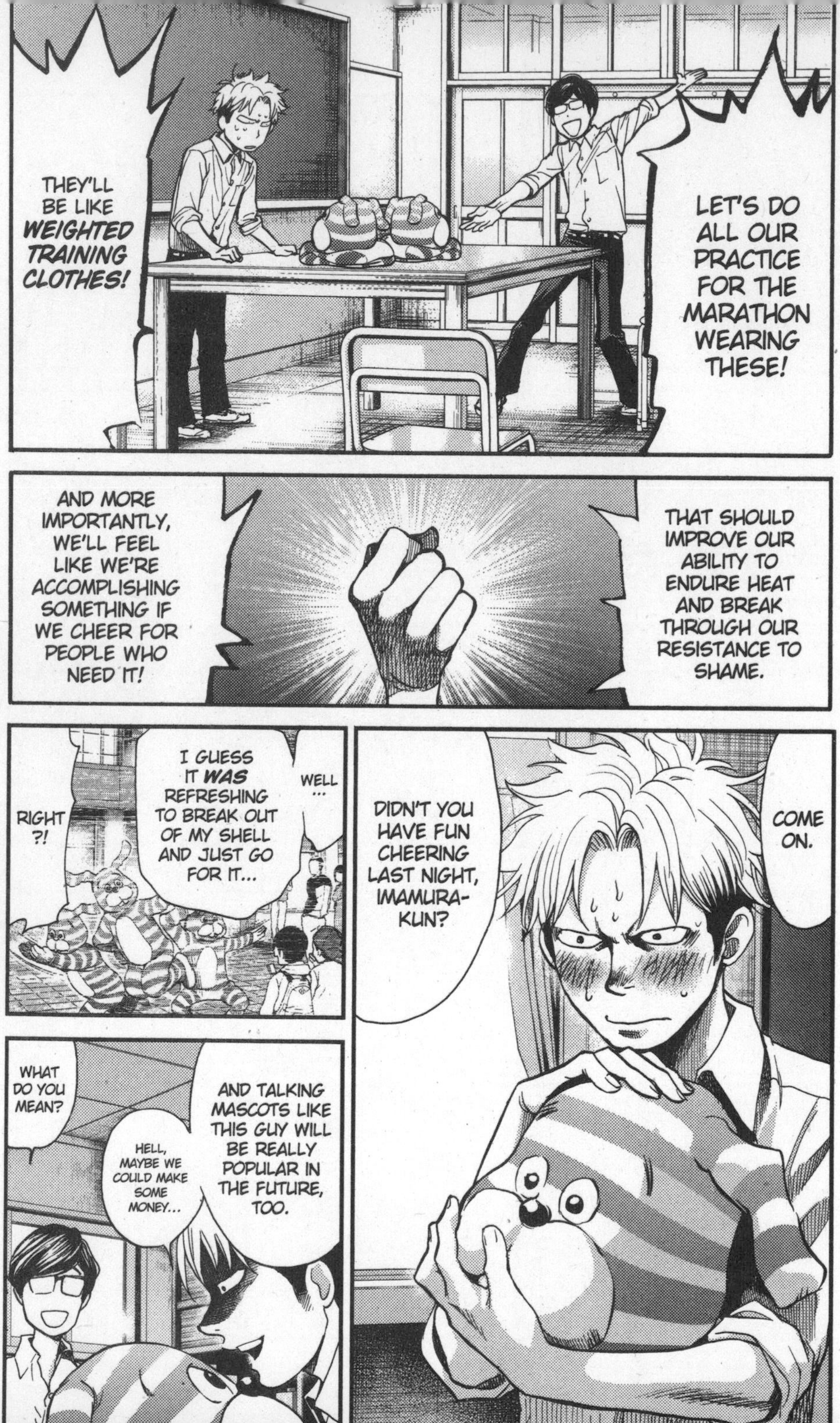
LET'S DO ALL OUR PRACTICE FOR THE MARATHON WEARING THESE!
THEY'LL BE LIKE ***WEIGHTED TRAINING CLOTHES!***
THAT SHOULD IMPROVE OUR ABILITY TO ENDURE HEAT AND BREAK THROUGH OUR RESISTANCE TO SHAME.
AND MORE IMPORTANTLY, WE'LL FEEL LIKE WE'RE ACCOMPLISHING SOMETHING IF WE CHEER FOR PEOPLE WHO NEED IT!
COME ON.
DIDN'T YOU HAVE FUN CHEERING LAST NIGHT, IMAMURA-KUN?
WELL ...
I GUESS IT ***WAS*** REFRESHING TO BREAK OUT OF MY SHELL AND JUST GO FOR IT...
RIGHT ?!
AND TALKING MASCOTS LIKE THIS GUY WILL BE REALLY POPULAR IN THE FUTURE, TOO.
WHAT DO YOU MEAN?
HELL, MAYBE WE COULD MAKE SOME MONEY...

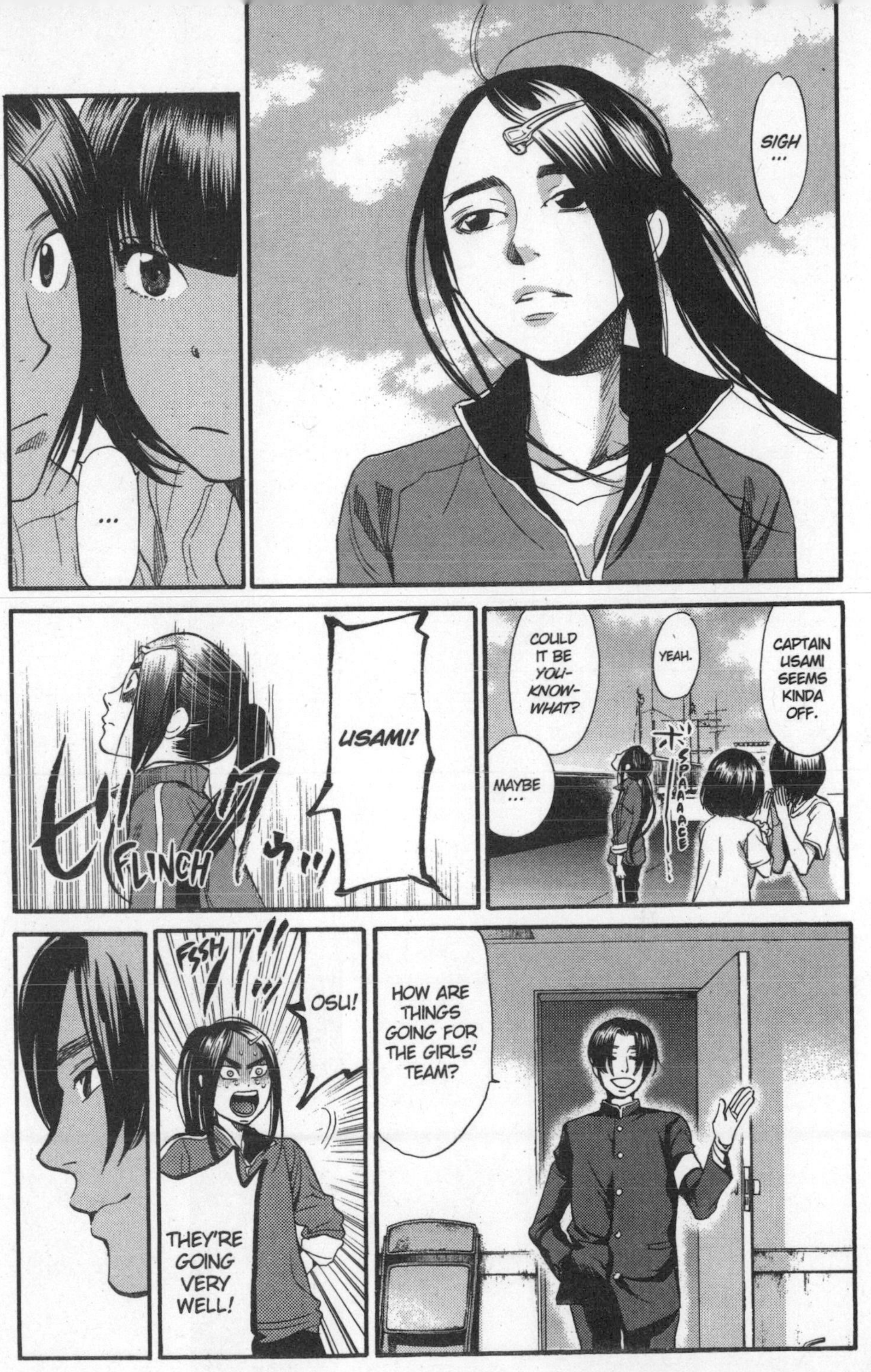
SIGH ...
...
CAPTAIN USAMI SEEMS KINDA OFF.
YEAH.
COULD IT BE YOU-KNOW-WHAT?
MAYBE ...
SPAAAACE
USAMI!
FLINCH
HOW ARE THINGS GOING FOR THE GIRLS' TEAM?
FSSH
OSU!
THEY'RE GOING VERY WELL!

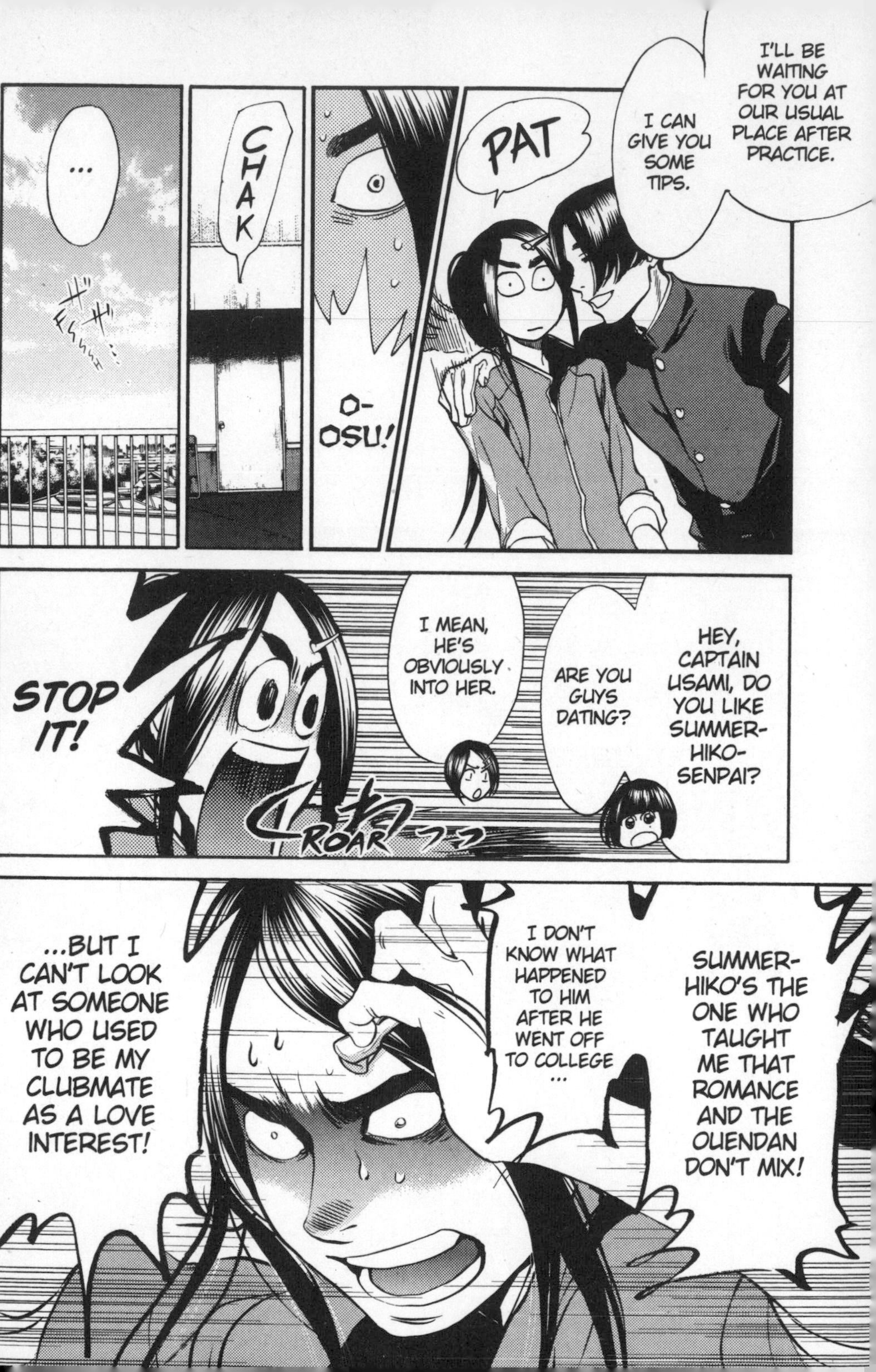
I'LL BE WAITING FOR YOU AT OUR USUAL PLACE AFTER PRACTICE.
I CAN GIVE YOU SOME TIPS.
PAT
O-OSU!
CHAK
...
HEY, CAPTAIN USAMI, DO YOU LIKE SUMMER-HIKO-SENPAI?
ARE YOU GUYS DATING?
I MEAN, HE'S OBVIOUSLY INTO HER.
STOP IT!
ROAR
SUMMER-HIKO'S THE ONE WHO TAUGHT ME THAT ROMANCE AND THE OUENDAN DON'T MIX!
I DON'T KNOW WHAT HAPPENED TO HIM AFTER HE WENT OFF TO COLLEGE ...
...BUT I CAN'T LOOK AT SOMEONE WHO USED TO BE MY CLUBMATE AS A LOVE INTEREST!

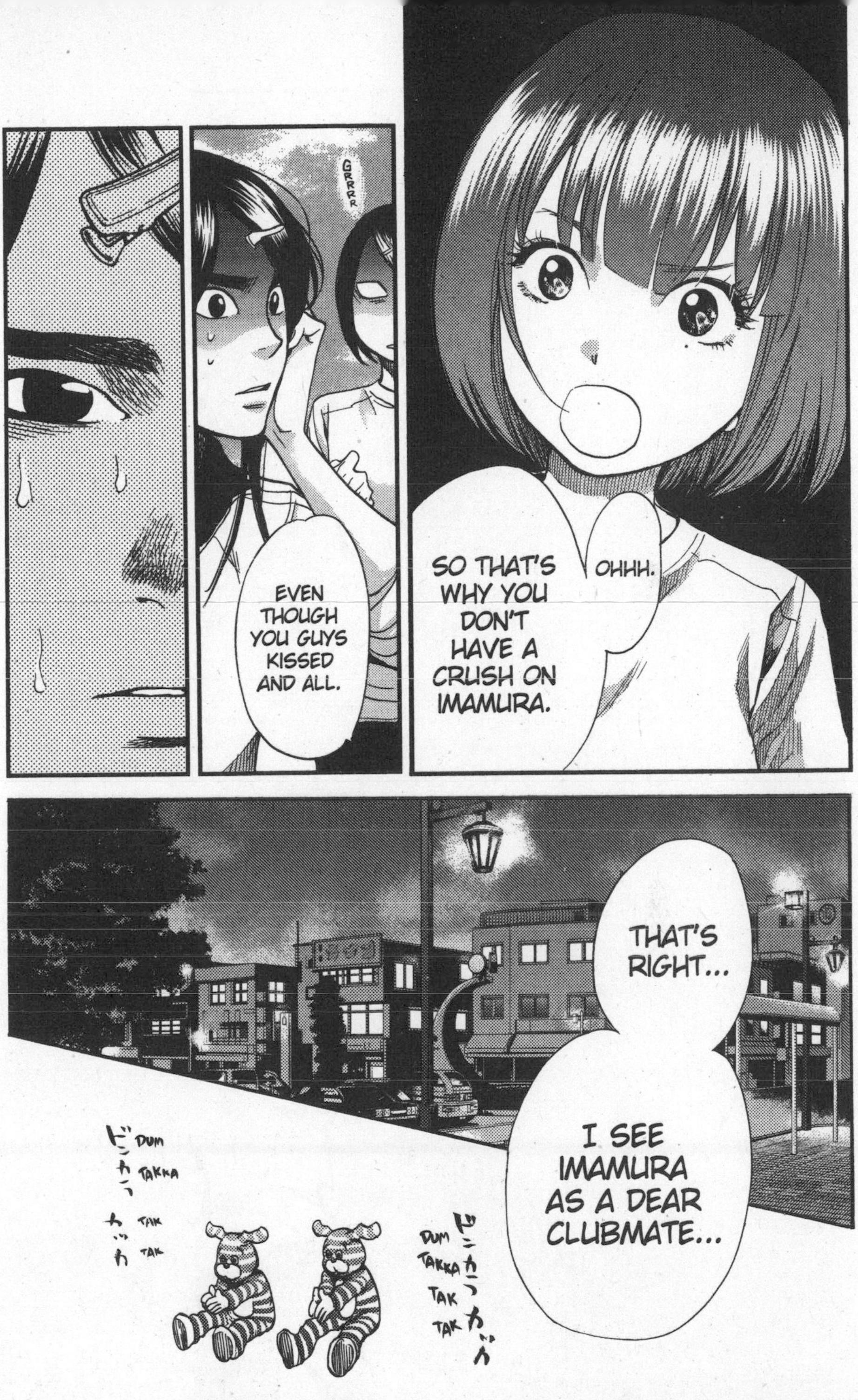
OHHH.
SO THAT'S WHY YOU DON'T HAVE A CRUSH ON IMAMURA.
GRRRR
EVEN THOUGH YOU GUYS KISSED AND ALL.
THAT'S RIGHT...
I SEE IMAMURA AS A DEAR CLUBMATE...
DUM TAKKA TAK TAK
DUM TAKKA TAK TAK

Again!!
アゲイン!!

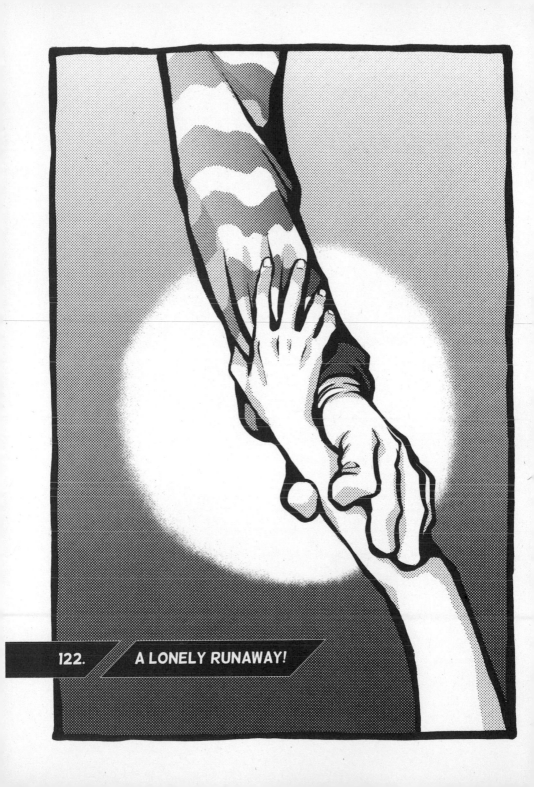

122. **A LONELY RUNAWAY!**

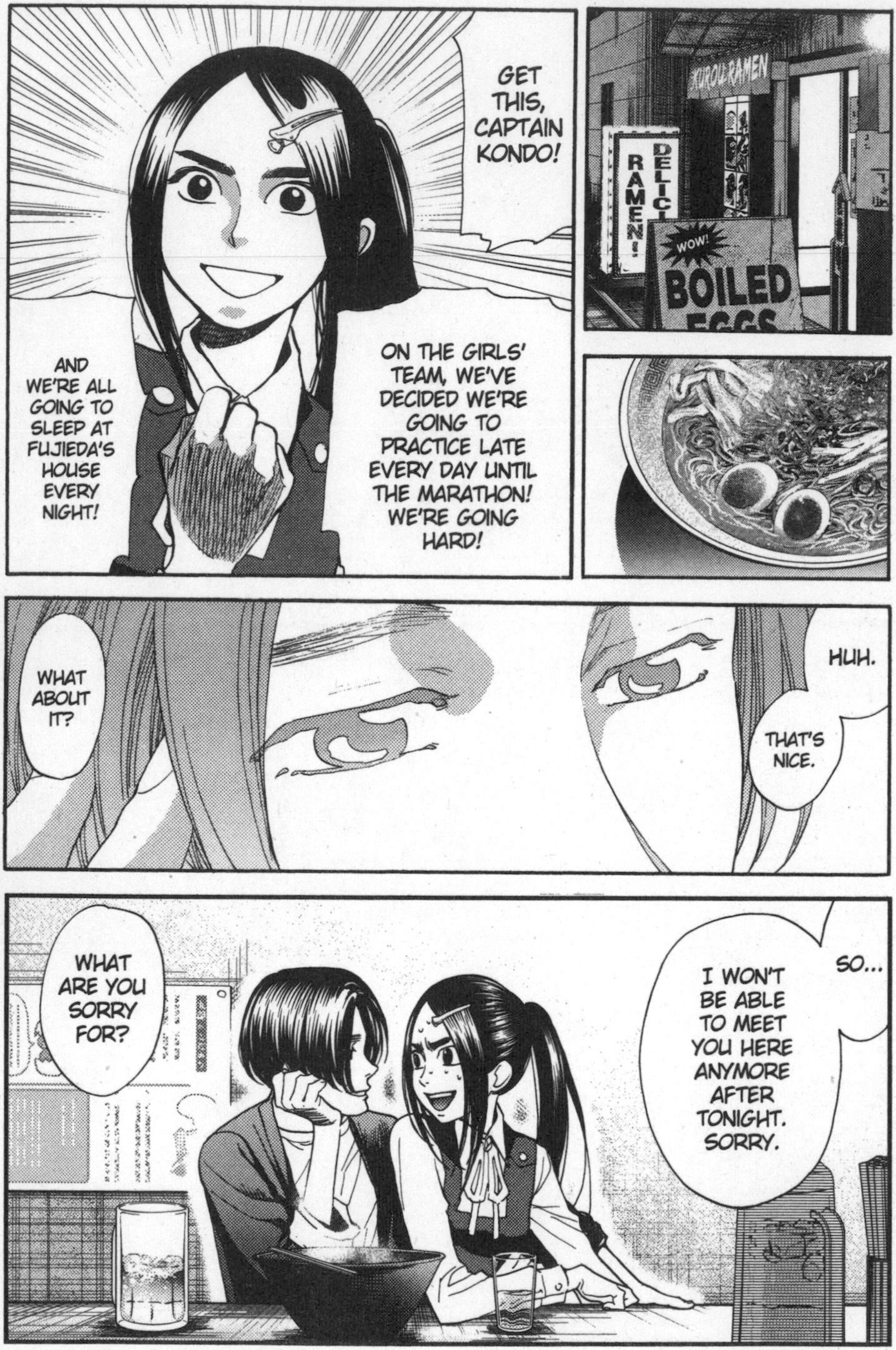
RAMEN!
WOW!
BOILED
GET THIS, CAPTAIN KONDO!
ON THE GIRLS' TEAM, WE'VE DECIDED WE'RE GOING TO PRACTICE LATE EVERY DAY UNTIL THE MARATHON! WE'RE GOING HARD!
AND WE'RE ALL GOING TO SLEEP AT FUJIEDA'S HOUSE EVERY NIGHT!
HUH.
THAT'S NICE.
WHAT ABOUT IT?
SO...
I WON'T BE ABLE TO MEET YOU HERE ANYMORE AFTER TONIGHT. SORRY.
WHAT ARE YOU SORRY FOR?

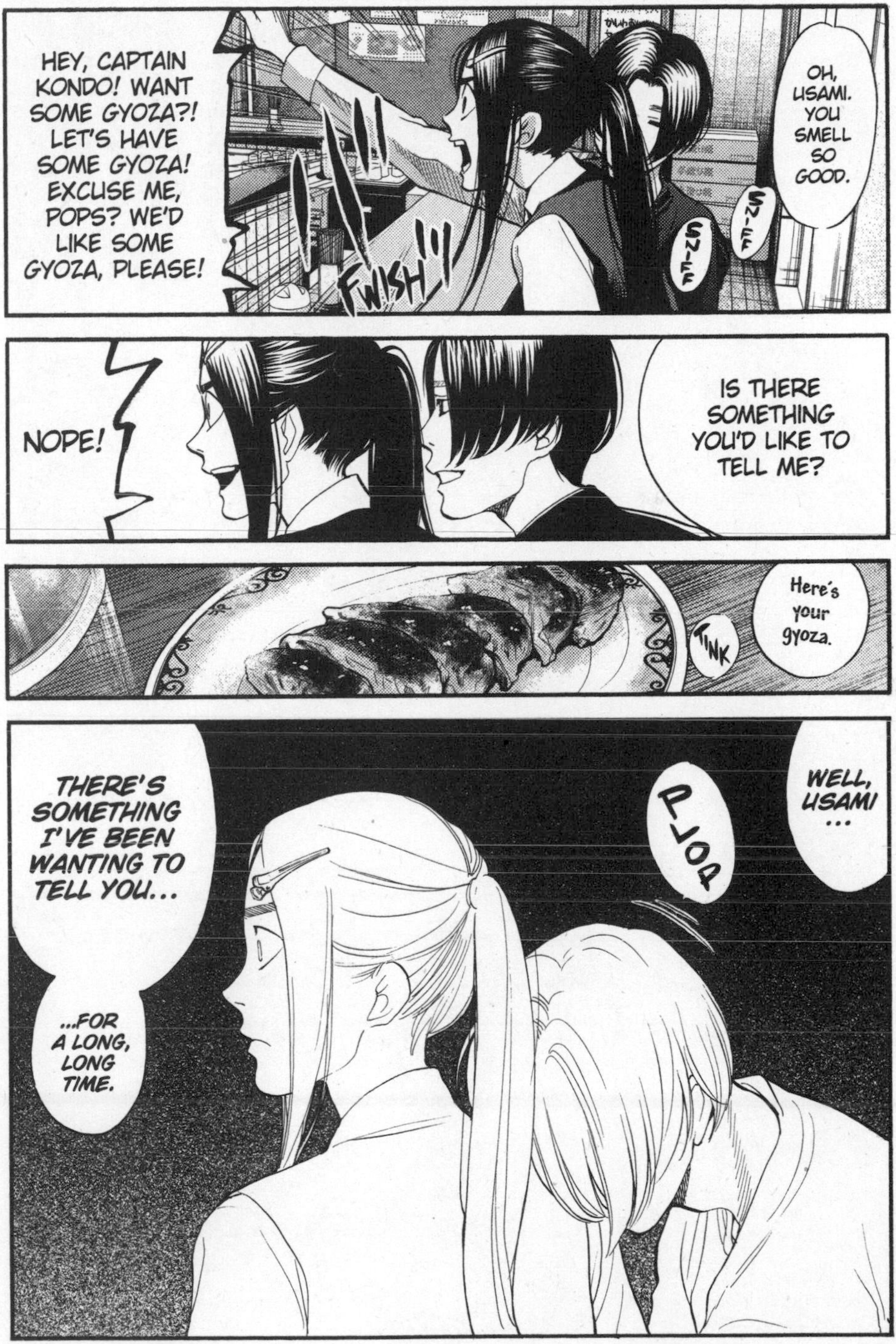
OH, USAMI. YOU SMELL SO GOOD.
SNIFF
SNIFF
FWISH
HEY, CAPTAIN KONDO! WANT SOME GYOZA?! LET'S HAVE SOME GYOZA! EXCUSE ME, POPS? WE'D LIKE SOME GYOZA, PLEASE!
IS THERE SOMETHING YOU'D LIKE TO TELL ME?
NOPE!
Here's your gyoza.
TINK
WELL, USAMI...
PLOP
THERE'S SOMETHING I'VE BEEN WANTING TO TELL YOU...
...FOR A LONG, LONG TIME.

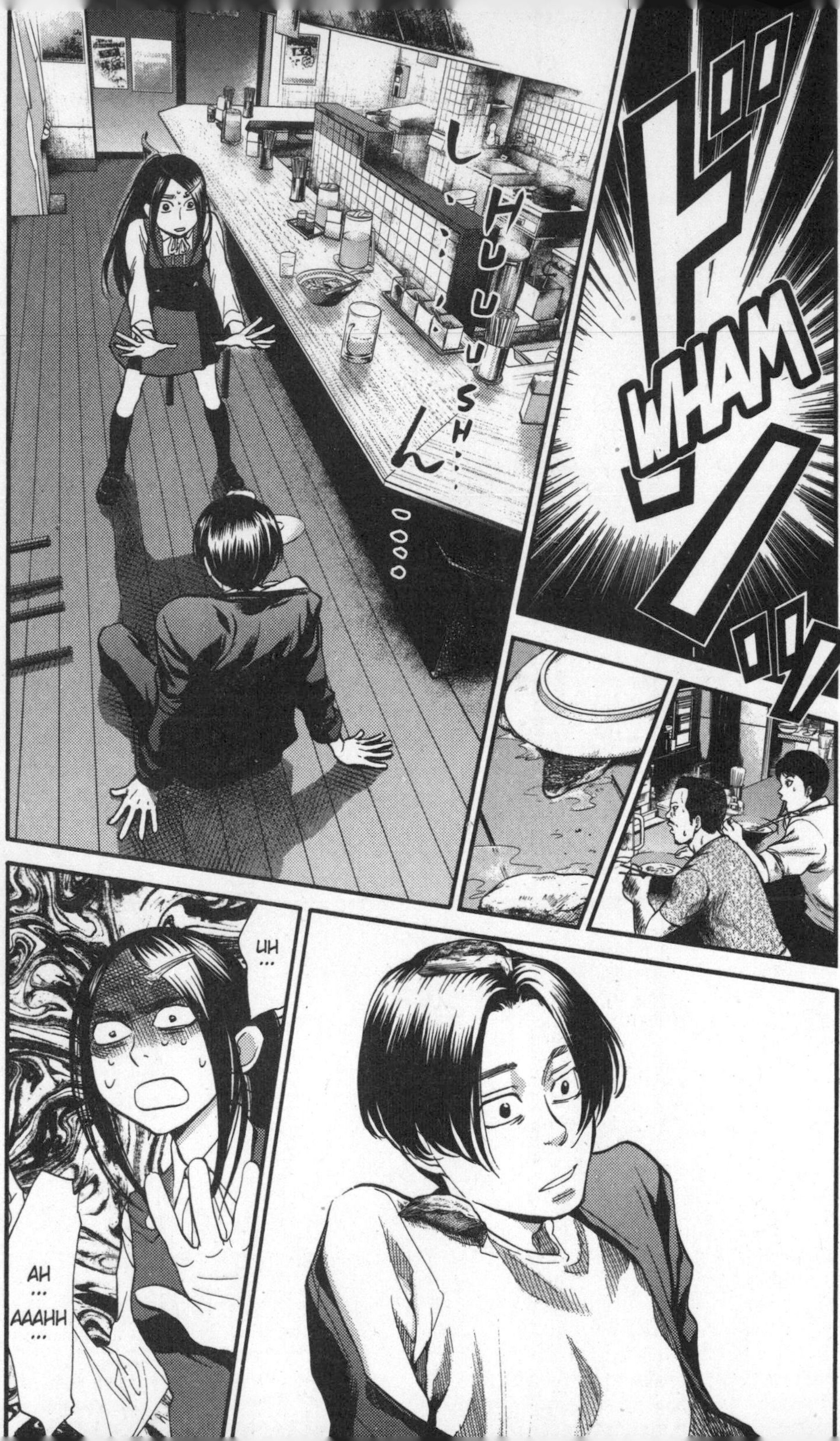
ドンッ
WHAM
しHUUUUSH...ん
UH...
AH... AAAHH...

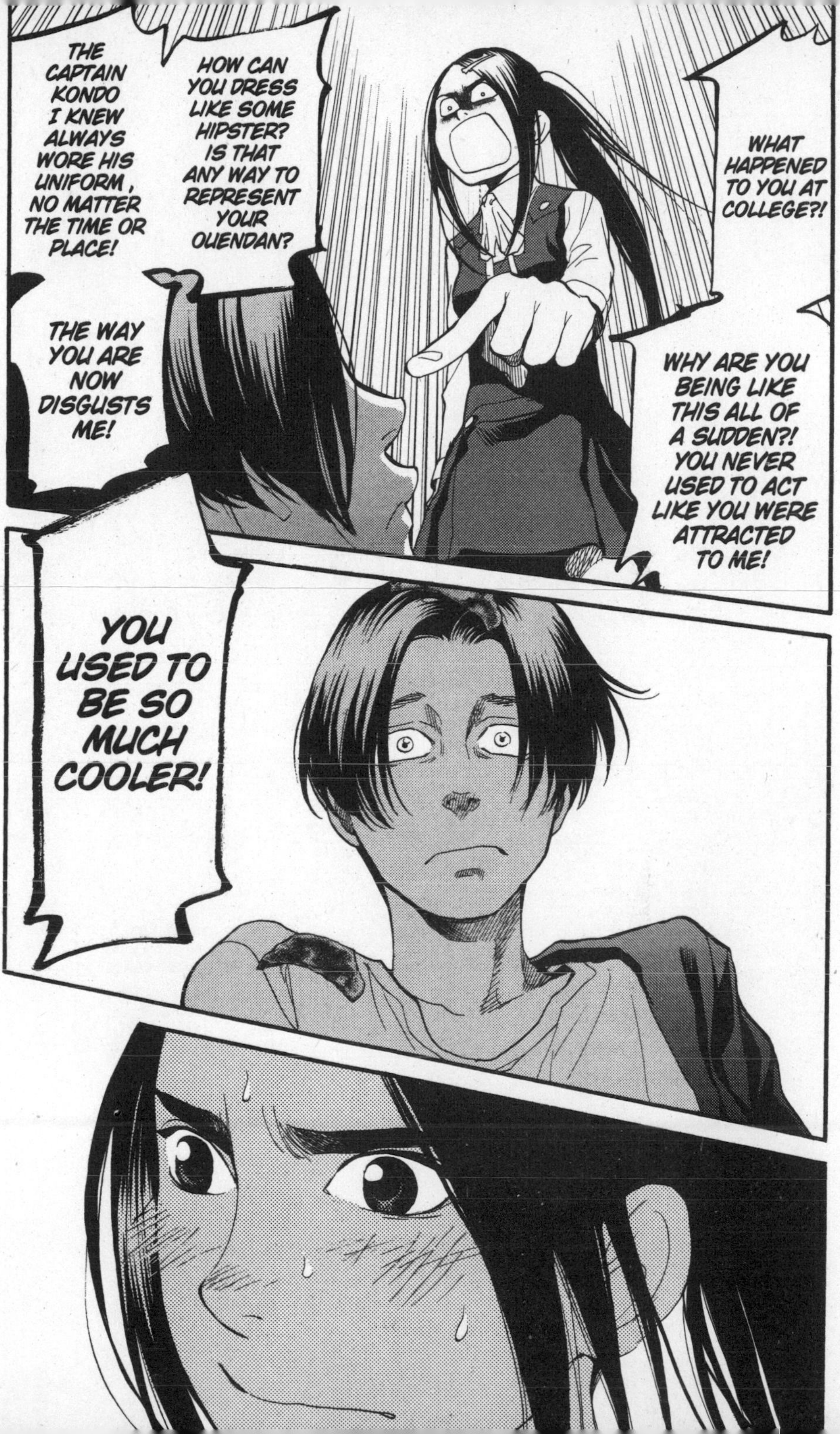
WHAT HAPPENED TO YOU AT COLLEGE?!
HOW CAN YOU DRESS LIKE SOME HIPSTER? IS THAT ANY WAY TO REPRESENT YOUR OUENDAN?
THE CAPTAIN KONDO I KNEW ALWAYS WORE HIS UNIFORM, NO MATTER THE TIME OR PLACE!
THE WAY YOU ARE NOW DISGUSTS ME!
WHY ARE YOU BEING LIKE THIS ALL OF A SUDDEN?! YOU NEVER USED TO ACT LIKE YOU WERE ATTRACTED TO ME!
YOU USED TO BE SO MUCH COOLER!

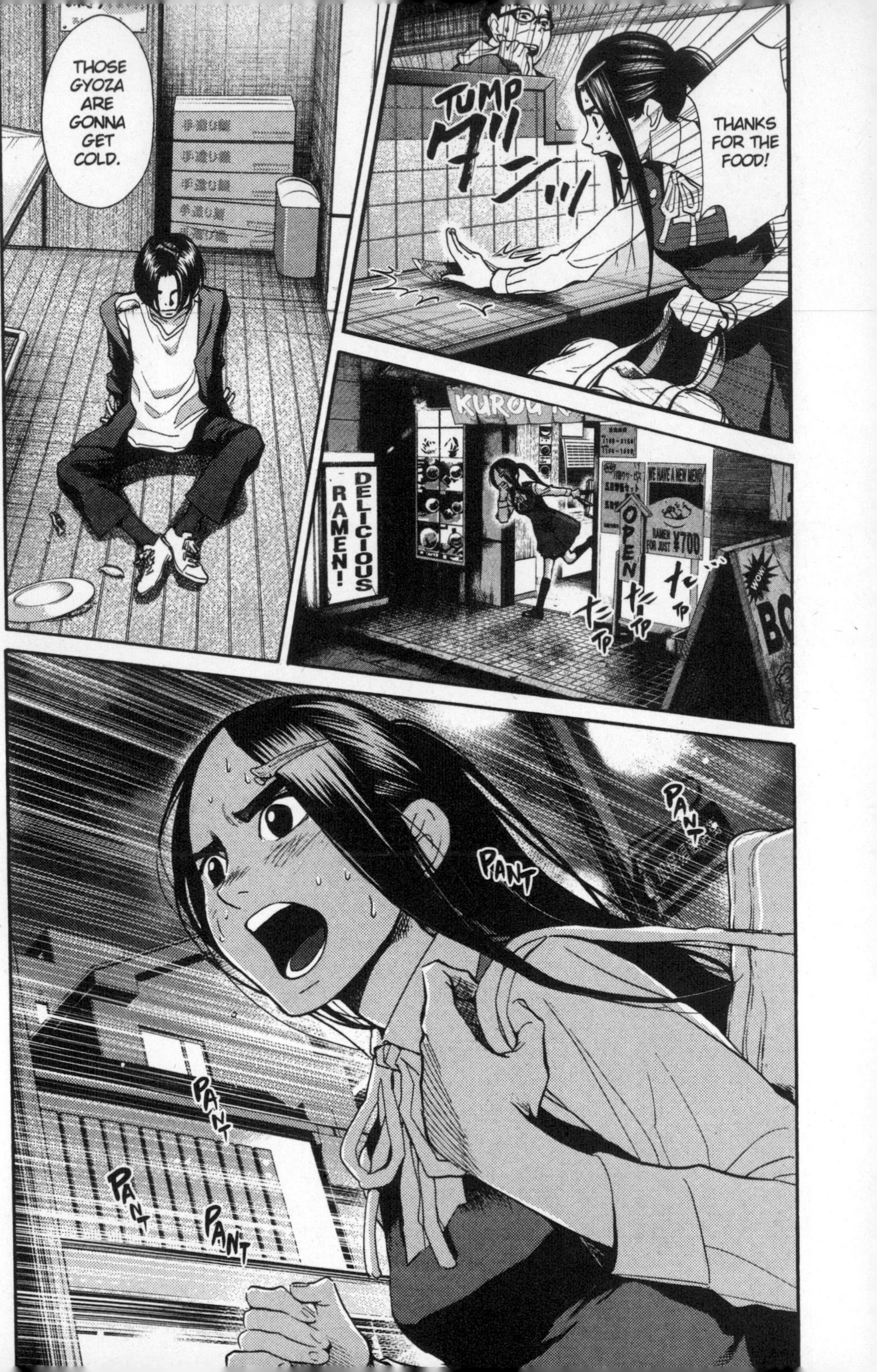
THANKS FOR THE FOOD!
TUMP
KUROU
WE HAVE A NEW MENU!
RAMEN FOR JUST ¥700
WOW!
OPEN
DELICIOUS RAMEN!
TP
TP
TP
THOSE GYOZA ARE GONNA GET COLD.
PANT
PANT
PANT
PANT
PANT

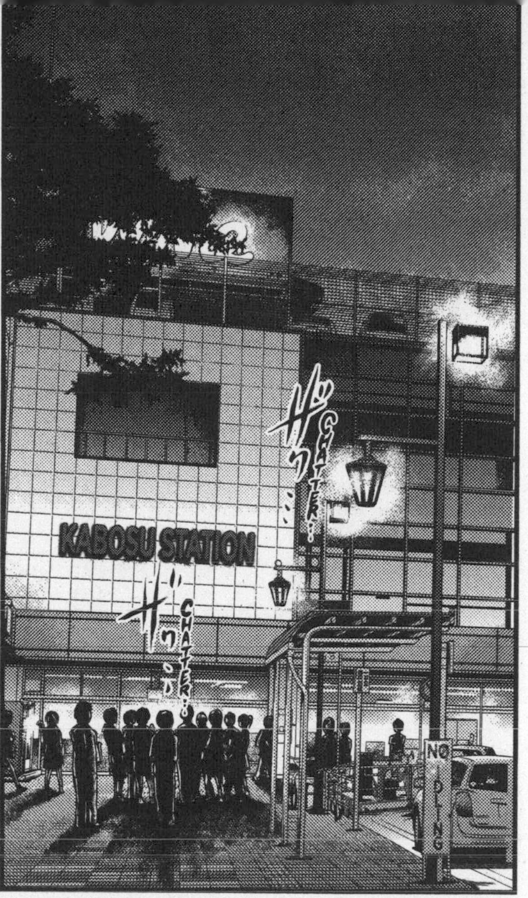

CHATTER...
KABOSU STATION
CHATTER...
NO IDLING

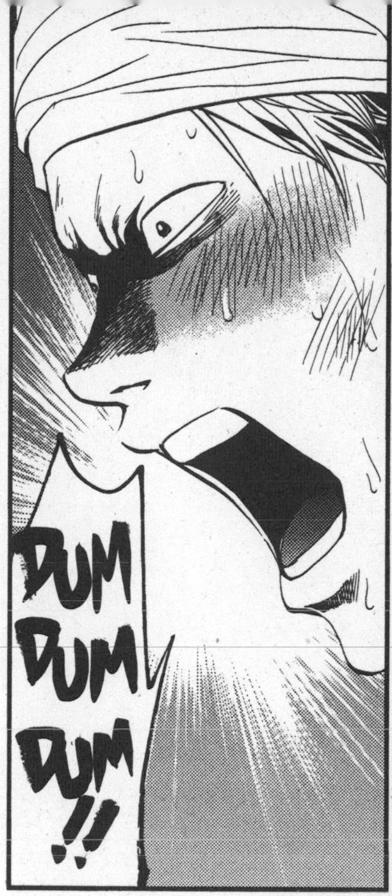

DUM DUM DUM DUM!!!

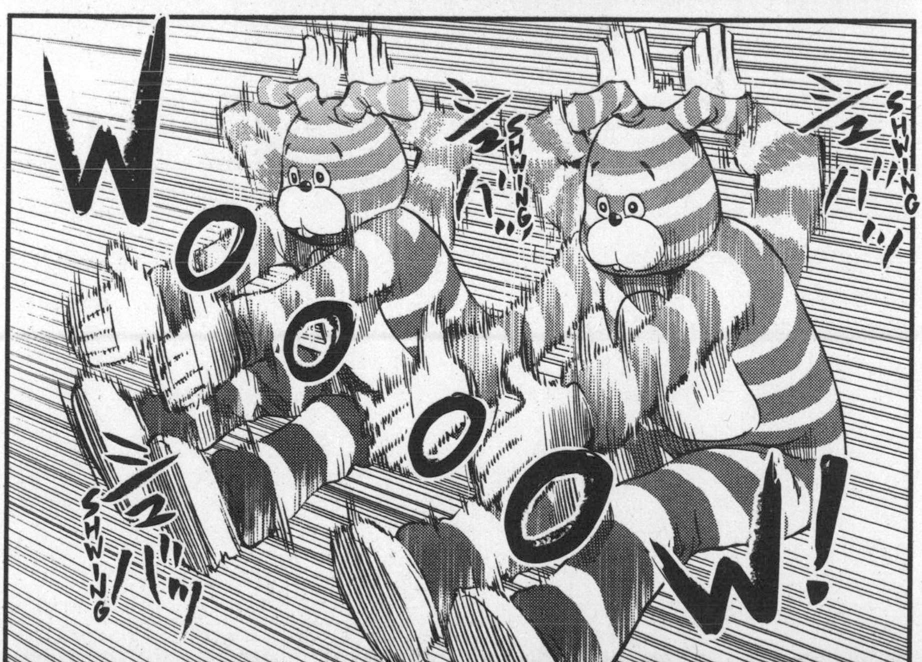

SHWING!
SHWING!
WOOOOOOOW!
SHWING!

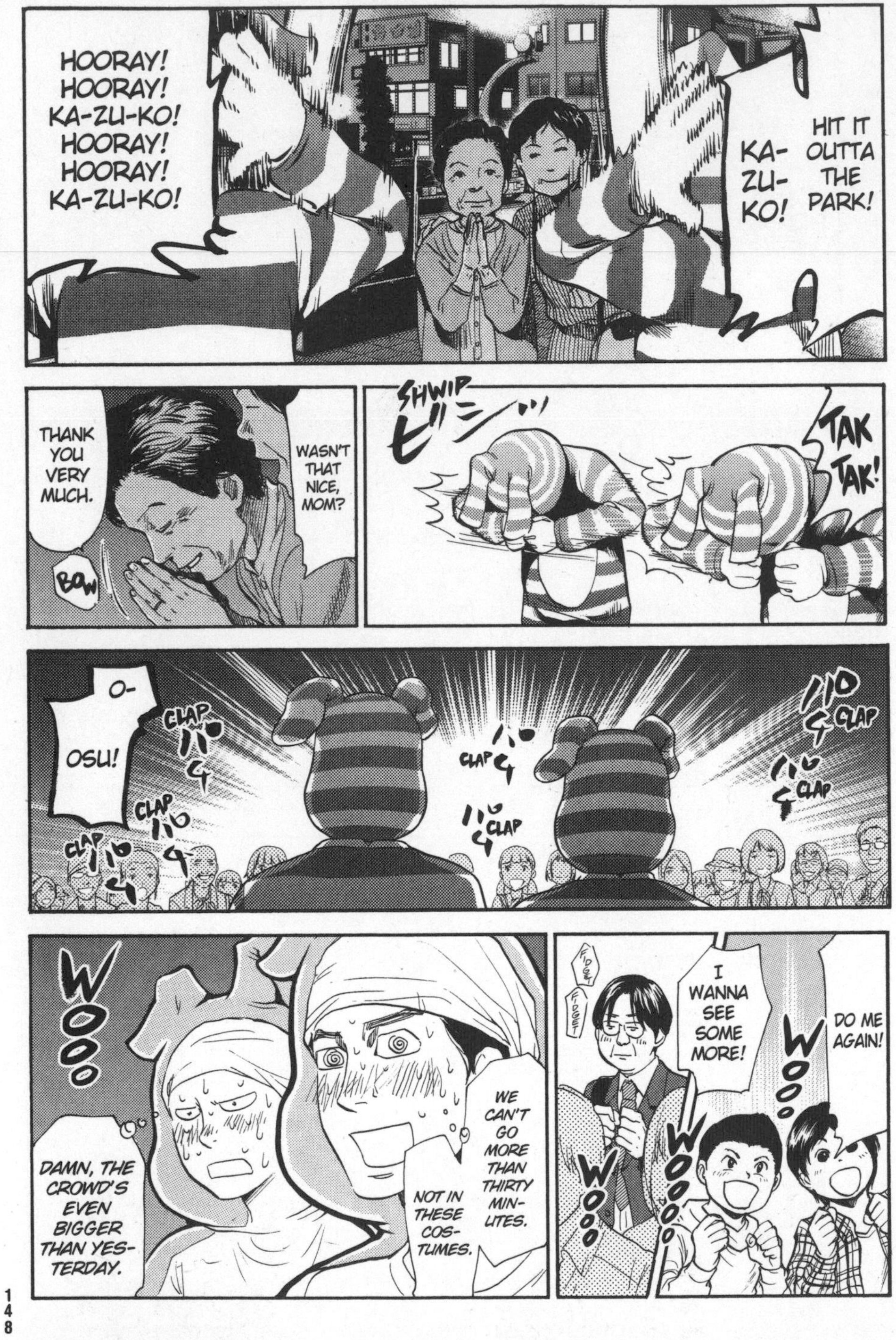
HIT IT OUTTA THE PARK!
KA-ZU-KO!
HOORAY! HOORAY! KA-ZU-KO! HOORAY! HOORAY! KA-ZU-KO!
TAK TAK!
SHWIP
WASN'T THAT NICE, MOM?
THANK YOU VERY MUCH.
BOW
CLAP
CLAP
CLAP
CLAP
CLAP
CLAP
CLAP
O-OSU!
DO ME AGAIN!
I WANNA SEE SOME MORE!
FIDGET FIDGET
WOOO
WOOO
WE CAN'T GO MORE THAN THIRTY MIN-UTES.
NOT IN THESE COS-TUMES.
DAMN, THE CROWD'S EVEN BIGGER THAN YES-TERDAY.
WOOO

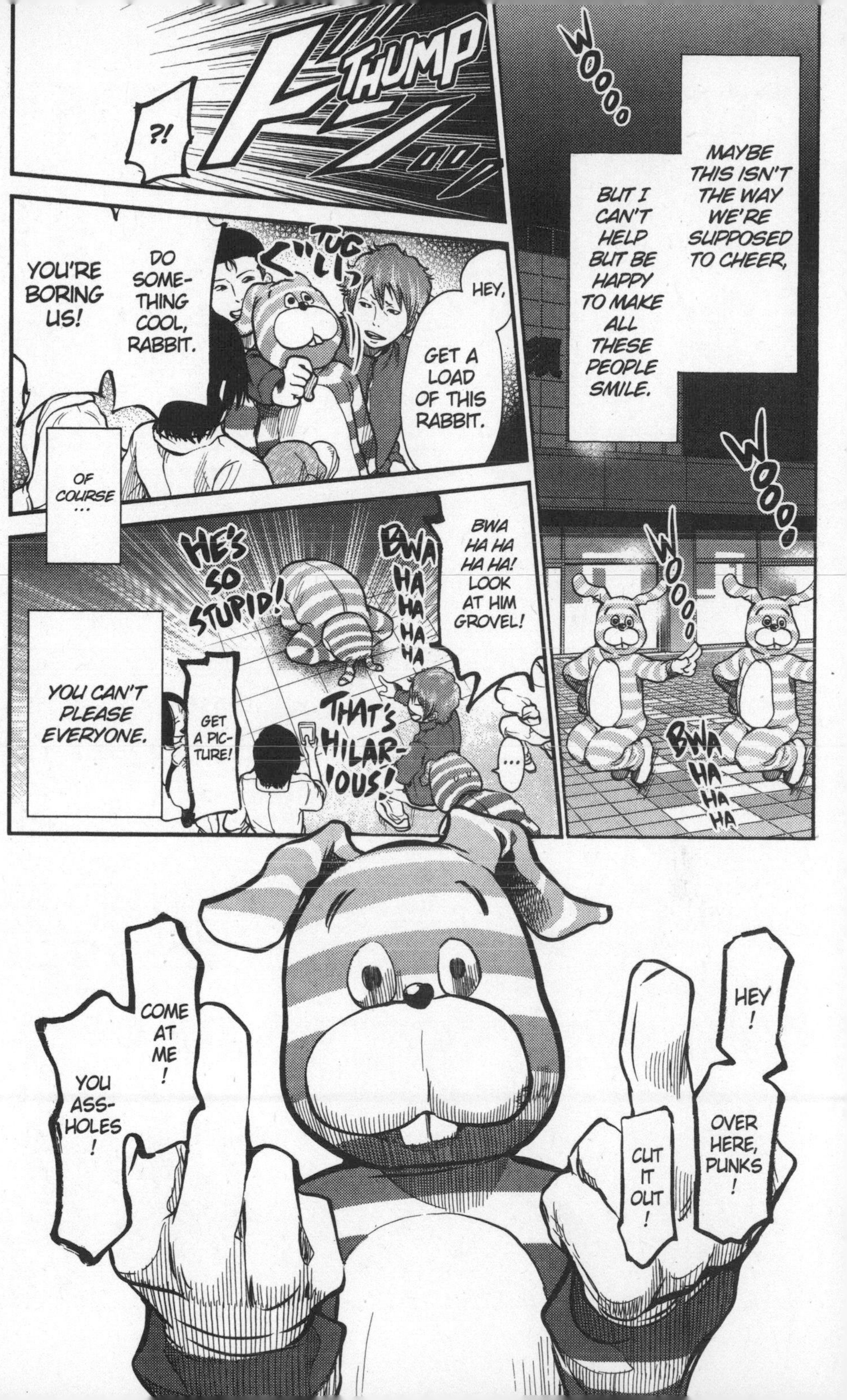
WOOOO
MAYBE THIS ISN'T THE WAY WE'RE SUPPOSED TO CHEER,
BUT I CAN'T HELP BUT BE HAPPY TO MAKE ALL THESE PEOPLE SMILE.
WOOOO
WOOOOO
BWA HA HA HA HA
THUMP
?!
HEY,
GET A LOAD OF THIS RABBIT.
TUG
DO SOME-THING COOL, RABBIT.
YOU'RE BORING US!
OF COURSE...
BWA HA HA HA HA! LOOK AT HIM GROVEL!
BWA HA HA HA HA HA
HE'S SO STUPID!
THAT'S HILAR-IOUS!
...
GET A PIC-TURE!
YOU CAN'T PLEASE EVERYONE.
HEY!
OVER HERE, PUNKS!
CUT IT OUT!
COME AT ME!
YOU ASS-HOLES!

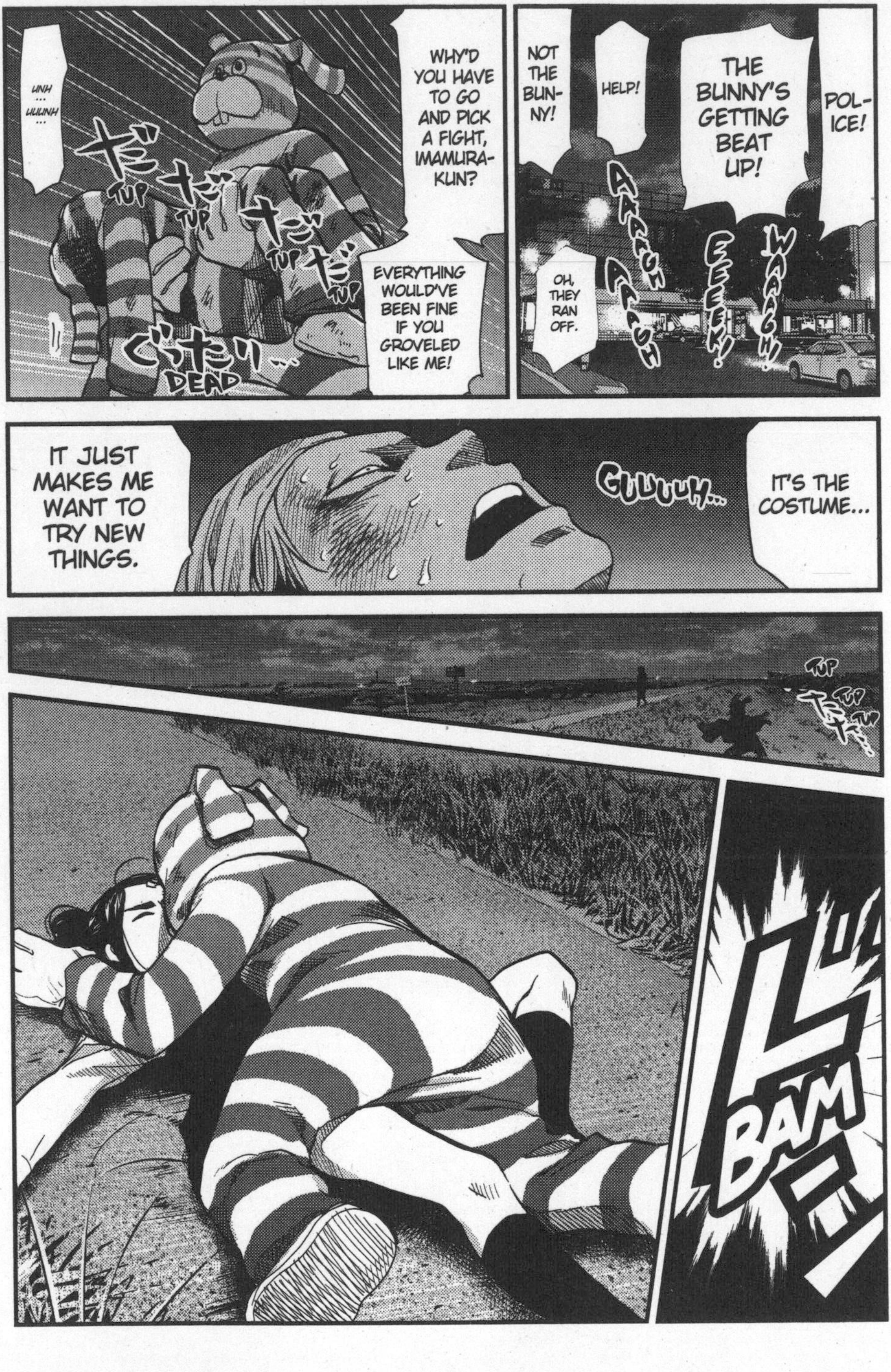
POL-ICE!
THE BUNNY'S GETTING BEAT UP!
HELP!
NOT THE BUN-NY!
WAAAGH!
EEEEEK!
AAARGH
AAAAGH
OH, THEY RAN OFF.
WHY'D YOU HAVE TO GO AND PICK A FIGHT, IMAMURA-KUN?
EVERYTHING WOULD'VE BEEN FINE IF YOU GROVELED LIKE ME!
UNH... UUUNH...
TUP
TUP
TUP
TUP
DEAD
IT'S THE COSTUME...
GUUUUH...
IT JUST MAKES ME WANT TO TRY NEW THINGS.
TUP
TUP
TUP
BAM

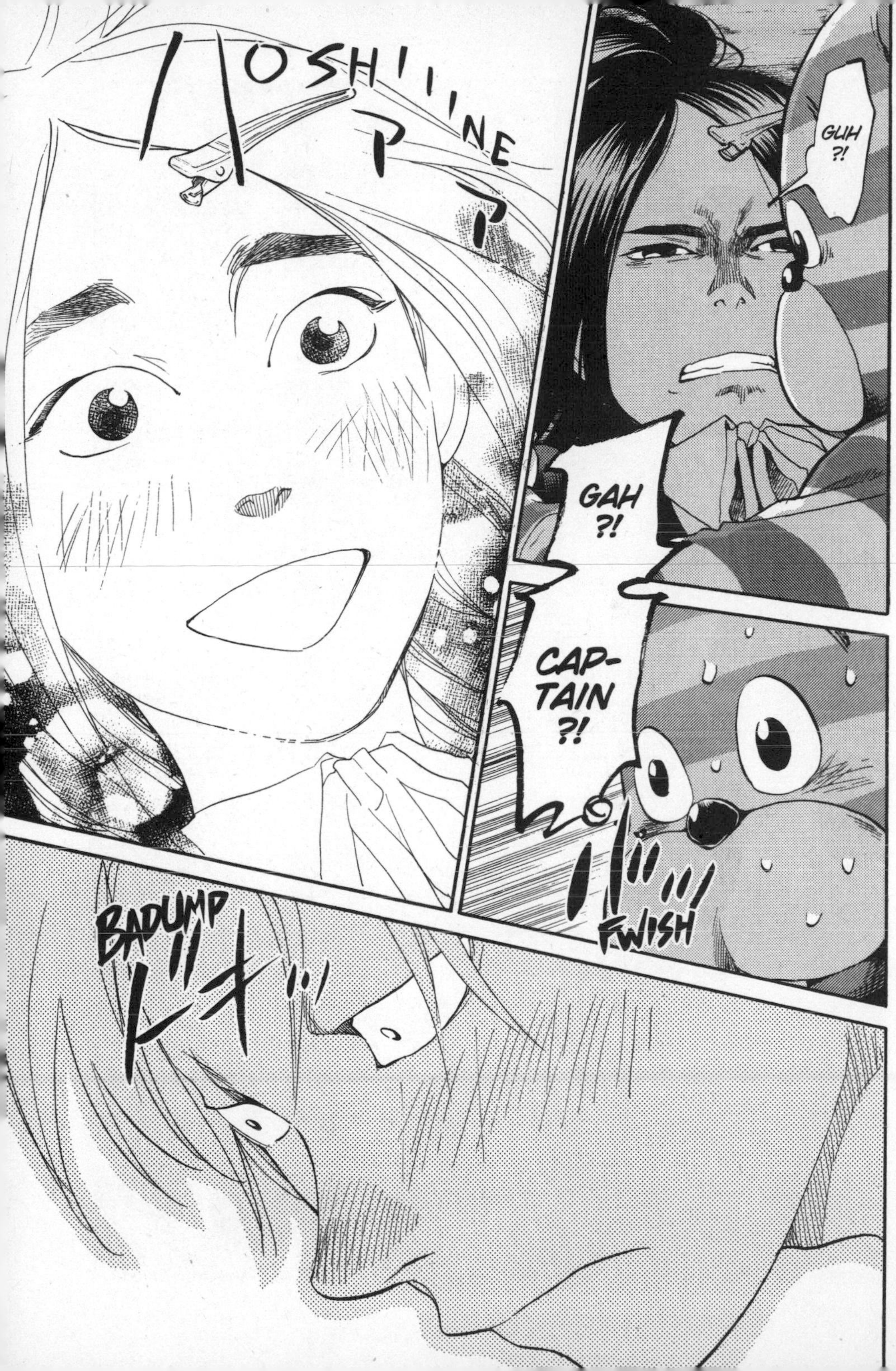
GUH ?!
GAH ?!
CAP-TAIN ?!
FWISH
HOSHIIINE
BADUMP

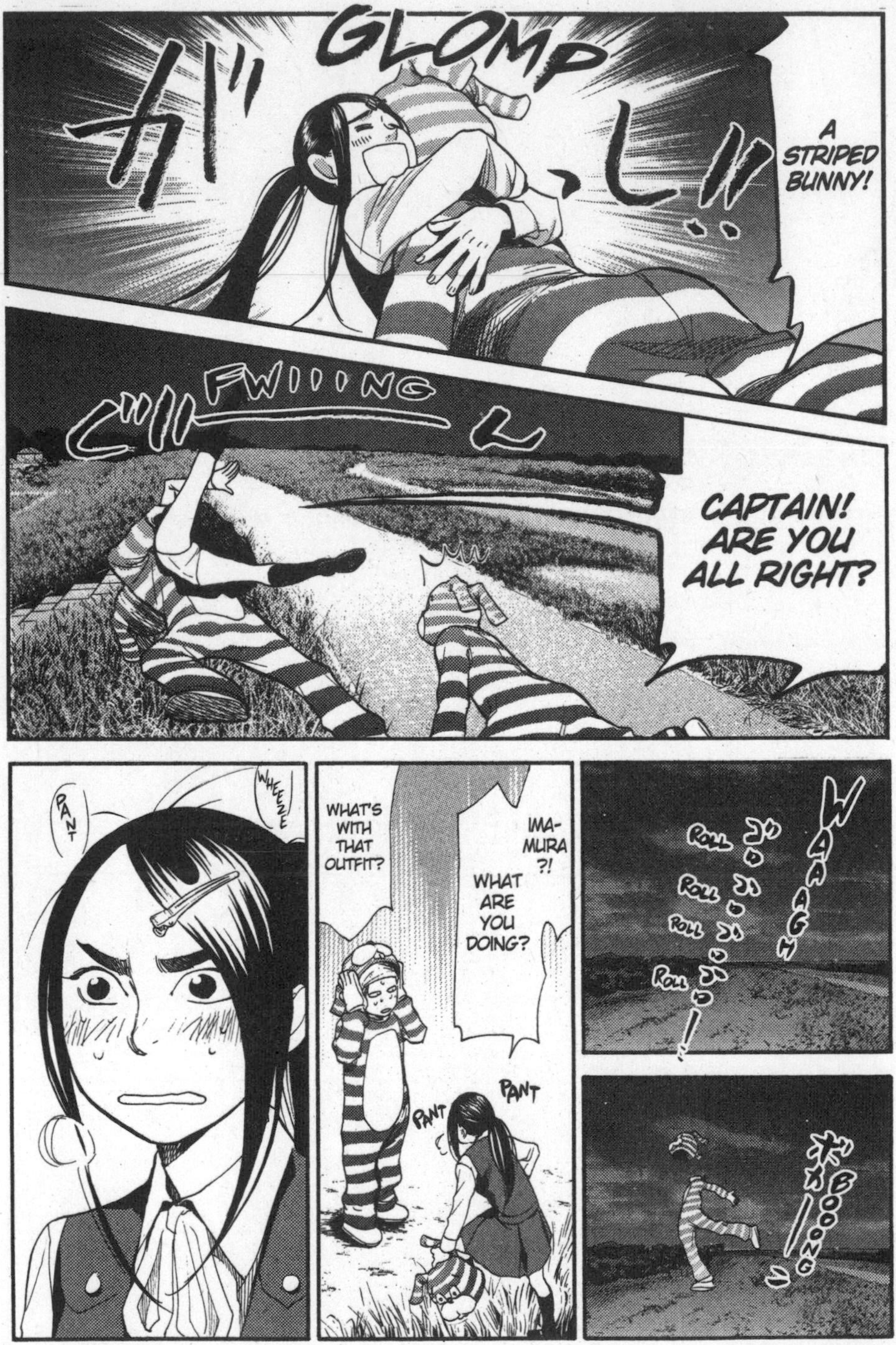
GLOMP
A STRIPED BUNNY!
FWIIING
CAPTAIN! ARE YOU ALL RIGHT?
WAAAGH
ROLL
ROLL
ROLL
ROLL
BOOOONG
IMAMURA?!
WHAT ARE YOU DOING?
WHAT'S WITH THAT OUTFIT?
PANT
PANT
WHEEZE
PANT

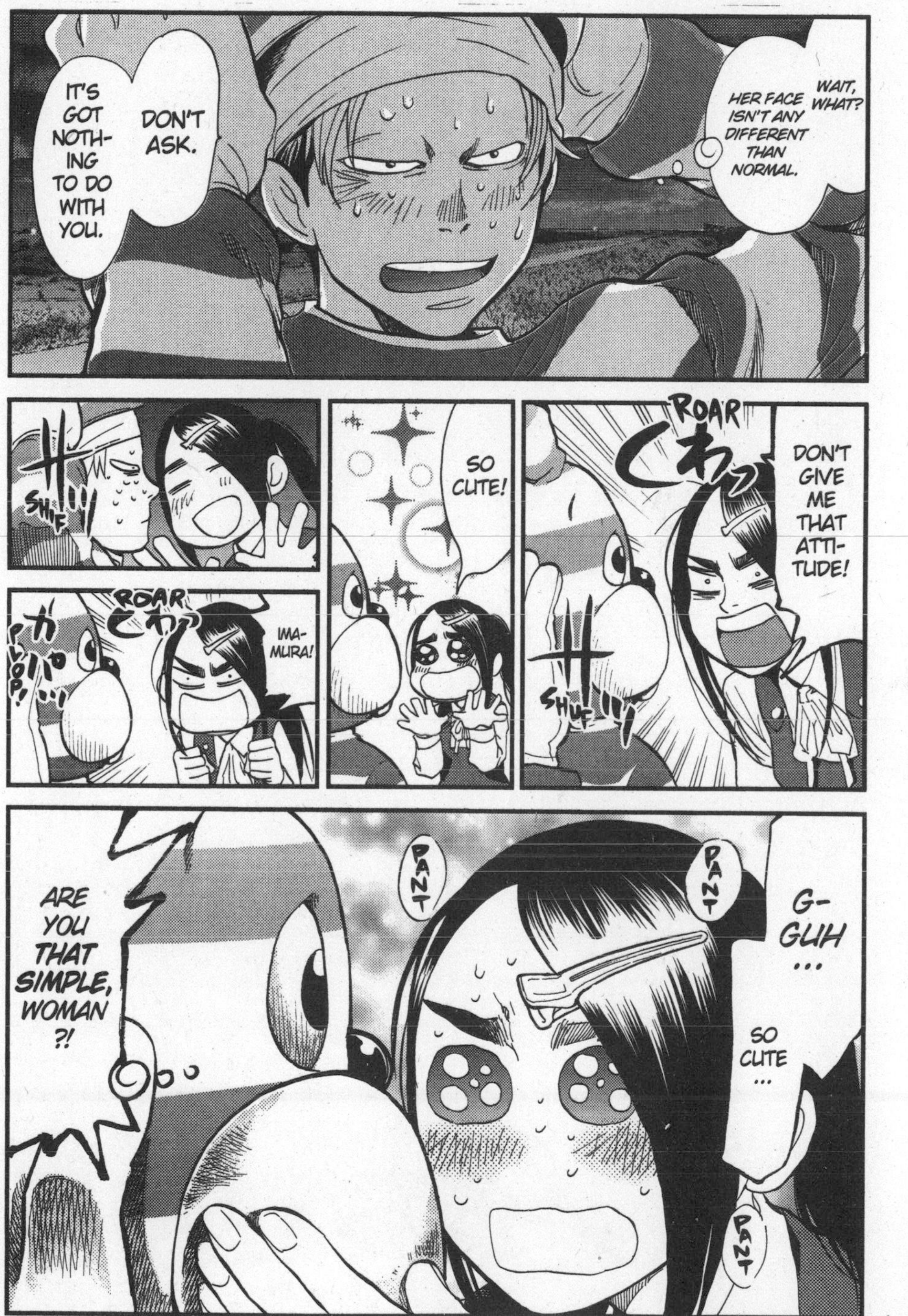
WAIT, WHAT?
HER FACE ISN'T ANY DIFFERENT THAN NORMAL.
DON'T ASK.
IT'S GOT NOTHING TO DO WITH YOU.
ROAR
くわっ
DON'T GIVE ME THAT ATTITUDE!
SHUF
SO CUTE!
SHUF
ROAR
くわっ
IMAMURA!
PLOP!
PANT
G-GUH...
SO CUTE...
PANT
PANT
ARE YOU THAT SIMPLE, WOMAN?!

Again!!

アゲイン!!

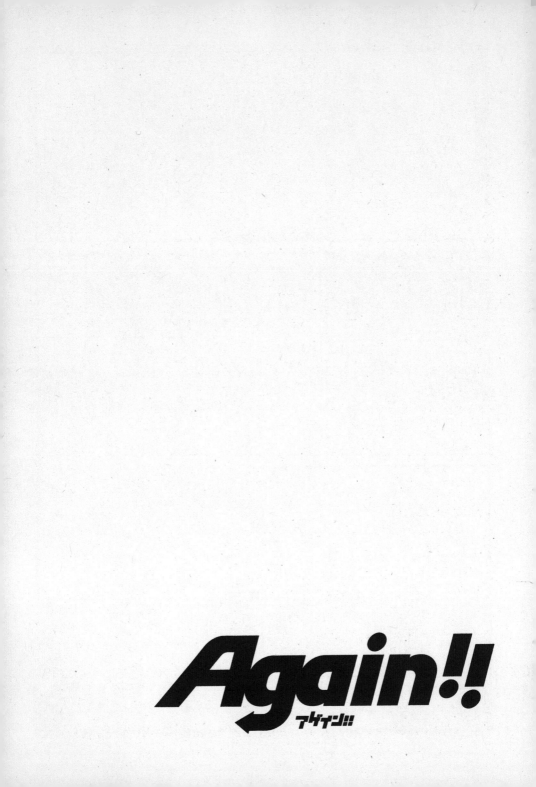

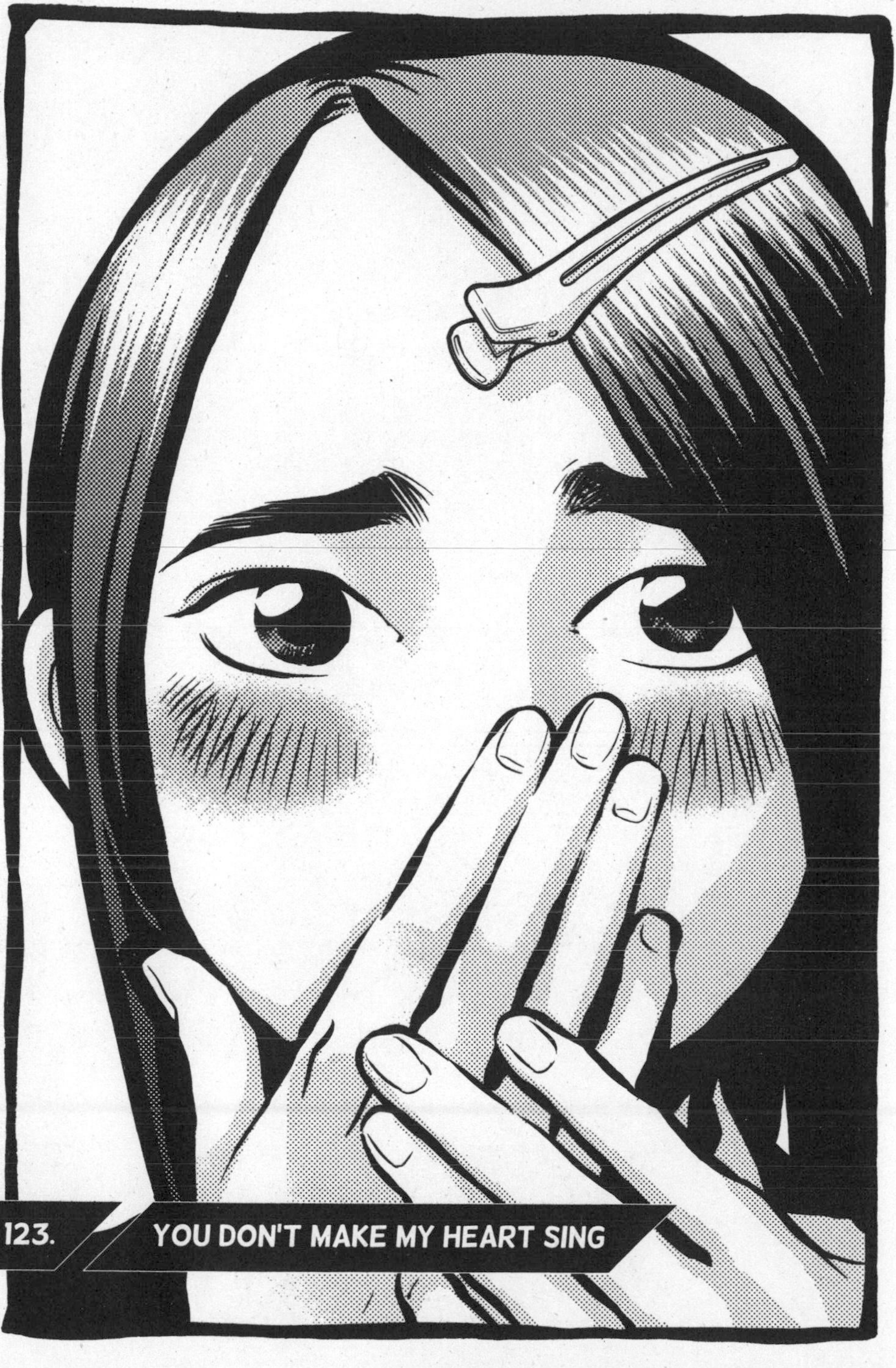

123. YOU DON'T MAKE MY HEART SING

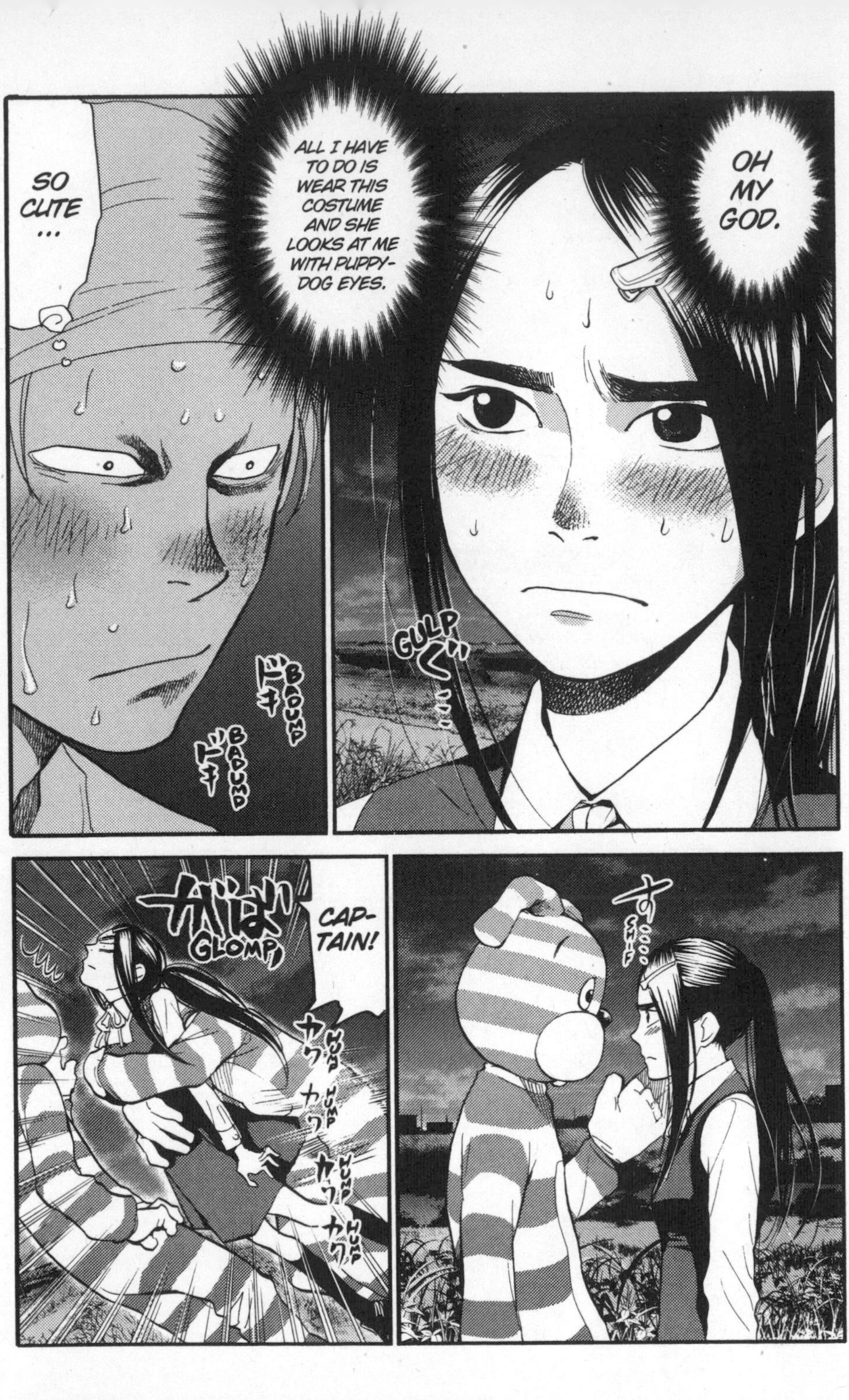
OH MY GOD.
ALL I HAVE TO DO IS WEAR THIS COSTUME AND SHE LOOKS AT ME WITH PUPPY-DOG EYES.
GULP
ぐ…
SO CUTE…
ドキ BADUMP
ドキ BADUMP
す… SNIF
CAP-TAIN!
がばっ GLOMP
カク HUMP
カク HUMP
カク HUMP
カク HUMP

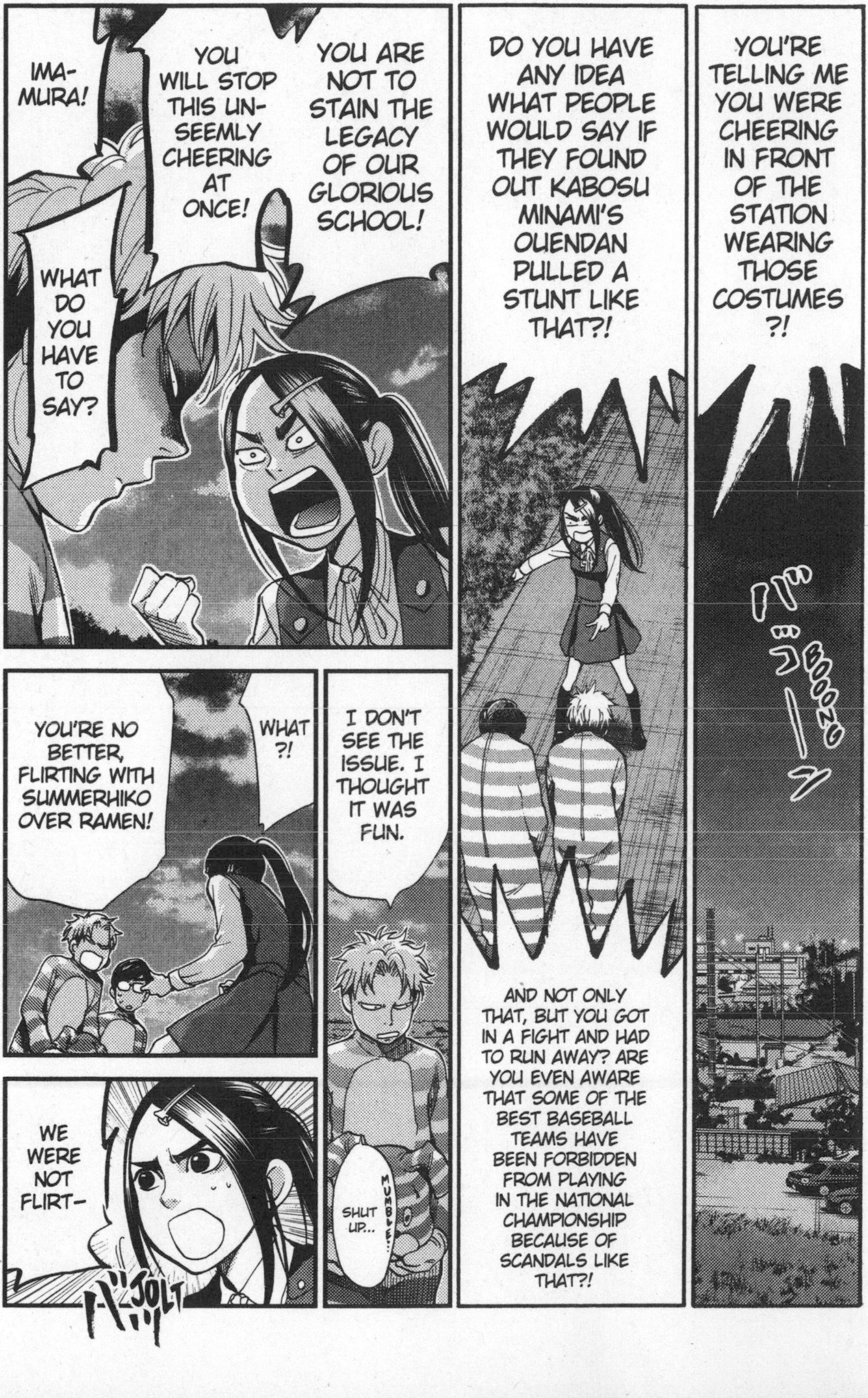
YOU'RE TELLING ME YOU WERE CHEERING IN FRONT OF THE STATION WEARING THOSE COSTUMES ?!
BOOONG
DO YOU HAVE ANY IDEA WHAT PEOPLE WOULD SAY IF THEY FOUND OUT KABOSU MINAMI'S OUENDAN PULLED A STUNT LIKE THAT?!
AND NOT ONLY THAT, BUT YOU GOT IN A FIGHT AND HAD TO RUN AWAY? ARE YOU EVEN AWARE THAT SOME OF THE BEST BASEBALL TEAMS HAVE BEEN FORBIDDEN FROM PLAYING IN THE NATIONAL CHAMPIONSHIP BECAUSE OF SCANDALS LIKE THAT?!
YOU ARE NOT TO STAIN THE LEGACY OF OUR GLORIOUS SCHOOL!
YOU WILL STOP THIS UN-SEEMLY CHEERING AT ONCE!
IMA-MURA!
WHAT DO YOU HAVE TO SAY?
I DON'T SEE THE ISSUE. I THOUGHT IT WAS FUN.
MUMBLE...
SHUT UP...
WHAT ?!
YOU'RE NO BETTER, FLIRTING WITH SUMMERHIKO OVER RAMEN!
WE WERE NOT FLIRT-
JOLT

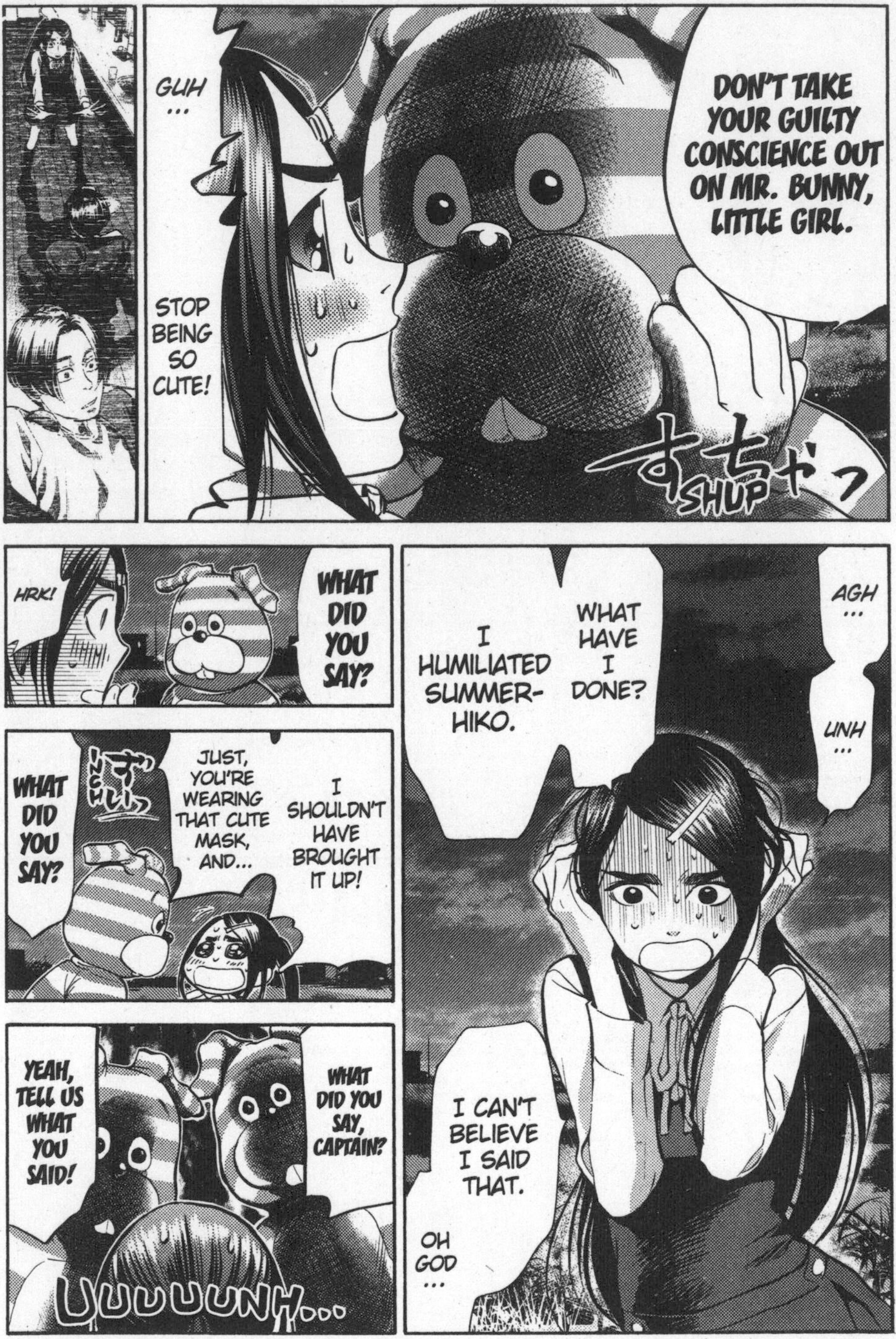
DON'T TAKE YOUR GUILTY CONSCIENCE OUT ON MR. BUNNY, LITTLE GIRL.
GUH ...
STOP BEING SO CUTE!
SHUP
AGH ...
WHAT HAVE I DONE?
I HUMILIATED SUMMER-HIKO.
UNH ...
I CAN'T BELIEVE I SAID THAT.
OH GOD ...
WHAT DID YOU SAY?
HRK!
I SHOULDN'T HAVE BROUGHT IT UP!
JUST, YOU'RE WEARING THAT CUTE MASK, AND...
INCH
WHAT DID YOU SAY?
WHAT DID YOU SAY, CAPTAIN?
YEAH, TELL US WHAT YOU SAID!
UUUUUNH...

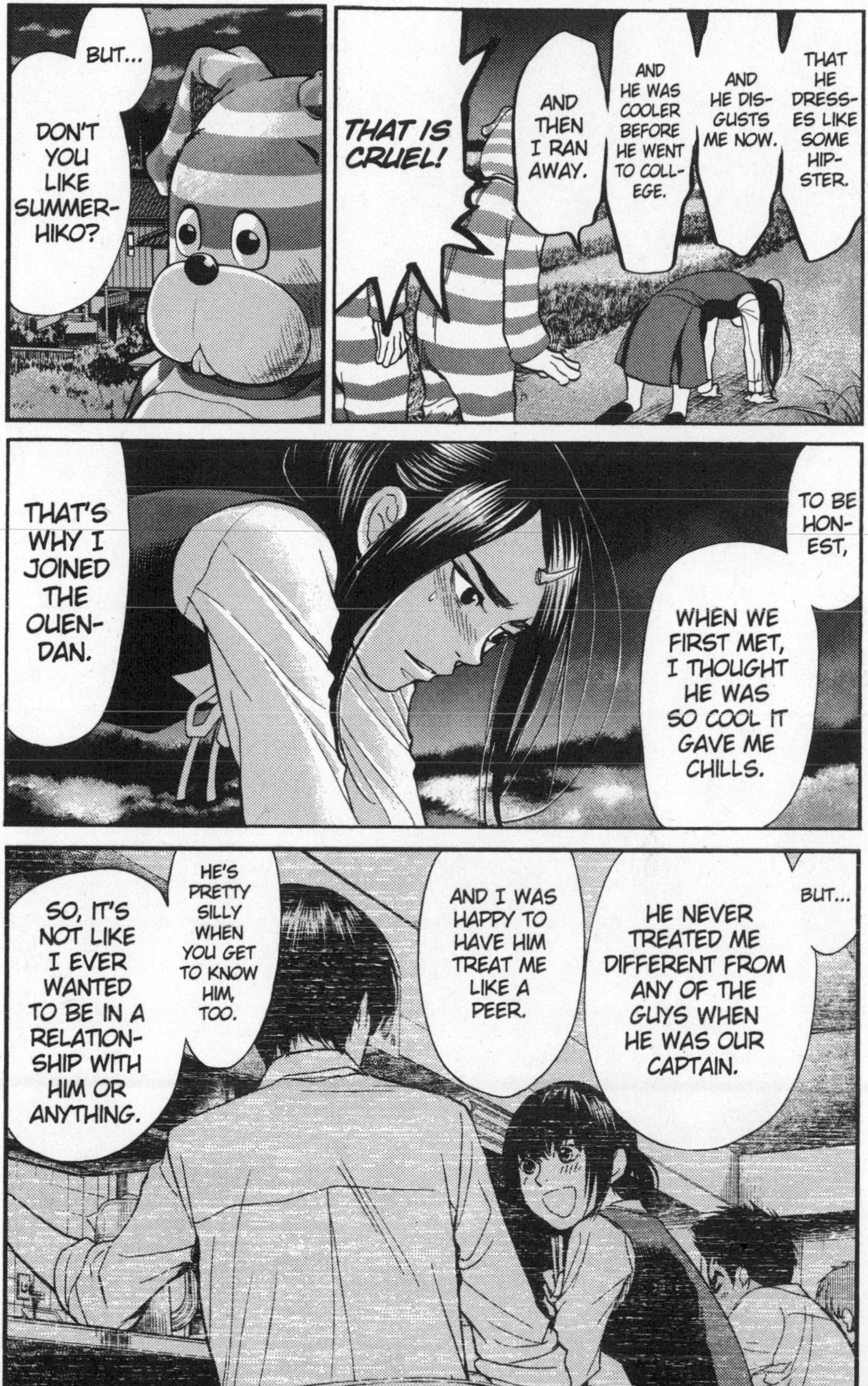
THAT HE DRESS-ES LIKE SOME HIP-STER.
AND HE DIS-GUSTS ME NOW.
AND HE WAS COOLER BEFORE HE WENT TO COLL-EGE.
AND THEN I RAN AWAY.
THAT IS CRUEL!
BUT...
DON'T YOU LIKE SUMMER-HIKO?
TO BE HON-EST,
WHEN WE FIRST MET, I THOUGHT HE WAS SO COOL IT GAVE ME CHILLS.
THAT'S WHY I JOINED THE OUEN-DAN.
BUT...
HE NEVER TREATED ME DIFFERENT FROM ANY OF THE GUYS WHEN HE WAS OUR CAPTAIN.
AND I WAS HAPPY TO HAVE HIM TREAT ME LIKE A PEER.
HE'S PRETTY SILLY WHEN YOU GET TO KNOW HIM, TOO.
SO, IT'S NOT LIKE I EVER WANTED TO BE IN A RELATION-SHIP WITH HIM OR ANYTHING.

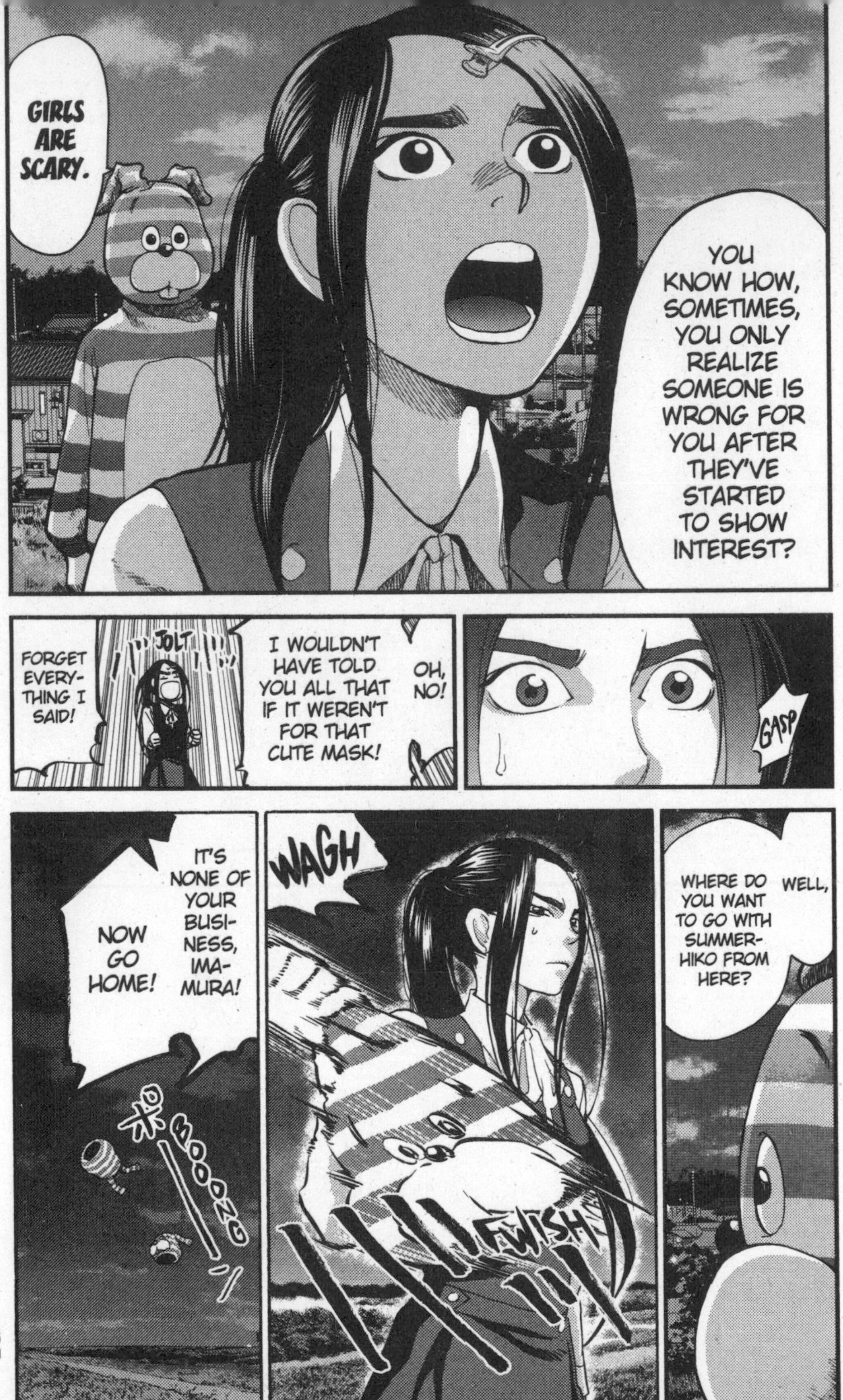
YOU KNOW HOW, SOMETIMES, YOU ONLY REALIZE SOMEONE IS WRONG FOR YOU AFTER THEY'VE STARTED TO SHOW INTEREST?
GIRLS ARE SCARY.
GASP
OH, NO!
I WOULDN'T HAVE TOLD YOU ALL THAT IF IT WEREN'T FOR THAT CUTE MASK!
JOLT
FORGET EVERYTHING I SAID!
WELL,
WHERE DO YOU WANT TO GO WITH SUMMERHIKO FROM HERE?
WAGH
FWISH
IT'S NONE OF YOUR BUSINESS, IMAMURA!
NOW GO HOME!
WOOONG

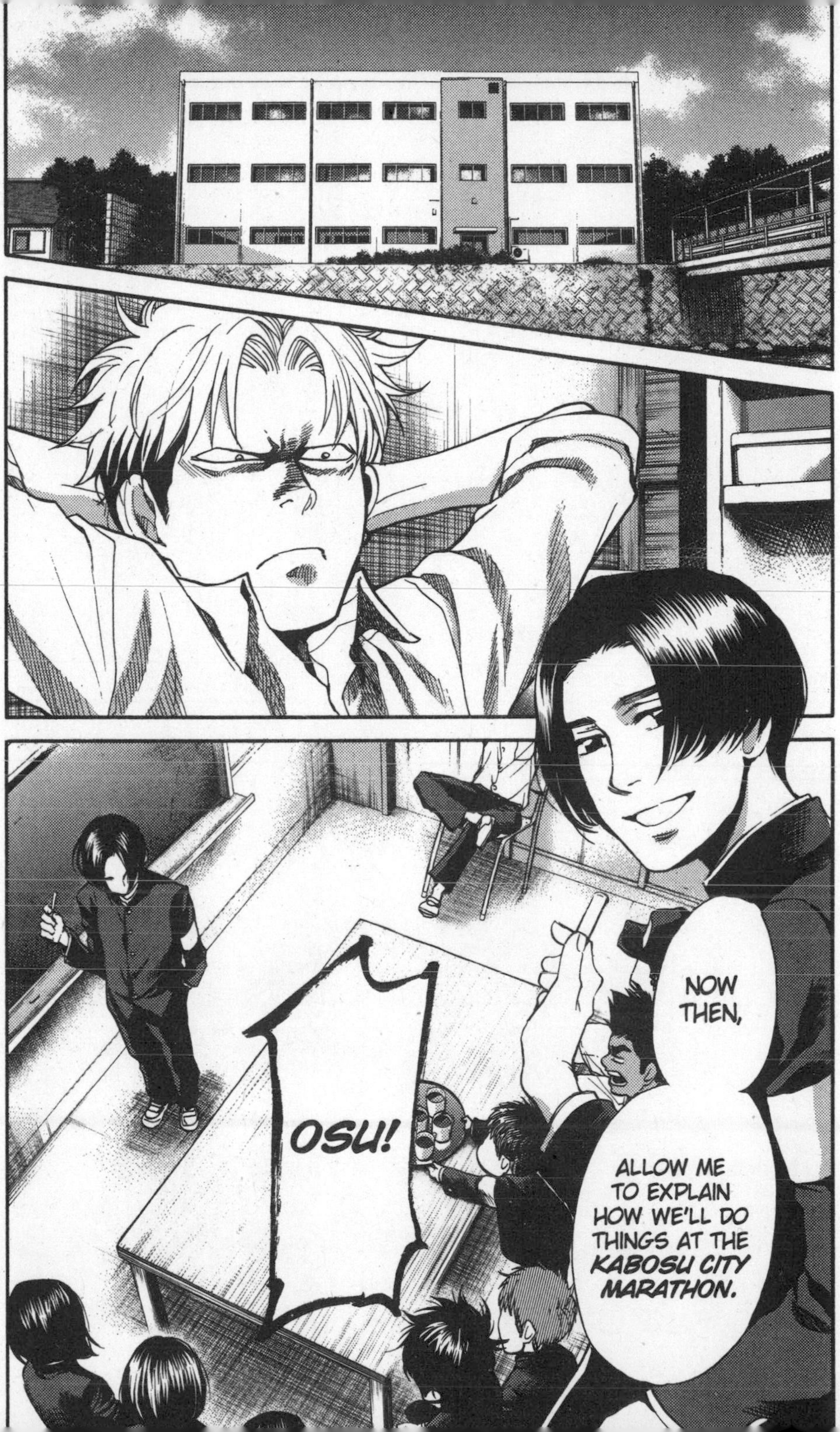
NOW THEN,
ALLOW ME TO EXPLAIN HOW WE'LL DO THINGS AT THE *KABOSU CITY MARATHON.*
OSU!

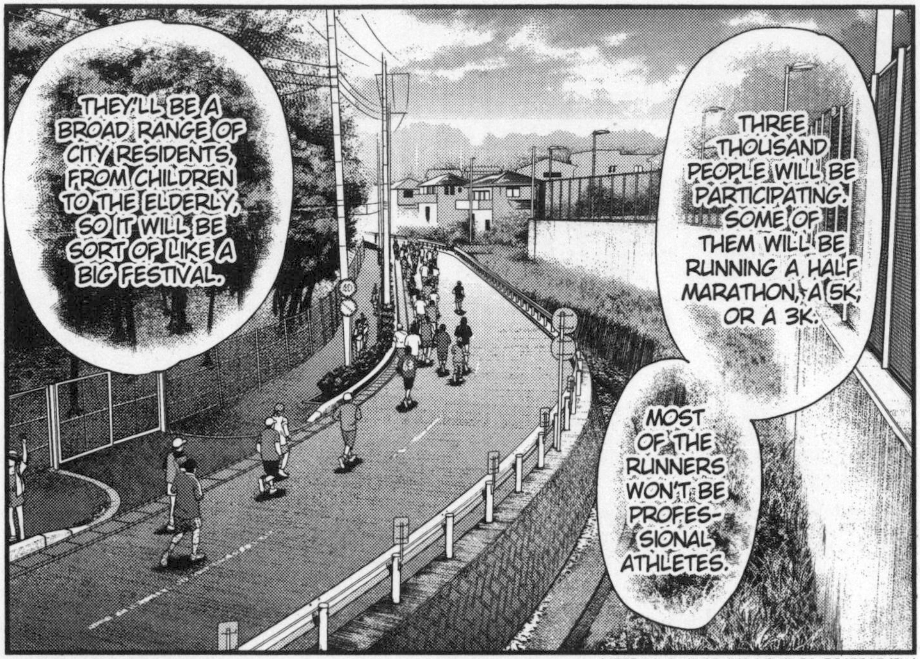
THREE THOUSAND PEOPLE WILL BE PARTICIPATING. SOME OF THEM WILL BE RUNNING A HALF MARATHON, A 5K, OR A 3K.
MOST OF THE RUNNERS WON'T BE PROFES-SIONAL ATHLETES.
THEY'LL BE A BROAD RANGE OF CITY RESIDENTS, FROM CHILDREN TO THE ELDERLY, SO IT WILL BE SORT OF LIKE A BIG FESTIVAL.
*APPROX. 3 MILES AND 1.8 MILES, RESPECTIVELY.

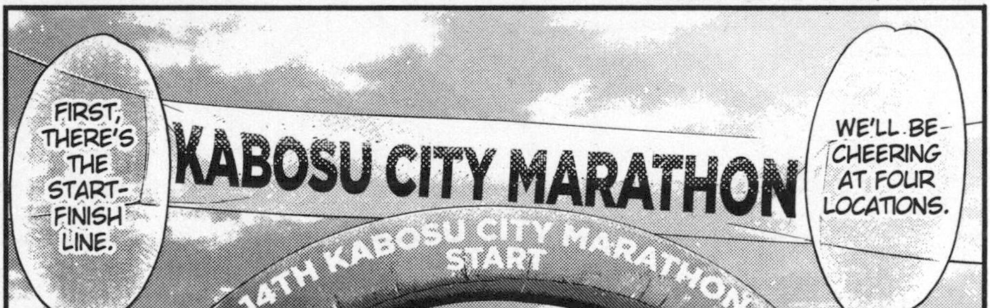
WE'LL BE CHEERING AT FOUR LOCATIONS.
KABOSU CITY MARATHON
14TH KABOSU CITY MARATHON START
FIRST, THERE'S THE START-FINISH LINE.

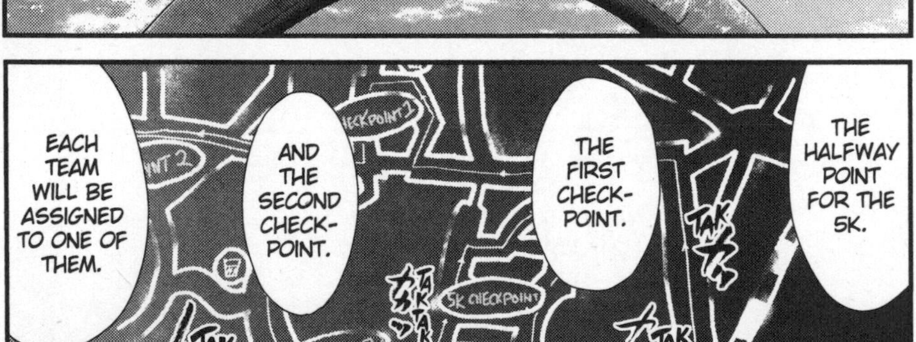
THE HALFWAY POINT FOR THE 5K.
TAK
TAK
THE FIRST CHECK-POINT.
5K CHECKPOINT
TAK TAK
AND THE SECOND CHECK-POINT.
CHECKPOINT 3
TAK
EACH TEAM WILL BE ASSIGNED TO ONE OF THEM.

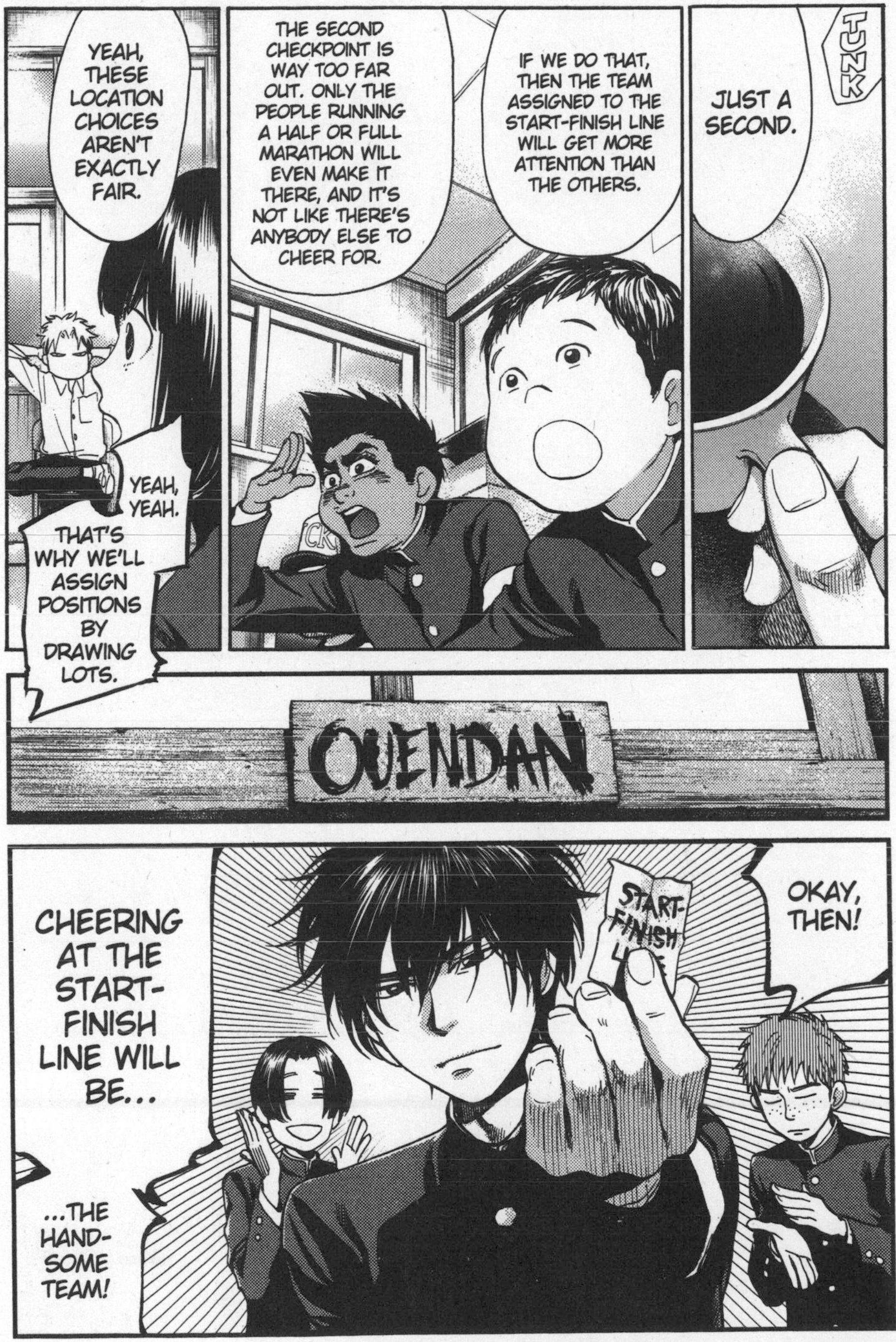
TUNK
JUST A SECOND.
IF WE DO THAT, THEN THE TEAM ASSIGNED TO THE START-FINISH LINE WILL GET MORE ATTENTION THAN THE OTHERS.
THE SECOND CHECKPOINT IS WAY TOO FAR OUT. ONLY THE PEOPLE RUNNING A HALF OR FULL MARATHON WILL EVEN MAKE IT THERE, AND IT'S NOT LIKE THERE'S ANYBODY ELSE TO CHEER FOR.
YEAH, THESE LOCATION CHOICES AREN'T EXACTLY FAIR.
YEAH, YEAH.
THAT'S WHY WE'LL ASSIGN POSITIONS BY DRAWING LOTS.
OUENDAN
OKAY, THEN!
START-FINISH
CHEERING AT THE START-FINISH LINE WILL BE...
...THE HANDSOME TEAM!

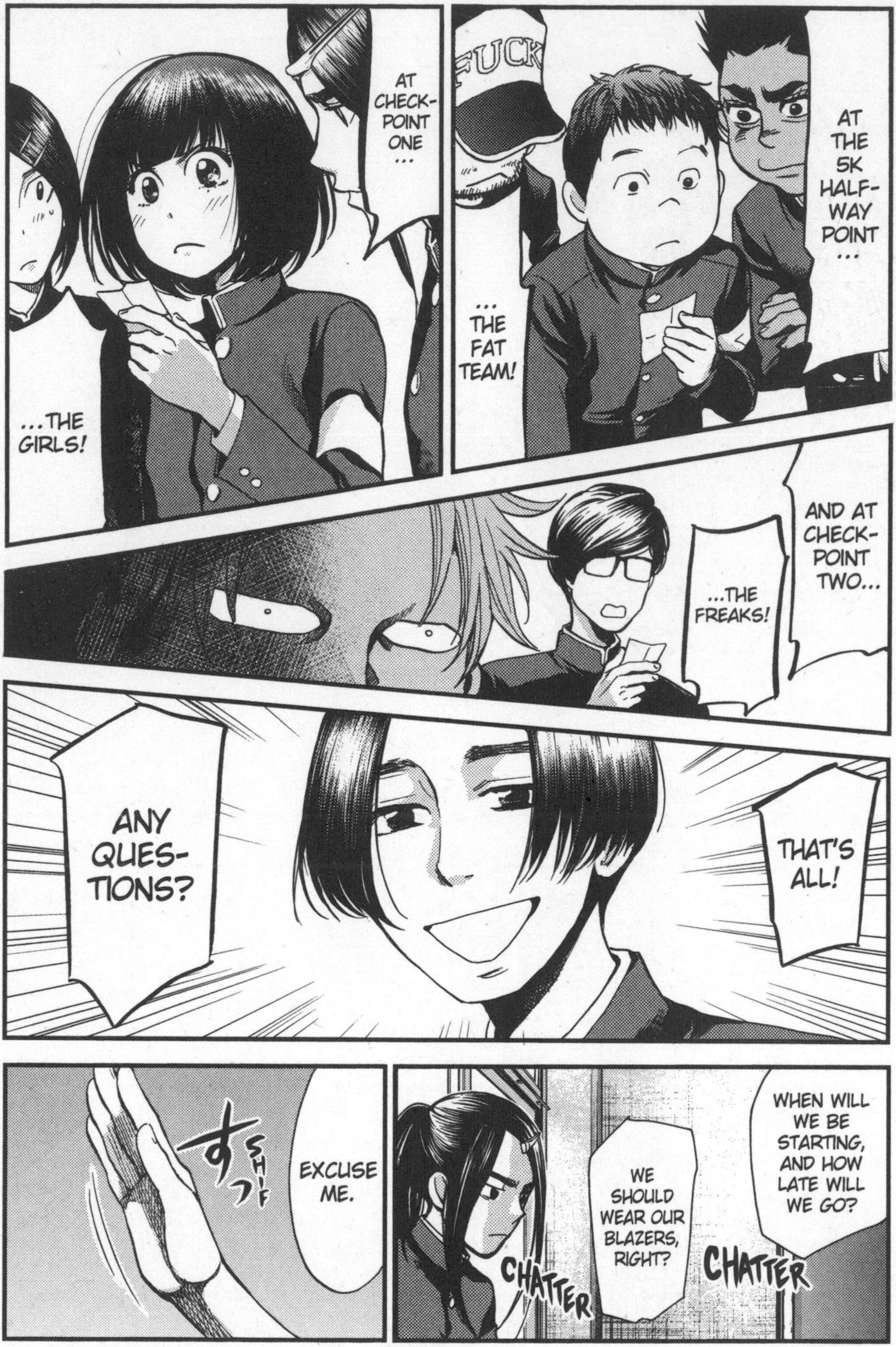
FUCK
AT THE 5K HALF-WAY POINT...
...THE FAT TEAM!
AT CHECK-POINT ONE...
...THE GIRLS!
AND AT CHECK-POINT TWO...
...THE FREAKS!
THAT'S ALL!
ANY QUES-TIONS?
WHEN WILL WE BE STARTING, AND HOW LATE WILL WE GO?
CHATTER
WE SHOULD WEAR OUR BLAZERS, RIGHT?
CHATTER
EXCUSE ME.
すっ SHIF

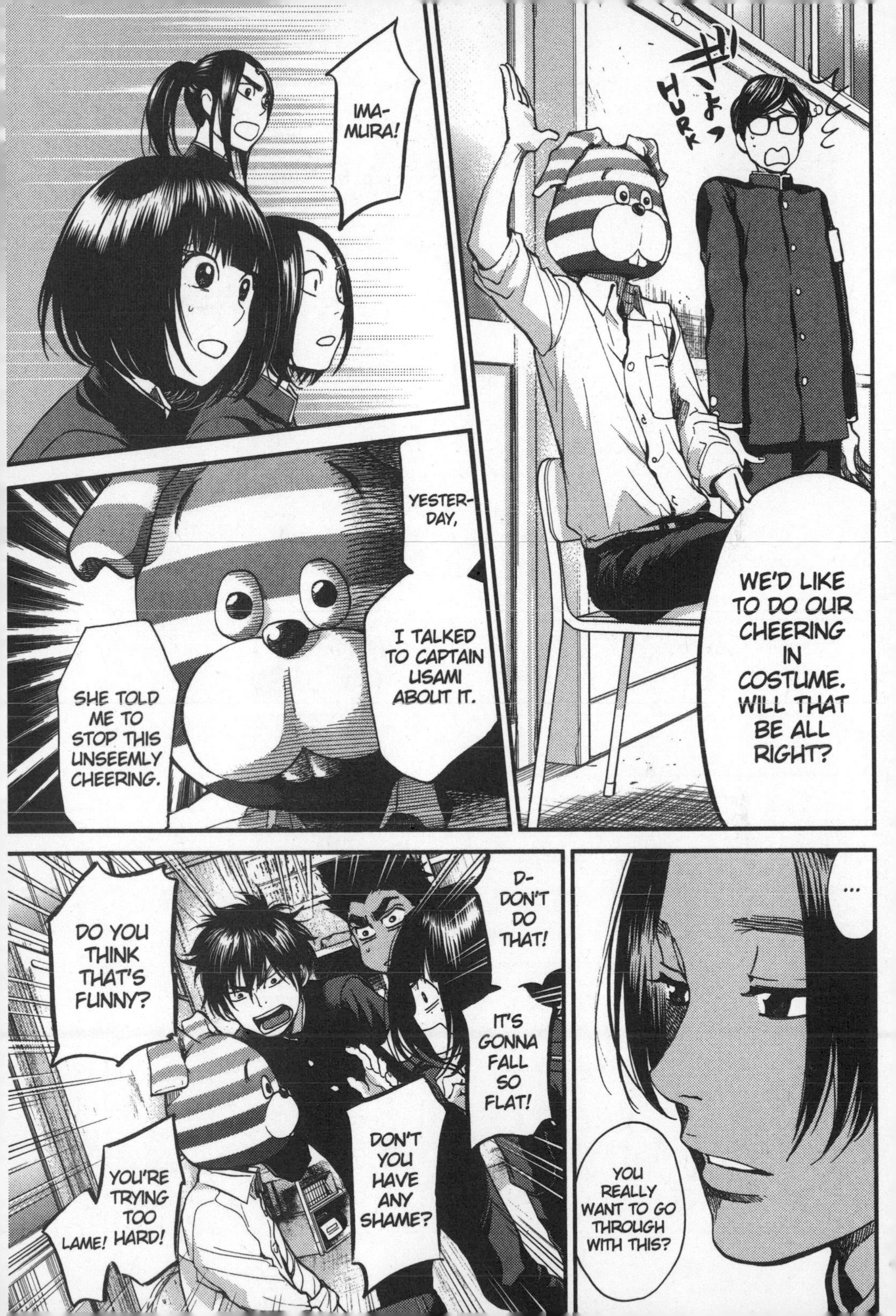
ギョッ
HURK
WE'D LIKE TO DO OUR CHEERING IN COSTUME. WILL THAT BE ALL RIGHT?
IMA-MURA!
YESTER-DAY,
I TALKED TO CAPTAIN USAMI ABOUT IT.
SHE TOLD ME TO STOP THIS UNSEEMLY CHEERING.
...
YOU REALLY WANT TO GO THROUGH WITH THIS?
D-DON'T DO THAT!
DO YOU THINK THAT'S FUNNY?
IT'S GONNA FALL SO FLAT!
DON'T YOU HAVE ANY SHAME?
YOU'RE TRYING TOO HARD!
LAME!

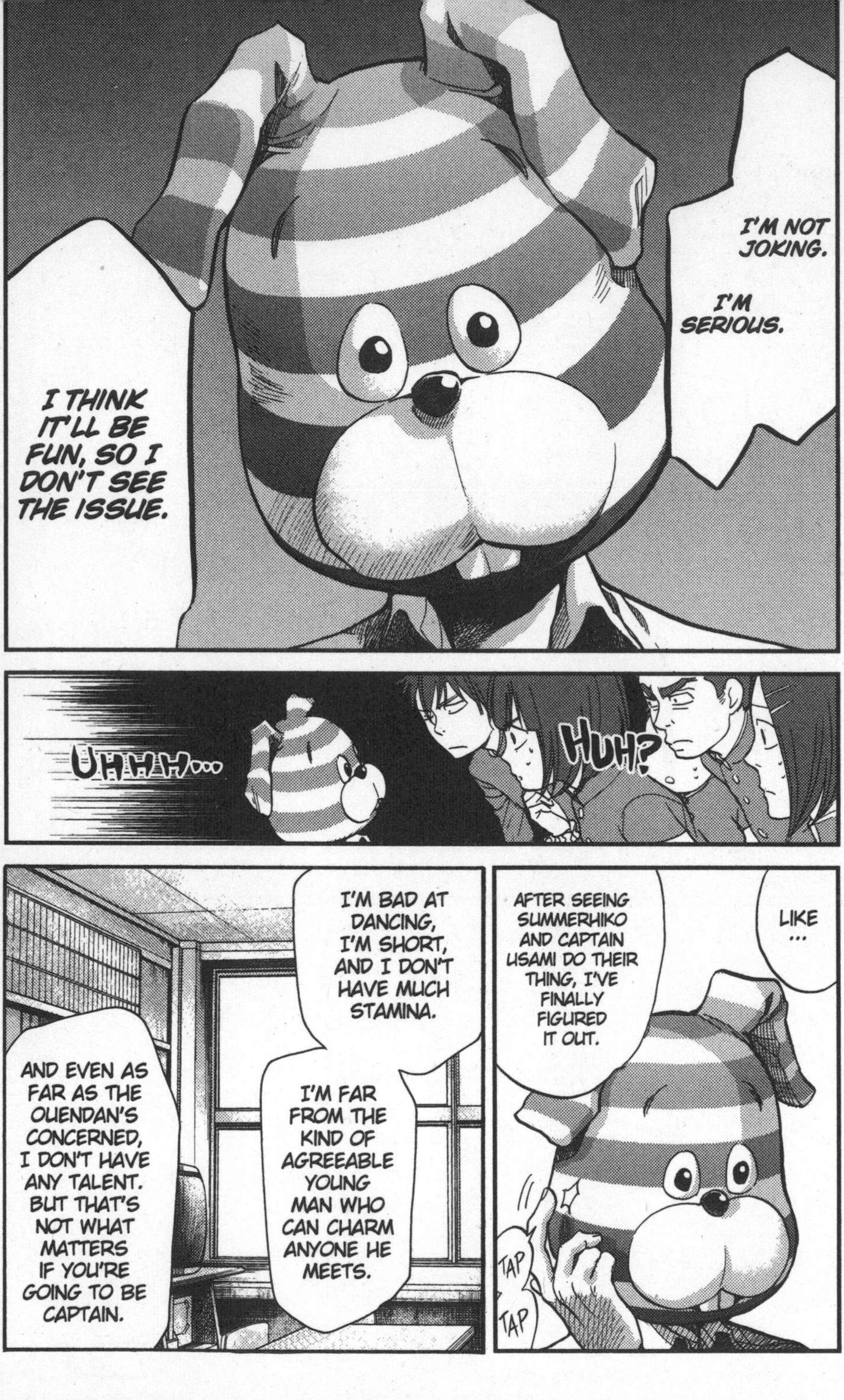
I'M NOT JOKING.
I'M SERIOUS.
I THINK IT'LL BE FUN, SO I DON'T SEE THE ISSUE.
HUH?
UHHH...
LIKE ...
AFTER SEEING SUMMERHIKO AND CAPTAIN USAMI DO THEIR THING, I'VE FINALLY FIGURED IT OUT.
TAP
TAP
I'M BAD AT DANCING, I'M SHORT, AND I DON'T HAVE MUCH STAMINA.
I'M FAR FROM THE KIND OF AGREEABLE YOUNG MAN WHO CAN CHARM ANYONE HE MEETS.
AND EVEN AS FAR AS THE OUENDAN'S CONCERNED, I DON'T HAVE ANY TALENT. BUT THAT'S NOT WHAT MATTERS IF YOU'RE GOING TO BE CAPTAIN.

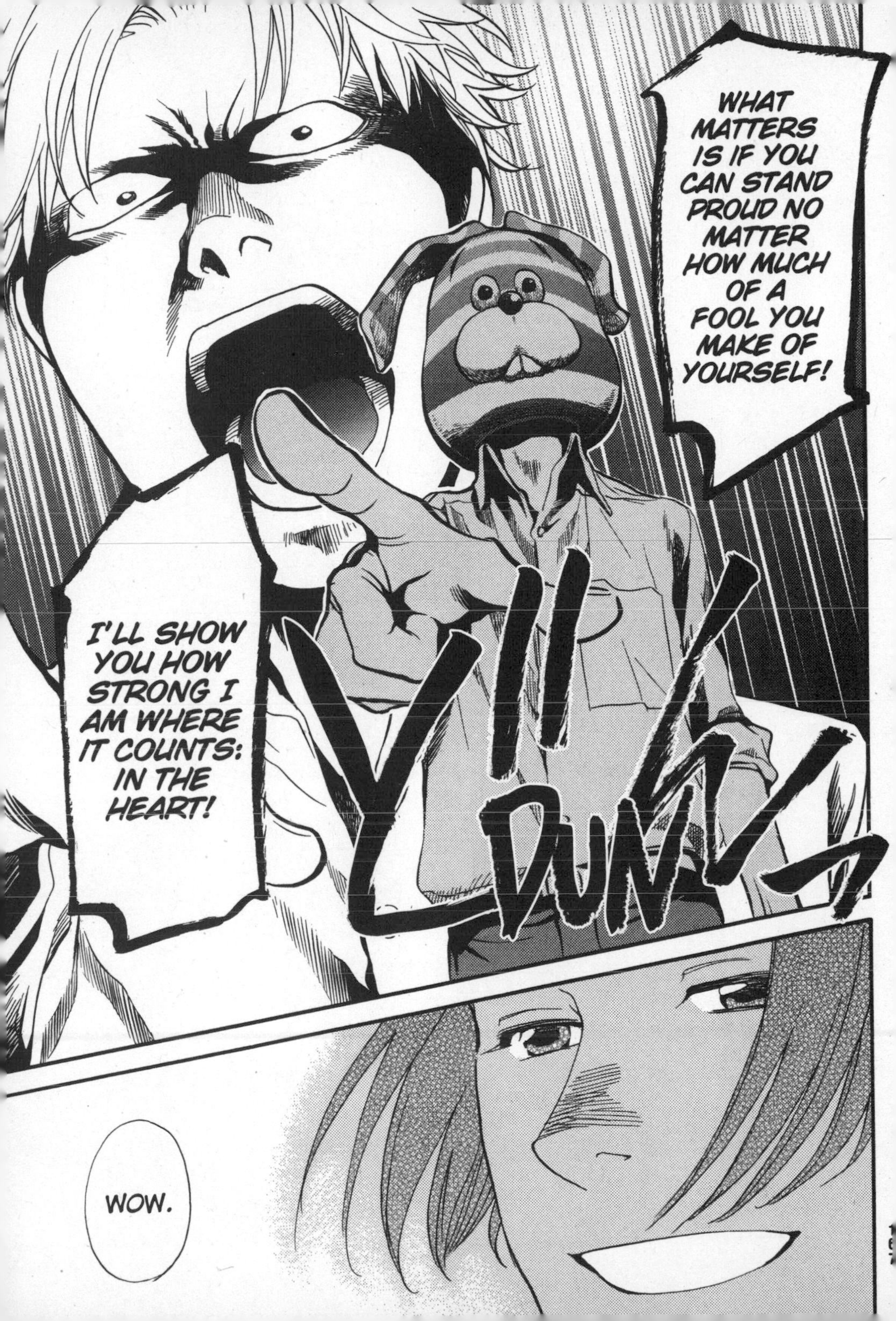
WHAT MATTERS IS IF YOU CAN STAND PROUD NO MATTER HOW MUCH OF A FOOL YOU MAKE OF YOURSELF!
I'LL SHOW YOU HOW STRONG I AM WHERE IT COUNTS: IN THE HEART!
DUN
WOW.

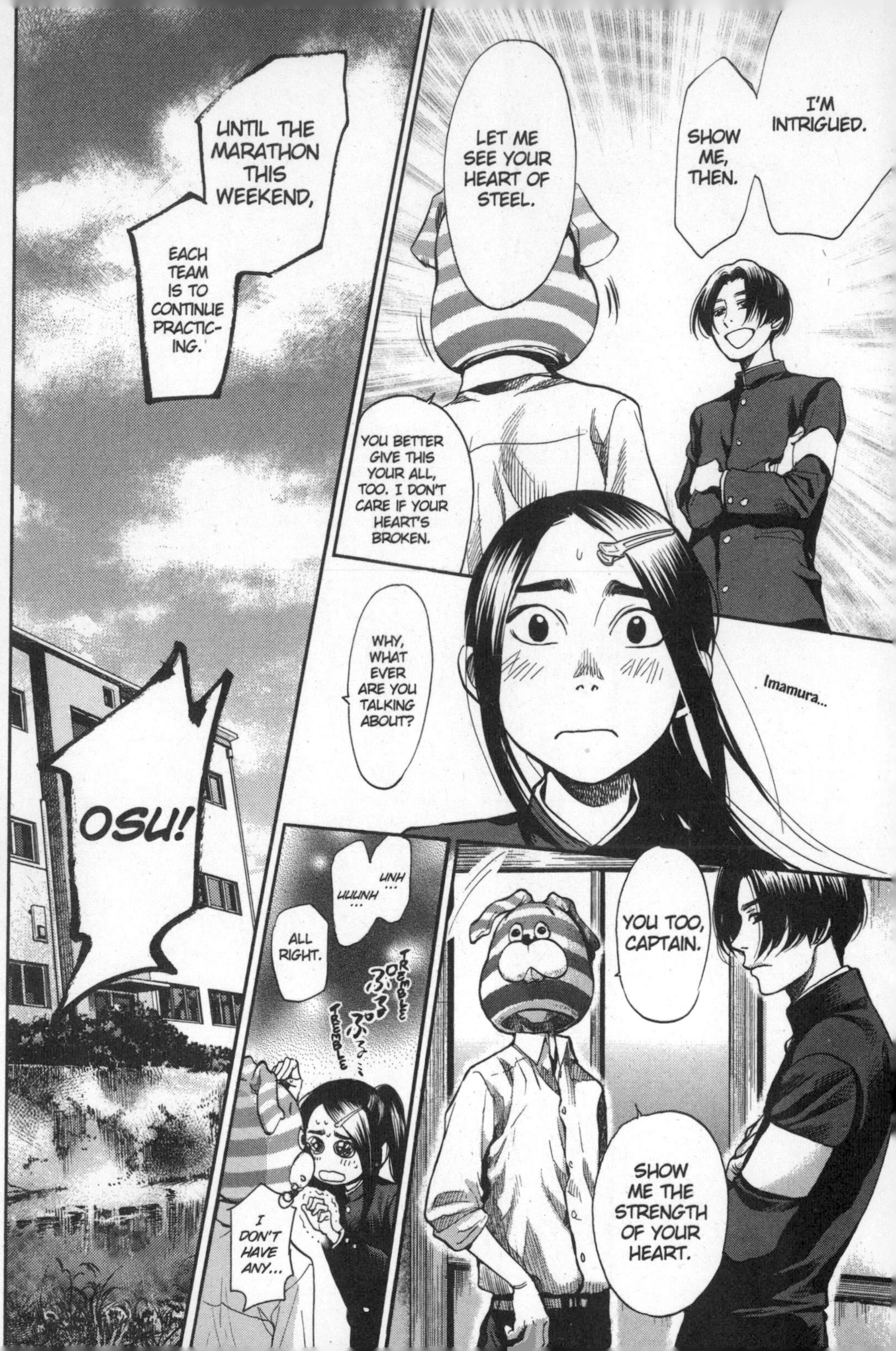
I'M INTRIGUED.
SHOW ME, THEN.
LET ME SEE YOUR HEART OF STEEL.
YOU BETTER GIVE THIS YOUR ALL, TOO. I DON'T CARE IF YOUR HEART'S BROKEN.
Imamura...
WHY, WHAT EVER ARE YOU TALKING ABOUT?
YOU TOO, CAPTAIN.
SHOW ME THE STRENGTH OF YOUR HEART.
UNH... UUUUNH...
ALL RIGHT.
TREMBLE
TREMBLE
I DON'T HAVE ANY...
UNTIL THE MARATHON THIS WEEKEND,
EACH TEAM IS TO CONTINUE PRACTICING.
OSU!

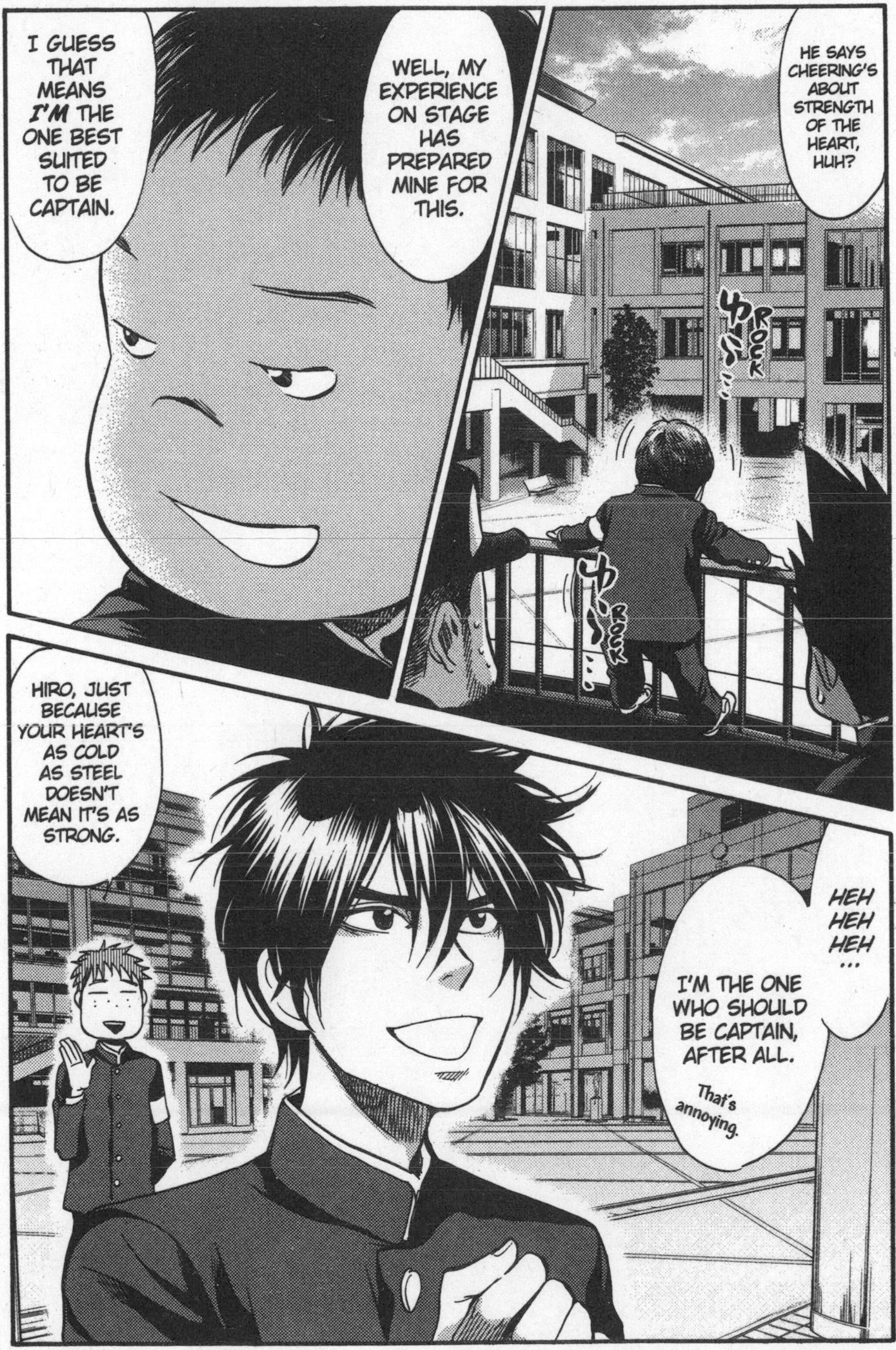
HE SAYS CHEERING'S ABOUT STRENGTH OF THE HEART, HUH?
ROCK
ROCK
WELL, MY EXPERIENCE ON STAGE HAS PREPARED MINE FOR THIS.
I GUESS THAT MEANS I'M THE ONE BEST SUITED TO BE CAPTAIN.
HIRO, JUST BECAUSE YOUR HEART'S AS COLD AS STEEL DOESN'T MEAN IT'S AS STRONG.
HEH HEH HEH...
I'M THE ONE WHO SHOULD BE CAPTAIN, AFTER ALL.
That's annoying.

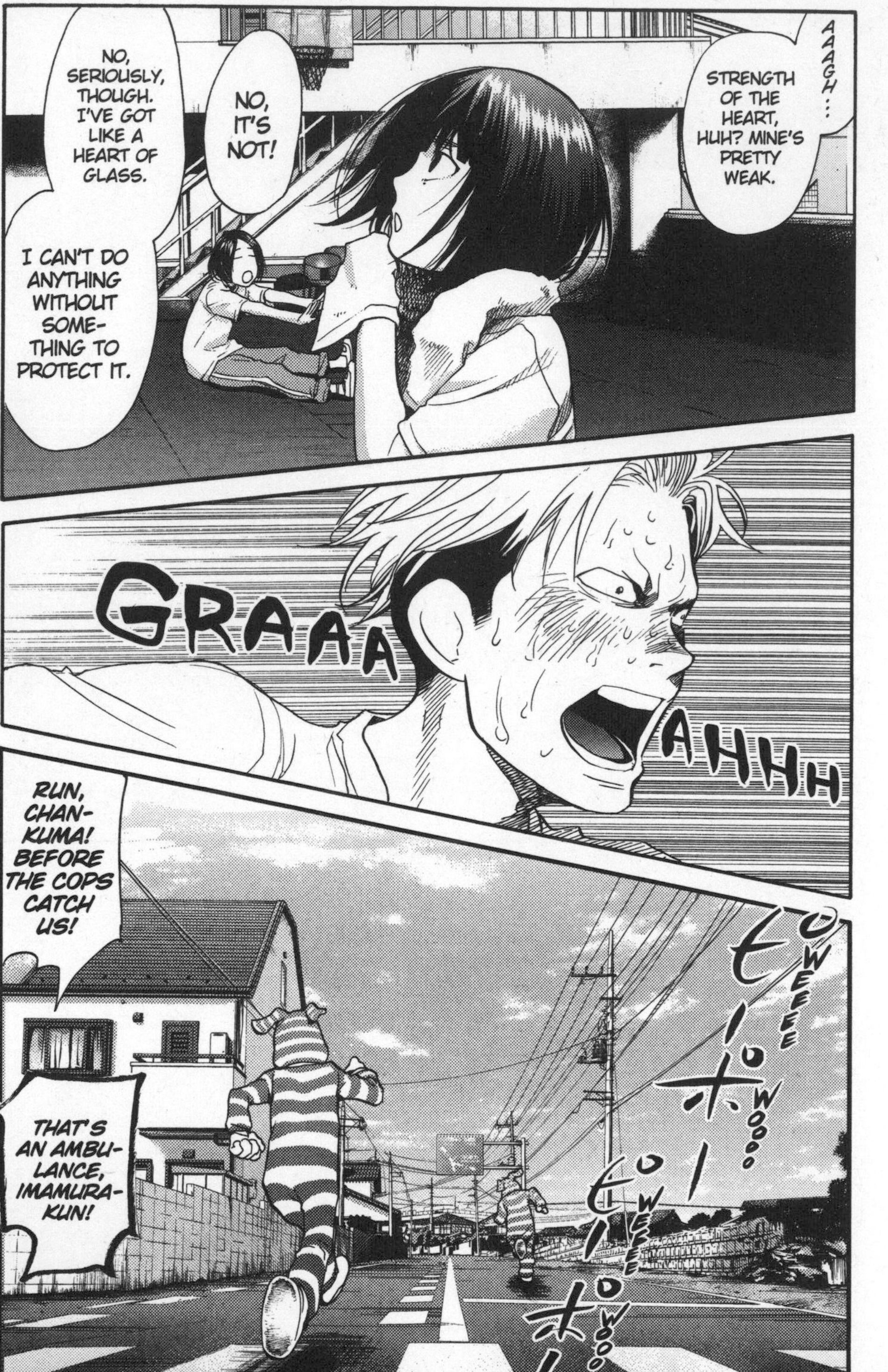
AAAGH...
STRENGTH OF THE HEART, HUH? MINE'S PRETTY WEAK.
NO, IT'S NOT!
NO, SERIOUSLY, THOUGH. I'VE GOT LIKE A HEART OF GLASS.
I CAN'T DO ANYTHING WITHOUT SOME-THING TO PROTECT IT.
GRAAAAHHHH
ピーポー
OWEEEE WOOOO...
ピーポー
OWEEEE WOOOO...
RUN, CHAN-KUMA! BEFORE THE COPS CATCH US!
THAT'S AN AMBU-LANCE, IMAMURA-KUN!

STRENGTH OF THE HEART

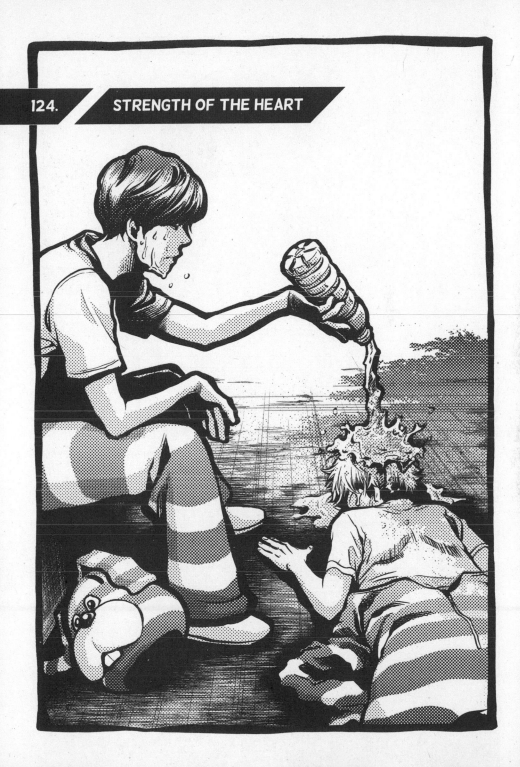

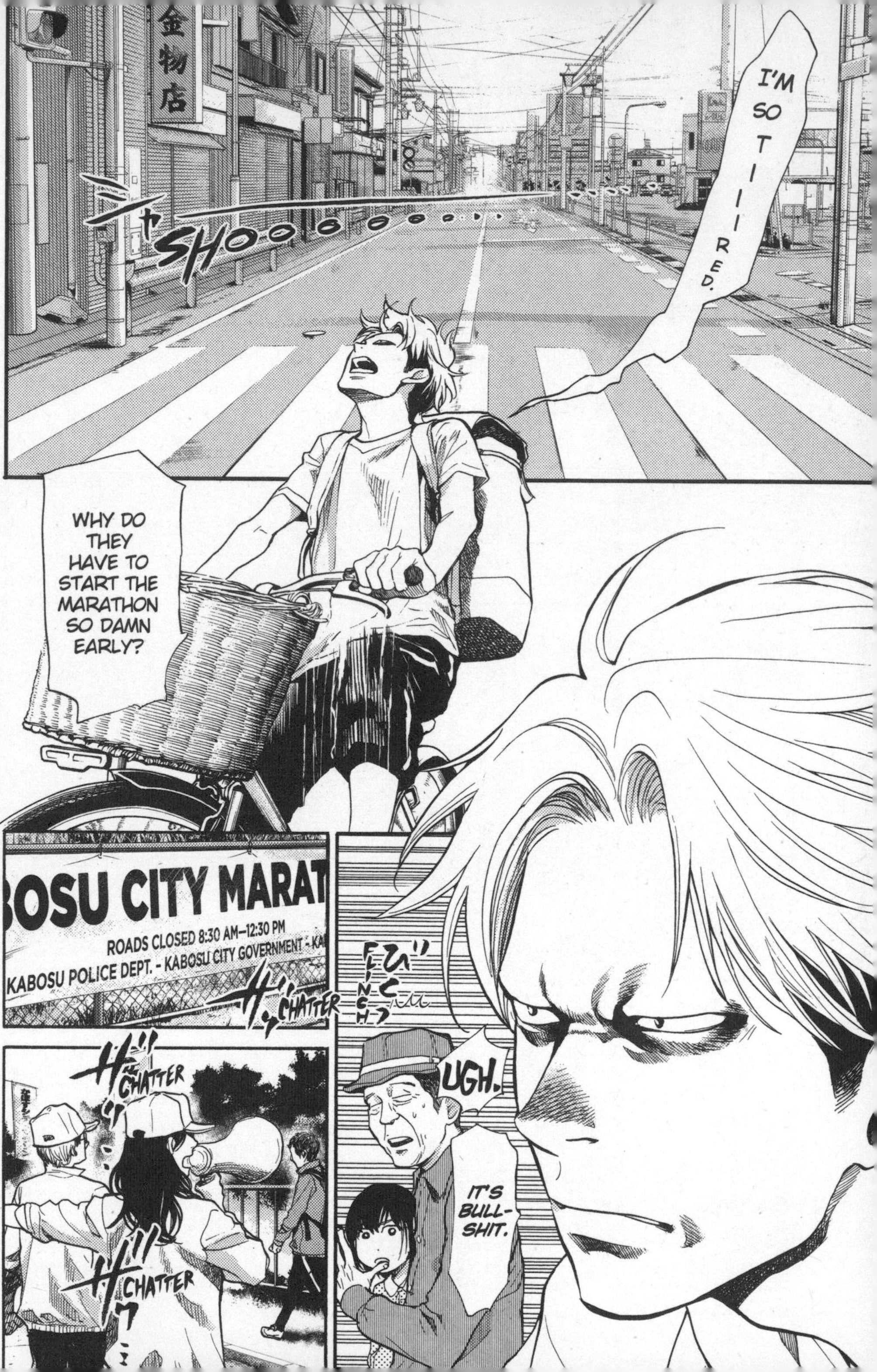
金物店
SHOOOOOOOO
I'M SO TIIIIRED.
WHY DO THEY HAVE TO START THE MARATHON SO DAMN EARLY?
FLINCH
UGH.
IT'S BULL-SHIT.
BOSU CITY MARAT
ROADS CLOSED 8:30 AM–12:30 PM
KABOSU POLICE DEPT. - KABOSU CITY GOVERNMENT - KA
CHATTER
CHATTER
CHATTER

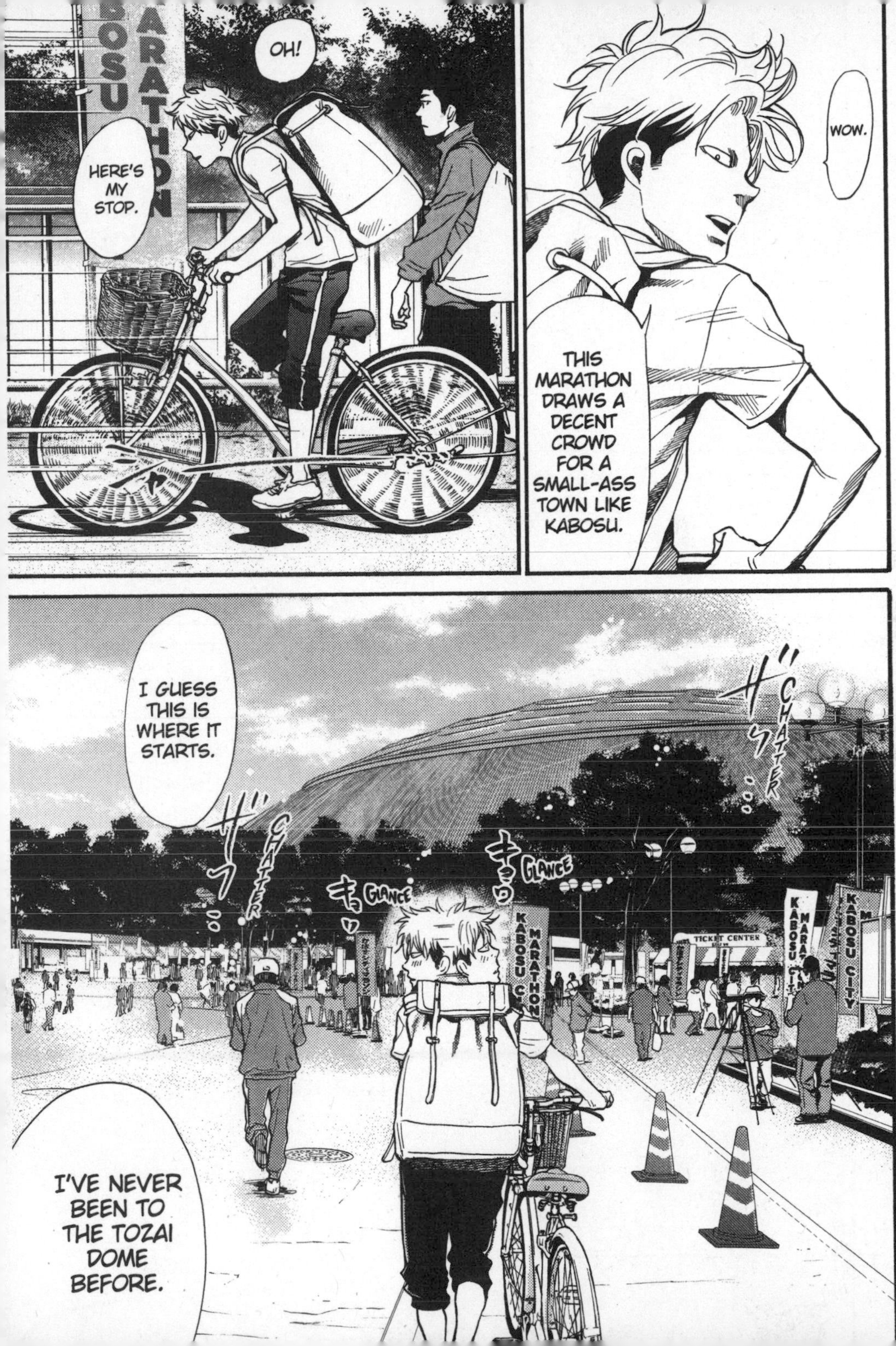
WOW.
THIS MARATHON DRAWS A DECENT CROWD FOR A SMALL-ASS TOWN LIKE KABOSU.
OH!
ARATHON
BOSU
HERE'S MY STOP.
CHATTER
I GUESS THIS IS WHERE IT STARTS.
CHATTER
GLANCE
GLANCE
KABOSU MARATHON
TICKET CENTER
KABOSU CITY
I'VE NEVER BEEN TO THE TOZAI DOME BEFORE.

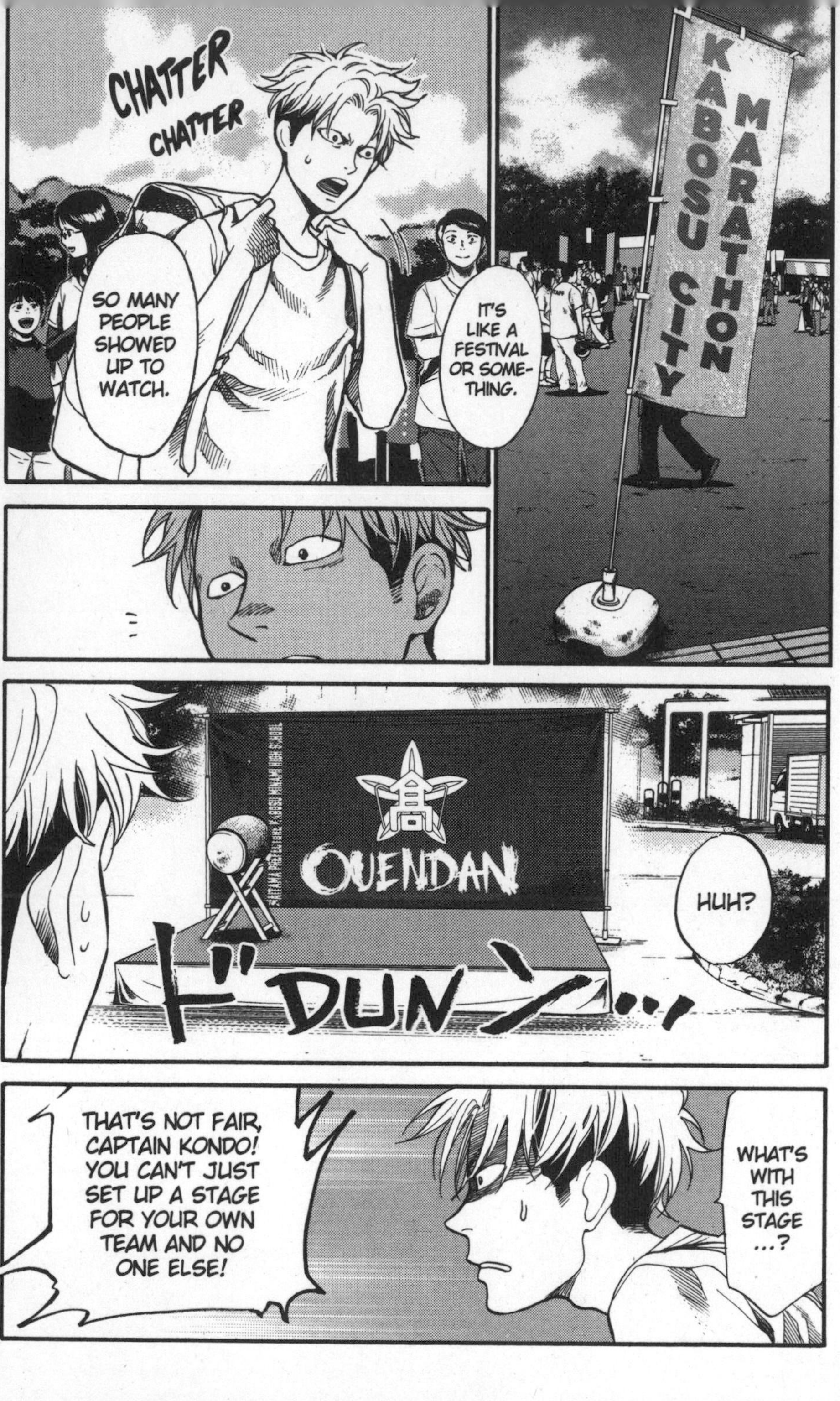
KABOSU CITY MARATHON
CHATTER CHATTER
IT'S LIKE A FESTIVAL OR SOME-THING.
SO MANY PEOPLE SHOWED UP TO WATCH.
HUH?
OUENDAN
ド DUN ン...!
WHAT'S WITH THIS STAGE ...?
THAT'S NOT FAIR, CAPTAIN KONDO! YOU CAN'T JUST SET UP A STAGE FOR YOUR OWN TEAM AND NO ONE ELSE!

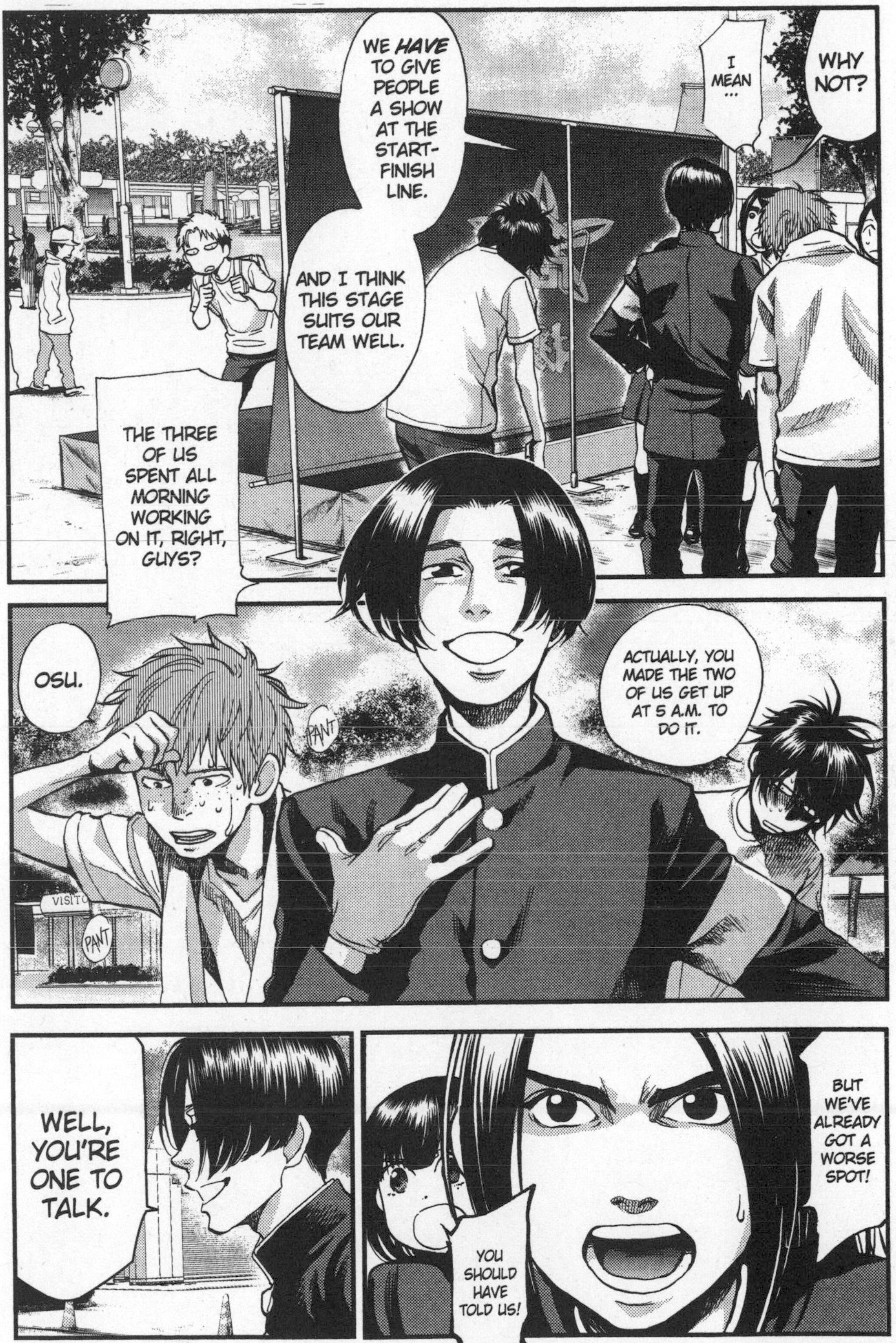
WHY NOT?
I MEAN ...
WE HAVE TO GIVE PEOPLE A SHOW AT THE START-FINISH LINE.
AND I THINK THIS STAGE SUITS OUR TEAM WELL.
THE THREE OF US SPENT ALL MORNING WORKING ON IT, RIGHT, GUYS?
ACTUALLY, YOU MADE THE TWO OF US GET UP AT 5 A.M. TO DO IT.
PANT
OSU.
PANT
BUT WE'VE ALREADY GOT A WORSE SPOT!
YOU SHOULD HAVE TOLD US!
WELL, YOU'RE ONE TO TALK.

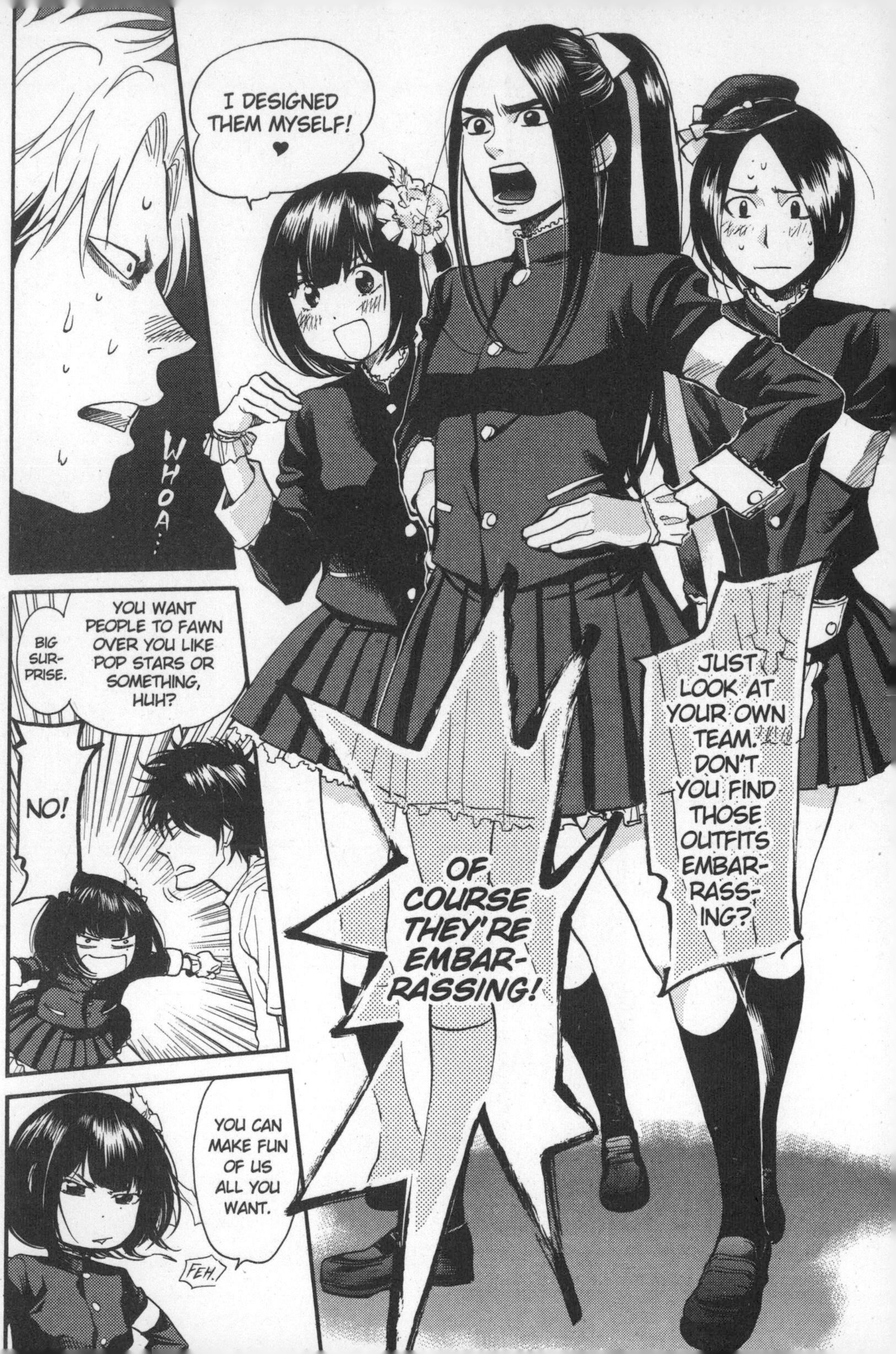
I DESIGNED THEM MYSELF! ♥
JUST LOOK AT YOUR OWN TEAM. DON'T YOU FIND THOSE OUTFITS EMBARRASSING?
OF COURSE THEY'RE EMBARRASSING!
WHOA..
YOU WANT PEOPLE TO FAWN OVER YOU LIKE POP STARS OR SOMETHING, HUH?
BIG SURPRISE.
NO!
YOU CAN MAKE FUN OF US ALL YOU WANT.
FEH.

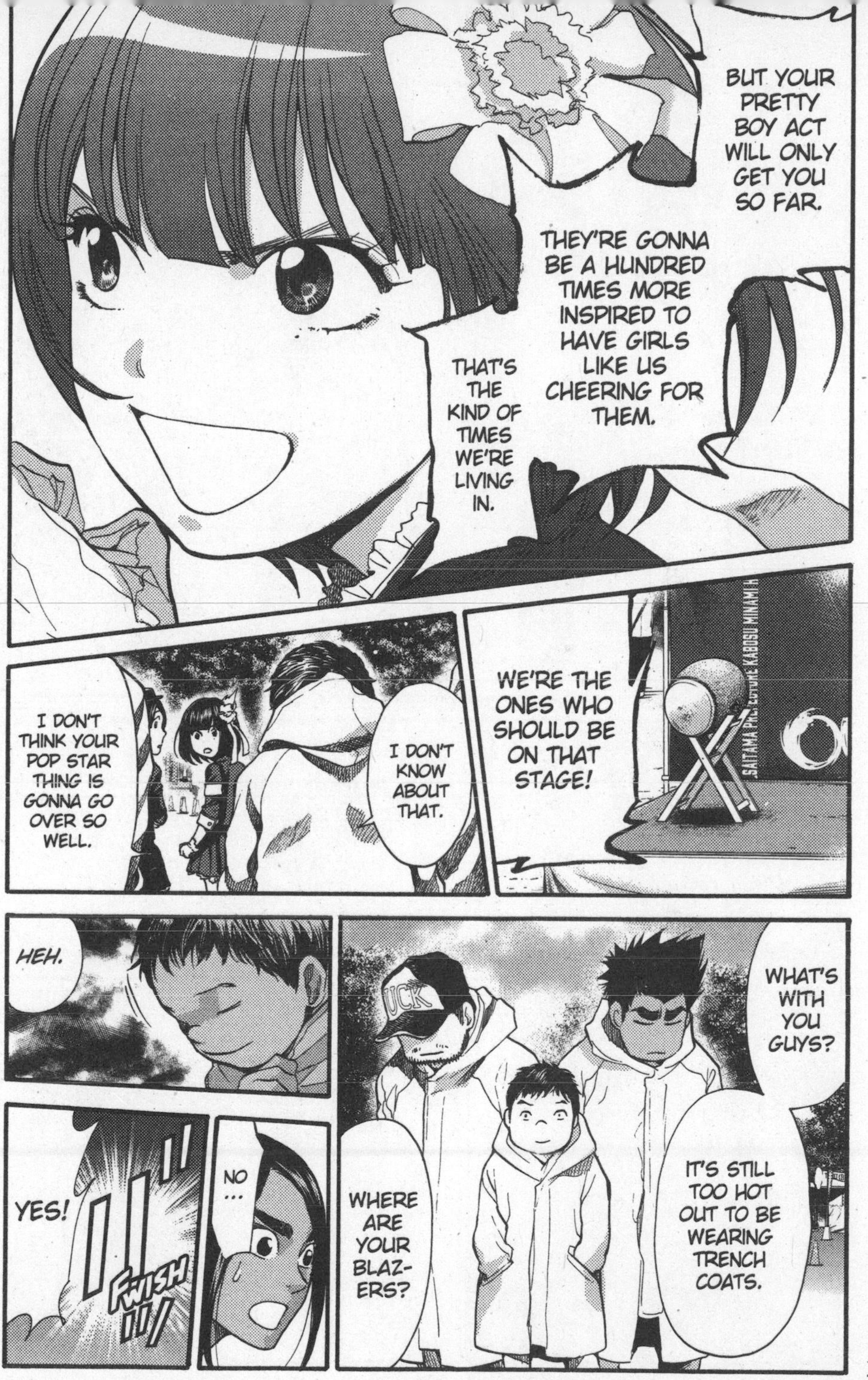
BUT YOUR PRETTY BOY ACT WILL ONLY GET YOU SO FAR.
THEY'RE GONNA BE A HUNDRED TIMES MORE INSPIRED TO HAVE GIRLS LIKE US CHEERING FOR THEM.
THAT'S THE KIND OF TIMES WE'RE LIVING IN.
WE'RE THE ONES WHO SHOULD BE ON THAT STAGE!
I DON'T KNOW ABOUT THAT.
I DON'T THINK YOUR POP STAR THING IS GONNA GO OVER SO WELL.
WHAT'S WITH YOU GUYS?
IT'S STILL TOO HOT OUT TO BE WEARING TRENCH COATS.
WHERE ARE YOUR BLAZERS?
HEH.
NO ...
YES!
FWISH

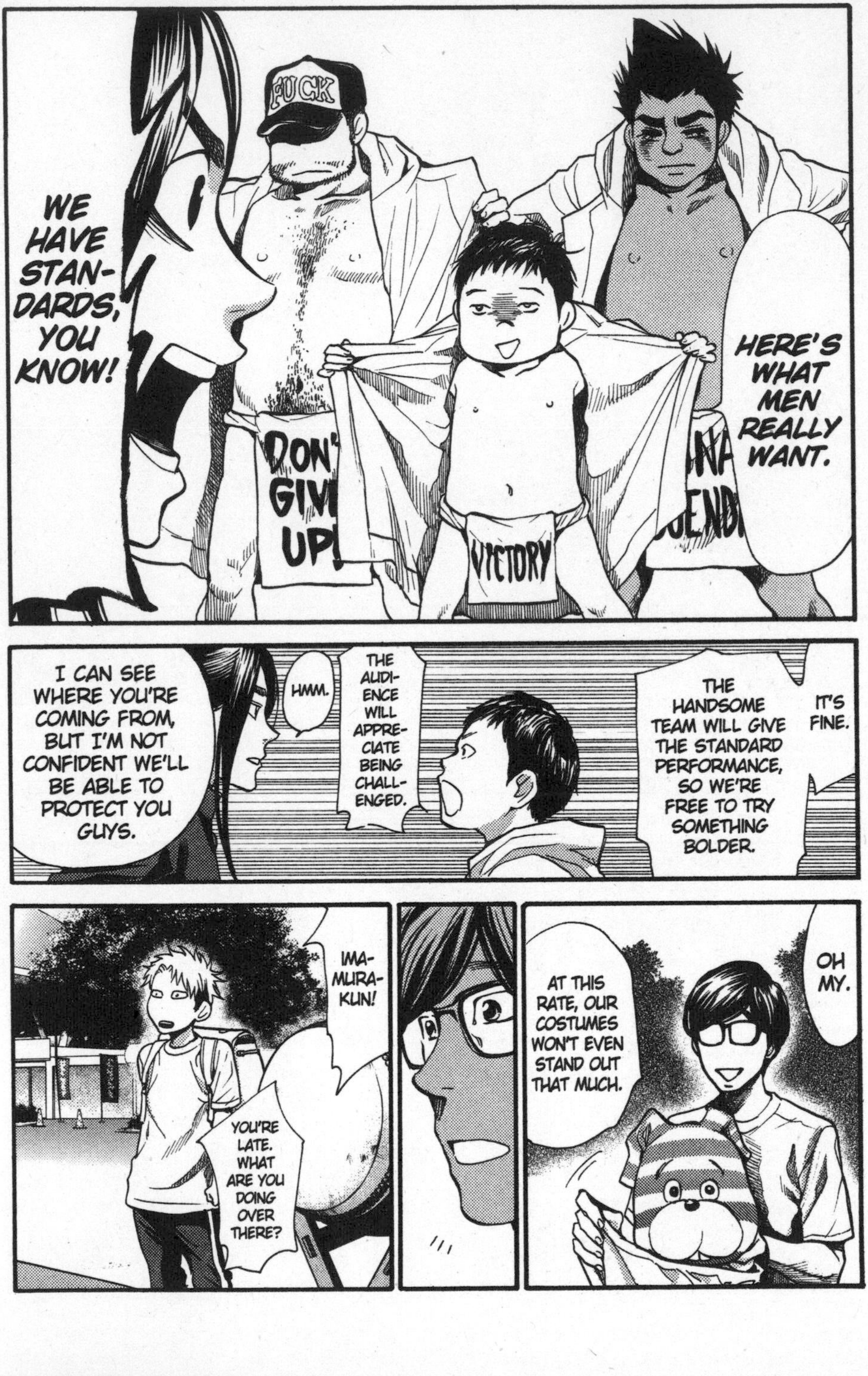
HERE'S WHAT MEN REALLY WANT.
FUCK
WE HAVE STAN-DARDS, YOU KNOW!
VICTORY
IT'S FINE.
THE HANDSOME TEAM WILL GIVE THE STANDARD PERFORMANCE, SO WE'RE FREE TO TRY SOMETHING BOLDER.
THE AUDI-ENCE WILL APPRE-CIATE BEING CHALL-ENGED.
HMM.
I CAN SEE WHERE YOU'RE COMING FROM, BUT I'M NOT CONFIDENT WE'LL BE ABLE TO PROTECT YOU GUYS.
OH MY.
AT THIS RATE, OUR COSTUMES WON'T EVEN STAND OUT THAT MUCH.
IMA-MURA-KUN!
YOU'RE LATE. WHAT ARE YOU DOING OVER THERE?

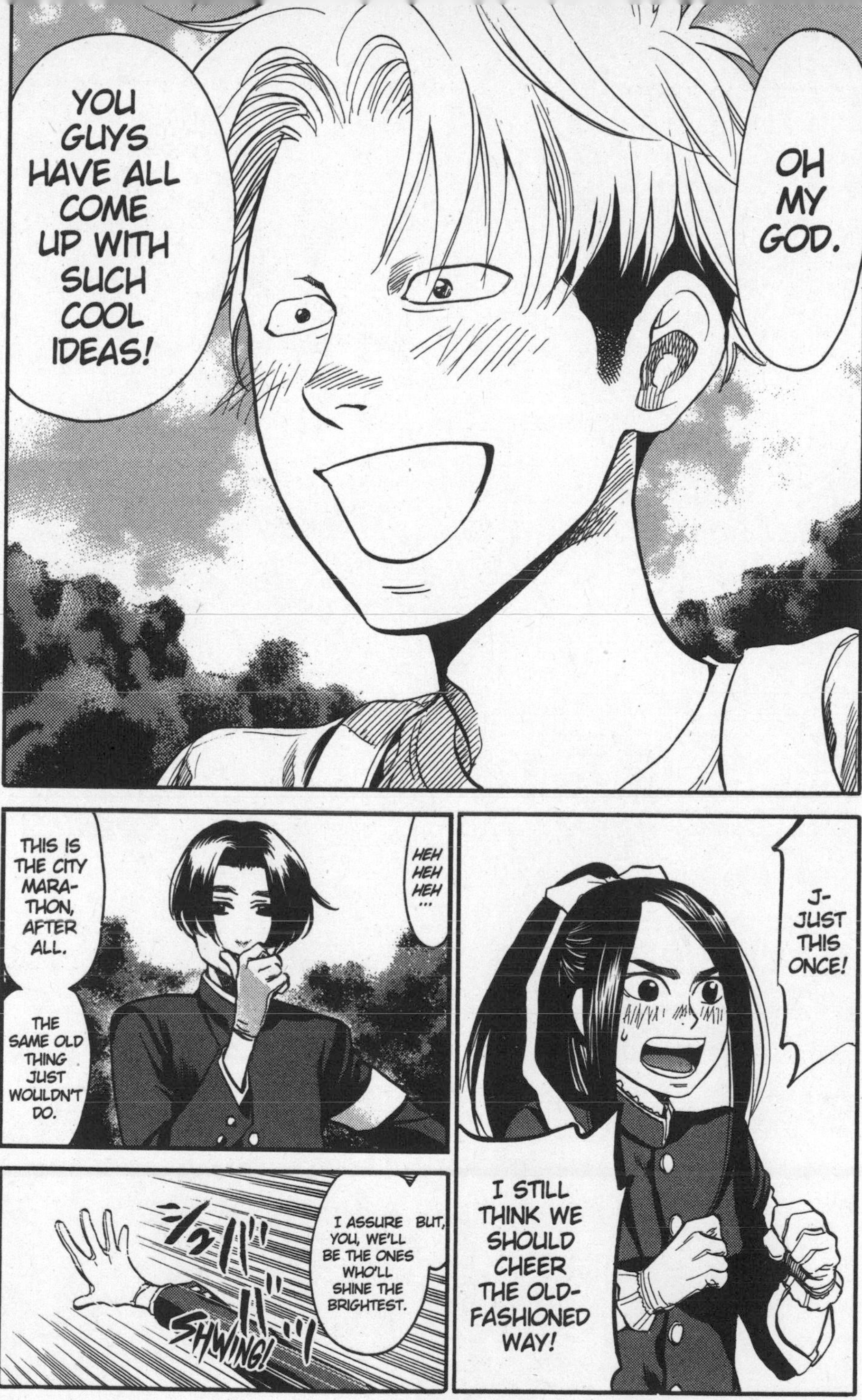
OH MY GOD.
YOU GUYS HAVE ALL COME UP WITH SUCH COOL IDEAS!
J-JUST THIS ONCE!
I STILL THINK WE SHOULD CHEER THE OLD-FASHIONED WAY!
HEH HEH HEH...
THIS IS THE CITY MARA-THON, AFTER ALL.
THE SAME OLD THING JUST WOULDN'T DO.
BUT, I ASSURE YOU, WE'LL BE THE ONES WHO'LL SHINE THE BRIGHTEST.
SHWING!

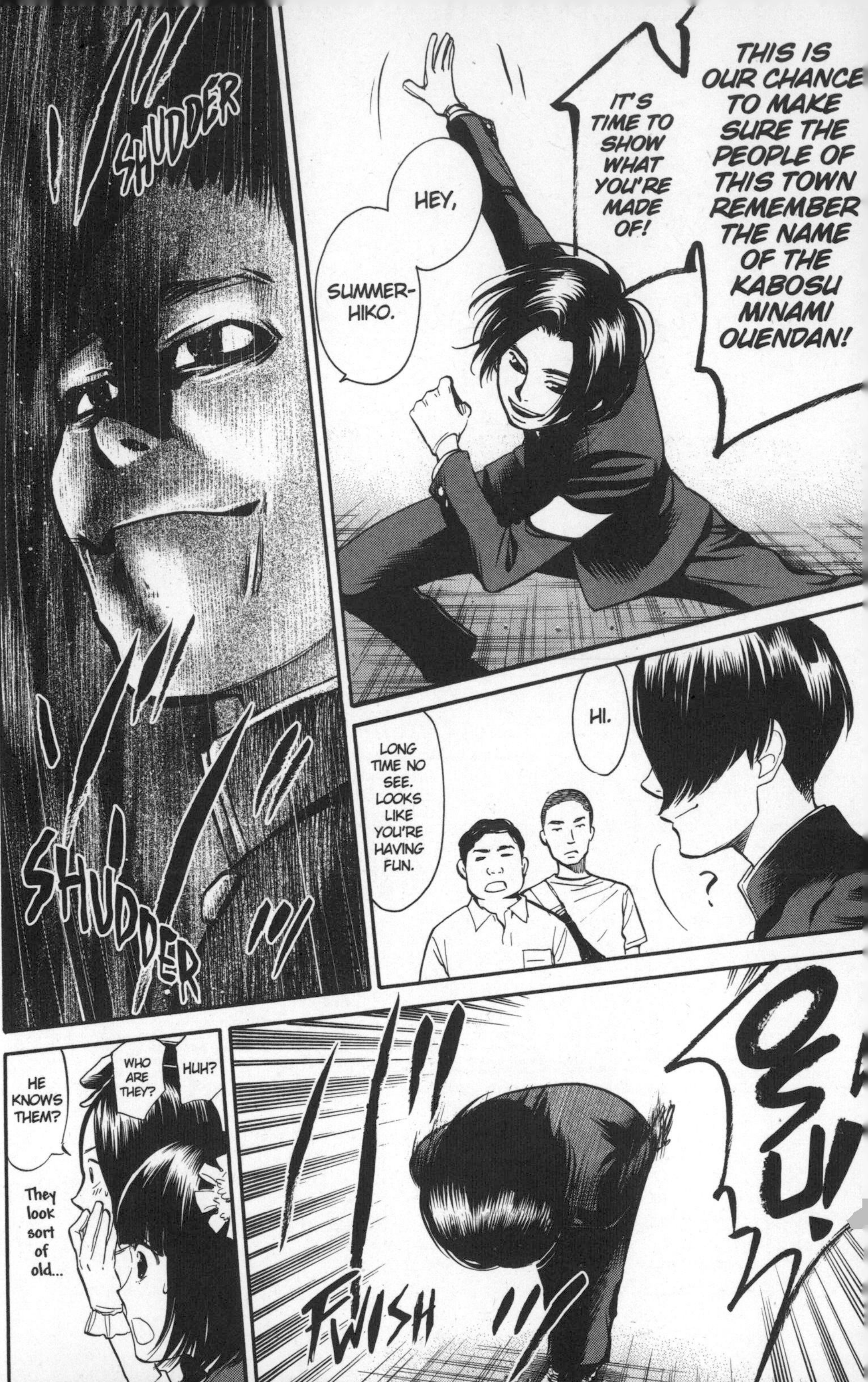
THIS IS OUR CHANCE TO MAKE SURE THE PEOPLE OF THIS TOWN REMEMBER THE NAME OF THE KABOSU MINAMI OUENDAN!
IT'S TIME TO SHOW WHAT YOU'RE MADE OF!
HEY,
SUMMER-HIKO.
HI.
LONG TIME NO SEE. LOOKS LIKE YOU'RE HAVING FUN.
?
SHUDDER
SHUDDER
OSU!
FWISH
HUH?
WHO ARE THEY?
HE KNOWS THEM?
They look sort of old...

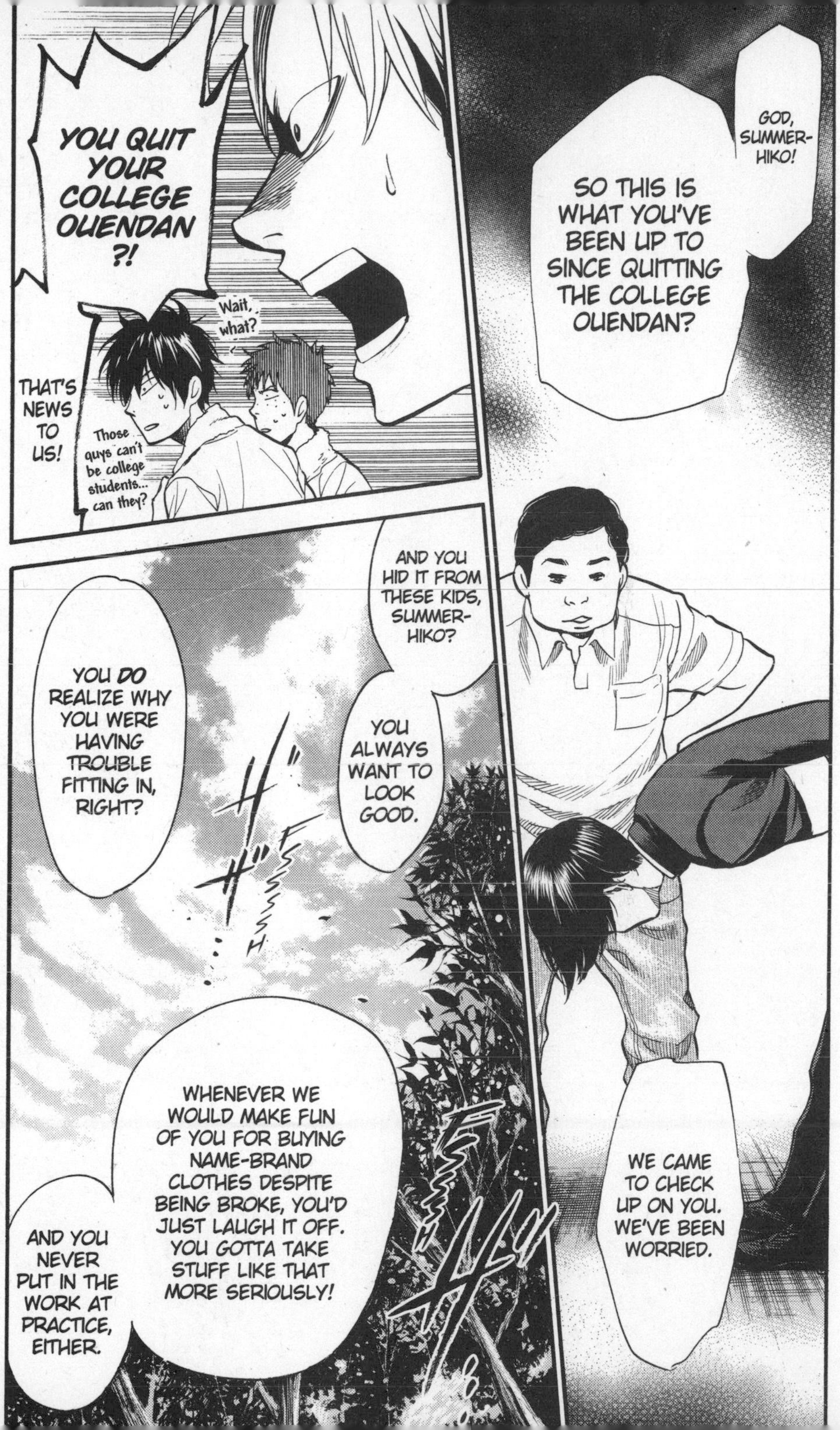
GOD, SUMMER-HIKO!
SO THIS IS WHAT YOU'VE BEEN UP TO SINCE QUITTING THE COLLEGE OUENDAN?
WE CAME TO CHECK UP ON YOU. WE'VE BEEN WORRIED.
YOU QUIT YOUR COLLEGE OUENDAN ?!
Wait, what?
THAT'S NEWS TO US!
Those guys can't be college students... can they?
AND YOU HID IT FROM THESE KIDS, SUMMER-HIKO?
YOU ALWAYS WANT TO LOOK GOOD.
YOU *DO* REALIZE WHY YOU WERE HAVING TROUBLE FITTING IN, RIGHT?
FSSSSSH
WHENEVER WE WOULD MAKE FUN OF YOU FOR BUYING NAME-BRAND CLOTHES DESPITE BEING BROKE, YOU'D JUST LAUGH IT OFF. YOU GOTTA TAKE STUFF LIKE THAT MORE SERIOUSLY!
AND YOU NEVER PUT IN THE WORK AT PRACTICE, EITHER.

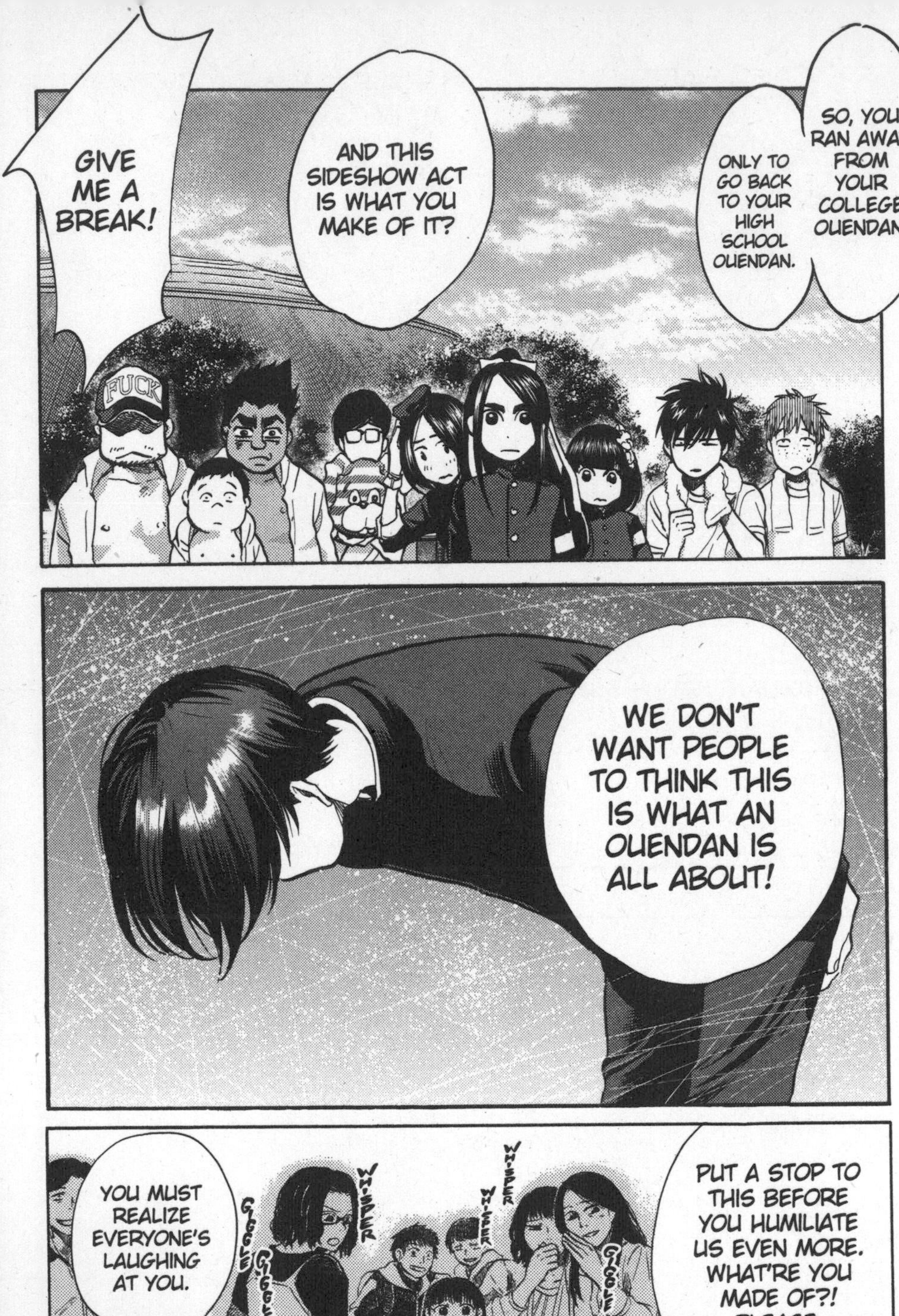

SO, YOU RAN AWAY FROM YOUR COLLEGE OUENDAN,
ONLY TO GO BACK TO YOUR HIGH SCHOOL OUENDAN.
AND THIS SIDESHOW ACT IS WHAT YOU MAKE OF IT?
GIVE ME A BREAK!
WE DON'T WANT PEOPLE TO THINK THIS IS WHAT AN OUENDAN IS ALL ABOUT!
PUT A STOP TO THIS BEFORE YOU HUMILIATE US EVEN MORE. WHAT'RE YOU MADE OF?! PLEASE.
GIGGLE
WHISPER
WHISPER
WHISPER
GIGGLE
GIGGLE
YOU MUST REALIZE EVERYONE'S LAUGHING AT YOU.

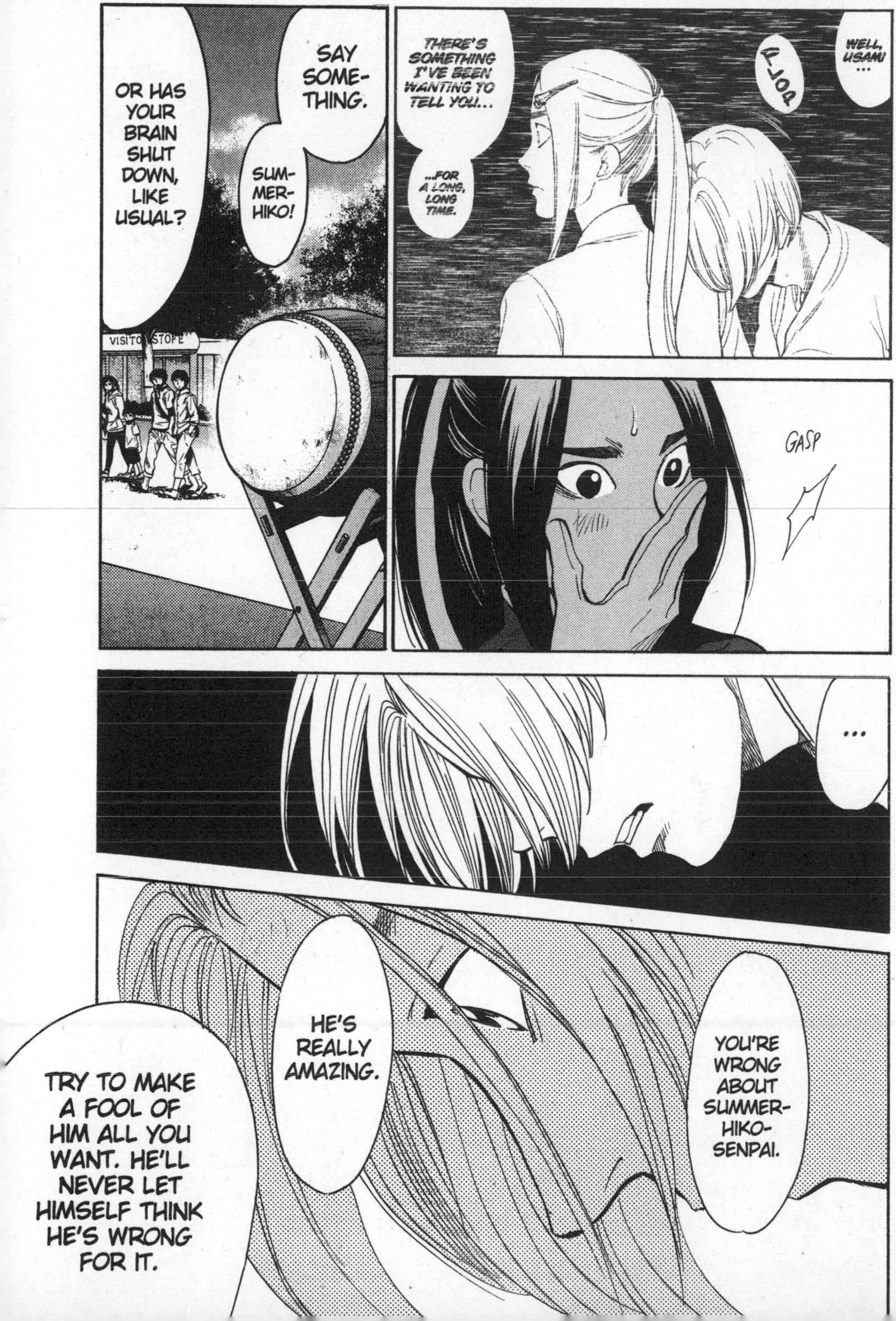
WELL, USAMI...
FLOA
THERE'S SOMETHING I'VE BEEN WANTING TO TELL YOU...
...FOR A LONG, LONG TIME.
GASP
SAY SOME-THING.
SUM-MER-HIKO!
OR HAS YOUR BRAIN SHUT DOWN, LIKE USUAL?
...
YOU'RE WRONG ABOUT SUMMER-HIKO-SENPAI.
HE'S REALLY AMAZING.
TRY TO MAKE A FOOL OF HIM ALL YOU WANT. HE'LL NEVER LET HIMSELF THINK HE'S WRONG FOR IT.

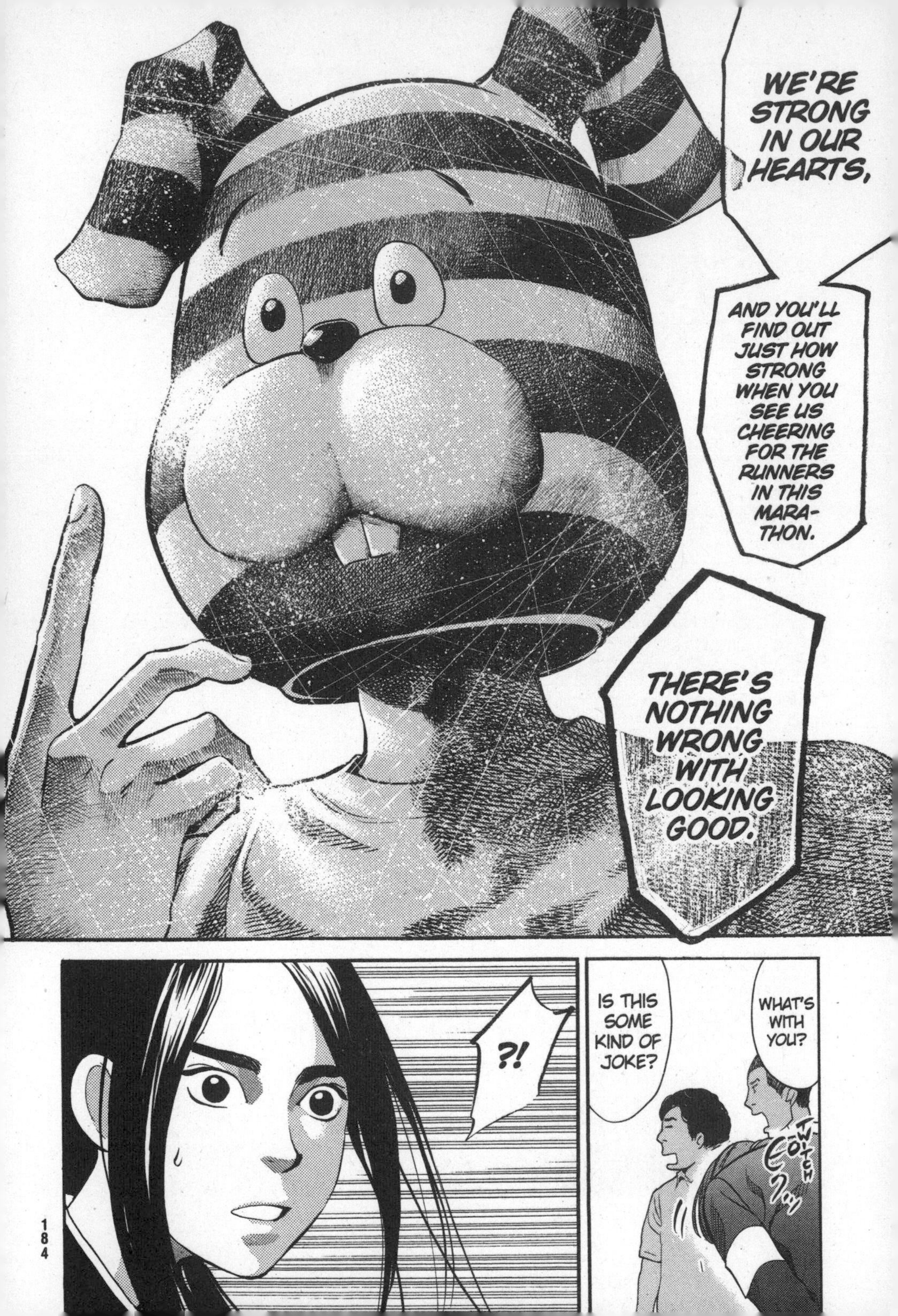
WE'RE STRONG IN OUR HEARTS,
AND YOU'LL FIND OUT JUST HOW STRONG WHEN YOU SEE US CHEERING FOR THE RUNNERS IN THIS MARA-THON.
THERE'S NOTHING WRONG WITH LOOKING GOOD.
WHAT'S WITH YOU?
IS THIS SOME KIND OF JOKE?
TWITCH
?!

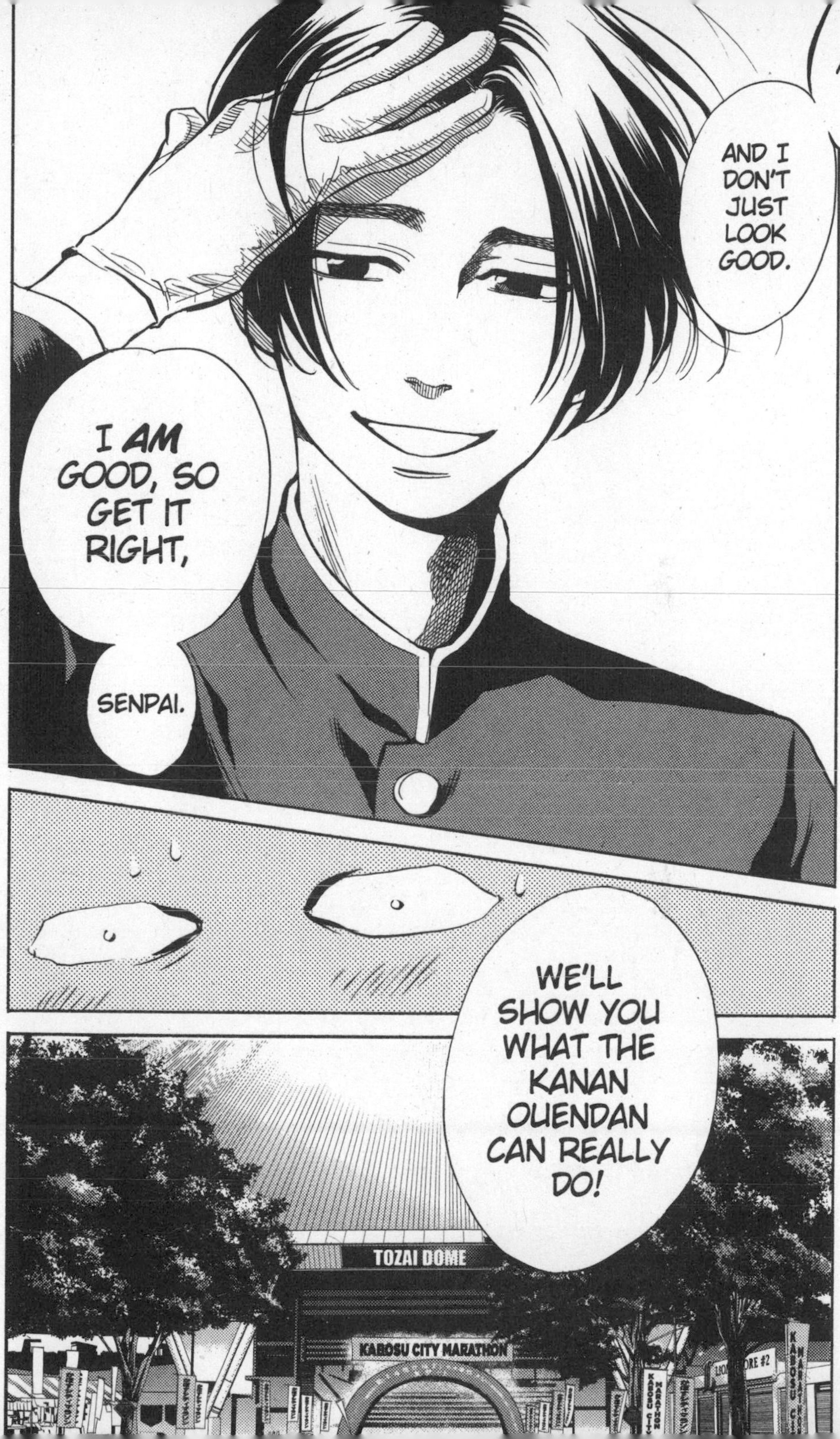
HEH.
AND I DON'T JUST LOOK GOOD.
I AM GOOD, SO GET IT RIGHT,
SENPAI.
WE'LL SHOW YOU WHAT THE KANAN OUENDAN CAN REALLY DO!
TOZAI DOME
KABOSU CITY MARATHON

TO BE CONTINUED IN VOLUME 12!

THIS IS THE AFTERWORD!

Volume 11! There are some things that only become visible once you've come this far.
And there are some things I can only do because I've walked this path.
I'm excited to draw Volume 12!

Mitsurou Kubo, January 2014

2014.1. 久保ミツロウ☆

☆ My Agent: Hiromi Sakitani

☆ Staff: Ema Yamanouchi

☆ My Assistants: Shunsuke Ono
                 Youko Mikuni
                 Hiromu Kitano
                 Koushi Tezuka
                 Kouhei Mihara
                 Rana Satou

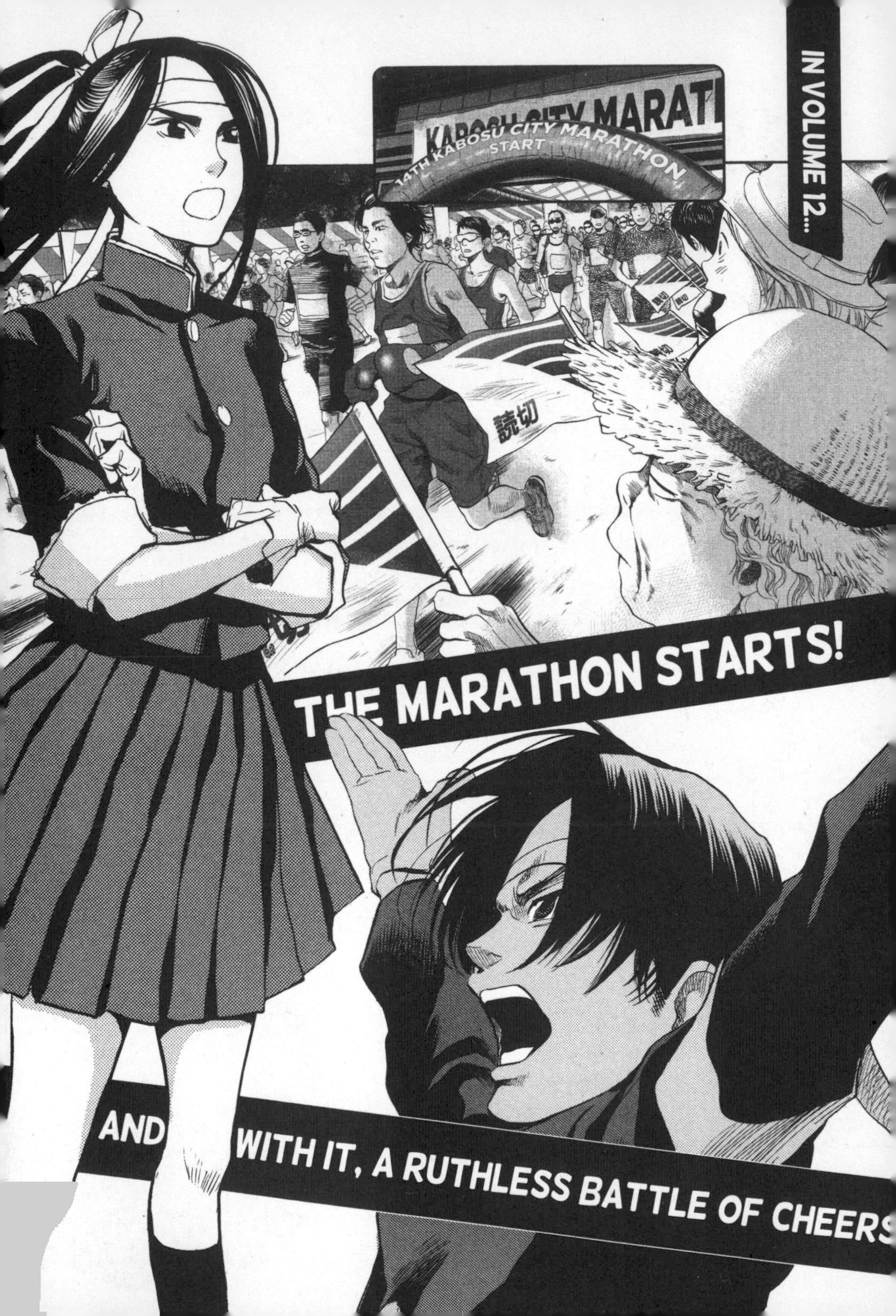
IN VOLUME 12...
14TH KABOSU CITY MARATHON
START
THE MARATHON STARTS!
AND WITH IT, A RUTHLESS BATTLE OF CHEERS

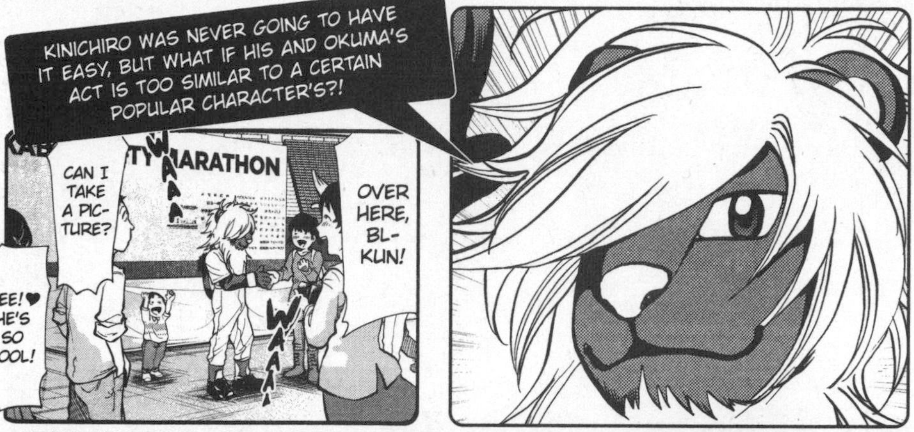
KINICHIRO WAS NEVER GOING TO HAVE IT EASY, BUT WHAT IF HIS AND OKUMA'S ACT IS TOO SIMILAR TO A CERTAIN POPULAR CHARACTER'S?!
OVER HERE, BL-KUN!
WAAA
WAAA
MARATHON
CAN I TAKE A PICTURE?
EEE!♥ HE'S SO COOL!

BAD LUCK? NO PROBLEM! IF NOBODY KNOWS WHO THEY ARE, THEY'LL JUST HAVE TO SHOW THEM!

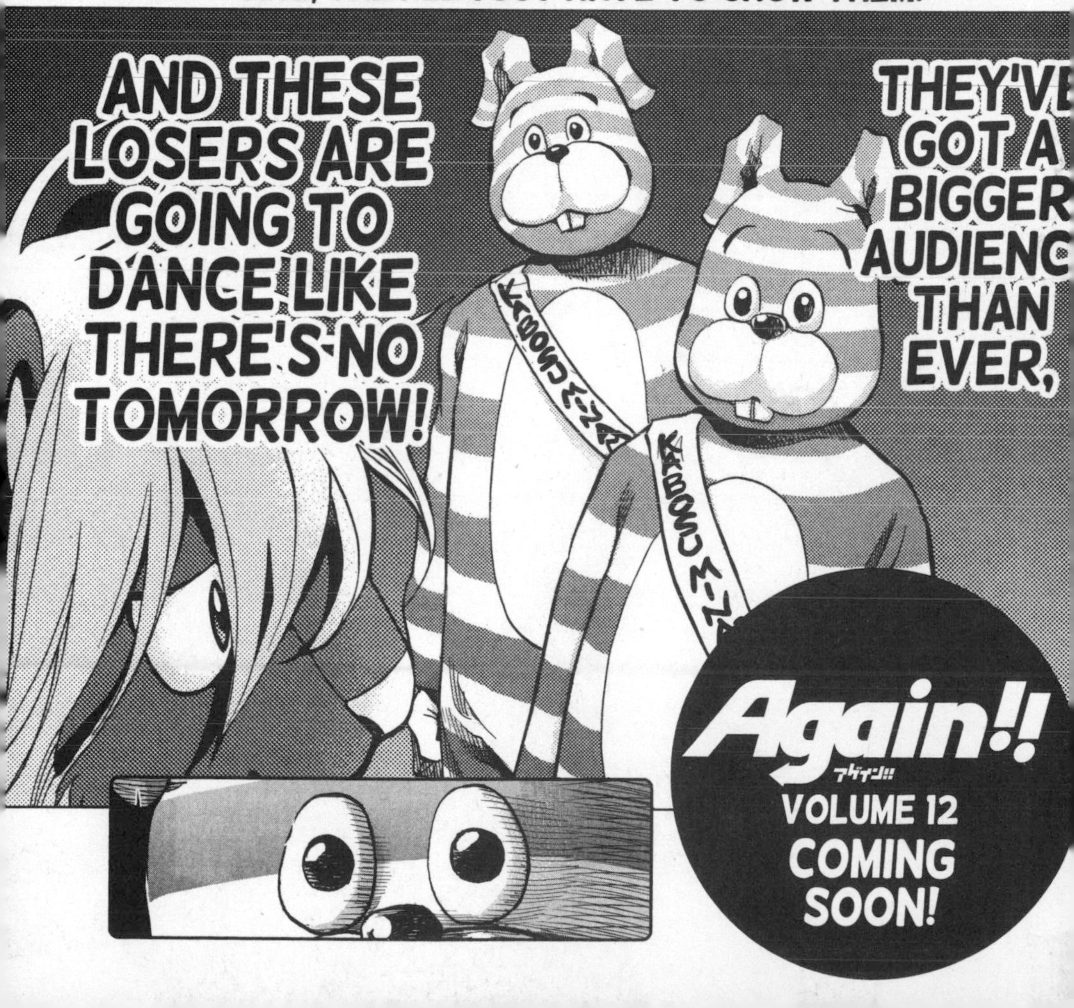
THEY'VE GOT A BIGGER AUDIENC THAN EVER,
AND THESE LOSERS ARE GOING TO DANCE LIKE THERE'S NO TOMORROW!
Again!!
アゲイン!!
VOLUME 12
COMING SOON!

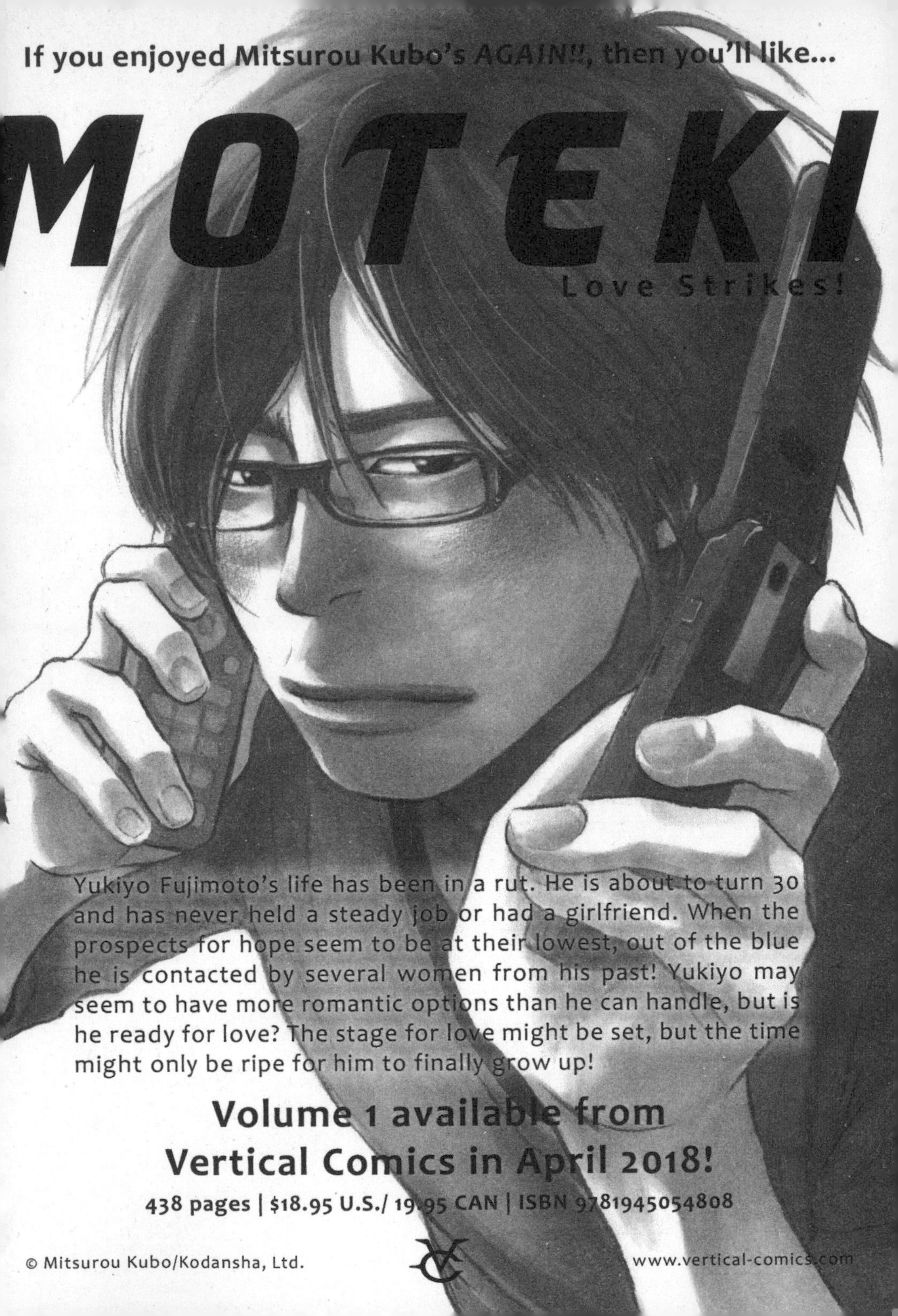
If you enjoyed Mitsurou Kubo's AGAIN!!, then you'll like...
MOTEKI
Love Strikes!
Yukiyo Fujimoto's life has been in a rut. He is about to turn 30 and has never held a steady job or had a girlfriend. When the prospects for hope seem to be at their lowest, out of the blue he is contacted by several women from his past! Yukiyo may seem to have more romantic options than he can handle, but is he ready for love? The stage for love might be set, but the time might only be ripe for him to finally grow up!
Volume 1 available from
Vertical Comics in April 2018!
438 pages | $18.95 U.S./ 19.95 CAN | ISBN 9781945054808
© Mitsurou Kubo/Kodansha, Ltd.
www.vertical-comics.com

Acclaimed screenwriter and director Mari Okada (*Maquia, anohana*) teams up with manga artist Nao Emoto (*Forget Me Not*) in this moving, funny, so-true-it's-embarrassing coming-of-age series!

When Kazusa enters high school, she joins the Literature Club, and leaps from reading innocent fiction to diving into the literary classics. But these novels are a bit more...*adult* than she was prepared for. Between euphemisms like fresh dewy grass and pork stew, crushing on the boy next door, and knowing you want to do that *one thing* before you die—discovering your budding sexuality is no easy feat! As if puberty wasn't awkward enough, the club consists of a brooding writer, the prettiest girl in school, an agreeable comrade, and an outspoken prude. Fumbling over their own discomforts, these five teens get thrown into chaos over three little letters: *S...E...X...!*

Anime coming soon!

O Maidens in Your Savage Season

Mari Okada Nao Emoto

KC KODANSHA COMICS

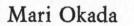

Again!! volume 11 is a work of fiction. Names, characters, places, and incidents are the products of the author's imagination or are used fictitiously. Any resemblance to actual events, locales, or persons, living or dead, is entirely coincidental.

A Kodansha Comics Trade Paperback Original.

Published in the United States by Kodansha Comics, an imprint of Kodansha USA Publishing, LLC, New York.

Publication rights for this English edition arranged through Kodansha Ltd., Tokyo.

First published in Japan in 2014 by Kodansha Ltd., Tokyo, as *Agein!!* volume 11

ISBN 978-1-63236-826-3

Printed in the United States of America.

www.kodanshacomics.com

9 8 7 6 5 4 3 2 1

Translator: Rose Padgett
Lettering: E. K. Weaver
Editing: Tiff Ferentini
Kodansha Comics edition cover design by Phil Balsman